The Wadsworth College Success™ Series

Living and Learning, by Gerald Corey, Cindy Corey, and Heidi Jo Corey (1997), ISBN: 0-534-50500-7

Orientation to College Learning, by Diana L. Van Blerkom (1995), ISBN: 0-534-24528-5

Learning Success: Being Your Best at College and Life, by Carl Wahlstrom and Brian K. Williams (1996), ISBN: 0-534-51346-8

The 'Net, the Web, and You: All You Really Need to Know About the Internet... and a Little Bit More, by Daniel J. Kurland (1996), ISBN: 0-534-51281-X

Learning Your Way Through College, by Robert N. Leamson (1995), ISBN: 0-534-24505-8

I Know What It Says... What Does It Mean? Critical Skills for Critical Reading, by Daniel J. Kurland (1995), ISBN: 0-534-24486-6

College Study Skills: Becoming a Strategic Learner, Second Edition, by Dianna L. Van Blerkhom (1997), ISBN: 0-534-51681-5

Integrating College Study Skills: Reasoning in Reading, Listening, and Writing, Fourth Edition, by Peter Elias Sotirou (1996), ISBN: 0-534-25686-4

Right From the Start: Managing Your Way to College Success, Second Edition, by Robert Holkeboer (1996), ISBN: 0-534-21570-X

Orientation to College: A Reader on Becoming an Educated Person, by Elizabeth Steltenpohl, Jane Shipton, and Sharon Villines (1996), ISBN: 0-534-26484-0

Foundations: A Reader for New College Students, by Virginia N. Gordon and Thomas L. Minnick (1996), ISBN: 0-534-25422-5

The Freshman Year Experience™ Series

Your College Experience: Strategies for Success, Second Concise Edition, by John N. Gardner and A. Jerome Jewler, with Mary-Jane McCarthy (1996), ISBN: 0-534-26520-0

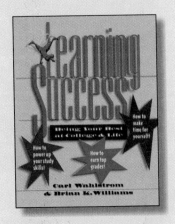

Your College Experience: Expanded Reader Edition, by John N. Gardner and A. Jerome Jewler (1997), ISBN: 0-534-51898-2

Your College Experience: Expanded Workbook Edition, by John N. Gardner and A. Jerome Jewler (1997), ISBN 0-534-51897-4

Success, Your Style! Left and Right Brain Techniques for Learners, By Nancy L. Matte and Susan Green Henderson (1995), ISBN: 0-534-24468-8

The Power to Learn: Helping Yourself to College Success, Second Edition, by William E. Campbell (1997), ISBN: 0-534-26354-2

The Senior Year Experience™ Series

Ready for the Real World, by William C. Hartel, Stephen W. Schwartz, Steven D. Blume, and John N. Gardner (1994), ISBN: 0-534-17712-3

Professional Development: The Dynamics of Success, Fifth Edition, by Mary Wilkes-Hull and C. Bruce Crosswait (1996), ISBN: 0-534-51160-0.

For more information or to purchase any of these Wadsworth texts, please contact your local bookseller.

Your College Experience

STRATEGIES FOR SUCCESS

Third Edition

John N. Gardner
Executive Director, University 101 and The National Resource Center
    for The Freshman Year Experience and Students in Transition
Professor, Library and Information Science
University of South Carolina, Columbia

A. Jerome Jewler
Professor, Journalism and Mass Communications
University of South Carolina, Columbia

Wadsworth Publishing Company
I⊤P® An International Thomson Publishing Company

Belmont, CA • Albany, NY • Bonn • Boston • Cincinnati • Detroit • Johannesburg • London • Madrid
Melbourne • Mexico City • New York • Paris • Singapore • Tokyo • Toronto • Washington

Editorial Assistant: *Ryan Vesely*
Development Editor: *Alan Venable*
Marketing Manager: *Chaun Hightower*
Senior Project Manager: *Debby Kramer*
Production: *Cecile Joyner, The Cooper Company*
Designers: *Ann Butler, Carolyn Deacy, 17th Street Studios*
Print Buyer: *Barbara Britton*
Permissions Editor: *Robert Kauser*
Copy Editor: *Melissa Andrews*
Cover Design: *Stephen Rapley*
Compositor: *Monotype Composition Co.*
Printer: *Johnson & Hardin Co.*
Cover Printer: *Phoenix Color Corp.*

Illustration Credits
John Nelson: Exercise, Journal, Box icons; chapter opening illustrations; and the illustrations on the following pages: 44, 61, 63, 81, 94, 103, 105, 112, 117, 129, 146, 166, 189, 191, 246, 251, 274, 284, 289, 305, 311, 326, 360, 362, 380.
Mary Ross: Illustrations on pages 49, 102, 121, 131, 134, 325
Jeff Tucker and Monotype Composition Co.: Freshman Survey graphs and graphs on pages 12, 90
Alexander Teshin Associates: All other illustrations

Printed in the United States of America
1 2 3 4 5 6 7 8 9 10

For more information, contact Wadsworth Publishing Company, 10 Davis Drive, Belmont, CA 94002, or electronically at http://www.thomson.com/wadsworth.html

International Thomson Publishing Europe
Berkshire House 168-173
High Holborn
London, WC1V 7AA, England

Thomas Nelson Australia
102 Dodds Street
South Melbourne 3205
Victoria, Australia

Nelson Canada
1120 Birchmount Road
Scarborough, Ontario
Canada M1K 5G4

International Thomson Editores
Campos Eliseos 385, Piso 7
Col. Polanco
11560 México D.F. México

Internationl Thomson Publishing GmbH
Königswinterer Strasse 418
53227 Bonn, Germany

International Thomson Publishing Asia
221 Henderson Road
#05-10 Henderson Building
Singapore 0315

International Thomson Publishing Japan
Hirakawacho Kyowa Building, 3F
2-2-1 Hirakawacho
Chiyoda-ku, Tokyo 102, Japan

International Thomson Publishing Southern Africa
Building 18, Constantia Park
240 Old Pretoria Road
Halfway House, 1685 South Africa

Library of Congress Cataloging-in-Publication Data
Your college experience : strategies for success / [edited by] John N. Gardner, A. Jerome Jewler—3rd ed.
   p. cm.
   Includes bibliographical references and index.
   ISBN 0-534-51894-X
   1. College student orientation—United States. 2. Study skills—United States. 3. Critical thinking—United States. 4. Success—United States. I. Gardner, John N. II. Jewler, A. Jerome.
LB2343.32.Y68 1997
378.1'98—dc20
                                  96-36217

We thank our wonderful families and colleagues for their patience over the past several years as we watched the newest edition of this book take shape. We thank our students for proving to us that the basic assumptions in this book really do work. We thank faculty, staff, and administrators at colleges and universities for believing in those same basic assumptions. Most important of all, we welcome all new students to their college experience and urge them, in the words of Tennyson, to be "strong in will, to strive, to seek, to find, and not to yield."

Brief Contents

Contents

In a World of Differences

■ A GLOBAL, FLEXIBLE APPROACH TO MEET THE NEEDS OF ALL NEW STUDENTS

In this third comprehensive edition of *Your College Experience*, we specifically address the concerns of many different types of students: commuting and residential, urban and suburban, "minority" and "majority," traditional and returning. At the same time we bear in mind that regardless of how an individual student may be grouped, he or she also shares many continuing and emerging needs with virtually all new college students:

- Building friendships, support groups, and contact with teachers
- Self-awareness and growth in terms of personal resources, goals, and commitment
- An analytic frame of mind that integrates individual study skills with focused critical thinking and an appreciation of the liberal arts
- Awareness of the new technology of computers and of the Internet, the World Wide Web, and e-mail as tools for learning and communicating
- Ways to make each dollar count and to avoid money management problems such as over-reliance on credit cards
- A clear idea of how diversity touches and enriches each of our lives

In view of these needs, this book supports a dynamic, holistic, timely program of study and an interactive, constructive classroom experience for each and every student.

■ NEW INTEGRATED FEATURES

In addition to making many changes in existing chapters (such as an expanded approach in "Diversity on Campus," now including issues of sexual orientation), we have called upon Linda J. Sax to update the Freshman Survey features as of 1996. We have also made two other pervasive changes: a new approach to critical thinking and expanded coverage of new technology.

A New Approach to Critical Thinking

In this edition, critical thinking is taught and presented through a simple but effective four-part framework developed by William T. Daly: abstract thinking, creative thinking, systematic thinking, and effective communication of thought (see pages 18 and 19). Exercises throughout the book, identified by the critical thinking icon 🎲 , help students practice and apply this approach to many areas of learning and personal development.

New Technology

With key advice from Daniel J. Kurland, author of *The 'Net, the Web, and You,* we have integrated Internet and technology coverage throughout the book, including such topics as the use of computers for gathering information, for studying, and for communicating by e-mail, Internet, and the World Wide Web. We also have called upon Steven Gilbert and Casey Green for late-breaking updates to Chapter 12 "Computing for College Success."

■ NEW CHAPTERS

We have brought new approaches to several topics. By combining the writing and speaking chapters and integrating critical thinking throughout, we have managed to add new coverage without increasing the overall length of the book. In fact, there are fewer chapters overall. New chapters include the following:

Money Management

In response to overwhelming demand, we have added a new chapter on money matters, including close attention to "the perils of plastic" (credit card abuses) especially for new college students.

The Liberal Arts

In "The Liberal Arts: Foundation for Lifelong Learning," Thorne Compton shows how a background in the liberal arts can be brought to bear on both creative and critical challenges, in school and beyond.

Relationships and Campus Involvement

Tom Carskadon and Nancy McCarley bring wisdom and humor to a new chapter on relationships. The chapter speaks to a broad range of student concerns and includes activities for traditional and nontraditional students.

■ PRINT TEACHING SUPPLEMENTS

Annotated Instructor's Edition

Instructors should have received (or may request) the *Annotated Instructor's Edition,* designed to make it easier to teach the course. It contains the complete text, along with teaching annotations about how to use the text and its exercises.

Instructor's Manual

Instructors may also obtain the separate instructor's guide for this text. It contains additional exercises and suggestions about how to approach each chapter, quiz master sheets to reinforce required reading when the occasion demands, and numerous transparency masters. There is certainly no uniformly right or wrong way to teach this course! Flexibility is key. We hope that the many added materials and suggestions will be helpful.

The Wadsworth College Success Course Guide

This general resource for instructors and administrators covers topics such as building campus support for a first-year course, creating and administering the course, and refining it in the future.

Additional Supplements

To enhance the book's integrated approach to critical thinking, we recommend William T. Daly's *Beyond Critical Thinking: Teaching the Thinking Skills Necessary to Academic and Professional Success*. It is available from The National Resource Center for the Freshman Year Experience and Students in Transition: Phone 803-777-6029, Fax 803-777-4699, or e-mail *ninal@rcce.sc.edu*. Please request Monograph #17.

■THE WADSWORTH COLLEGE SUCCESS WEBSITE

The Wadsworth website for College Success is in part a tool for instructors and students to communicate with the authors and with other instructors and students around the country. It also provides interactive enrichment for traditional students, adult learners, urban learners, commuters, students planning transfer, and others. The Wadsworth College Success newsletter, *Keystone,* is also published on the site. The site can be reached from *http://www.wadsworth.com*

■RESOURCES FOR BUILDING YOUR OWN COURSE MATERIALS

Building Your Own Customized Book

It is possible for you to build your own campus-specific custom book by selecting chapters from this and/or other Wadsworth College Success books, and combining them with your own campus materials. For immediate assistance and information regarding content, quantities, binding options, and prices of customized texts or bundled products, contact the ITP Custom Solution Center at 1-800-254-6724.

Additional Optional Chapters

In a customized book you may also include additional chapters not contained in this text. Optional chapters deal with leadership, women in college, returning students, living on campus, assertiveness, wellness, and critical thinking. To inspect the complete set of optional Gardner/Jewler custom chapters or other Wadsworth College Success materials, contact your local Wadsworth/ITP sales representative.

The Reader/Workbook Option

Your College Experience is now also available in a new alternative format, splitting the book into a separate Reader and Workbook. The Reader contains articles written by experts on topics such as assertiveness, career planning, managing stress, and much more. The Workbook contains all the exercises found in Gardner and Jewler's best selling text *Your College Experience*, Third Edition, plus chapter quizzes, chapter review questions, and chapter journal questions. Designed to be used in tandem, these texts will allow students to both learn and practice the skills necessary to achieve a lifetime of success. Contact your local Wadsworth/ITP sales representative for sample copies.

■VIDEO SUPPLEMENTS

Wadsworth's Film and Video Policy and New Video Series

The Wadsworth Film and Video policy is one way to enhance your course presentations. In addition, Wadsworth is developing a new series of short videos on key topics such as time management, stress, and general study skills. Ask your local Wadsworth/ITP sales representative for more details.

The SCETV Video Series

The video series *Your College Experience: Strategies for Success* is produced by the University of South Carolina and South Carolina Educational Television. Twelve 5- to 7-minute video programs, based on the text, are designed to teach, inform, motivate, and stimulate lively group discussion. The series is highly adaptable to many educational settings. To order or to request information, call or write: The National Resource Center for The Freshman Year Experience and Students in Transition at 1728 College St., University of South Carolina, Columbia, SC 29208. Or call 803-777-6029 or fax 803-777-4699.

■INSTRUCTOR TRAINING

Teacher Training Seminars with Wadsworth Authors

Held several times a year in various regions, these workshops allow you to interact with the author and develop your teaching skills in general.

Additional Training and Seminar Information

Additional training is available through the National Resource Center for the Freshman Year Experience and Students in Transition at the University of

South Carolina at 803-777-6029 or by calling Jerry Jewler at 803-787-7174 (e-mail: *jewler-a.jerome@sc.edu*).

▋ACKNOWLEDGMENTS

First thanks must go to the many continuing adopters of the text who have kept in touch with us about their evolving needs by direct communication or by responding to our occasional surveys.

Thanks also to the following astute reviewers for this new edition: Mona J. Casady, Southwest Missouri State University; Kathy Jones, University of California, Riverside; Frances M. Kavenik, University of Wisconsin—Parkside; Molly M. Thacker, Radford University; Esther J. Winter, Northwest Missouri State University. We also thank the reviewers from past editions: Peter Biegel, Purdue University; Mary Jo Boehms, Jackson State Community College; Sandy Darnell, Rappahanock Community College; David Entin, NYC Technical College; Barbara Greenstein, The College of New Jersey; Elizabeth Hall, Texas Tech University; Michael Johnson, Western Kentucky University; Wendy J. Palmquist, Plymouth State College; Lauren Pernetti, Kent State University; Nancy Sonleitner, University of Oklahoma; John Steingoss, University of Toledo; James Stepp, University of Maine at Presque Isle; and Michael Stoune, Texas Tech University.

We are grateful for new major contributions to the book from Tom Carskadon, Nancy McCarley, H. Thorne Compton, William T. Daly, and Daniel J. Kurland.

For us, *Your College Experience* continues to be an exhilarating collaboration with colleagues, students, and friends across the country.

John N. Gardner

A. Jerome Jewler

A Student's Guide to Learning

On the next few pages, you will find excerpts from the Third Edition of Your College Experience: Strategies for Success, *the freshman seminar/orientation* text that has helped thousands of entering students put their college careers on a successful track. We invite you to take a few moments to review these pages. They highlight the major text themes and illustrate the carefully constructed learning tools found throughout this book.

Note, in particular, the material on critical thinking—an important factor in academic success—the many group activities, and the stimulating interactive activities that abound in this text.

By following the guidelines and exercises in this empowering book, you will greatly enhance your ability to learn as well as adjust to college life. Throughout, we share with you our many years of teaching experience to help you gain the insights, skills, and strategies you'll need to make a success of your college years.

■A SYSTEMATIC APPROACH

The text provides you with a systematic approach to dealing effectively with the challenges you face upon entering college.

Twenty-One Steps That Ensure Success

The first chapter offers a list, excerpted here, of 21 suggestions for a fulfilling college experience. The list covers everything from advisors to study habits to health to reasonable expectations.

■KEYS TO SUCCESS IN COLLEGE

Researchers have identified certain things students can do to ensure success. Ironically, students are often unaware of what these "persistence factors"—or keys to success—are and how much they really matter. Here are twenty-one basic things you can do to thrive in college. This book is built on these suggestions and will show you how to implement them. With a pencil, checkmark (✔) every item that you think will be particularly important or difficult for you. Later, after you've accomplished them, come back and turn the checkmark into an ✗.

1. **Find and get to know one individual on campus who cares about your survival.** It takes only one. It might be the leader of your orientation seminar or some other instructor, an academic advisor, someone at the career or counseling center, an advisor to a student organization or group, or someone where you have an on-campus job. You may have to take the initiative to establish this relationship—but it will be well worth it.

2. **Learn what helping resources your campus offers and where they are located.** Most campuses have academic and personal support services that are free and confidential. Successful people use them.

3. **Understand why you are in college.** Identify specific goals. This chapter introduces you to a useful goal-setting process.

4. **Set up a daily schedule and stick to it.** If you can't do it alone, find someone in your academic skills or personal counseling center. Get a daytimer or "week-at-a-glance" calendar from your bookstore. Chapter 4 will

Four Aspects of Critical Thinking: Improving Your Powers

The single most important goal of higher education is to help you learn to think more critically and creatively. This involves training yourself to go beyond common sense and personal opinion when you try to analyze a problem or to communicate ideas to others. It means freeing yourself of your emotional attachments to certain ideas and relying on factual information and conscious, systematic reasoning. It means basing what you think and say on knowledge gained through careful reading and ordered study.

Higher education goes beyond memorizing facts. This is not to say that facts are unimportant. Nothing substitutes for thorough, truthful information. But equally important are your abilities to judge the truth of supposed facts and to think logically from the facts. Such thinking is often referred to as *critical thinking*.

For you to develop critical thinking skills, your teachers will ask more open-ended questions—Why? How? and What if? Rather than expecting you to absorb knowledge like a sponge, teachers will encourage you to think problems through, analyze, conceptualize, ask questions, be questioned, and reflect on how certain beliefs might compare to others. In addition to memorizing facts and figures for a final examination, you will be challenged to apply what you have learned to the real world. College

Each of these abilities corresponds roughly to a step in an overall process. Throughout this book we will be asking you to practice and improve your abilities in each of these steps, largely through exercises that require you to think about an issue and then write or speak about it. To a great extent, critical thinking results from first carefully reading what others have written about a topic and then writing or speaking in response. Think about how far along you are in each of the following areas:

1. **Making abstractions out of details.** From large amounts of facts or information learn to find the big ideas, the patterns and abstractions behind the facts. What are the general and recurring truths or arguments reflected in the details? What are the key ideas? Even fields like medicine, which involve countless facts of biology, culminate in general ideas: the principle of circulation; the basic patterns of cell biology; the principles of genetics. In essence, what larger concepts do the details suggest? What is the speaker or writer really saying?

2. **Finding new possibilities.** Practice creative thinking to discover the meaning and implications of abstractions. What questions do the large ideas suggest? Avoid making im-

Improving Your Powers of Critical Thinking

This excerpted Critical Thinking box focuses on one of the key aspects of your success in college—the ability to sort through the unimportant and the misleading, and to think logically about all the information you will be receiving. Critical Thinking boxes are a new feature of this edition.

The cube symbol identifies Critical Thinking boxes. (A bicyclist symbol accompanies topics of interest to commuting students and a wavy arrow identifies helpful hints and other useful information.)

Focus on Technology

In addition to Chapter 12 "Computing for College Success," the text contains many other exercises and suggestions about making the best use of important new technology such as the Internet and the World Wide Web.

Internet Resources

Finding information on the Internet depends on knowing where to look for it. It helps to know the existence and uses of a number of electronic resources—both in general and in your field of interest:

Databases (both public and commercial)

Abstract services (which provide summaries of journal articles or other information)

Specialized on-line library collections

Professional associations

Gopher/Veronica: for locating documents, files, information, or data from or about a specific education, governmental, or nonprofit organization or association. The search program Veronica can be of service here.

WAIS: for specific documents or to search the content of a certain type of document or database.

World Wide Web: for locating documents, files, information, or data from or about a

■THE IMPORTANCE OF PERSONAL CONTACT

Throughout the book, we emphasize the value of personal contact, through the use of personal stories, collective problem-solving, study group suggestions, and discussions on student–advisor–teacher relationships.

Student–Teacher Relationships

As in this excerpt from the chapter covering the student–teacher connection (Chapter 2), we provide frequent and concrete advice on how to make the most out of your interactions with instructors, advisors, and counselors.

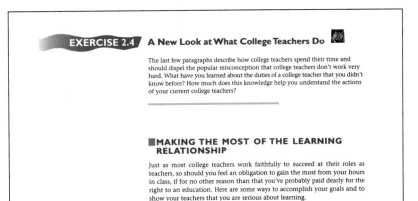

EXERCISE 2.4 A New Look at What College Teachers Do

The last few paragraphs describe how college teachers spend their time and should dispel the popular misconception that college teachers don't work very hard. What have you learned about the duties of a college teacher that you didn't know before? How much does this knowledge help you understand the actions of your current college teachers?

■MAKING THE MOST OF THE LEARNING RELATIONSHIP

Just as most college teachers work faithfully to succeed at their roles as teachers, so should you feel an obligation to gain the most from your hours in class, if for no other reason than that you've probably paid dearly for the right to an education. Here are some ways to accomplish your goals and to show your teachers that you are serious about learning.

Group Exercises

This exercise from Chapter 16 "A Personal System of Values" is just one of many in the book that utilizes group dynamics.

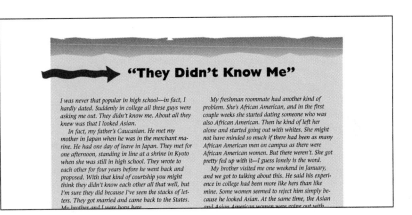

EXERCISE 16.3 Shared Values?

List all the reasons you chose to attend college. Look back at your responses to Chapter 1, Exercises 1.1 and 1.2, regarding your reasons for attending college. Share your reasons in a small group. Attempt to arrive at a consensus about the five most important reasons for people in general to choose college. Then rank the top five, from most important to least important.

Share your final rankings with other groups in the class. How similar were the results of the groups? How different? How easy or hard was it to reach a consensus in your group? In other groups? What does the exercise tell you about the consistency or inconsistency of values among members of the class?

Personal Stories

We relate several personal stories that allow you to see the college experience through the lives of others. You may be surprised to find that these interesting accounts will show you that your concerns and experiences are often shared by others.

"They Didn't Know Me"

I was never that popular in high school—in fact, I hardly dated. Suddenly in college all these guys were asking me out. They didn't know me. About all they knew was that I looked Asian.

In fact, my father's Caucasian. He met my mother in Japan when he was in the merchant marine. He had one day of leave in Japan. They met for one afternoon, standing in line at a shrine in Kyoto when she was still in high school. They wrote to each other for four years before he went back and proposed. With that kind of courtship you might think they didn't know each other all that well, but I'm sure they did because I've seen the stacks of letters. They got married and came back to the States. My brother and I were born here.

My freshman roommate had another kind of problem. She's African American, and in the first couple weeks she started dating someone who was also African American. Then he kind of left her alone and started going out with whites. She might not have minded so much if there had been as many African American men on campus as there were African American women. But there weren't. She got pretty fed up with it—I guess lonely is the word.

My brother visited me one weekend in January, and we got to talking about this. He said his experience in college had been more like hers than like mine. Some women seemed to reject him simply because he looked Asian. At the same time, the Asian and Asian American women were going out with

The Freshman Survey

The text encourages you to compare your views with those of other first-year students throughout the country. Reports throughout the text from Higher Education Research Institute at UCLA give you concrete national data.

FRESHMAN SURVEY
Linda J. Sax

Changing Interest in Business and Health-Related Majors

Between 1966 and 1987, the proportion of first-year students interested in business careers doubled, as the first graph shows. Although interest in business careers has declined steadily since the proportion of women planning business careers increased sixfold. Indeed, in some business specializations, women now outnumber men. For several years more women than men have

■ACTIVITIES THAT CULTIVATE WRITING AND SPEAKING SKILLS

Realizing the importance of effective writing and speaking (employers are asking for these skills more and more often), we have included numerous activities and discussions to help you achieve proficiency in these two critical areas.

Writing Integrated Throughout

This exercise from Chapter 10 "Writing and Speaking" reinforces the connection between the two modes of communication. Goal-oriented writing exercises appear throughout the text.

EXERCISE 10.4 Introduce Yourself

To try your hand at speaking in front of the class, prepare a 3-minute presentation introducing yourself to your classmates. Bring or wear a "prop" that characterizes or caricatures you. For example, if you like to ski, wear your goggles; if you flip burgers on the weekends, wear your apron and carry a spatula. You can talk about your hometown, your high school days, your family, your reasons for going to college, or some other topic your instructor suggests.

JOURNAL

Write about yourself as a writer. How do you proceed when given a writing assignment? How well does your method work? What are your strengths and weaknesses as a writer? What suggestions have instructors made to you about your writing? Now think of yourself as a speaker and answer the same questions. Do you consider yourself a better writer or speaker? Explain why.

Journals

At the end of each chapter is a journal activity, such as the one shown here from the chapter on writing and speaking, that offers an opportunity for writing practice. Journal entries are an excellent vehicle for helping you to reflect, organize, and set goals. The diverse and interesting journal exercises found throughout this book can help you begin the rewarding lifelong habit of practicing systematic reflections and, if you wish, keeping a regular journal.

Your College Experience

Keys to Success

John N. Gardner
University of South Carolina

I just stood in line for an hour and spent over a hundred dollars on three books. Now I'm broke and have three exams scheduled for the same week in October. First week of college and I'm already stressing out.

At least I've met a few interesting people. Wish I had the time to talk to them!

Chapter Goals

After reading this chapter, you will have a clearer sense of the value of college. You will also be aware of specific factors that can contribute to your success. The chapter activities will help you see how these factors apply to you as an individual and will get you started on a goal-setting process that supports success.

You've just taken another major step in life: You've decided to invest in a college education. Will the results be worth the investment? That depends on one thing more than any other: the goals you set as you begin. Before you read on, take a few moments now to consider what you hope to accomplish.

EXERCISE 1.1 Your Reasons for Attending College

List three reasons you've entered college.

1. _____

2. _____

3. _____

Which one of these three is the most important? Why?

_____

_____

_____

_____

We'll come back to this soon.

Note: Many of the exercises in this book are marked by one or more of the following icons: ✐ indicates a writing exercise; 🖼 indicates an exercise involving class or small group discussion; 🎲 indicates a critical thinking exercise; 💻 indicates an exercise involving computer technology.

Less Todd/photo courtesy of Duke University

■ WHO ARE YOU, ANYWAY?

People attend college for different reasons. Which one of the following sounds *most* like you? Which may also apply?

- You did just fine in high school and are ready for everything college can throw at you. You're also ready for a lot more personal freedom.
- You're not really sure what you're after. You just want to test the waters, find what's out there, try a few courses, and see what happens.
- You know exactly what you want to study. You have a career in mind, and you can see yourself making your mark on the world.
- You started a few other things before you got around to college—job, marriage, kids. Your attention feels a bit divided.
- You know why you're in college but wonder how well you'll fit in.
- You're wondering how you're going to raise the money you need and still keep up with a full college course load.
- You like attending college locally, but you wonder how you're going to deal with commuting and living at home.
- You're proud to be the first in your family to get this far academically. You don't plan to stop until you graduate.
- You've just had a major life change: You've lost your job, your marriage has ended, or your last child has "left the nest."
- You tried college a long time ago but weren't motivated. Now you've screwed up your courage to finally return.
- Your parents expected you to go to college. Everyone else in your high school group did.

 **Why You Decided on College**

In a small group discuss the list of reasons on page 3 for attending college. Which ones seem most relevant to you personally? Would you need to write a different statement to accurately describe your own situation? What would it be?

Do any of your goals in Exercise 1.1 relate to the statement that best describes you? How? Discuss this with the group as well.

Today's Student Body

For most of us college is a necessity, not an option. New technologies and the information explosion are changing the workplace so drastically that few people will be able to support themselves and their families well without at least some education beyond high school. That may not have been true for earlier generations, but it's true for yours.

In 1900 fewer than 2 percent of Americans of traditional college age attended college. Today more than 50 percent attend, with over 3,500 colleges serving more than 14 million students. Over 55 percent of college entrants start in two-year colleges, and more often than not these students combine studies at a local school with work or family commitments. At the same time, four-year schools are admitting increasing numbers of increasingly diverse students. Adult students also are enrolling in college in record-breaking numbers, and by the end of the 1990s, over one-third of college students will be over 25.

Although a higher percentage of high school graduates in the United States (or people with equivalent education) choose college than in any other country in the world, 40 percent of students who start in four-year programs never earn their degrees. Of those who do, about one-third will take up to ten years to do so. In two-year colleges, up to half of the entering class will drop out by the end of the first year.

Dealing with Freedom

Of those who quit, about three-fourths are in good academic standing. Clearly, a lot besides academic talent will affect your success in college.

One problem is simply choosing the courses you will need to complete in order to graduate. Today's students often face a staggering number of course and program options, and most need an advisor to help them choose and coordinate courses.

This book won't take the place of a living, breathing advisor or counselor, but it will help you avoid some common pitfalls and support your academic goals and enjoyment of college in the broadest sense.

Eliminate the Negatives

A self-fulfilling prophecy is something you predict is going to happen, and by thinking that's how things will turn out, you greatly increase the chances that they will. For instance, if you decide that today just isn't going to be

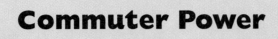

Commuter Power

About how many of America's 14.5 million college students would you guess are commuters? (The answer appears at the top of page 22.)

a. 2.83 million (20 percent)

b. 5.66 million (40 percent)

c. 8.49 million (60 percent)

d. 11.32 million (80 percent)

1. **The fact that you commute may work to your advantage in some ways.** In others you will need to work harder than the campus resident. Look over the twenty-one "persistence factors" on pages 7–11. Do you think any of these will be harder for you to achieve because you commute?

2. **Interact fully with your campus.** Use the goal-setting process to ensure that you do *get involved* in a campus activity, do *explore* campus resources, and do *find* someone on campus who knows and cares about you.

3. **If you are living at home with your parents, negotiate home responsibilities up front.** Your parents may need to understand that your college work will take more time than high school. You may not have as much time to devote to family errands and chores as before.

your day, chances are it won't be. You'll look for ways that things can go wrong—and you'll find them. Do any of these apply to you?

- Fear of too much freedom or not being able to manage your time
- Anxiety over adjusting to a new environment
- Fear that college will be too difficult
- Homesickness
- Lack of good study habits
- Difficulty in understanding instructors
- Fear of competition from brighter, younger, or older students
- Fear of disappointing people or not getting their support
- Problems with new living arrangements
- Worry over choosing the wrong major
- Shyness
- The feeling that you may have to cheat to survive
- Fear of being perceived by other students as a klutz
- Problems in juggling work, family, and studies
- Inability to pay for college

If some of these concerns sound familiar, take comfort: Most other entering students share the same fears. Each of the worries is attached to a negative self-fulfilling prophecy that you can exchange for a positive one. That's basically what setting goals is all about.

The New Majority

American women were at one time barred from higher education. In 1833 Oberlin College became the first to admit women, as well as African Americans. It was only when publicly funded, land grant universities were founded under the Morrill Act of 1862 that "coeducation" became at all common. And only in the last twenty-five years have most men's colleges become schools for men and women, with fully integrated degree programs, residences, and curricula. Facing social and financial pressures, many formerly all-women's colleges have also opened their admissions to men. Women now make up the majority of college students—about 54 percent.

Photo by David Gonzales

EXERCISE 1.3   The Good, the Bad, the Not-So-Bad

Think about things that have happened already this term.

1. Name one thing that's been fun or easy.

   _____

2. Name one thing that was hard that you knew would be hard.

   _____

3. Name one thing that was hard that you *didn't* know would be hard.

   _____

4. Name one thing that you expect to happen and think will be hard.

   _____

5. Name one thing that's been *too* easy!

   _____

Share your answers in a group. What problems do you have in common with other people in your class? What problems seem to be yours alone? How are these problems likely to be influenced (for better or worse) by self-fulfilling prophecies?

EXERCISE 1.4 **Solving a Problem**

What has been your biggest unresolved problem to date in college? What steps have you attempted to solve this? Write a letter or memo to your instructor about these two questions.

■KEYS TO SUCCESS IN COLLEGE

Researchers have identified certain things students can do to ensure success. Ironically, students are often unaware of what these "persistence factors"— or keys to success—are and how much they really matter. Here are twenty-one basic things you can do to thrive in college. This book is built on these suggestions and will show you how to implement them. With a pencil, checkmark (✔) every item that you think will be particularly important or difficult for you. Later, after you've accomplished them, come back and turn the checkmark into an ✘.

1. **Find and get to know one individual on campus who cares about your survival.** It takes only one. It might be the leader of your orientation seminar or some other instructor, an academic advisor, someone at the career or counseling center, an advisor to a student organization or group, or someone where you have an on-campus job. You may have to take the initiative to establish this relationship—but it will be well worth it.

2. **Learn what helping resources your campus offers and where they are located.** Most campuses have academic and personal support services that are free and confidential. Successful people use them.

3. **Understand why you are in college.** Identify specific goals. This chapter introduces you to a useful goal-setting process.

4. **Set up a daily schedule and stick to it.** If you can't do it alone, find someone in your academic skills or personal counseling center. Get a daytimer or "week-at-a-glance" calendar from your bookstore. Chapter 4 will get you started at assigning sufficient time for study, work, sleep, and recreation. If you have family or work obligations, find ways to balance them with academic demands.

5. **If you're attending classes full-time, try not to work more than 20 hours a week.** Most people begin a downhill slide beyond 20 hours. If you need more money, talk to a financial aid officer. Also, students who work on campus tend to do better in classes and are more likely to stay enrolled than those working off campus. Visit your college placement office.

6. **Assess and improve your study habits.** Find out about your own learning style. This will help you learn how to take better notes in class, read more efficiently, and do better on tests. If your campus has an academic skills center, pay a visit.

7. **Join at least one study group.** Studies have shown that students who study in groups often get the highest grades and survive college better.

8. **See your instructors outside class.** It's okay to go for help. Students who interact with instructors outside class tend to stay in college longer.

Tips for "Minority" Students

The "minority" population of the United States is growing so fast that the common use of the term to denote Americans of non-European ancestry is rapidly becoming outdated. For the present, however, students of non-European ancestry still often find themselves in a distinct minority on campus.

Some of the twenty-one keys to success are particularly important for most students of color, especially the keys related to establishing contact with faculty and other students. Focus on those keys. Don't let yourself become isolated. Form or join study groups. Visit your instructors outside class. Take advantage of support services. Join activities outside class.

1. **Keep that "I can do it" attitude and stay in college.** A positive attitude matters.

2. **Shoot for an A. Grades matter.** If you're not already thinking about getting a master's degree or doctorate now, you probably will in the future. Your undergraduate GPA will be an important part of your application to graduate school and jobs.

3. **Attend college full-time if you can.** If you work, look for a campus job and try to work no more than 20 hours a week. Ask at your financial aid office for information about work–study programs, grants, and scholarships.

4. **Take advantage of minority support services.** Your campus may have centers for minority students. Visit these places and introduce yourself. Ask for help with problems. Take advantage of mentoring programs.

5. **Don't be afraid to take math and science courses or to go into math- and science-based fields.** Scholarships for minority students may be available for math and science careers.

6. **Practice for standardized tests.** Anyone can improve his or her performance on tests such as the ACT, SAT, or GRE. Enroll in test preparation sessions, especially if you're heading for graduate school.

7. **Choose a career with long-term pay-offs.** Shoot for being a teacher, not a teacher's aide; a lawyer, not a paralegal; a doctor or registered nurse, not a doctor's or nurse's assistant. Be sure that your course work matches your goal.

9. **Develop critical thinking skills.** Challenge. Ask why. Look for unusual solutions to ordinary problems and ordinary solutions to unusual problems. (See "Four Aspects of Critical Thinking" on pages 18–19.)

10. **Choose teachers who involve you in the learning process.** Take classes in which you can actively participate and develop your critical thinking skills. Unfortunately, most students choose their classes based on what will fit best in their schedule. Ask upper-class students who the best instructors are.

11. **Know how to find information on your campus, including at the library.** The library isn't as formidable as it might seem, and it offers a wealth of resources.

12. **Improve your writing.** Employers want graduates who can write. Write every day—the more you write, the better you will write. Do the journal and other writing assignments in this book.

13. **Find a great academic advisor or counselor.** The right advisor will support and guide you.

14. **Visit the career center early in your first term.** See a career counselor before you get too far along in college, even if you have chosen your academic major.

8. **Explore alternative learning activities and environments.** Find out about co-op opportunities, internships, and exchange programs. Consider spending a semester at a historically black college. Studying at another school may not cost any more than being at your present school.

9. **Maintain connections with your "home base."** But be aware of the changes you may be going through and the impact of those changes on family and friends. They may put pressure on you to stay the same or accuse you of "selling out" for being a successful student. Use campus e-mail or a commercial on-line service to stay in touch with parents and friends at other schools.

10. **Be proud of your heritage and culture.** In college you may hear racist remarks and witness or be the target of behaviors rooted in ignorance, bigotry, fear,

Photo courtesy of Bill Denison

and hatred. Stand tall. Be proud. Refuse to tolerate such behaviors.

Take courses in African American, Hispanic, and other cultural studies. Help other minority students. Make friends with students from different racial and ethnic backgrounds. Get to know minority faculty and administrators. Get involved in sensitizing others to cultural diversity.

15. **Make at least one or two close friends among your peers.** Choose your friends for their own merits, not for what they can do for you. In college, as in life, you become like those with whom you associate.

16. **If you're not assertive enough, take assertiveness training.** Check at your counseling center for workshops on assertiveness training. Learn how to stand up for your rights in a way that respects the rights of others.

17. **Get involved in campus activities.** Visit the campus (or student) activities office—usually found in the student union. Work for the campus newspaper or radio station. Join a club or support group. Play intramural sports. Most campus organizations welcome newcomers—you're their lifeblood. Students who join even one group are more likely to graduate.

18. **Take your health seriously.** How much sleep you get, what you eat, whether you exercise, and what decisions you make about drugs, alcohol, and sex all contribute to your well-being. Be good to yourself and you'll be happier and more successful. Find healthy ways to deal with stress. Your counseling center can help.

19. **Polish your computer skills.** At the very least, you should be comfortable with basic file manipulation, the use of a standard word processing program, and e-mail.

"Am I Smart Enough?"— Tips for Returning Students

1. **Don't doubt your abilities.** Recent studies have shown learning ability does not decline with age. In fact, verbal ability actually increases as one grows older.

2. **Expect teachers to be glad to see you.** Most will welcome you because your practical life experiences will enrich the class. Your experiences will also be good material for written assignments.

3. **If school seems stressful, enroll part-time.** Adjust the number of courses you're taking to control the amount of strain.

4. **Enlist the support of your spouse, partner, or family.** Seek adjustments in household routines and duties. Let family members know when you'll need extra time for exams. An actively supportive partner is a great ally. A nonsupportive partner who interferes with study time can reduce your success in college. If your partner feels threatened and seems to undermine what you are doing, sit down and discuss the problem. Or seek counseling. Changes in relationships between partners often go hand in hand with enormous growth.

5. **Find faculty and staff support on campus. Find out about child care.** If your school has special advisors for adult students, they will know the most about weekend and evening courses. Look for adult advocates in student affairs or continuing education programs.

6. **Develop peer support.** Find out about classes and organizations where you can meet other adult learners. Or put an ad in the campus paper and form your own group. Find a classmate to meet for coffee, study with, or exchange notes with if one of you has to miss a lecture.

7. **Take review courses or a course in how to study.** Most adults have let their study habits become rusty. After learning the study skills tools in this book, consider taking a longer study skills course. You may need to review basic math or languages. Fortunately, relearning something is much easier than learning new material. Look for review courses on campus or in adult programs at local high schools.

8. **Embrace new technologies.** Ask how to use word processors at the campus computing center, computerized library search or journal access programs, or e-mail. The computer skills you develop on campus will be valuable in later employment.

9. **Be realistic.** Weigh your expectations about grades against your other important commitments.

Photo courtesy of Berea College

20. **Show up for class.** When asked what they would do differently if they could do it all over again, most seniors say, "go to class." Instructors tend to test on what they discuss in class, as well as grade in part on the basis of class attendance and participation. Be there.

21. **Try to have realistic expectations.** At first you may not make the grades you could be making or made in high school. If you were a star athlete in high school, you might not be in college. This book can help you develop more realistic goals.

Do most of these suggestions sound simple? They are.

EXERCISE 1.5 Focusing on Your Concerns

Go back and browse the table of contents of this book. Find at least one chapter that addresses each of your most important concerns.

■ THE VALUE OF COLLEGE

Few decisions will have as great an impact on your life as your decision to go to college. In addition to increasing your knowledge and self-understanding, college will expand your career horizons and can help you make the right career decisions. It will probably also affect your views on family matters, social issues, community service, politics, health, recreation, and consumer issues.

Education, Careers, and Income

Will your college education lead to greater income? Consider the information in Figure 1.1, which shows average pay in 1993 dollars, for 25- to 34-year-old full-time, year-round workers.

Facing a job market that places a higher premium on education and technical knowledge, young men with only a high school education have found that they are making less than their counterparts did from 1974 to the present. High school-educated women have held their own on salaries since the 1970s. Although college-educated females' wages have increased more quickly than those of their male counterparts, much of that overall gain has come from working more hours.

According to a report by the Carnegie Commission on Higher Education, as a college graduate you will have a more continuous, less erratic job history; will be promoted more often; and are much less likely to become unemployed than nongraduates. You are also likely to be happier with your work than those who didn't attend college.

Critics of higher education occasionally point out that some people with college degrees are unemployed or underemployed (particularly due to the recession of the early 1990s), but you have only to look at the employment figures of high school graduates and high school dropouts to see that the better educated you are, the better your opportunities. As the saying goes, "If you think education is expensive, try ignorance."

Figure 1.1 Higher Education = Higher Pay

The graphs show average pay for male and female full-time, year-round workers, ages 25 to 34, from 1974 to 1993. The earnings gap between high school- and college-educated workers is growing.

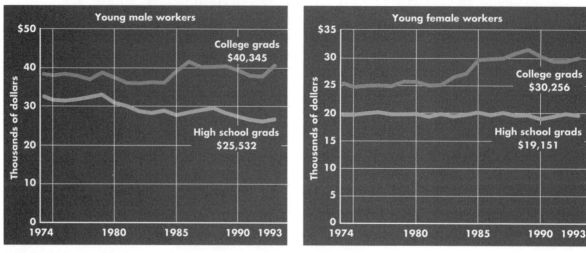

SOURCE: U.S. Bureau of the Census, 1994. Amounts are expressed in terms of 1993 dollars.

The Broader Benefits of a College Education

Of course college will affect you in many ways besides financially. How will you change in ways that differ from those of people who decided to go directly to work, join the military, or do something else rather than go to college? The evidence from many studies suggests:

- College has a strong positive impact on how effectively people think. Expect to increase significantly your knowledge, intellect, tolerance, and interest in lifelong learning.

- College educates the *whole* person. It gives students the opportunity to clarify and improve their sense of possibility and self-worth. This self-esteem is one of the principal benefits of college and may help you realize how you might make a difference in the world.

- You will tend to be more adaptable, more future-oriented, more liberal in your outlook, more interested in political and public affairs, and less prone to criminal activity.

- College has an important influence on family life. You will tend to delay getting married and having children, to have fewer children, and to share child-care and household responsibilities. You will also tend to devote more energy to child rearing. You will have a slightly lower divorce rate than non-college-educated people, and your children generally will have greater abilities and achieve more than children of non-college-educated parents.

- In addition to making more money, you will be a more efficient consumer. Chances are you will save more money, make better investments, and spend more money on home, intellectual, and cultural interests and on your children. You will also be more able to deal with bureaucracies, the legal system, tax laws and requirements, and advertising claims.

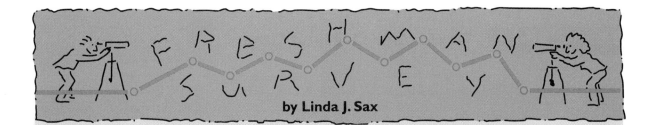

by Linda J. Sax

College, Money, and Career

In the previous decade, entering students increasingly thought of college as a link to jobs and money. As the figure shows, in Fall 1995, 72.3 percent of first-year students indicated that making more money was a very important factor in their decision to attend college.

Students increasingly view college as a means to financial security and career development rather than as a chance for intellectual growth and personal development. Although some might interpret this as an indication that they have become more materialistic, the economic upheaval that has shaken the nation for the past two decades suggests that students are simply being realistic about the future.

High inflation in the late 1970s, severe recession in the 1980s, and a dramatic economic restructuring in the 1990s have had significant effects on the job market. Today's college graduates are sometimes referred to as "Generation X"—recipients of bachelor's degrees who face limited career opportunities and often must resort to jobs for which they are "overqualified."

Although the economy is expected to improve by the time you graduate from college, the 1990s is a time of significant change for American workers. Corporations across the country are hiring fewer new workers and reducing overall employment. Increased competition both at home and abroad means that American businesses—both large corporations and small firms—are making every effort to work faster, wiser, and smarter, *and with fewer people*.

How are students of the 1990s reacting to the possibility of an economically troubled future?

Reasons for Attending College, 1980–1995 (percentage of freshmen indicating "very important")

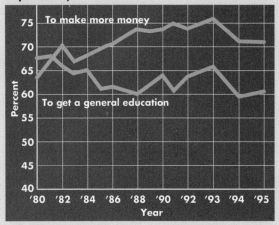

SOURCE: *Higher Education Research Institute, UCLA*

One common response among undergraduates is to build a portfolio of skills, contacts, experiences, and credentials to present to potential employers. A growing number of students are making choices about college and majors based in part on what they think will protect them in the job market of the twenty-first century.

Linda J. Sax, associate director of UCLA's Higher Education Research Institute and the Cooperative Institutional Research Program (CIRP) Freshman Survey project, wrote the Freshman Survey reports that appear throughout this book. The CIRP Freshman Survey results are based on data collected by the Higher Education Research Institute each year from hundreds of thousands of college students at campuses across the country.

- For leisure you will spend less time and money on television and movies and more time on continuing education, hobbies, community and civic affairs, and vacations.

- You are likely to be more concerned with wellness and preventive health care. Through diet, exercise, stress management, a positive attitude, and other factors, you will live longer and suffer fewer disabilities.

EXERCISE 1.6 Goals: Your Own and Others'

Look back at the reasons for attending college you listed in Exercise 1.1. Did your list include any long-term goals—say, something you want to achieve five or ten years from now? Compare your goals to the benefits of higher education just listed. Add a long-term goal to your list, or make other changes that now seem appropriate.

In small groups, compare your goals with the goals of others in the group. Do you share the same goals? How do you differ? Compare your findings with those of other groups in the class.

■SKILLS AND RESOURCES

Whatever your goals, you'll get off to the best start if you know your own strengths and also know where to look for help when you need it. In later chapters we'll focus on specific study skills. For now, let's take an informal preliminary look at your basic study skills.

EXERCISE 1.7 Assessing Your Basic Skills

Think about your strengths and weaknesses in areas such as reading, writing, and math. Have you ever consciously thought about exactly how you approach listening in class, taking notes, writing papers, reading textbooks, and studying for tests?

For each item below, rank yourself either 1 (very strong); 2 (okay); or 3 (not strong).

_____ Taking notes in class

_____ Learning facts and concepts from textbooks

_____ Reading comprehension

_____ Computer literacy (word processing)

_____ Time management

_____ Oral presentation skills

_____ Studying for tests

_____ Writing

_____ Math and science skills

If you found yourself writing some 3's, you'll want to look for help on campus. Keep this in mind as you do the next exercise.

Most college campuses offer a multitude of support and recreational resources. The box on page 15 lists typical support services on a college campus, along with the types of services they offer. If a vital support service is not offered on your campus, ask that it be made available. Many colleges will welcome petitions to extend support services.

Where to Go for Help

College support services are not always located where you might think or named what you might expect. If you're not certain where to look for a particular service, there are several ways to begin. You might ask your academic advisor or counselor, consult your college catalog and phone directory, or call or visit the office of student services (called student affairs at some schools) for assistance. The majority of these services are free.

- **Academic Advisement Center**
  Guidance about choosing classes
  Information on degree requirements

- **Academic Skills Center**
  Improve study skills and memory skills
  Help on how to study for exams
  Individual tutoring

- **Academic Computing Center**
  Minicourses and handouts on campus and other computer resources

- **Adult Re-Entry Center**
  Programs for returning students
  Supportive contacts with other adult students
  Information about services such as child care

- **Career Planning and Placement**
  Career materials library
  Career interest assessments
  Career goal counseling
  Computerized guidance programs
  Assistance finding a major
  Full-time, part-time, co-op, internship, and campus job listings
  Opportunities for graduating students to interview with employers
  Help with resumes and job interview skills

- **Chaplains**
  Worship services and fellowship
  Personal counseling

- **Commuter and Off-Campus Services**
  Listings of nearby available housing
  Roommate listings

Orientation to the community
Maps, information on public transportation, babysitting lists, and so forth

- **Counseling Center**
  Confidential psychological counseling on personal and interpersonal concerns ranging from roommate problems to prolonged states of depression
  Programs on managing stress

- **Financial Aid and Scholarship Center**
  Information about financial aid programs, scholarships, and grants

- **Health Center and Enrichment Services**
  Tips on personal nutrition, weight control, exercise, and sexuality
  Information on substance abuse programs, adult children of alcoholics, and general health care, often including a pharmacy

- **Housing Center**
  Assistance in locating on- or off-campus housing

- **Legal Services**
  Legal services for students (If your school is affiliated with a law school, check to see whether senior students in the law school are available for counseling.)

- **Math Center**
  Help with math courses

- **Physical Education Center**
  Free or inexpensive facilities for exercise
  Recreational sports facilities and equipment for swimming, racket sports, basketball, archery, weight training, dance, and so on

- **Services for Students with Disabilities**
  Support in overcoming physical barriers or learning disabilities

- **Writing Center**
  Help with writing papers and reports

EXERCISE 1.8   **Finding Out About Campus Resources**

Make a list of types of campus support services or resources you might be interested in. Include not only "serious" support needs but also things that will help you relax and enjoy campus life to the fullest.

1. _____

2. _____

3. _____

4. _____

5. _____

Pool your list with others in your class. Use a campus map, student handbook, or other tools to find out which are available on your campus.

EXERCISE 1.9   **Critical Thinking—"Unnatural Acts"?**

William T. Daly proposes that the critical thinking skills discussed in the box on pages 18 and 19 ("Improving Your Powers") are "unnatural acts"—not things that people do easily or without training. Do you agree? In what ways has your previous education or other experiences prepared you to form abstractions? To generate new ideas or foresee new possibilities? To question the facts or logic of what other people write and say? To examine the logic or evidence behind your own written or spoken arguments?

■SETTING GOALS

College is an ideal time to begin fulfilling short- and long-term goals. Begin to test some of your short-term goals. It's okay if you don't yet know what you want to do with the rest of your life or what you should be majoring in. Be patient. Practice setting and achieving some short-term goals by means of the following process:*

1. **Select a goal. State it in measurable terms.** Be specific about what you want to achieve and when (not "improve my study skills" but "master the double-entry system of note-taking by the end of October").

2. **Determine whether the goal is achievable.** Do you have enough time to pursue it, and more important, do you have the necessary skills, strengths, and resources? Modify the goal as needed to make it achievable.

*Adapted from *Human Potential Seminars* by James D. McHolland and Roy W. Trueblood, Evanston, Illinois, 1972. Used by permission of the authors.

Don't put off making contact until everyone seems too busy. Get to know as many people as you can before you and they slide into isolated routines.

Photo courtesy of David Gonzales

3. **Be certain you genuinely want to achieve this goal.** Don't set out to work toward something only because you feel you should or because others tell you it's the thing to do. Be sure that your goal will not have a negative impact on yourself or others and that it is consistent with your most important basic values.

4. **Identify why this goal is worthwhile.** Be sure that it has the potential to give you a sense of accomplishment.

5. **Anticipate and identify difficulties you might encounter.** Plan ways to overcome these problems.

6. **Devise strategies and steps for achieving the goal.** What will you need to do to begin? What comes next? What may you need to avoid? Set a timeline for the steps.

EXERCISE 1.10 **Set a Short-Term Goal**

Review your responses to the previous exercises in this chapter. Pick one problem that you can resolve as a short-term goal. (Ask your instructor whether this will overlap with work assigned later in the course.)

Start by discussing this goal with your group. Identify how this short-term goal relates to your long-term goal of doing well in college.

In group discussion and writing, complete the six steps for achieving a short-term goal. Establish a date (perhaps a week or a month from now) when you will determine whether the goal has been achieved. At that time set at least one new goal.

Be sure your goal is:

- Something you genuinely want to achieve
- Written down in measurable terms
- Achievable

Four Aspects of Critical Thinking: Improving Your Powers

The single most important goal of higher education is to help you learn to think more critically and creatively. This involves training yourself to go beyond common sense and personal opinion when you try to analyze a problem or to communicate ideas to others. It means freeing yourself of your emotional attachments to certain ideas and relying on factual information and conscious, systematic reasoning. It means basing what you think and say on knowledge gained through careful reading and ordered study.

Higher education goes beyond memorizing facts. This is not to say that facts are unimportant. Nothing substitutes for thorough, truthful information. But equally important are your abilities to judge the truth of supposed facts and to think logically from the facts. Such thinking is often referred to as *critical thinking*.

For you to develop critical thinking skills, your teachers will ask more open-ended questions—Why? How? and What if? Rather than expecting you to absorb knowledge like a sponge, teachers will encourage you to think problems through, analyze, conceptualize, ask questions, be questioned, and reflect on how certain beliefs might compare to others. In addition to memorizing facts and figures for a final examination, you will be challenged to apply what you have learned to the real world. College instructors will reward you more quickly and more handsomely for higher-level thinking skills than for anything else you do in class.

FOUR ASPECTS OF CRITICAL THINKING*

Critical thinking involves skills that take effort to learn and practice. Although there is no easy formula, the process may be simplified if we break it down into four general stages or abilities:

- abstract thinking
- creative thinking
- systematic thinking
- precise communication of thought

Each of these abilities corresponds roughly to a step in an overall process. Throughout this book we will be asking you to practice and improve your abilities in each of these steps, largely through exercises that require you to think about an issue and then write or speak about it. To a great extent, critical thinking results from first carefully reading what others have written about a topic and then writing or speaking in response. Think about how far along you are in each of the following areas:

1. **Making abstractions out of details.** From large amounts of facts or information learn to find the big ideas, the patterns and abstractions behind the facts. What are the general and recurring truths or arguments reflected in the details? What are the key ideas? Even fields like medicine, which involve countless facts of biology, culminate in general ideas: the principle of circulation; the basic patterns of cell biology; the principles of genetics. In essence, what larger concepts do the details suggest? What is the speaker or writer really saying?

2. **Finding new possibilities.** Practice creative thinking to discover the meaning and implications of abstractions. What questions do the large ideas suggest? Avoid making immediate decisions. Put off closure. Reject nothing at first. If the facts of economic history seem to show that free markets (the free exchange of goods and services among free people) lead to economic growth, what new questions can you ask about how to create more free markets? Can you apply this idea to the country as a whole? To your city? To your campus? Brainstorm questions. Brainstorm answers. Is the universe round? Astronomers entertain what may seem to others to be wild ideas. But so did the early geographers who proposed that the earth was round. Look for many possible answers rather than the elusive (and probably nonexistent) "one correct solution."

3. **Organizing new ideas and possibilities in a logical order.** Love is blind. The ideas you are most in love with may be wrong. In the long run you must weigh ideas more carefully than your emotions may at first accept. What do the facts really suggest? What is the logic of your thinking? In what ways do small conclusions or newly discovered facts lead to new abstractions, new broad ideas? Two hundred years ago someone thought about the fact that milkmaids rarely contracted smallpox. That observation led to the first inoculations against a devastating disease. It's not enough to dream up a new idea. It must be tested against the facts. Ideas that don't stand up under scrutiny must be discarded or modified so that they are consistent with the broader truth. Here dedicated research makes the difference. Is there some important additional information that needs to be gathered and evaluated before it is possible to reach a conclusion? Ultimately, what new abstractions and new conclusions have resulted from your thinking?

4. **Precisely communicating your ideas to others.** Organize your ideas to show others how your conclusions follow from your assumptions and the facts. Are your conclusions well supported? If you seem to be relying mainly on your personal opinions, experiences, or emotions to convince others, how can you broaden your support with reliable sources? Consider what your audience will need to know to follow your line of reasoning and to be persuaded through speech and writing.

WILL COLLEGE DEVELOP YOUR CRITICAL THINKING SKILLS?

None of us ever completely masters the four basic steps. Great scientists make great mistakes.

(Consider the famous nineteenth-century French physician Paul Broca who thought he could judge the relative intelligence of different races simply by comparing the sizes of people's brains, as measured by cranial capacity of the skull. He was embarrassed to find that Europeans' brains *weren't* the largest!) But colleges and universities are communities of people who are committed to trying. Be confident that effort pays off.

The more you associate with others who practice critical thinking skills, the more opportunity you will have to practice them yourself. The more you read, the better you will write. The more you write, the more you will be able to both think and speak. No miracle, no luck, no gift is involved. Begin by recognizing that some ideas have more logical and empirical validity than others, and that one of your obligations as an educated citizen is to be able to distinguish the valid from the invalid.

CAN THIS BOOK IMPROVE YOUR THINKING?

This book suggests ways to improve your thinking, both on your own and in the company of others. Certain exercises are marked with the icon 🎲 to let you know that they specifically target one or more of the four basic steps. Each time you complete one of these critical thinking exercises, turn back to this section and reconsider how what you have done has helped you to become a better thinker.

*For many of the ideas in this section we are indebted to William T. Daly, professor of political science at Stockton State College, New Jersey. We recommend his article "Thinking as an Unnatural Act" in the *Journal of Developmental Education*, 18(2), Winter 1994. For his complete monograph, see *Teaching Independent Thinking*. Columbia, SC: National Resource Center for the Freshman Year Experience and Students in Transition, 1995.

A First-Year Journal

Each chapter in this book ends with a journal assignment such as the one on page 21. It's important to get into the habit of asking questions as you read and keeping track of your thoughts in writing. Periodically throughout this book you should be asking yourself questions like these:

1. **What do I think of what I just read?**
2. **What did I learn?**
3. **How do I react to what I've learned?**
4. **What is there here that I can apply to my own life?**

Each journal assignment poses questions to help you focus your thoughts. Use them if they stimulate your thinking. If other, related questions concern you more, write about those instead.

Your instructor may ask you to write these entries strictly for your own private reading and reflection or as a hand-in assignment. Instructors who ask to read your journal entries generally do so because they know this to be an excellent means of private communication between you and them.

Depending on your instructor's preferences, you may record your journal entries on separate

Photo by David Gonzales

looseleaf sheets, on typed pages, or in a journal notebook. Whatever the format, be sure to collect and keep these writings so that you can periodically review them, especially at the end of the term and later in your college career.

Also be certain to:

- Identify and explore potential problems
- Create a specific set of steps for achieving the goal
- Set a schedule for the steps
- Set a date for completion

In completing this exercise, you are learning a goal-setting process that with practice can become a lifelong skill. Apply this process at least three times this term and you will have mastered a technique that will help you all your life.

This book will ask you to use this goal-setting process in later chapters. Look for other chances to use it. Point these out to your instructor and other members of the class.

Photo courtesy of University of Utah

JOURNAL

Which of the "keys to success" listed in this chapter have you already begun to incorporate into your college life? Which others can you start working on soon?

If you are a returning student, write some advice to the younger students in your class. If you are a younger student, give the adults the benefit of your knowledge about how to study effectively. Consider sharing these thoughts in class.

SUGGESTIONS FOR FURTHER READING

Astin, A. W., Linda J. Sax, Kathryn M. Maboney, and William S. Korn. *The American Freshman: National Norms for Fall 1995*. Los Angeles: Higher Education Research Institute, University of California.

Bird, Caroline. *The Case Against College*. New York: McKay, 1975.

Boyer, E. L. *College: The Undergraduate Experience in America*. New York: Harper & Row, 1987.

Erikson, Erik. *Identity: Youth and Crisis*. New York: Norton, 1968.

Friedan, Betty. *The Feminine Mystique*. New York: Dell, 1962.

Hartel, William C., et al. *Ready for the Real World*. Belmont, Calif.: Wadsworth, 1994.

Parks, Sharon. *The Critical Years: Young Adults and the Search for Meaning, Faith and Commitment*. New York: HarperCollins, 1991.

Sheehy, Gail. *Passages: Predictable Crises of Adult Life*. New York: Dutton, 1974.

Upcraft, L., and J. N. Gardner. *The Freshman Year Experience*. San Francisco: Jossey-Bass, 1989.

ANSWER (to question in box on page 5): **d.** commuters account for 11.32 million of America's 14.5 million college students. That number is more than the combined populations of Norway and Israel. There are more commuter students than there are people in the greater Boston and Philadelphia areas combined. If all commuter students parked in the same parking lot, the lot would have to be larger than the city of Boston. No wonder parking is often cited by commuters as one of their major problems!

Exploring the Student–Teacher Connection

A. Jerome Jewler
University of South Carolina

She's so smart; how can I talk to her? Walks in and starts talking about her passion for geology; then asks us questions about things I've never even thought about. We have to have a conference with her during office hours to talk about how we're doing. Alone. And mine is today. I'm doing all right in the course, I think. But what in the world am I going to say to her?

Chapter Goals

After completing this chapter, you'll know how a positive relationship with an instructor can make learning easier and more interesting. You'll know more about what a college instructor does and understand the difference between "good and bad teaching" and "good and bad learning," as well as the differences between high school and college teachers. You should have a better idea of what college teachers expect of their students and understand the significance of academic freedom.

Quite often, theater can be more revealing than real life, or so it seemed as I walked along a New York City street after being blown away by a performance of David Mamet's play *Oleanna.*

This brief two-character drama gives us John, a college professor who does not really believe in teaching but relishes the opportunity to lay down the law. John has never forgotten how he hated his own pompous, unfeeling college instructors. Yet somehow, in a sort of twisted form of revenge, he has become one of them.

The other character, Carol, is a student. Although earnest in her quest for education, she appears to be confused about its purpose. Her belief is that teachers ought to teach, that they owe it to students; but she seems to resent the fact that they know things she does not.

As one drama critic explains, John teaches not in order to lead, but to hear himself talk; he listens admiringly as his brain disposes of the problems and uncertainties of others. When he explains something, however, it only sounds more confusing.

He has the power; the pupil has the responsibility. "I'm not here to teach you," he explains to Carol, "I'm here to tell you what I think." He describes higher education as a game in which those who hold the power (the teachers) test the powerless (the students) by asking idiotic questions that only measure one's ability to "retain and spout back information." Pure nonsense, John tells Carol.

Yet when she fails to understand anything he says, Carol revolts. She reports him, alleging incompetence, sexual harassment, and a number of other violations that threaten his career as a professor. She reprimands him for forgetting just how hard she has worked to get to college and how he is depriving her of her natural right to learning by "one low grade that keeps us out of graduate school . . . one capricious or inventive answer on our parts, which, perhaps, you don't find amusing." Now he understands what it is to be subject to that power, she concludes.

In a scene from David Mamet's Oleanna, *Carol tries to get a clear message from her professor about how he is reacting to her work. The play probes the complexities of the college teacher–student relationship.*

Ken Friedman/photo courtesy of American Conservatory Theater of San Francisco

EXERCISE 2.1 **Is the Power Struggle for Real?**

Mamet's *Oleanna* makes some bold assertions about the relationship between college instructor and student. Do you agree that instructors hold absolute power over students, that whether a student passes or fails is sometimes subject to the whims of the instructor? Another related question: Do you believe that higher education is a game of memorizing and regurgitating information? Write your thoughts about this issue, and be prepared to share them in class.

■ THE TEACHER'S CHALLENGE

Although some teachers may be involved in power trips, the majority of us look on teaching as a challenge to help students develop themselves as more literate individuals and as critical thinkers by presenting them with challenges of their own.

I experienced this challenge from a different perspective when I signed up for an undergraduate acting course, a subject not related to my discipline of mass communications, but rather to an avocation—theater—that I have pursued seriously for the last eight years.

I called the instructor ahead of time to ask how she would feel about having a middle-aged professor in the class. I had been fortunate to have been cast in a local show under her direction and I respected her talent greatly. Her first words were, quite frankly, a surprise to me.

"Are you going to be serious about this?" she asked.

"Of course I'm going to be serious!" I told her. "Matter of fact, it's going to be a real pleasure to be a student again, to have a chance to learn more about a field I find exciting, personally rewarding, and mind broadening."

Later, as I pondered her question, I found it to be quite appropriate. As teachers, we want every student to be "serious" about what takes place in our classroom. So the very next term, I gave my class a new assignment to turn in. It was this:

EXERCISE 2.2　How Serious Are You Going to Be?

Using this course or another you are currently taking, write a paper that answers this question:

Just how serious are you planning to be about this course?

Consult the syllabus. List topics or aspects of the course you believe you will find particularly challenging, as well as topics or aspects you believe will be easy for you. Note any foreseeable problems that the syllabus suggests (deadlines, reading assignments, work load, and so on), and suggest how they might be solved. Also state, in detail, just what you believe you will gain from the successful completion of this course and how you might apply that knowledge in future endeavors.

What Your Instructors Expect

Note that I asked my students for their input—for feedback about how they saw the challenges of my course and, to some extent, how I was managing the class. I'm not the only college instructor who does this. But were you ever asked to do this in high school? If you believe that high school teachers were supposed to have all the answers and that their main purpose was to transmit those answers to you, it may come as a mild shock to know that most college teachers view education as more of an exchange of ideas than as one-way communication. To new college students, it may come as a shock to hear that knowledge is no longer etched in stone, that new ideas are welcomed, that traditional ways of thinking may not be the best; to college teachers, that makes good sense. If all questions were already answered, what would be the point of further scholarship?

Fortunately or otherwise, this new attitude toward learning is hardly the only difference you'll be aware of during your first term in college.

In high school you were taught by individuals who took courses in teaching. Strangely, your college instructors may never have taken such courses, but focused instead on learning in their fields. If your teacher has a doctoral degree, he or she has written a dissertation, a book-length document about some question that has not been studied in such detail before.

But that just begins to tell the differences between high school and college teachers. Can you guess other differences? Generally, college teachers:

- Will supplement textbook assignments with related information from other sources
- Will give quizzes and exams covering both assigned readings and lectures
- Will insist there is more than one way to interpret information, may question conclusions of other scholars, and may accept several different opinions from students regarding some question of the day
- May never check to see if you are taking adequate notes

- May or may not take attendance—or count it in determining grades

What's more, college teachers are likely to expect much more of you than your high school teachers did. They may:

- Be more demanding in how much they ask you to read, how many quizzes they give, and how much participation they expect in class.
- Expect you to be aware of topics related to their field and the particular course as well as the material for the course itself.
- Be sympathetic to excuses you may have for missing class or assigned work, but hold firm to high standards for grading. You may be on good terms with your instructor and find you have failed the course because you did not complete some part of the assigned work!

EXERCISE 2.3 | What Do College Teachers Expect of Students?

Look back over the lists of differences between high school and college teachers. Then list five to ten qualities and behaviors you believe college teachers want in their students. Compare your response with that of several classmates. Consider asking one of your teachers to comment as well.

What Your Instructors Do

To understand why college teachers approach learning in this manner, it helps to know more about their lives beyond the classroom and the financial constraints they have been under in recent years. According to Jacques Barzun, American historian and educator and former provost of Columbia University, college teaching is

> *backbreaking work that would fray the nerves of an ox. . . . An hour of teaching is certainly the equivalent of a whole morning of office work. The pace, the concentration, the output of energy in office work are child's play, compared with handling a class, and the smaller the class, the harder the work. Tutoring a single person—as someone has said—makes you understand what a dynamo feels like when it is discharging into a non-conductor.*

Faced with the reality of shrinking budgets, colleges and universities have been demanding more of their faculty: more teaching, more committee assignments, more publications, and more service to the college and community. Yet, despite other demands on their time, effective teachers know that teaching takes time and patience, that it goes beyond the classroom, spilling over into student conferences, academic advising, and career counseling. Thus, while the average teacher may spend 9–15 hours in the classroom each week, he or she probably works another 60 or more hours between Monday and Monday.

To stay current in their fields, college teachers are constantly reading books, journals, and magazines. They update lecture notes, which takes more time than delivering the lecture. They may conduct experiments in their fields, review manuscripts for journals, or write articles and books. They may address community and professional groups, as well as consult with private corporations or government agencies. They advise students on academic courses, career paths, personal problems, or specific class assignments. In the time left, they'll work as administrators on campus, serve on committees, grade papers, and still find time to be responsible parents and providers to their own families.

EXERCISE 2.4   **A New Look at What College Teachers Do**

The last few paragraphs describe how college teachers spend their time and should dispel the popular misconception that college teachers don't work very hard. What have you learned about the duties of a college teacher that you didn't know before? How much does this knowledge help you understand the actions of your current college teachers?

■ MAKING THE MOST OF THE LEARNING RELATIONSHIP

Just as most college teachers work faithfully to succeed at their roles as teachers, so should you feel an obligation to gain the most from your hours in class, if for no other reason than that you've probably paid dearly for the right to an education. Here are some ways to accomplish your goals and to show your teachers that you are serious about learning.

1. **Make it a point to attend class regularly and on time.** If you must miss a class, you'll need to ask another student for notes. That's okay as long as the student agrees and you don't make a habit of it. But remember, learning is easier when you are there every day. Save your cuts for emergencies; you will have them. When you know you will be absent, let your instructor know in advance. Depending on the size of the class, you may choose to do so by a written note delivered to the instructor's office, a phone message, an e-mail, or in person at the end of a class period.

2. **Sit near the front.** Studies indicate that students who do so tend to earn better grades. That should be no surprise; sitting up front forces you to focus, to listen, and to participate.

3. **Speak up!** Although you may be nervous about challenging instructors when you don't agree with them or about asking questions when you want clarification, you'll find that most of your comments will be appreciated.

4. **See a teacher outside of class when you need help.** Instructors are required to keep office hours for you. If possible, make an appointment by phone or at the end of class. Doing so will make the conference more convenient for both parties.

■ TEACHING AND LEARNING: A TWO-WAY CHALLENGE

What other effects did that undergraduate acting course have on my teaching? At first I felt awkward and isolated sitting on a bare stage with twenty or so people who were much younger than I. But things improved rapidly. I played a scene with a woman less than half my age, and a young chap slapped me on the back when I finished and exclaimed, "That was great, man!" I became a player in the chatter that goes on during lulls in instruction. I became part of their group. In addition, I was able to watch a teacher who came to class prepared, who set reasonable deadlines for assignments and made it clear how failure to meet those deadlines would throw the entire class schedule out of whack, who went out of her way to be certain students were developing the acting skills appropriate for this course, and who used her knowledge of the plays and playwrights we were assigned to instill in us a new way of thinking about those works. I learned not only how you students feel sitting "out there" but also how much energy and preparation it takes to keep a class interesting day after day after day.

What's more, seeing another teacher in action, I became aware of how motivating to students teachers can be when they take the time to bring out the best in each of them. As in any group, ability levels ran the gamut, yet I never felt a single individual was slighted because he or she didn't perform as well as someone else. Like any good teacher, this one believed in the importance of establishing a comfortable, positive relationship with each student in the class. If put into words, this relationship might be summed up as follows: "As long as you make an effort to do the assigned work to the best of your ability, as long as you listen to my advice and attempt to improve your understanding of this work, and as long as you demonstrate persistence to learn throughout this class, you're worth the time it's taking me to help you."

Effective teachers constantly attempt to challenge their students. They make an effort to connect with you and to establish a relationship that will support both their goals and yours. As a professor of advertising, I'm struck by the fact that one of the new trends we're talking about is called "relationship marketing." Many relatively new companies that have enjoyed rapid growth—Ben and Jerry's, The Body Shop, Nike—have discovered the rewards of nurturing a long-term relationship with their customers, who in turn support them through loyalty to their brands.

Critical to the building of such relationships are a number of avenues for two-way communication between company and consumer. In fact, companies are learning to be good listeners. They encourage consumers to talk to them through 800 numbers, surveys and panels, seminars, and trade shows.

Now change the word *company* to *teacher* and the word *consumer* to *student* and you begin to see the value of building long-term relationships to foster learning. Many of your instructors may encourage such relationships through teaching techniques that stress class participation (discussions, presentations). Some may write extensive comments on your written assignments and quizzes. Others may even ask you to write your feelings, anonymously, about the class and drop them off at the end of the hour. During a major study of teaching at Harvard University, one of the many suggestions for fostering relationships that could improve learning in the classroom was a simple feedback exercise called "The One-Minute Paper." At the end of each class, students were asked to write what they felt was the main issue of that class and what the unanswered questions were for the next class. Remarkably, as students became aware they would be asked to do this daily, they found themselves beginning to listen more deliberately for "the main issue" each day! Even though the responses were unsigned, most students wanted to let the professor know they were listening.

The One-Minute Paper

Whether or not your teacher asks for it, choose one of your classes and consider writing at the end of each class what you thought was the main issue of the day and what the unanswered questions are for the next class. During the next class, see if those questions are answered. If not, consider raising your hand to ask them. Try this for a week. Did this help you master the information in the class? In what way?

COMMUNICATION AND ACADEMIC FREEDOM

Although academic freedom has its origins in the Middle Ages, it continues to be a burning issue. You may have college teachers who don't give a hoot if the basketball team has a winning season, who criticize the college administration for its lenient admissions policies, or who argue that you're wasting your time watching TV sitcoms and soaps. As college instructors, we believe in the freedom to speak our thoughts, whether it be in a classroom discussion about economic policy or at a public rally on abortion or gay rights. What matters more than what we believe is our right to proclaim that belief to others without fear. Think of where education would be if we were governed by more stringent rules regarding free speech! On the other hand, no one says you must think as we do.

Colleges and universities have promoted the advancement of knowledge by granting scholars virtually unlimited freedom of inquiry, as long as human lives, rights, and privacy are not violated. Such freedom is not usually possible in other professions.

Some teachers may insult a politician you admire or speak sarcastically about the president. In college, as in life, you must tolerate opinions vastly different from your own. You need not accept such ideas, but you must learn to evaluate them for yourself, instead of basing your judgments on what others have always told you is right.

FINDING THE RIGHT TEACHER

When students were asked in a survey to rank the characteristics of good teaching, they listed clarity and organization at the top. Close in importance were those things that help "humanize" the teacher: high levels of interaction with students outside the classroom, a genuine effort to make courses interesting, frequent examples and analogies in teaching, references to contemporary issues as appropriate, and relating the course to other fields of study.

In fact, studies of teaching confirm that the best learning takes place when the teacher involves students in the learning, through class discussion, library research, oral presentations, and small discussion groups that report their findings to the rest of the class. Add enthusiasm and clear, well-organized presentations, and the fact that students appreciate teachers who assign more work and more difficult work, and you have a complete picture of the effective teacher: one who is actively involved with students, who comes to class prepared, who gives students a voice in the classroom, and who is academically demanding but highly nurturing. One teaching expert likens teaching to coaching, explaining that a good teacher challenges students and works them hard, but somehow students know that this same teacher cares about their success.

Most college teachers are busy people who enjoy contact with their students. That's one reason they chose to become teachers.

Photo © Charles Gupton/Stock Boston

EXERCISE 2.6

Describing Your Ideal Teacher

Jot down some adjectives that describe the best teachers you have ever had. Now jot down some adjectives that describe the worst teachers you have ever had. Be prepared to explain why you chose these words to describe good teachers and poor teachers.

Best Teacher

Worst Teacher

_____

_____

_____

_____

_____

How do you find great teachers? Ask. Ask other students, especially juniors and seniors in your major. Ask your academic advisor. If you enroll in a class and your "gut feeling" tells you on the first day that there is going to be a conflict with your style of learning and this teacher's approach to the topic, consider changing sections immediately. Visit a teacher before you register for class; by asking about the class, you'll learn more about the person, too.

You can often discover what fellow students think of a course or a professor from student evaluations. Student groups at many schools make these evaluations available at the library, on-line, or as handouts at registration.

Finding a Mentor

In his study of the aging process in men, Yale psychiatrist Daniel J. Levinson discovered several things about those who tended to be successful in life:

- They had developed a dream in adolescence, an idealized conception of what they wanted to become.
- They went on to find a mentor—an older successful individual—who personified that dream.
- They also cultivated friendships with a few other people who encouraged, nurtured, and supported them in their pursuit of that dream.[*]

A mentor is a person who, in some respect, is now what you hope to be in the future. What mentors have you had previously? What specific qualities have you tried to emulate? Do you have a mentor right now? If you do, what might you do to make more use of him or her? What are you looking for in a college mentor?

[*]D. J. Levinson et al., *The Seasons of a Man's Life* (New York: Ballantine Books, 1978).

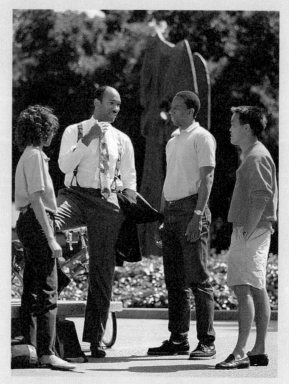

Photo © David Weintraub/Photo Researchers, Inc.

However, use these evaluations with caution. They may not represent the views of all students taking a course or of students sharing your own special concerns and standards.

What if you get a bad instructor? See if you are beyond the point in the term when you can drop the course without being penalized. Arrange a meeting to see if you can work things out. Getting to know the teacher as a person may help you cope with the way the course is taught.

If things are really bad, you might consider sharing your concerns with higher levels of authority, in keeping with the prescribed chain of command (department head, dean, and so on). Keep in mind, however, that a teacher's freedom to grade is a sacrosanct right, and no one can make teachers change their grades against their will. Don't let a bad instructor sour you on the rest of college. Even a bad course will be over and done with by the end of the term.

EXERCISE 2.7 Interviewing a Teacher

Choose a teacher to interview—perhaps your favorite instructor or one you'd like to know more about. You may even wish to choose an instructor whose course is giving you problems, in hopes that you can find out how to resolve those problems in the course of the interview. Make an appointment for the interview and prepare your questions before you go, but also be ready to "go with the flow" of your conversation. Then write a paper about what you learned and what surprised you the most.

Suggested Questions

1. What was your first year of college like?
2. At what point in your life did you decide to teach? Why?
3. What steps did you take to become a teacher in your field?
4. What do you like most about teaching? Least?
5. What are some of the things that keep you busiest outside the classroom?
6. What do you expect from your students? What should they expect from you?

Dr. Eliot Engel of North Carolina State University believes teaching is very much like farming. We cultivate our crops in the fall and harvest them in the spring, he explains. We boast of the sprouts that burst into vibrant bloom and sigh over those that withered on the vine, believing like a farmer that luck had much to do with the blooms, and our own failure with the blights. Engel warns that a society blighted by a dearth of great teachers soon finds itself in danger of growing nothing but a bunch of blooming idiots. He continues:

> *Great teachers know their subjects well. But they also know their students well. In fact, great teaching fundamentally consists of constructing a bridge from the subject taught to the student learning it. Both sides of that bridge must be surveyed with equal care if the subject matter of the teacher is to connect with the gray matter of the student. But great teachers transcend simply knowing their subjects and students well. They also admire both deeply.* *

That's a far cry from the relationship of the instructor and student in Mamet's *Oleanna*, discussed at the beginning of the chapter. Mamet's professor seems to instill fear in his student. He might have listened to Albert Einstein, who said, "The worst thing seems to be for schools to work with methods of fear, force and artificial authority. Such treatment destroys the healthy feelings, the integrity, and the self-confidence of pupils."

Finally, if you doubt the value of a well-taught class, one in which you know the instructor is working hard to make learning enjoyable, heed the words of Alfred North Whitehead, noted American philosopher, mathematician, and logician, writing in the *Atlantic Monthly* in 1928: "The university imparts information, but it imparts it imaginatively. . . . A university which fails in this respect has no reason for existence. . . . A university is imaginative or it is nothing—at least nothing useful."

Perhaps it is this imaginative imparting of information that distinguishes the best teachers from all the rest. What do you think?

*From a column in the *Dickens Dispatch,* the newsletter of the North Carolina Dickens Club, January 1989.

EXERCISE 2.8   Patching a Less-Than-Perfect Student–Teacher Relationship

When you approach one of your teachers to explain that you missed class because you were stressed out by the breakup of a long-term relationship, which resulted in pounding headaches, stomach upsets, and extreme fatigue, your teacher tells you that's no excuse. He adds that stress is natural, that people end relationships all the time, and that you should be ashamed for acting like a baby about it.

Although he grudgingly agrees to let you off the hook, you come away feeling angry, embarrassed, and insecure about your behavior. You're determined to write him a note about it, but you need some expert information on stress so that you won't sound like you're begging for sympathy. For starters, check out the information on stress in Chapter 19. Using critical thinking strategies, read Chapter 19 and then:

1. Abstract the main ideas from the chapter and write them down.

2. Brainstorm ways to defend your position that stress is sometimes unavoidable, but that you are learning to get it under control.

3. Organize your defense in a logical manner. Consider what you would agree with, what you would disagree with, and how to support what you believe is right. Don't be too apologetic, but at the same time don't argue about everything. Use your newfound knowledge to assert your beliefs in a way that shows respect for your teacher.

4. Look at what you have written. Put it away for a few days. Then get it out, revise it, and turn it in.

EXERCISE 2.9   A Teaching Experience

Chapters 20 and 21 include some useful information on sexuality and alcohol and drugs. Choose either topic, and read the chapter carefully to prepare a 5-minute presentation to your class on some aspect of either topic. Consult Chapter 10, "Writing and Speaking for Success." Employ note-taking and the critical thinking process to:

1. Abstract the main ideas.

2. Brainstorm various ways to present the material so that students will find it interesting.

3. Organize your best ideas into a logical method of presentation.

4. Write yourself lecture notes so that you'll be able to do good, interactive teaching on the topic.

5. Teach.

EXERCISE 2.10   Finding Faculty E-Mail Addresses

More and more, students communicate with their instructors using e-mail. Although e-mail is often a poor substitute for an office visit, it is useful for specific questions or other short communications.

To send e-mail, just as with regular mail, you have to know someone's address. Find the e-mail addresses of your instructors on the campus network, or ask them for their e-mail addresses on the first day of class.

JOURNAL

Obviously your college teachers are different from your high school teachers. What differences have you observed? How are you reacting to those differences? Describe one or more of your instructors. What do you like most about them? Least? Explain why. What further questions do you have about college teachers and how to deal with them? Which of these would you like to raise in class?

SUGGESTIONS FOR FURTHER READING

Distinguished Teachers on Effective Teaching. New Directions for Teaching and Learning, #28. San Francisco: Jossey-Bass, 1986.

Freedman, Samuel G. *Small Victories. The Real World of a Teacher, Her Students, and Their High School*. New York: Harper Perennial, 1991.

Guide to Effective Teaching. A national report on eighty-one outstanding college teachers and how they teach: lectures, computer, case studies, peer teaching, simulations, self-pacing, multimedia, field study, problem solving, and research. New Rochelle, N.Y.: Change Magazine Press, 1978.

Mamet, David. *Oleanna*. New York: Pantheon Books, 1992.

Pirsig, Robert. *Zen and the Art of Motorcycle Maintenance: An Inquiry into Values*. New York: Morrow, 1974.

Surviving College

Al Siebert
Counseling Psychologist

*S*ometimes I think I'll never
make it to graduation. So
much can happen between now and
then—and knowing my luck, a lot
of it probably will be more than I
can handle.

Chapter Goals

After reading this chapter, you will have learned about six approaches to help you survive and be successful, not only in college but throughout life. You will gain insights into the personality characteristics of survivors and will be asked to apply these to activities designed to enhance your chances of success.

First-year students often feel bewildered and disoriented when they start college. For students coming directly from high school, it is the biggest transition of their lives thus far. Older students who have not taken classes or studied for years have many fears and concerns. Almost all students wonder, "Will I survive? Will I make it through to graduation?"

These are legitimate concerns because you are starting a journey that many of your entering classmates will not complete. A reality of college is that surviving and succeeding take more than simply passing tests in the classroom. You must also face—and overcome—other, nonacademic tests. Some of your brightest classmates will not survive because they don't recognize the difference between surviving academic challenges and surviving life's challenges.

To attain a college degree, you must have skills for coping with life as well as good study skills. You must handle the academic program and also deal with all the challenges that will test your emotional strength, attitudes, and character.

Survivors always have fascinated me. When I was in the army, I knew there was something special about the paratroopers who were combat survivors. Later, when I was in graduate school, I took advantage of the interviewing and personality research skills I had learned to study survivors in more depth. The more I learned, the more fascinated I became with the emotional strength and good spirits of some survivors of horrible experiences.

■ SIX SURVIVAL TESTS

There are six tests you need to pass in order to increase your chances of survival and success in college:

- Test 1: Making the transition from a teaching environment to a learning environment
- Test 2: Dealing with newfound freedom

- Test 3: Replacing feelings of discouragement with optimistic self-talk
- Test 4: Building healthy self-esteem
- Test 5: Developing empathy for roommates, fellow students, and even instructors
- Test 6: Learning how to learn from experience

The following guidelines and suggestions will help you not only to survive but to profit from these nonacademic tests.

Test 1: Making the Transition from a Teaching Environment to a Learning Environment

In high school your teachers were evaluated based on how much they taught you in their classes. You were in a teaching environment.

College, however, is a learning environment. How much you learn in any college course is primarily your responsibility, not the instructor's. This will be a challenge because many college instructors have never taken classes on how to teach. They focused instead on their academic areas of interest. You may find yourself working harder to learn in a course taught by an instructor who is brilliant in his or her field but is not very skillful at teaching the subject.

Curiosity is the key to doing well in a learning environment. In high school you could wait passively for a teacher to tell you what to learn. In college, however, your most valuable learning comes from asking questions and searching for answers. An essential skill developed by successful college students is that of asking and answering questions. They actively seek and find useful information. They do not sit back and wait for someone to tell them what they need to know.

EXERCISE 3.1 **How College Differs from High School**

At your high school commencement, was anyone in your graduating class honored for being the best at asking questions? Probably not. Make a list comparing all the ways college is different from high school. Include what it is like to become a new student again after being a senior.

Compare your lists with other class members. See if you agree on differences between a teaching environment and a learning environment.

High School (Teaching)

_____

_____

_____

_____

_____

_____

College (Learning)

_____

_____

_____

_____

_____

_____

Adult students: If high school seems a long way back, modify this exercise by listing and talking about other changes you face in starting college.

Test 2: Dealing with Newfound Freedom

Many students flounder in college because they cannot overcome ingrained habits. They probably came to college because they were told to. They go through orientation waiting to be told what to do; wait for an advisor to tell them what courses to take; wait for an instructor to tell them what to study.

For students conditioned to accept such controls over their lives, the freedom of the college environment can be overwhelming. And unless they can develop their own controls, they may party too much, study too little, have unsafe sex, drink too much or start taking drugs, and spend themselves into bankruptcy. Freedom includes the freedom to use, or waste, time. But spending too much time watching soap operas, surfing the World Wide Web, or engaging in on-line chat groups can leave little time for the job of being a student.

Students who pass the "freedom test" are those who feel personally responsible for how well they do in college. The primary control over what they do is inside them. They have an internal guidance system that they follow in the absence of external controls.

EXERCISE 3.2 — Being Responsible for Your Success

For each of the following pairs of statements, which one do you believe is more true than the other?

1a. My grades in college will reflect how well I study, pass tests, and do the course work.

1b. Instructors decide what grade a student gets. How hard I study doesn't affect my grades very much.

2a. My career success will be determined by how competent I become.

2b. Real career success is determined more by fate than hard work.

3a. I expect my college roommates to be interesting and friendly.

3b. You're lucky if you get a good roommate.

In this attitude test, there are no right or wrong answers. The real issue here is understanding that whatever you believe becomes a self-fulfilling prophecy. If you believe the "a" statements—that your actions determine your success in college—your belief will be proven true. If you believe the "b" statements and expect your fate in college to be determined by forces beyond your control, your belief will be proven true.

Write about how much you do or don't feel responsible for your success in college and in life.

Test 3: Replacing Feelings of Discouragement with Optimistic Self-Talk

Most college students feel discouraged at times. For example, in high school you may have gotten good grades with little studying, but in college you get a C– on your first test even though you studied hard. That first low grade can be a major shock. Your old habits don't work here. You feel discouraged. You think maybe you aren't college material and conclude that your situation is hopeless. The question is, what happens next?

The first step is to recognize that discouragement is a perfectly normal human emotion. The next step is to recognize the value of positive self-talk. Students who overcome discouragement replace pessimistic self-talk with optimistic statements. Research by Martin Seligman and other psychologists shows that you can learn to be optimistic about your future efforts. Optimism is an essential skill for overcoming difficult challenges in college. The best copers in college see setbacks and difficulties as temporary. They learn from the negative experience, expect to do better next time, repeat positive statements to themselves, and take action to do better.

EXERCISE 3.3 Turning Pessimism into Optimism

List several pessimistic statements you've heard from other students, and some that you may have said yourself.

1. _____
2. _____
3. _____
4. _____

Write down and rehearse three or four optimistic statements that you can repeat to yourself if you feel hopeless or discouraged.

1. _____
2. _____
3. _____
4. _____

Don't be misled, however, into believing that all negative thinking should be replaced by positive thoughts. A very trusting person who thinks in only positive ways runs blindly into unexpected problems that others avoid. Some negative thinking may increase your chances for success.

The best survivors in college spend less time "surviving" because they anticipate and avoid difficulties better than other students. To do this requires being able to think in both optimistic and pessimistic ways.

David McClelland, a famous Harvard psychologist, discovered that college students destined to have the most career success do the following:

1. Daydream about possible accomplishments.
2. Try to anticipate all the things that could keep them from succeeding.
3. Take steps to avoid potential problems and get around all the blocks and barriers.

In other words, successful students use pessimism in productive ways. Negative thinking gives their optimistic thinking a better chance of leading to successful action.

Daydreaming? Evidence suggests that those who daydream some about what they hope to become are more likely to reach their goals.

Photo by David Gonzales

EXERCISE 3.4 A Different Approach to Setting a Goal

This is a slightly different approach to goal setting than the one you learned in Chapter 1. It integrates the benefits of both positive and negative thinking. Start by thinking about a goal you have in one of your courses. Ask yourself if the goal is one you believe you really can reach with good effort. Then use McClelland's three-step approach to see if you can improve your chances of reaching it. For example, if your goal is to get an A on a written assignment, you should do the following:

1. Think about how good it will feel to have completed your research, to have prepared a well-organized outline for your topic, and to be in the final stages of writing the paper.

2. Consider the time period between the present and the due date. How far along are you in this project? Have you checked to see if your topic offers adequate opportunities for research? Have you set a timetable for accomplishing each portion of the project? Have you asked your instructor to comment on the appropriateness of your topic or the focus of your paper? Will you find yourself putting off the inevitable because of laziness, invitations to "take a weekend off," or other distractions?

3. Address the possible stumbling blocks you have listed above, work out ways to overcome them, and put a schedule in writing in your calendar. Stick to it.

Now choose your goal and write your three steps.

Test 4: Building Healthy Self-Esteem

To survive emotionally as a first-year college student requires healthy self-esteem. As a high school senior you had status, were invited to parties, may have held a student body office, and were recognized for achievements in school, sports, or music. Adult students have enjoyed the status gained from their jobs and community activities. But when you start college many of these external sources of esteem no longer exist. You may feel awkward and inadequate for the first time in years.

Students who relied on external sources (praise from parents, compliments from friends, job title, and so on) for feelings of esteem may be devastated because they find they lack inner self-esteem. Those students who survive "starting all over" have strong *conscious* self-esteem and self-confidence. Self-esteem is like a thick blanket of energy around you. If other students put you down, you can compare your opinion of yourself with theirs, decide that you like yours better, and shrug off the barb without feeling wounded.

Healthy self-esteem determines how much you learn after you have done poorly on a test or a paper. Students with weak self-esteem can't handle negative feedback very well. They will blame an instructor for a low grade or claim that the low grade was caused by something that kept them from doing well. Healthy self-esteem lets you examine your failings and shortcomings in a way that leads to improvement. It also allows you to better accept compliments.

EXERCISE 3.5 Self-Esteem

A Make a list of all the things you like and appreciate about yourself. Silently practice positive self-talk about yourself.

B Get together with several friends and interview each other about what each of you likes and appreciates about yourself. Practice giving and receiving compliments.

C In a small group discuss the following:

1. Why does a person with weak self-esteem get nervous when complimented? Why does a person who brags all the time seem to be trying to hide feelings of weak self-esteem?

2. If having strong self-esteem is so important, why do so many parents admonish and scold a child who brags or feels proud about something? If having healthy self-esteem is desirable, why do so many parents react as though it is undesirable?

Test 5: Developing Empathy for Roommates, Fellow Students, and Even Instructors

When someone acts or talks in a way that upsets you, take a deep breath and work to understand how things look from his or her point of view. The ability to understand ways of acting, thinking, and living that you disagree with is a high-level empathy skill. Empathy does not mean, however, that you agree with or approve of the other person's views or actions. It means only that you comprehend.

Discuss the following questions in a small group: Why do you think negative thinking is seen so negatively in our culture? Why are people with positive attitudes usually so negative about people with negative attitudes? Is it ever okay to be negative? Is it phony to be always positive?

Think of a negative roommate or classmate as a teacher in the school of life. The way to learn new skills from associating with a bothersome person is to stop blaming that person for your reactions and to ask yourself, "What advantages, benefits, and payoffs does he or she get from being negative all the time?" One big payoff, for example, is attention. Look at the person's negative behavior with curiosity and empathy and attempt to guess the payoffs that person may have in mind.

Next ask yourself, "How could I react differently so that I'm in control of my feelings?" Here are some possibilities:

1. Say, "You may be right." Then change the subject.

2. Ask him or her to also say something positive.

3. Play with this person's negative way of thinking by giving him or her a dose of his or her own medicine. Plan ahead, and after hearing a negative comment say, "You know, it is much worse than you realize." Then list three negative things about college, life, and the world that he or she has overlooked.

4. Learn to be active, not reactive. Before the person says anything negative, ask him or her to point out what could go wrong with your plans.

The key to coping well with any difficult person is to experiment. Play, learn, and develop response choices. Regain control. And silently thank the negative person for providing you with an opportunity to learn a valuable lesson.

Test 6: Learning How to Learn from Experience

Many years spent in the classroom conditioned you first to learn a lesson and then to take a test. In the school of life, however, the sequence is reversed: First you take the test and then you learn a lesson.

Learning from experience is the learning you do on your own. It is what you learn after you've taken the history or biology test and know you could have done better. Psychologists have studied learning for almost a hundred years and have identified the following steps as the way to learn from an incident or an "experience":

1. If it is upsetting, handle your feelings first. Cry, tell a friend, or write about your feelings in a journal.

2. Reflect on the experience. Mentally replay it as if remembering a dream. The observing part of your mind manages your learning.

3. Put it into words. Write everything that happened in a journal or tell someone.

4. Ask yourself, "What can I learn from this? What is the lesson here?"

5. Ask yourself, "Next time, what could I do differently?"

6. Imagine yourself handling the situation differently, better, and getting a desirable outcome.

7. Mentally rehearse handling the situation well just in case anything like this should ever occur again.

College students who are unable to learn from experience react to something that upsets or distresses them by assigning blame or acting the victim. You can see this when classmates who fail a test blame the instructor, dwelling on all the things the instructor and the college did to cause them to fail. In contrast, students who learn from experience and spend their time thinking about "the next time" expect to do better on the next test and usually do.

When you learn the steps for self-managed learning, you develop confidence in yourself. You anticipate either handling something well or, if you don't, you expect to learn something useful.

EXERCISE 3.7 **Learning from Experience**

Think about an unpleasant experience when someone put you down and you didn't handle it well. Based on the steps for learning from experience, what will you do or say the next time it happens? Mentally rehearse what you will do the next time in a similar situation. Discuss your plan with others in a small group and get their reactions.

■ THE FINAL EXAM: DEVELOPING A TALENT FOR SERENDIPITY

Several hundred years ago writer Horace Walpole coined the word *serendipity* to describe a special talent some people have for changing an accident or misfortune into a lucky happening.

The best sign of having mastered the tests for survival in college occurs when you convert a difficult situation into something you feel thankful you went through. One college student, for example, was raised hearing her parents tell her she would become a nurse. She wasn't enthusiastic about nursing but went along with what they said. It wasn't until she started doing clinical assignments in nursing school that she realized she just couldn't go ahead with her parents' plans.

Finally, after much anguish, sleeplessness, and an upset stomach, she told her parents she had always wanted to be a writer. Her parents were surprised but accepted her decision. She switched majors and is now a successful journalist writing about health and medicine. She discovered that her prenursing background gave her an advantage over other journalists in health care topics.

When you instruct your brain to find a creative solution, it has a tendency to do just that. If you define an adverse situation too narrowly and think of it only as "bad luck," then a serendipitous solution won't be able to penetrate your thinking.

Your mind will build either barriers or bridges to your future. Your survival and success in college are determined by how well you handle your feelings, cope with pressures and adversities, and learn the lessons you won't always be taught in classes. And be reassured that students who survive and cope well with the nonacademic tests in college are not better than or different from you. Their success is due to skills that almost any student can learn and develop.

EXERCISE 3.8   The College Survival Final Exam

A Try looking for the hidden good in a bad situation. What if your computer crashes and you lose part of a paper you've been writing? By asking yourself, "How can I turn this to my advantage?" or "What unusual opportunity has this created?" you will activate your brain to discover how to convert the disaster into something positive.

B Discuss the following: When ice skater Nancy Kerrigan was clubbed in the leg a few weeks before the 1994 Winter Olympics, was that a major misfortune? Good luck? All the publicity she received led to her signing commercial contracts worth over $2 million before the Olympic competition even started. How can an incident be both bad luck and good luck?

C Do you think that your chances of surviving in college will be improved by passing the six nonacademic tests described in this chapter? Why? Why not?

JOURNAL

Evaluate yourself on how well you've done on the "tests" that life will give during your time in college. State your answer in the form of several paragraphs of thought rather than in the form of a numerical score.

SUGGESTIONS FOR FURTHER READING

Seligman, Martin. *Learned Optimism: How to Change Your Mind and Your Life.* New York: Knopf, 1991.

Siebert, Al. *The Survivor Personality.* Portland, Ore.: Practical Psychology Press, 1993.

Siebert, Al, and Bernadine Gilpin. *The Adult Student's Guide to Survival and Success: Time for College,* 2nd ed. Portland, Ore.: Practical Psychology Press, 1992.

Walter, Timothy L., and Al Siebert. *Student Success: How to Succeed in College and Still Have Time for Your Friends,* 7th ed. New York: Harcourt Brace, 1996.

Time Management: The Foundation of Academic Success

Kenneth F. Long
University of Windsor

Mary-Jane McCarthy
Middlesex Community College

L et's see . . . it's Wednesday. Wednesday!! That big review session's at four and I need to go to work. I can't work tonight; I've got a history quiz at nine tomorrow and I need to read two chapters for it. Got to pick up Susie at daycare in 2 hours. Better write this all down in my calendar. Now where's that calendar??

Chapter Goals

After reading this chapter, you should understand that time management is one of the keys to success—in college and in life. You will be familiar with methods of controlling your time and know a time management method that works for you. If you commute, you should adapt a time management system that includes your special needs.

Time management is one of the keys to success in college. Yet many students entering college are weak in this area. Perhaps it's because they did well in high school without consciously practicing time management or because in most high schools students had little control over their own time.

In certain high school courses students are not expected to take much responsibility for controlling their own use of time. College is different. Once courses are selected, you are personally responsible for allocating time to attend classes, to complete assignments, to study for tests, and so on. Generally, it's even your decision whether to show up for class—on time or at all! College offers a great deal of freedom. In turn, it requires you to take personal responsibility for planning and managing your time. The central aim of this chapter is to show you how to develop and stick to a time management program.

First, let's examine your personal approaches to the use of time.

EXERCISE 4.1 Assessing Your Skills

For each set of statements below, circle the number of the one that best describes you.

1. I like my watch to be set exactly at the correct time.
2. I like my watch to be set a few minutes ahead of the correct time.
3. Most of the time, I don't wear a watch.

1. I tend to arrive at most functions at least 5 minutes early.
2. I tend to arrive at most functions exactly on time.
3. I tend to arrive at most functions a little late.

1. In the course of my daily activities I tend to walk and talk quite fast.
2. In the course of my daily activities I tend to take my time.
3. In the course of my daily activities I tend to walk and talk slowly.

1. In high school I almost always completed my daily assignments.
2. In high school I usually completed my daily assignments.
3. In high school I often failed to complete my daily assignments.

1. I like to finish assignments and reports with a little time to spare.
2. I tend to finish assignments and reports exactly on the due dates.
3. I sometimes finish assignments and reports a little late.

1. I rarely spend more than 15 minutes at a time on the telephone.
2. I sometimes spend more than 15 minutes at a time on the telephone.
3. I often spend more than 15 minutes at a time on the telephone.

1. I rarely spend more than an hour eating a meal.
2. I sometimes spend more than an hour eating a meal.
3. I usually spend more than an hour eating a meal.

1. I never watch more than 1½ hours of TV on a weeknight.
2. I sometimes watch more than 1½ hours of TV on a weeknight.
3. I usually watch more than 1½ hours of TV on a weeknight.

1. I never spend more than an hour surfing the Web or talking on a chat line at any one time.
2. I sometimes spend more than an hour surfing the Web or talking on a chat line at any one time.
3. I usually spend more than an hour surfing the Web or talking on a chat line at any one time.

Now add up the numbers that you have circled: _____

The higher the total, the more you need to work on time management skills now that you are in college. If your total is over 10, you probably need to adjust your priorities and begin to take more responsibility for managing your time.

Time management involves planning, judgment, anticipation, and commitment. First, you must know what your goals are and where you will need to be at some future time. Second, you must decide where your priorities lie and how to satisfy competing interests. Third, you must make plans that anticipate future needs as well as possible changes. Finally, you must commit yourself to placing yourself in control of your time and carrying out your plans.

■SETTING PRIORITIES

To manage your time in college, you must first set priorities. The decision to attend college is a commitment to being a professional student for the next few years. Any professional—businessperson, athlete, doctor, or student—attends to his or her professional responsibilities above most other things in life. Usually work comes *before* pleasure. As a student, you must identify your priorities and develop a system for living each day accordingly.

A Rank the following pursuits in order of their importance to you. In the left-hand column write 1 beside the most important, 2 beside the second most important, and so on. Next, under "Estimated Hours," record the amount of time per week you believe you spend at this pursuit. Be honest, now!

Rank		Estimated Hours	Actual Hours
_____	Class attendance	_____	_____
_____	Relaxation	_____	_____
_____	Volunteer service	_____	_____
_____	Time with family	_____	_____
_____	Exercise	_____	_____
_____	Clubs/organizations	_____	_____
_____	Required reading	_____	_____
_____	Hobbies or entertainment	_____	_____
_____	Time with girlfriend/boyfriend or spouse	_____	_____
_____	Studying	_____	_____
_____	Surfing the Web or sending e-mail to friends	_____	_____
_____	Working at a job	_____	_____
_____	Religious activities	_____	_____
_____	Shopping	_____	_____
_____	Household responsibilities	_____	_____
_____	Nonrequired reading	_____	_____
_____	Sleeping	_____	_____
_____	Other: _____	_____	_____

B Monitor the amount of time you spend at each pursuit over the course of one week, and record the total figures under "Actual Hours." Compare your estimates with the actual figures. Are there any important differences? If so, how do you explain them?

C Discuss your rankings and your use of time with your peers and your instructor. How are your choices and habits similar to or different from theirs?

D From this information, use the first step in the critical thinking process outlined in Chapter 1 to summarize what time management means to you. Second, brainstorm (alone or with a friend who has also completed the first step) ways to solve the problem of having too much to do in too little time. Come up with lots of solutions. Reject nothing. Third, go back over your ideas and pick and choose carefully. Drop the ones that aren't working and systematically organize what's left in logical order. Finally, use this rough outline—along with what you learn from the balance of this chapter—to write a preliminary plan for managing your time that can be understood by others.

TAKING CONTROL IN THE FIRST WEEK: THE TIMETABLE AND MASTER PLAN

By the time we get to college, some of us are already better than others at setting priorities. Let's first consider a student who has some problems setting priorities. Joe is a well-intentioned, promising student who happens to be in danger of failing his first semester. He complains about having too much work and not enough time. Unfortunately, like many students, Joe wastes many hours every day. How does this happen?

First, Joe socializes at the drop of a hat. Naturally he wants to be popular, so he is available when anyone calls. He also likes to enjoy himself and often stays out fairly late, even during the week. To catch up on his sleep, he sometimes skips his 8:00 class, figuring he can make it up later. Other times Joe makes it to class even when he is still tired and manages to take notes, usually from the back of the room. In general, Joe's social life makes it hard for him to keep up with his studies.

Joe is a person of good character, as shown by his other activities. He is a frequent volunteer at a children's center and never disappoints his little friends. He also writes an occasional column for the student newspaper and faithfully meets his deadlines, usually at the expense of his studies. This is when Joe complains about never having enough time.

Of course Joe has the same number of hours in each day as you or I. But rather than controlling the various attractions of college life, Joe lets them control him. Rather than deciding what his basic responsibilities are, he proceeds on a vague agenda of personal preferences.

By contrast, Carmen is a more aware, committed student. Let's see how she handles priorities. Carmen's first step each semester is to create a personal timetable and master plan (see Figure 4.1). The timetable is determined mostly by her course selections and other fixed responsibilities (shaded in the figure). Note that her timetable includes five courses, the typical load for full-time students on the semester system. (If you work long hours or have significant family responsibilities, you should take on a smaller course load.)

The classroom time for Carmen's five courses (History, College 101, Geology, Psychology, and Expository Writing) totals only 16 hours per week. That leaves her with lots of free time, right? Well, no. To that figure Carmen adds 2 hours outside of class for *every hour* in class. Thus, based on her 16 hours in class, she plans for 32 more hours of schoolwork outside of class, for a total of 48 hours. A 48-hour work week?! Who says college students have it easy? Obviously both Joe and Carmen have to schedule their time wisely and efficiently.

Carmen begins by scheduling 17 hours of study time into her normal weekday hours (see Figure 4.1). Her trick is to use the many hours tucked into the day between her widely scheduled classes. For instance, on Tuesdays and Thursdays she gets an early (but not too early) start; completing 4 of the 6 hours of study for Psychology. Now look at Monday, Wednesday, and Friday mornings, which are more complex. Carmen knows that it is best to review right after class, so on Mondays and Wednesdays she uses the hour between College 101 and Geology to review her notes from the two classes she has already attended on those mornings. Nor does she waste the time after lunch on Monday before her Geology lab at 2:00.

Since Tuesday evening is her 3-hour writing workshop, Carmen schedules time for writing right before the workshop and again the following afternoon. Although short bursts of study are sometimes ideal for review, writing requires longer, uninterrupted periods.

Figure 4.1 Carmen's Timetable and Master Plan

	Sunday	Monday	Tuesday	Wednesday	Thursday	Friday	Saturday
6:00							
7:00							
8:00		History		History		History	
9:00		College 101	Read/ Study Psych.	College 101	Read/ Study Psych.	College 101	
10:00		Review Hist. & College 101	↓	Review Hist. & College 101	↓		
11:00		Geology	Psych.	Geology	Psych.		
12:00		LUNCH	↓	LUNCH	↓	LUNCH	
1:00		Study Geology	LUNCH	Study Geology, etc.	LUNCH	Read/ Study History,	
2:00		Geology Lab	Work on Writing			College 101, etc.	
3:00		↓		↓		↓	
4:00			↓	Work on Writing			
5:00				↓			
6:00	Library Job		Expository Writing			Library Job	
7:00			Workshop				
8:00				Library Job			
9:00	↓		↓	↓		↓	
10:00							

Total class hours: 16
Total study hours needed: 16 x 2 = 32

Total study hours allotted: 17
Additional study hours needed: 15

Now that she has accounted for 17 of the 32 study hours, Carmen should be able to find time for the additional 15 hours. When will she add these hours or, on certain weeks, put in even longer hours as her courses may require? The master plan makes it clear that Carmen will most likely be using many Thursday afternoons as well as evenings and weekends to meet her basic commitment. Oh, no, the weekends?! Sad but true. You should plan to work a good portion of many weekends. But take heart—it's worth it. Once you have met your academic (and other) commitments, the free time left over will be all yours. It will relax you totally, letting you enjoy yourself and return refreshed to your studies.

Let's review the steps Carmen followed to gain control from the first day of college:

- Step 1: She obtained a blank timetable form or purchased a calendar organized by day and hour, which often provides blank timetable forms as well.

- Step 2: As soon as she was registered in her courses, she filled in the days and times for each course. She also made a list of buildings and room numbers, consulted a campus map, and took a tour before the first day of class. Colleges frequently organize these tours for new students.

- Step 3: She began to organize her class hours according to effective strategies for study, also including some time for nonacademic pursuits.

You may want to put your schedule on your computer using Personal Information Management (PIM) software or a spreadsheet program. Writing and revising the schedule, however, should not become a goal in itself. The real concern is that you make and keep a schedule, not how you write it.

EXERCISE 4.3 Your Timetable and Master Plan

Photocopy Figure 4.2 and construct your own timetable and master plan. First, fill in your scheduled commitments: classes, job, child care, and other activities. Then block out study hours according to the suggestions discussed previously. Share and discuss these with your peers and instructors. Check particularly to see if your work schedule or family responsibilities are too demanding and prevent you from putting in the necessary study hours.

If you are a commuter, you may wish to do Exercise 4.7 on pages 63–65 before creating your timetable and master plan.

ORGANIZING THE TERM: THE WEEKLY ASSIGNMENT PLAN

Weekly assignment plans are the next important tool for staying in control. These add into the timetable all your assignments and tests. In the first week of classes you may receive course outlines, or *syllabi,* that explain the nature and purpose of each course and state the criteria and due dates of all assignments. Use these syllabi to structure your weekly study plans. If the instructor does not provide a syllabus, ask him or her for the specific study requirements for that week and mark them on your timetable. If the course syllabus doesn't give due dates, don't be bashful. Ask the instructor, and write the dates on your copy of the syllabus.

Figure 4.2 Timetable and Master Plan

(1) List all class meeting times and other fixed obligations (work, scheduled family responsibilities, and so forth.
(2) Try to reserve about 1 hour of daytime study for each class hour. (3) Reserve time for meals, exercise, free time.
(4) Try to plan a minimum of 1 hour additional study in evenings or on weekends for each class.

	Sunday	Monday	Tuesday	Wednesday	Thursday	Friday	Saturday
6:00							
7:00							
8:00							
9:00							
10:00							
11:00							
12:00							
1:00							
2:00							
3:00							
4:00							
5:00							
6:00							
7:00							
8:00							
9:00							
10:00							
11:00							
12:00							

To see the "big picture" of your work load this term, fill in the assignment preview sheet in Figure 4.3, listing all tests, reports, and other deadline-related activities.

Use photocopies of your timetable as weekly assignment plans, one sheet for each week. Carefully study all of the course outlines, and write in the due dates of all tests, papers, and special assignments. After you have recorded due dates, note on the weekly assignment sheet when you will begin to work on each major project, paper, report, or exam. Then schedule planning time during each subsequent week. You may wish to buy a large desk-size calendar for scheduling this information. The large size lets you describe your tasks in detail and view an entire week's or month's work at a glance.

Complete this early in the term. Typically, the first two or three weeks will be free of due dates, but the midterm (fifth through seventh weeks) will be full. This lets you see in advance what planning is necessary to handle these demanding weeks.

Let's look at a week for Carmen when she will face preparing for three tests while also turning in two essays (see Figure 4.4). Carmen keeps her timetable where she can consult it often, but she knows that good time management is flexible. She will generally stick to her routine, but when things are going well, she will slack off a bit. She also knows that certain days and weeks will be unusually demanding.

In order to manage this week, she will need to have done some planning and a lot of studying in advance. Note her early wakeup on Monday for a "final" study session. In other words, Carmen has studied all the important material prior to Monday morning. (Later chapters will say more about long-term study for exams.) The same will be true for the lab test on Monday afternoon. Now look at 1:30 on Tuesday. All Carmen can do here is proofread and make minor revisions. This means that the essay itself was researched, written, and revised some days earlier—certainly not the day before, in the midst of preparing for and taking tests on Monday and Tuesday morning!

The rest of the week is not so difficult, but note that for the history essay, only the final draft and proofing stages are planned for. Once again, success depends on Carmen's completing the bulk of the work for this essay well before this week. Only by crafting a detailed weekly plan for each week of the semester can Carmen—and you—see in advance how to get everything done well and on time. You don't want to find yourself scrambling to write an essay when you need to be studying for a test!

Your master plan and weekly assignment plans should be completed no later than Monday morning of the second week of classes so that you can continue to plan, anticipate, judge, and use your time effectively. Purchase a pocket calendar at your bookstore that you can use and carry everywhere.

Note how versatile the weekly assignment plan is: It reminds you, on a week-to-week basis, of your major assignments during the term. The master plan serves a more global purpose: It tells you when you must be in class and encourages you to structure the hours outside of class. You should have access to both plans at all times for reference.

Figure 4.3 Term Assignment Preview

	Course	Assignment	Due date
Week 1: ____ to ____ (date) (date)			
Week 2: ____ to ____			
Week 3: ____ to ____			
Week 4: ____ to ____			
Week 5: ____ to ____			
Week 6: ____ to ____			
Week 7: ____ to ____			
Week 8: ____ to ____			

	Course	Assignment	Due date

Week 9: _____ to _____

Week 10: _____ to _____

Week 11: _____ to _____

Week 12: _____ to _____

Week 13: _____ to _____

Week 14: _____ to _____

Week 15: _____ to _____

Week 16: _____ to _____

© 1997 Wadsworth Publishing Company

Figure 4.4 Carmen's Timetable and Master Plan—Week 6

	Sunday	Monday	Tuesday	Wednesday	Thursday	Friday	Saturday
6:00							
7:00		Final Study College 101					
8:00		History		History		History ESSAY DUE	
9:00		College 101 TEST	Read/ Study Psych/	College 101	Read/ Study Psych.	College 101	
10:00		Review Hist. & College 101	for Test ↓	Review Hist. & College 101	↓		
11:00		Geology	Psych. TEST	Geology	Psych.		
12:00		LUNCH	↓	LUNCH	↓	LUNCH	
1:00		Study Geology Final Review	LUNCH Work	Study Geology, etc.	LUNCH	Read/ Study History,	
2:00		Geology Lab	on Writing Review	↓		College 101, etc.	
3:00		TEST ↓	and Proofread Essay			↓	
4:00			↓	History Essay			
5:00				Final Draft			
6:00	Library Job	Study for	Expository Writing		Review and	Library Job	
7:00		Psych. Test	Workshop ESSAY DUE		Proofread History Essay		
8:00		↓	↓	Library Job			
9:00	↓			↓		↓	
10:00							
11:00							
12:00							

Time management is a life-long skill. The better the job you have after college, the more likely that you'll be managing your own and possibly other people's time.

Photo by David Gonzales

Guidelines for Scheduling

1. Examine your toughest weeks. Can you finish some of these assignments early in order to free up some time to study for tests?
2. Break large assignments like term papers down into smaller steps (choosing a topic, doing research, writing an outline, writing a first draft, and so on). Add deadlines in your schedule for each of these smaller portions of the project.
3. Start working on assignments days before they are due. Good student time managers frequently finish assignments before actual due dates to allow for emergencies.
4. Allocate specific times for potentially repetitive tasks. You might, for instance, check your e-mail at the beginning and end of the day, not every hour.
5. No schedule is of any use if you do not use the time allocated to a specific task productively. This includes learning how to search a library catalog, access e-mail, or use a word processor effectively.

ORGANIZING THE DAY: THE DAILY PLAN

With master and weekly plans in place, it will be easy for you to plan each day as a 24-hour package. Let's look at one of Carmen's daily plans. This daily plan is nothing more than a note that she has written to herself the prior evening (see Figure 4.5).

Being a good student does not necessarily mean grinding away at studies and doing little else. By planning her time carefully, Carmen is able to balance her academics with a modest amount of recreation. By working two-

Figure 4.5 Carmen's Daily Plan

Thursday

7:00 — Up

Scheduling early classes and rising early will give you a jump on the day.

8:00 - 9:00 — Review science and hist. notes with Rob over breakfast

Rob is also a well-organized student — a good study partner.

9:00 - 10:00 — Read/study psych. in library, review notes from last lecture

Reading and reviewing notes will help prepare you for class.

11:00 - 12:30 — Psych. lecture

12:30 - 12:45 — Review/Recall/Recite

As you will discover, to prevent forgetting it's very important to review as soon after class as possible.

12:45 - 1:45 — Lunch

1:45 - 2:30 — Bookstore for supplies; textbook

Right after lunch is a good time for miscellaneous activity. It's hard to study on a full stomach.

2:30 - 4:00 — Read/study history

Always take a short break in the middle of a study session to maintain alertness.

4:00 - 5:30 — 25 min. jog with Alice; shower, sauna

Regular exercise is important. It actually aids studying by promoting alertness.

5:30 - 6:30 — Dinner

6:30 - 7:15 — Free time

Schedule free time. It keeps you balanced emotionally.

7:15 - 10:00 — Study for hist. quiz, prepare for College 101, write schedule for Friday

In extended study sessions schedule a variety of activities, each with a specific objective.

"Do Not Disturb"

Read how one single-parent commuter handles distractions:

I made it a point to select one area of the house for serious study. I selected a specific block of time to study. When I entered the room, I would place a red sign outside my door to signal the kids that I was not to be disturbed.

My kids didn't buy into this right away, but they soon learned that I was not going to alter this strategy. I was amazed at how soon they adjusted. Later they were a big help in keeping me on schedule.

I feel much better about working at home because I am no longer under pressure to get things done in a piecemeal fashion. My children feel better too. They feel that they have a part to play in helping me with my studies.

thirds of her class and study hours into the normal working day, she has reduced the additional studying she will need to do to about 15 hours. Thus a few hours spent studying each evening should cover most of the required study time. Her weekends can be somewhat free, as can selected regular times during the week, for other commitments and interests.

Note that Carmen honors the age-old principle "Sound mind, sound body." Her timetable includes two commitments to exercise, and she'll work out once more on the weekend. Your schedule should also include regular exercise time of at least an hour (including shower) three times a week. Research consistently shows that regular exercise gives you more, not less, energy.

EXERCISE 4.5 Starting Your Time Management System

A Review your assignment preview sheet from Exercise 4.4. Then begin to structure a schedule allowing you time to finish all your assignments. Be sure to try to find time during your hours on campus to study. Try to follow this schedule for a week.

B Jot down what you found to be the main obstacles to your time management system. Working with your peers, make a list of the obstacles each of you encountered during the week. Brainstorm strategies for overcoming these obstacles and share them with the rest of the class.

C Choose partners. Decide how you might be able to help each other overcome particular obstacles. Plan to take a few minutes before class one day each week to discuss your progress.

Reduce Distractions

If you study in the living room, in front of the television, or in other places associated with leisure, you may be giving the message that your study isn't serious. Studying at times associated with meals or family interaction can signal others that you want to be approached. Studying while lying on your bed, walking around the house, or listening to the radio can signal to others that you really aren't studying.

Use proper study habits to *reduce* distractions. Set aside specific study times at locations not associated with socialization. Behave in a way that is consistent with academic work and that signals others not to disturb you.

EXERCISE 4.6

Study Time Without Distractions

Whether you live on campus or at home, there will be distractions that interfere with your ability to study. List the things that tend to distract you the most. Then, using the goal-setting process in Chapter 1, work in small groups to brainstorm ways to avoid distractions and send signals to distractors that you are not to be disturbed.

ON CAMPUS

Study location: _____ time: _____ to _____

Potential distractors (human and physical):

_____

_____

Actions against physical distractions:

_____

_____

Signals to human distractors:

_____

_____

AT HOME (OFF-CAMPUS OR ON-CAMPUS RESIDENCE)

Study location: _____ time: _____ to _____

Potential distractors (human and physical):

_____

_____

Actions against physical distractions:

_____

_____

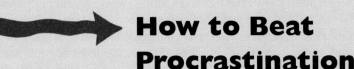

How to Beat Procrastination

Procrastination may be your single greatest enemy. Getting started when it's time to start takes self-discipline and self-control. Here are some ways to beat procrastination:

1. Say to yourself, "A mature person is capable and responsible and is a self-starter. I'm that kind of person if I start now." Then start!

2. On a 3 × 5 notecard write out a list of everything you need to do. Check off things as you get them done. Use the list to focus on the things that aren't getting done. Move them to the top of your next day's list and make up your mind to do them. Working from a list will give you a feeling of accomplishment and lead you to do more.

3. Break big jobs down into smaller steps. Tackle short, easy-to-accomplish tasks first.

4. Apply the goal-setting technique described in Chapter 1 to whatever you are putting off.

5. Promise yourself a suitable reward (an apple, a phone call, a walk) whenever you finish something that was hard to undertake.

6. Take control of your study environment. Eliminate distractions—including the ones you love! Say no to friends who want your attention at *their* convenience. Agree to meet them at a specific time later. Let them be your reward for doing what you must do now. Don't make phone calls during planned study sessions. Close your door.

Signals to human distractors:

_____

_____

■TIME MANAGEMENT FOR COMMUTERS

If you are a commuter you probably have less time for college than students who live on campus. Not only do you spend more time traveling, but you are also more likely to have commitments to family and work that seriously compete with your class and study time. Your greatest problems probably occur during exam time or when papers and projects are due. In addition to the time management strategies already described, you can do other things to manage your time efficiently.

Be Realistic in Your Time Management Plans

To keep your problems to a minimum, be realistic. As you fill out your daily and weekly plans, be sure to allow time for travel, family, work, or other responsibilities. If there is really not enough time to meet your commitments and carry the hoped-for number of courses, reduce your course load. Be sure to do so before the "drop date," and be certain you don't become ineligible for any full-time financial aid. Take care to record the critical exam dates and assignment due dates on your family calendar to avoid conflicts. Let your family know ahead of time the days or weeks that you will need more time of your own.

EXERCISE 4.7 — Do Commuters Have Time for Success?

The following shows how typical *residential* first-year students allocate their time on a weekday.*

Activity	Hours per Day
Class time	3
Studying	3
Employment	¼
Idle leisure	3
Social	2¼
Travel (between classes)	1
Eating	1½
Grooming	1
Resting	6½
Recreation	1½
Other	1

Notice that new students who live on campus devote almost 7 hours each day to socializing, recreation, and leisure pursuits. How might a commuter use those 7 hours? The following chart lists some activities that commuters may have to carry out on a typical weekday. If you are a commuter, estimate the time you take for each. Write your response in the "Hours per Day" column.

Activity	Hours per Day
Class time	_____
Studying	_____
Employment	_____
Travel	
Home to college	_____
Between classes	_____
College to work	_____
Work to home	_____
Other	_____
Total travel	_____

*Data adapted from David W. Desmond and David S. Glenwick, "Time-Budgeting Practices of College Students: A Developmental Analysis of Activity Patterns," *Journal of College Student Personnel* 28, no. 4 (1987): 318–23.

Activity	Hours per Day
Home responsibilities	
Shopping	_____
Meals	_____
Housecleaning	_____
Laundry	_____
Other	_____
Total home	_____
Family responsibilities	
General time	_____
Child care	_____
Care for elderly or disabled	_____
Other	_____
Total family	_____
Civic responsibilities	
Volunteer work	_____
Other	_____
Total civic	_____
Personal	
Grooming/dressing	_____
Newspaper	_____
Rest	_____
Other	_____
Total personal	_____
Other	_____
Total time for all responsibilities	_____

Do you need to make some adjustments? What are they? Use the goal-setting process in Chapter 1 to help yourself make them.

Don't Be a "Blockhead"

As a commuter you may tend to use block scheduling, running all your classes together without any breaks or attending school only one or two days a week. You may be doing this to cut down travel costs and have more free time on other days.

However, you may be unaware of problems associated with block scheduling. Fatigue can kill your efforts in classes held later in the day. You will probably tend to forget lecture material because you don't have enough time between classes to digest information. You may also sometimes feel compelled to miss one class in order to prepare for another. If you are on a two-day schedule (for example, all your classes on Tuesday and Thursday), you will find it difficult to finish assignments between one class meeting and the next. And if you are on a one-day schedule and fall ill on that day, the consequences of missing all your classes that week can be devastating. You will also feel stress when all your midterm or final exams fall on the same day. With back-to-back block scheduling, you may not have even a free period between several exams.

For a more effective schedule:

1. **Arrange a "double-up" schedule.** Try to schedule classes in which instructors teach the same course at different times or on different days. This will give you a chance to catch up if you miss a class. Ask your instructors if you can attend an alternate class.

2. **Split your schedule.** Try to alternate classes with free periods. This will give you time to prepare for the next class, visit the library, talk and study with other students, meet with a teacher, or just recoup.

3. **Seek a flexible schedule.** Look for teachers who will allow you flexibility in completing assignments. Find out about independent study, correspondence, and televised courses.

Follow a Routine

Humans have a built-in biological clock that helps them establish a rhythm and routine. Some psychologists believe this natural rhythm is thrown out of sync when events conflict with our biological expectations.

Perhaps the best-known example of this problem is jet lag. Similarly, many shift workers such as nurses and police officers are less productive and more lethargic and irritable as they adapt to new time schedules. Commuting students likewise may have time lag problems when they adjust their schedules to satisfy competing obligations or when block scheduling requires them to vary their schedules. For instance, if you study 2 hours every night Monday through Thursday, then engage in leisure activities during these times Friday through Sunday, you are likely to have trouble getting back into studying on Monday evening. Like the victim of jet lag, you confuse your body about whether it should study, play, or vegetate during this time of day. Likewise, students who sleep in on weekends often find it hard to make it to Monday morning classes.

As a commuter you face more schedule challenges than the residential student. Keep your biological clock running smoothly by establishing as much routine as possible.

EXERCISE 4.8 **Student Telephone Directory**

Devise a telephone directory and keep it handy. Begin with phone numbers for any of the following that apply:

1. All instructors (include e-mail address) _____

_____

2. Campus security/local police _____

3. Campus lost and found _____

4. Campus health service _____

5. Dean of students _____

6. Campus counseling center _____

7. Campus legal services _____

8. Child-care centers _____

9. Emergency road service _____

10. Landlord (home and work) _____

11. Employer (home and work) _____

12. Campus tutorial center or learning center _____

13. Campus commuter student service center (if available) _____

14. Neighbor _____

15. Local taxi service _____

16. Public library _____

17. Friends and study mates (for each class) _____

_____

_____

_____

18. College FAX numbers (to FAX a paper long distance if you get stuck) _____

_____

Also place your class schedule and the number for campus security in a convenient place at home so that people can reach you in an emergency. See if your campus has a telephone directory on-line and learn the quickest way to access it. What telephone numbers or e-mail addresses does it include? What does it not include?

■ TIME AND CRITICAL THINKING

You may be tempted to think that most college assignments can and should be done quickly and that, once they are done, instructors simply have to mark them right or wrong. However, most questions worthy of study in college do not have clear and immediate yes or no answers; if they did, no one would be paying scholars to spend years doing careful research. Good critical thinkers have a high tolerance for uncertainty. Confronted by a difficult question they begin by saying, "I don't know." They suspend judgment until they can gather information and take the time it requires to find and verify an answer.

Thus, effective time management doesn't always mean making decisions or finishing projects quickly. Effective critical thinkers resist finalizing their thoughts on important questions until they feel they have developed the best answer possible. This is not an argument in favor of ignoring deadlines. But it does suggest the value of beginning the research, reading, and even the writing phases of a project *early,* so that you will have time to change direction if necessary as you gather new insights.

You will generally do your best if you start writing an essay well before it is due, maybe even before you feel you've done all the study needed to complete your paper. Give your thoughts time to "incubate"—like eggs preparing to hatch. Allow time to visit the library more than once.

Sometimes insights come unexpectedly, when you're barely thinking about a problem. One well-known example of this involves a famous chemist's discovery:

> *According to legend, one evening in 1865, August Kekulé, who had become absorbed in unlocking the molecular structure of the six-carbon chemical benzene (C_6H_6) was sitting half-asleep in front of his fireplace, idly staring into the fire. As his mind wandered, he seemed to see atoms in the fire dancing around in snakelike movements. Suddenly one of the snakes seized its own tail and whirled around in a circular motion. Kekulé awoke and spent the rest of the night working out what he had seen. He proposed that benzene is a ring of six carbon atoms, having alternating single and double bonds, with each carbon bonded to one hydrogen atom.*
>
> *Of his experience he wrote, "Let us learn to dream, gentlemen, then perhaps we shall find the truth. But let us beware of publishing our dreams till they have been tested by the waking understanding."**

JOURNAL

How would you evaluate yourself as a time manager right now? Are you more like Carmen or Joe? What do you see as your greatest asset in terms of time management? What do you think will be the greatest hindrance to effectively managing your time? How do you intend to deal with this hindrance? How might you use your assets to overcome your weaknesses?

SUGGESTIONS FOR FURTHER READING

Fanning, Tony, and Robbie Fanning. *Get It All Done and Still Be Human: A Personal Time Management Workshop.* Menlo Park, Calif.: Open Chain, 1990.

Hunt, Diane, and Pam Hait. *The Tao of Time.* New York: Henry Holt, 1989.

MacKenzie, Alec. *The Time Trap: The New Version of the 20-Year Classic on Time Management.* New York: AMACOM (Div. of American Management Association), 1990.

Sotiriou, Peter Elias. *Integrating College Study Skills: Reasoning in Reading, Listening, and Writing,* 4th ed. Belmont, Calif.: Wadsworth, 1996. See Chapter 2, "Your Learning Inventory: Your Learning Style, Study Time, and Study Area."

*From G. Tyler Miller, Jr., and David G. Lygre, *Chemistry: A Contemporary Approach,* 3rd ed. Belmont, CA: Wadsworth, 1991.

Learning Styles

Steven Blume
Marietta College

*M*y friend Janet always
sleeps through U.S. history.
That is totally weird because I could
listen to Dr. Moroney lecture on
Grant and Lee all day. Janet says
she likes discussion classes. Those
freak me out. I guess there's more
than one way to learn. I hope so.

Chapter Goals

After completing this chapter, you should know how and why you prefer to learn as you do and why some of your teachers may be more difficult to understand than others. The chapter suggests how you can make adjustments to overcome difficulties in learning, and how studying with students who have different learning styles can help you.

In high school, certain subjects appealed to you more than others. For one thing, some came easier than others. Perhaps you found history easier than mathematics, or biology easier than English. Part of the explanation for that has to do with what is called your *learning style*—that is, the way you acquire knowledge.

Learning style affects not only how you process material as you study but how you absorb it. Some students learn more effectively through visual means, others through listening to lectures, and still others through class discussion, hands-on experience, memorization, or various combinations of these.

Your particular learning style may make you much more comfortable and successful in some areas than in others. Consider Mark, whose favorite subject is history. Mark generally receives B's on his history exams, and he is satisfied with his performance. One of the things he likes best about history is the study of historical movements—the development of ideas as they inform historical events. When he studies for his exams, he analyzes those events, trying to determine what is responsible for the various social, political, and historical changes he has been reading about. Although he recognizes the importance of names and dates, they are less significant and interesting to him than the analysis of why certain events occurred and what effects have resulted from such occurrences. For example, he studies to understand *why* the pilgrims came to America and *how* they created the Plymouth Plantation rather than to discover who the leaders of the emigration were, who the first settlers were, when they arrived in America, what crops they grew, and what treaties they signed with the Indians. What he is interested in and how he studies are integral parts of his learning style.

Mark is also taking Introductory Biology, and as is natural for him, he studied for his biology exam in the same way he studied for his history test. Unfortunately, he was able to use very little of the knowledge gained from his studying and thus received an F on his biology exam. Instead of studying facts, committing important terminology to memory, and learning definitions, Mark had stressed concepts when he studied, and this *analytical learning style* turned out to be inappropriate for this course, or at least for the way his instructor taught the course.

One student's analytical style may thrive on the complexities of history. Another's satisfaction at mastering facts and understanding how they are related may lead her into science.

Walter Calahan/Earlham College

Photo courtesy of State University of West Georgia

The reverse can also be true. Another student, Anne, has a *factual learning style* that makes her comfortable with memorizing facts. Anne would do very well on that same biology test and yet find the history exam that stressed concepts and analysis of material very difficult. Just as we all have different skills, so we have different learning styles. Although no one learning style is inherently better than another, it is important to be able to work comfortably no matter what style is required in a given course. An awareness of your learning style can be helpful in emphasizing your strengths and helping you compensate for your weaknesses.

In this chapter, we'll examine learning styles of students both in and out of the classroom, as well as discuss the teaching styles of professors.

AN INFORMAL MEASURE OF LEARNING STYLE

To begin to define your own learning style and to understand how it affects your responses in class, do the following exercise.

EXERCISE 5.1 Your Learning Style: A Quick Indication

A List three or four of your favorite courses from high school or college:

1. _____

2. _____

3. _____

4. _____

What did these courses have in common? Did they tend to be hands-on courses? Lecture courses? Discussion courses? What were the exams like? Do you see a pattern from one course to the next? For example, did your favorite courses tend to use information-oriented tests such as multiple-choice or true-false? Or did they often include broader essay exams? Did the tests cover small units of material or facts, or did they draw on larger chunks of material?

Now list three or four of your least favorite courses from high school or college:

1. _____

2. _____

3. _____

4. _____

What did these courses and their exams have in common? How did they tend to differ from the courses you liked?

What conclusions can you draw about your preferences for learning based on these common elements in course presentation or exams? Do you prefer to make lists and memorize facts or to analyze the material, searching for concepts and considering broader implications? If you prefer the former, your learning style is more factual, like Anne's; if you prefer the latter, your learning style is more analytical, like Mark's. Can you understand why Anne prefers biology and Mark prefers history?

B After doing part A, form a small group with two or three other members of the class. Brainstorm about what courses you are taking that seem to require factual learning styles, analytical learning styles, or a combination of both. Prepare an oral group presentation to the class about your conclusions and the reasons for them. What is the best way to prepare for an exam in these classes, and why? (Read the rest of this chapter before you give your presentation.)

If you prefer listening to lectures, taking notes, and reading your notes aloud to yourself, you have a more *auditory learning style.* You might even read your notes into a tape recorder and play them back when you study for an exam. If you prefer instructors who outline their lectures on the blackboard or who make liberal use of the board by illustrating the important points they are trying to make, you have a more *visual learning style.* You probably find that copying and recopying your notes helps you learn the material better. If you learn best by a "hands-on" approach, you may prefer a *kinesthetic, or physical, learning style.*

Being more aware of your learning style preferences can help you exploit your strengths in preparing for classes and also help you better understand why you may be having difficulty with some of your courses and what you might do to improve.

■MORE FORMAL MEASURES OF LEARNING STYLE

A number of instruments can help you determine more effectively just what your preferred learning style is and better understand other learning styles as well.

Classroom Behavior

One approach is based on the ways in which students behave in the classroom. For instance, psychologists Tony Grasha and Sheryl Riechmann have put together the *Grasha-Riechmann* instrument. This tool assesses six learning styles based on classroom behavior: (1) *competitive,* (2) *collaborative,* (3) *participant,* (4) *avoidant,* (5) *dependent,* and (6) *independent.*

To understand which classroom learning style you are most comfortable with, you need to answer certain questions. For example, do you find the study questions or review questions passed out by your instructor helpful? Do you enjoy and find helpful studying with and learning from other students in your class? Do you like it when the instructor engages the class in discussion? If so, then you probably have a more collaborative, participant, and dependent learning style and will work best with an instructor who has a correspondent teaching style. On the other hand, you may prefer an instructor who lectures in class with minimal class participation. You may feel that straightforward study of your lecture notes and textbook is the most effective means of study. If so, your learning style is more competitive, independent, and avoidant.

Personality Preferences

Another approach explores basic personality preferences that make people interested in different things and draw them to different fields and lifestyles. The *Myers-Briggs Type Indicator,* based on Carl Jung's theory of psychological types, uses four scales:

- **EI (Extroversion/Introversion).** This scale describes two opposite preferences depending on whether you like to focus your attention on the outer or the inner world.
- **SN (Sensing/Intuition).** This scale describes opposite ways you acquire information—that is, whether you find out about things through facts or through intuition.

- **TF (Thinking/Feeling).** This scale describes how you make decisions, whether by analysis and weighing of evidence or through your feelings.
- **JP (Judging/Perceiving).** This scale describes the way you relate to the outer world, whether in a planned, orderly way or in a flexible, spontaneous way.

You will often feel most comfortable around people who share your preferences, and you will probably be most comfortable in a classroom where the instructor's preferences for perceiving and processing information are most like yours. But the Myers-Briggs instrument also emphasizes our ability to cultivate in ourselves all processes on the scale.

EXERCISE 5.2 / Assessing Your Learning Style

PERSONAL STYLE INVENTORY

Just as every person has differently shaped feet and toes from every other person, so we all have differently "shaped" personalities. Just as no person's foot shape is "right" or "wrong," so no person's personality shape is right or wrong. The purpose of this inventory is to give you a picture of the shape of your preferences, but that shape, while different from the shapes of other persons' personalities, has nothing to do with mental health or mental problems.

The following items are arranged in pairs (*a* and *b*), and each member of the pair represents a preference you may or may not hold. Rate your preference for each item by giving it a score of 0 to 5 (0 meaning you *really* feel negative about it or strongly about the other member of the pair, 5 meaning you *strongly* prefer it or do not prefer the other member of the pair). The scores for *a* and *b* must add up to 5 (0 and 5, 1 and 4, or 2 and 3). Do not use fractions such as 2½.

I prefer:

_____	1a. making decisions after finding out what others think	_____	1b. making decisions without consulting others
_____	2a. being called imaginative or intuitive	_____	2b. being called factual and accurate
_____	3a. making decisions about people in organizations based on available data and systematic analysis of situations	_____	3b. making decisions about people in organizations based on empathy, feelings, and understanding of their needs and values
_____	4a. allowing commitments to occur if others want to make them	_____	4b. pushing for definite commitments to ensure that they are made
_____	5a. quiet, thoughtful time alone	_____	5b. active, energetic time with people
_____	6a. using methods I know well that are effective to get the job done	_____	6b. trying to think of new methods of doing tasks when confronted with them
_____	7a. drawing conclusions based on unemotional logic and careful step-by-step analysis	_____	7b. drawing conclusions based on what I feel and believe about life and people from past experiences
_____	8a. avoiding making deadlines	_____	8b. setting a schedule and sticking to it
_____	9a. inner thoughts and feelings others cannot see	_____	9b. activities and occurrences in which others join

_____ 10a. the abstract or theoretical		_____ 10b. the concrete or real	
_____ 11a. helping others explore their feelings		_____ 11b. helping others make logical decisions	
_____ 12a. communicating little of my inner thinking and feelings		_____ 12b. communicating freely my inner thinking and feelings	
_____ 13a. planning ahead based on projections		_____ 13b. planning as necessities arise, just before carrying out the plans	
_____ 14a. meeting new people		_____ 14b. being alone or with one person I know well	
_____ 15a. ideas		_____ 15b. facts	
_____ 16a. convictions		_____ 16b. verifiable conclusions	
_____ 17a. keeping appointments and notes about commitments in notebooks or in appointment books as much as possible		_____ 17b. using appointment books and notebooks as minimally as possible (although I may use them)	
_____ 18a. carrying out carefully laid, detailed plans with precision		_____ 18b. designing plans and structures without necessarily carrying them out	
_____ 19a. being free to do things on the spur of the moment		_____ 19b. knowing well in advance what I am expected to do	
_____ 20a. experiencing emotional situations, discussions, movies		_____ 20b. using my ability to analyze situations	

PERSONAL STYLE INVENTORY SCORING

Instructions: Transfer your scores for each item of each pair to the appropriate blanks. Be careful to check the _a_ and _b_ letters to be sure you are recording scores in the right blank spaces. Then total the scores for each dimension.

Dimension		**Dimension**	
I	**E**	**N**	**S**
1b. _____	1a. _____	2a. _____	2b. _____
5a. _____	5b. _____	6b. _____	6a. _____
9a. _____	9b. _____	10a. _____	10b. _____
12a. _____	12b. _____	15a. _____	15b. _____
14b. _____	14a. _____	18b. _____	18a. _____
TOTALS: I _____	E _____	N _____	S _____

Dimension		**Dimension**	
T	**F**	**P**	**J**
3a. _____	3b. _____	4a. _____	4b. _____
7a. _____	7b. _____	8a. _____	8b. _____
11b. _____	11a. _____	13b. _____	13a. _____
16b. _____	16a. _____	17b. _____	17a. _____
20b. _____	20a. _____	19a. _____	19b. _____
TOTALS: T _____	F _____	P _____	J _____

PERSONAL STYLE INVENTORY INTERPRETATION

Letters on the score sheet stand for:

I — Introversion	**E** — Extroversion
N — Intuition	**S** — Sensing
T — Thinking	**F** — Feeling
P — Perceiving	**J** — Judging

If your score is: *The likely interpretation is:*

12–13	balance in the strengths of the dimensions
14–15	some strength in the dimension; some weakness in the other member of the pair
16–19	definite strength in the dimension; definite weakness in the other member of the pair
20–25	considerable strength in the dimension; considerable weakness in the other member of the pair

Your typology is those four dimensions for which you had scores of 14 or more, although the relative strengths of all the dimensions actually constitute your typology. Scores of 12 or 13 show relative balance in a pair so that either member could be part of the typology.

DIMENSIONS OF THE TYPOLOGY

The following four pairs of dimensions are present to some degree in all people. It is the extremes that are described here. The strength of a dimension is indicated by the score for that dimension and will determine how closely the strengths and weaknesses described fit the participant's personality.

INTROVERSION/EXTROVERSION

Persons more introverted than extroverted tend to make decisions somewhat independently of culture, people, or things around them. They are quiet, diligent at working alone, and socially reserved. They may dislike being interrupted while working and may tend to forget names and faces.

Extroverted persons are attuned to the culture, people, and things around them. The extrovert is outgoing, socially free, interested in variety and in working with people. The extrovert may become impatient with long, slow tasks and does not mind being interrupted by people.

INTUITION/SENSING

The intuitive person prefers possibilities, theories, invention, and the new and becomes bored with nitty-gritty details and facts unrelated to concepts. The intuitive person thinks and discusses in spontaneous leaps of intuition that may neglect details. Problem solving comes easily for this individual, although there may be a tendency to make errors of fact.

The sensing type prefers the concrete, factual, tangible here-and-now, becoming impatient with theory and the abstract, mistrusting intuition. The sensing type thinks in detail, remembering real facts, but possibly missing a conception of the overall.

THINKING/FEELING

The thinker makes judgments based on logic, analysis, and evidence, avoiding decisions based on feelings and values. As a result, the thinker is more interested in logic, analysis, and verifiable conclusions than in empathy, values, and personal warmth. The thinker may step on others' feelings and needs without realizing it, neglecting to take into consideration the values of others.

The feeler makes judgments based on empathy, warmth, and personal values. As a consequence, feelers are more interested in people and feelings than in impersonal logic, analysis, and things, and in harmony more than in being on top or achieving impersonal goals. The feeler gets along well with people in general.

PERCEIVING/JUDGING

The perceiver is a gatherer, always wanting to know more before deciding, holding off decisions and judgments. As a consequence, the perceiver is open, flexible, adaptive, nonjudgmental, able to see and appreciate all sides of issues, always welcoming new perspectives. However, perceivers are also difficult to pin down and may become involved in many tasks that do not reach closure, so that they may become frustrated at times. Even when they finish tasks, perceivers will tend to look back at them and wonder whether they could have been done another way. The perceiver wishes to roll with life rather than change it.

The judger is decisive, firm, and sure, setting goals and sticking to them. The judger wants to make decisions and get on to the next project. When a project does not yet have closure, judgers will leave it behind and go on to new tasks.

STRENGTHS AND WEAKNESSES OF THE TYPES

Each person has strengths and weaknesses as a result of these dimensions. Committees and organizations with a preponderance of one type will have the same strengths and weaknesses.

	Possible Strengths	**Possible Weaknesses**
Introvert	is independent	avoids others
	works alone	is secretive
	reflects	loses opportunities to act
	works with ideas	is misunderstood by others
	avoids generalizations	dislikes being interrupted
	is careful before acting	
Extrovert	interacts with others	does not work without people
	is open	needs change, variety
	acts, does	is impulsive
	is well understood	is impatient with routine
Intuitor	sees possibilities	is inattentive to detail, precision
	works out new ideas	is inattentive to the actual and practical
	works with the complicated	is impatient with the tedious
	solves novel problems	loses sight of the here-and-now
		jumps to conclusions
Senser	attends to detail	does not see possibilities
	is practical	loses the overall in details
	has memory for detail, fact	mistrusts intuition
	is patient	is frustrated with the complicated
	is systematic	prefers not to imagine future
Feeler	considers others' feelings	is not guided by logic
	understands needs, values	is not objective
	is interested in conciliation	is less organized
	demonstrates feelings	is overly accepting
	persuades, arouses	bases judgments on feelings

A good study group shares a common goal of success for all its members. It also asks each member to contribute according to his or her own special perspective and style.

Dollarhide/Monkmeyer Press Photo

	Possible Strengths	**Possible Weaknesses**
Thinker	is logical, analytical	does not notice people's feelings
	is objective	misunderstands others' values
	is organized	is uninterested in conciliation
	has critical ability	does not show feelings
	is just	shows less mercy
	stands firm	is uninterested in persuading
Perceiver	compromises	is indecisive
	sees all sides of issues	does not plan
	is flexible	does not control circumstances
	decides based on all data	is easily distracted from tasks
	is not judgmental	does not finish projects
Judger	decides	is stubborn
	plans	is inflexible
	orders	decides with insufficient data
	makes quick decisions	is controlled by task or plans
	remains with a task	wishes not to interrupt work

NOTE: This exercise is an abridgment of the Personal Style Inventory by Dr. R. Craig Hogan and Dr. David W. Champagne, adapted and reproduced with permission from Organization Design and Development, Inc., 2002 Renaissance Blvd., Suite 100, King of Prussia, Pa., 19406. For information on using the complete instrument, please write to the above address.

As you reflect on your performance on the previous exercise, keep in mind that your score merely suggests your preferences; it does not stereotype or pigeonhole you. Remember, too, that no one learning style is inherently preferable to another and that everyone knows and uses a range of styles. The fact that many of us exhibit behaviors that seem to contradict our preferences shows that we each embrace a wide range of possibilities.

Using Knowledge of Your Learning Style

Discovering your own strengths empowers you to recognize what you already do well. Discovering your weaknesses is also useful, because it is to your advantage to cultivate your less dominant learning styles. While certain disciplines and certain instructors may take approaches that favor certain styles, no course is going to be entirely sensing or entirely intuitive, entirely thinking or entirely feeling, just as you are not entirely one thing or another. You can also use your learning style data to determine how to study more effectively. Diagram? Study aloud? Annotate texts in margins? Focus on details or concepts?

■STUDY GROUPS AND LEARNING STYLE

Knowing your own learning style preference can help you to study more effectively with other students. When you form a study group, seek out students with some opposite learning preferences, but be sure, too, that you have some preferences in common. The best teamwork seems to come from people who differ on one or two preferences. If you prefer intuitive fact gathering, you might benefit from the details brought forth by a sensing type.

If you are in a math class, don't always try to solve problems alone. Share your ideas in a group. Talk about the steps you went through to solve a problem, and share study techniques that worked for you. In other classes study for exams by comparing notes and reviewing the main points covered in class.

EXERCISE 5.3 | **Working with Other Learning Styles**

A Form a group with one or two other students whose learning style preferences are different from yours in one or two dimensions. Review the chart in Exercise 5.2 on strengths and weaknesses and make some notes about yours so that you can find the best "match" with other study group members:

Strengths: _____

_____

_____

_____

Weaknessess: _____

_____

_____

_____

How to Develop Other Learning Styles

The key ingredient in developing your less dominant style is awareness. Try to develop one process at a time.

RAISING YOUR SENSING (S) LEARNING STYLE

1. Whenever you walk, try to notice and jot down specific details of the scenery—shapes of leaves; size, color, and types of rocks; and so on.

2. Three or four times a day pay careful attention to, and then describe to a friend, what someone else is wearing.

3. Do a jigsaw puzzle.

4. Break down a physical activity into its component parts.

5. Describe in detail something you just saw, such as a picture, a room, or the like.

RAISING YOUR INTUITIVE (N) LEARNING STYLE

1. Imagine a given situation or circumstance in a new light by considering, "What if . . . ?" For example, what if the pilgrims had landed in California—how would their lifestyle have changed? What if you had gone to a bigger (smaller) school? What if X were your roommate instead of Y?

2. Pretend you saw an article ten years from now about your hometown, your lifestyle, American values, or the like. What would it say?

3. Read a novel and imagine yourself as one of the characters. What would happen to you following the novel's conclusion?

RAISING YOUR FEELING (F) LEARNING STYLE

1. Write down a feeling statement about your class, your day, your job, or your emotions, and make sure you use a simile. For example, "I feel like a puppy that's just been scolded." Note that if you use *think* in a statement, it's not a feeling statement. Write down five feeling statements every day.

2. Write down what matters most in your relationship with someone or something else.

RAISING YOUR THINKING (T) LEARNING STYLE

1. Have someone write down a problem that's bothering him or her or a problem related to the college or your environment. Then answer questions that explain who, what, where, when, and why, and provide the details that back up each response. Doing this every day for 15 or 20 minutes will teach you how to be objective.

How will your strengths help others? What strengths will you look for in others that will help you?

How I can help others: _____

_____

_____

How others can help me: _____

_____

_____

In your next session, ask that each person share his or her strengths and weaknesses and talk about how the group might work for everyone's benefit.

B Try working on an assignment with someone who has a preference that is opposite of your own on either the sensing/intuitive or thinking/feeling scale. Discuss how this worked. Did you get more out of the assignment? Did you consider more issues than you might have alone? Did you learn something about how to study? What did you discover about the other person's learning style?

■ DEALING WITH YOUR TEACHERS' LEARNING/TEACHING STYLES

Just as your learning style affects how you study, perform, and react to various courses and disciplines, so your instructor's teaching style affects what and how he or she teaches. Some awareness of your instructor's teaching style may also help you study and prepare for exams. The syllabus for the course, the lecture, and the discussion questions, as well as handouts, assignments, and exams, can provide some helpful hints not only about your instructor's teaching style but also about ways you can use the strengths of your own learning style or compensate enough to perform effectively in the class.

Clues to Teachers' Teaching Styles

The best clue to your instructor's teaching style is the language he or she uses. If your learning style is more visual, you can sense those clues more easily from printed material such as the syllabus or course handouts. If your learning style is more auditory, pay attention to the language your instructor uses when lecturing, asking discussion questions, or phrasing oral test questions.

For example, earlier we discussed two ways of receiving and processing information: (1) sensing, that is, factual and informational, and (2) intuitive, that is, analytical and conceptual. An instructor who uses words such as *define, diagram, label, list, outline,* and *summarize* will tend to have a more sensing teaching style. He or she will want you to be extremely specific and provide primarily factual information. Words such as these really ask for very restricted answers. (See Chapter 8, pages 123–126, for more on the meaning of each of these terms.) Whereas Anne will be very comfortable with this instructor, Mark will be less so. Recognizing his instructor's teaching style, however, would be to Mark's benefit, since he would have a better idea of what to expect. He could then adjust his approach to the material in order to perform satisfactorily in class and on exams.

On the other hand, an instructor whose syllabus or lecture is sprinkled with words such as *concept, theme, idea, theory,* and *interpretation* will tend to have a much more intuitive and analytical learning style and expect similar kinds of responses from students. On exams or on assignments, he or she may use terms such as *describe, compare, contrast, criticize, discuss, evaluate, explain, interpret, justify,* or *relate.* (Again, see Chapter 8 for definitions.) You may notice that instead of asking you to provide factual data or information, these words ask you to act on that information—that is, to use it in relation to other pieces of information, to evaluate it, or to examine it in terms of your own experience. An instructor who uses these words has a much more intuitive teaching style and will expect more analytical, imaginative, and conceptual responses. He or she will expect you to see that information in a new context rather than simply restate the facts as they have been given to you or as they appear in the textbook.

Mark will, of course, feel far more comfortable with this instructor. Anne will have to recognize when she studies in this course that learning the facts is not enough. She will be expected to see them in other contexts, to think about their relationships to one another. While this may not be easy for her, she can certainly adapt to it if the instructor's teaching style and expectations demand it.

Exam Preparation and Learning/Teaching Style

Understanding learning styles can help you to perceive more clearly the expectations of an instructor whose teaching style is incompatible with your learning style and thus allow you to prepare more effectively for his or her exam. You saw earlier, for example, how Mark's learning style, essentially an intuitive (N) style, was suited to his history course but not to his biology exam. By contrast Anne's more sensing (S) style was suited to the biology course but not the history course. In order to perform better on that biology exam, Mark would need to modify his way of studying.

Let me illustrate further with an experience of my own. When I was learning about the Myers-Briggs Type Indicator, I attended a workshop for college instructors. Those of us attending the workshop were divided into two groups, sensing and intuitive. Each group was given a five-page essay about the effects of divorce on young children and asked to construct a short exam based on the reading. The sensing group was then asked to take the exam constructed by the intuitive group while the intuitive group was asked to take the exam constructed by the sensing group.

In dealing with the questions, we could not believe that both groups had read and discussed the same essay. Those of us in the intuitive group had been asked to construct lists of details and respond to much factual data that we had regarded as less essential than the more analytical and conceptual themes of the essay. And those in the sensing group were quite taken aback by the very broad thematic questions my group had asked about the implications of divorce on the children and the larger questions about the children's future.

It would have been much easier for those who favored sensing to respond to an exam constructed by other sensing people, and vice versa. That same situation has probably been true for you in classes and will continue to be true—you will be most comfortable in a course taught by an instructor with a teaching style similar to your learning style.

EXERCISE 5.4   Exams and Learning Styles

As a class, select some piece of writing such as a newspaper article or short magazine piece. Read the article. Then divide into groups in which people of similar learning styles are together. Within each group create a short test based on the reading. Reconvene as a class and compare the tests from the various groups. Did the different learning styles of the groups have any influence on the kinds of tests they created?

EXERCISE 5.5   Assessing Your Courses and Instructors

Take some time over the next few days to think about the courses you are taking now. How well does your preferred learning style fit the style reflected in the syllabus, handouts, lectures, and study questions in at least two of your courses? Ask several of your instructors how *they* teach and learn best.

Do any of the key sensing words mentioned previously (*define, diagram,* and so on) or some close approximation of them appear? If so, list them and place a check mark next to each of them each time the word appears. Do any of the key intuition words (*describe, compare,* and so on) or similar words appear? List them also and note their frequency. Listen carefully in class. What key words do you hear? Write these down also. Which type of word do you hear most frequently? That will begin to give you some idea of each instructor's learning/teaching style. You may also wish to assess your academic advisor's preferences.

INSTRUCTOR/COURSE 1: _____

Sensing Words   **Intuition Words**

_____   _____

_____   _____

_____   _____

_____   _____

_____   _____

_____   _____

_____   _____

Instructor's preferred style: Sensing _____   Intuition _____

Other teaching style observations: _____

_____

_____

_____

_____

_____

_____

INSTRUCTOR/COURSE 2: _____

Sensing Words   **Intuition Words**

_____   _____

_____   _____

_____   _____

_____   _____

_____   _____

_____   _____

_____   _____

Instructor's preferred style: Sensing _____   Intuition _____

Other teaching style observations: _____

_____

_____

_____

_____

_____

How does your learning style as measured in Exercise 5.2 fit with the learning/teaching style of each instructor? Which courses will require some adjustment on your part? Discuss these problems with other students in class. Keep these problems in mind as you complete the next three chapters, which focus on your study skills.

Are there things your instructors could be doing to help you take advantage of your strengths and learn more efficiently? In class discuss what these ideas are and how you might convey them to the appropriate instructor.

If your instructor's teaching style is compatible with your learning style, then you should be able to perform well simply by keeping up with your work. If your instructor's style is incompatible with yours, you might consider either mastering more factual material or interpreting or analyzing that material in order to be better prepared for exams or papers. In any case a greater awareness of both your learning style *and* your instructor's teaching style can be of real benefit.

A variety of additional tests can help you learn more about your learning style. These are generally available through your career planning or learning center. A guidance counselor will both administer the test and help you interpret the results. Ask about the following:

- The Myers-Briggs Type Indicator
- The complete Hogan/Champagne Personal Style Inventory
- The Kolb Learning Style Inventory

EXERCISE 5.6 Learning Styles and Critical Thinking

Can your learning preferences affect the ease or difficulty with which you complete the four stages of critical thinking? Think about it. It may be easier for intuitive (N) learners to find abstractions amid details and brainstorm possibilities (steps 1 and 2), whereas sensing (S) learners may do well in step 3 where they can list ideas into some logical order. Thinking (T) learners may also find step 3 comes naturally to them, whereas feeling (F) learners may complete step 3 by prioritizing their values, rather than by the logic of the situation. As you complete this exercise, note first how your learning style preferences have made it easy or difficult for you to complete the steps of the critical thinking process and then how your learning style preferences affect your thinking on the following issue.

Imagine that your college newspaper has run a story detailing a new structure for teaching courses. To cut costs and accommodate students who wish to complete their education faster, the administration is considering dividing the year into four equal terms of thirteen weeks each. One term would run January through March, a second term would run April through June, a third July through September, and a fourth October through December. Any holidays—such as Christmas and Thanksgiving—would be shortened to no more than two days to accommodate the schedule. Faculty would teach only three terms a year, on a rotating basis, meaning that some courses might not be available year round. While most students would attend classes only three out of four terms, students would have the option of graduating early if they attended all four terms. Due to a slightly shorter schedule, class length would increase by roughly 10 minutes a period. The average student course load would be four courses per term.

The highly popular president of your student government, who is in favor of the proposal, has asked you to take a stand on this issue at a campuswide meeting. Using the principles of critical thinking, meet with three or four other students (ask your instructor if he or she can group you by opposite N/S and T/F preferences) and complete the first three steps. Then complete the final step.

1. List the broad *abstract* ideas inherent in this proposal to change the school term. What are the truths or arguments here? What are the key ideas? What larger concepts do the details suggest? What is the administration really trying to accomplish?

2. Find new *possibilities*. What questions do the large ideas suggest? What new questions can you ask about the value of adjusting the schedule? What other possibilities might there be besides dividing the year into four equal parts? What are some possible effects of such a change on students? On faculty? Avoid making immediate decisions. Put off closure. Reject nothing at first.

3. *Organize* new ideas and possibilities in a logical order. In what direction do the facts really point? What are the best solutions? To leave the schedule alone? To offer options? Is there some important additional information that needs to be gathered and evaluated before it is possible to reach a conclusion? Ultimately, what new abstractions and new conclusions have resulted from your thinking?

4. Using the results of the group thinking process, write a paper that precisely *communicates* your ideas to others. Are your conclusions well supported? Make certain your conclusions take all parties (the majority of students, faculty, and others) into account. At the end of the paper, state whether you believe your learning style made any of these steps easy or difficult to follow and why.

JOURNAL

What's your learning style? How are you trying to adapt your style to the teaching styles of some of your instructors and academic advisors? Outside class do you tend to associate with people who have learning styles similar to your own or with people whose learning styles are different? Thinking about this may help you uncover some clues about compatibility between you and some of the significant people in your life, in both short-term and long-term relationships.

SUGGESTIONS FOR FURTHER READING

Lawrence, Gordon. *People Types and Tiger Stripes*. Gainesville, Fla.: Center for the Application of Psychological Types, 1982.

Malone, John C., Jr. *Theories of Learning: A Historical Approach*. Belmont, Calif.: Wadsworth, 1991.

Perry, William. *Forms of Intellectual and Ethical Development in the College Years: A Scheme*. New York: Holt, Rinehart & Winston, 1970.

CHAPTER 6

Listening and Learning in the Classroom

Kenneth F. Long
University of Windsor

Mary-Jane McCarthy
Middlesex Community College

I'm looking over my notes from psych. "Personalities affecting behaviors . . . something . . . something . . . abnormal." What does that mean? I guess I write too fast. What does this say? "Ask Sarah to go out Friday." That's not psych. These notes are useless. I'd better get them from somebody else.

Chapter Goals

This chapter provides you with a proven system for taking good notes in lectures—one that you can use to prepare for class, get the most out of class, and draw on as you review material for tests.

Learn to make every minute count. That means not merely *attending* classes but making the most of the time you spend *in* your classes. Participate in the activity of the classroom, taking meaningful, efficient notes that will enhance your ability to abstract ideas, find new possibilities, organize ideas, and recall the material once the class is over.

Lecturing is only one mode of teaching, and for a variety of reasons including the relatively short attention span of many people, it is often not the best. However, to succeed in college, you should know what lecturing entails and how to deal with it. The lecture method is teacher-dominated (they talk, you listen), is information-laden (you take notes and study later), and allows for large amounts of material to be covered quickly. (We almost said "efficiently," but if most students aren't really listening after 15 minutes, it can hardly be called efficient, can it?)

Lectures can seduce you into taking a passive role in the classroom. Some students have a second self, a "stenographer," who tries to write down everything a teacher says. For them a full notebook creates a false sense of security. In reality, indiscriminate note-taking wastes a lot of time because it leaves all of the learning for later and invites forgetting. It's not enough to say, "I'll write everything down and worry about what's important later." Improper note-taking encourages intellectual laziness in the classroom and gets in the way of active listening—and learning. Not surprisingly, poor note-taking skills often correlate with poor grades. Look at the students with good grades and you will usually find good note-taking skills, too.

EXERCISE 6.1 Your Note-Taking IQ

Mark each of the following statements either T (true) or F (false).

_____ 1. If you can't tell what is really important in a lecture, you should write down everything the instructor says.

_____ 2. If an instructor moves through the material very fast, it is better to tape record the lecture and not worry so much about listening in class.

Should schools abandon the lecture system? Like other skilled performers and communicators, a good lecture can stimulate many minds, each in its own direction.

Rogers/Monkmeyer Press Photo

———— 3. If the instructor puts an outline on the board or on an overhead projector, you should copy it down immediately.

———— 4. In a class that is mainly discussion, it is best just to listen and talk rather than to take notes.

———— 5. The best way to take notes is to use a formal outlining system with Roman numerals, letters, and numbers.

The correct answers are given on page 90. Discuss the answers with your instructor or in small groups.

■ NOTE-TAKING AND FORGETTING

As an undergraduate, one of this chapter's authors was dismayed to find himself studying material over and over again, rereading chapters that seemed almost new, laboring over notes that were only a month old. Some years after college, he learned something unforgettable about forgetting. He read about an experiment (discussed in Pauk, 1989) involving people who were tested at various intervals after reading a textbook chapter. Researchers discovered that most forgetting takes place in the first 24 hours and then tapers off (see Figure 6.1). Within two weeks almost 70 percent of the material is lost.

Because many instructors draw the bulk of their test items from the content of their lectures, remembering what is presented in the classroom is crucial to doing well on exams. A note-taking system that lessens the forgetting curve of the first 24 hours and organizes the information for later recall can greatly improve your chances for success on exams.

Listening and Learning in the Classroom

Figure 6.1 Learning and Forgetting

Psychologists have studied human forgetting in many laboratory experiments. Here are the "forgetting curves" for three kinds of material: poetry, prose, and nonsense syllables. The curves are basically similar. The shallower curves for prose and poetry indicate that meaningful material is forgotten more slowly than nonmeaningful information. Poetry, which contains internal cues such as rhyme and rhythm, is forgotten less quickly that prose.

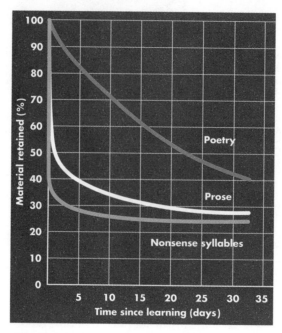

SOURCE: *Used with permission from Wayne Weiten,* Psychology: Themes and Variations *(Pacific Grove, Calif.: Brooks/Cole, 1989, p. 254. Based on data from D. van Guilford, Van Nostrand, 1939).*

■ A SOUND APPROACH TO NOTE-TAKING IN LECTURES

Although the lecture system itself may not induce active learning and retention, there are things you can do to make it more efficient. An organized, planned approach to the lecture includes three phases: before, during, and after the lecture. The objectives will be (1) increased on-the-spot learning, (2) longer attention span, (3) better retention of information, and (4) better notes for later study, particularly at exam time.

Before the Lecture: Reading and Warming Up

If a lecture is a demanding intellectual encounter, then you need to be ready intellectually. You wouldn't go in cold to give a speech, interview for a job, plead your case in court, or compete in sports. For each of these situations you would prepare in some way and set out with attention focused. So always prepare for class, especially when you are not asked, apparently, to do

ANSWERS (to Exercise 6.1): All the statements are false.

You'll get more out of a lecture if you prepare ahead of time. Stay abreast of the readings. Get your own ideas flowing by reviewing notes from the previous lecture. What questions were left unanswered? Where should today's session begin?

Photo by David Gonzales

anything more than listen and take notes. Active listening, learning, and remembering begin *before* the lecture.

1. **Do the Assigned Reading.** Many students blame lecturers for seeming disorganized or confusing, when in fact the student has not done the reading that the lecture required. Some instructors explicitly assign readings for each class session and refer frequently to readings; others will simply hand out a syllabus and assume you are keeping up. Either way, doing the assigned readings helps you to listen well, and active listening in turn promotes good reading. So keep up with your reading and most lectures will come alive—that is, the lectures will answer questions you may have had as you read. If you go into a lecture without having done the reading, the material will be unfamiliar and perhaps overwhelming.

2. **Warm Up for Class.** If you have read well and taken good notes, this should be easy. Warm up by referring to the underlinings in your readings (see Chapter 7) and/or to the recall columns (see page 93) in your previous class notes. This gets you ready to pay attention, understand, and remember.

During the Lecture: Taking the Right Kind of Notes

Now that you're ready for class, you need to develop your listening and note-taking skills.

1. **Identify the Main Ideas.** Good lecturers always present certain key points in their lectures. The first principle of effective note-taking is to identify and write down the four or five most important ideas that the lecture is built around. Although some supporting details may be important as well, your note-taking focus should be on the main ideas. These may be buried in detail, statistics, anecdotes, or problems to solve, but you need to locate and record them for later study.

Listening and Learning in the Classroom

© 1992, Chuck Savage/photo courtesy of Beloit College

A good lecture is an exploration. As part of the expedition, think critically about the direction of a teacher's thought. Try to predict where the lecture is heading and why. What are the major landmarks and key ideas along the way?

As you listen, keep these two frames of thinking in mind: general material (main idea) and specific information (supporting details). Every good lecturer is trying to express one or several main ideas. This is your general frame of reference. For example, in a psychology lecture on learning curves, you would likely formulate a main idea statement like the following: "There are three learning curves presented in this study." Then you would be alert for the specifics that would explain this general statement: "prose, poetry, and nonsense syllables."

Lecturers sometimes announce the purpose or offer an outline, thus providing you with the skeleton of main ideas and details. Some change their tone of voice or repeat themselves at each key idea. Some ask questions or promote discussion. These are all clues to what is important. Ask yourself, "What does my instructor want me to know at the end of today's session?"

Certainly not everything needs to be written down. Because of insecurity or inexperience, some first-year students try to write everything down—they stop being a thinker and let the stenographer take over. Don't fall into this trap. Be an *active listener,* always searching for main ideas and for the connections among them—those general assertions that must be supported by specific comments. After a week's practice, as you get to know your instructors, you will have better, and *shorter,* notes.

Unfortunately, some of your instructors may teach in a manner that makes it difficult to take good notes. You can still use the same techniques, however, to organize the lectures for your own use. Even though some of your instructors may not teach as you would like them to, you are ultimately responsible for making sense of what they said.

When a lecture is disorganized, you must strive to organize what is being said into general and specific frameworks; and when this order is not apparent, you need to take notes on where the gaps in the lecture's organization lie. After the lecture you may need to consult your reading material or your classmates in order to try to fill in these gaps.

2. **Leave Space for a Recall Column.** In addition to helping you listen well, notes provide an important study device for tests and exams. This is the second principle of effective note-taking. In anticipation of this, treat each page of your notes as part of an exam-taking system.

On each page of notepaper draw a vertical line to divide the page into two columns (see Figure 6.2). (Looseleaf is a good choice, but write on one side only.) The column on the left, about 2½ inches wide, is called the "recall column" and remains blank while you take notes during class in the column on the right. The momentarily blank recall column, you will discover, is an incredibly powerful study device that reduces forgetting, helps you warm up for class, and promotes understanding in class. It also lets you review efficiently right after class. This recall column is essentially the place where you can sift through your note material to determine main ideas and important details.

Computer Notes in Class?

More and more, students bring laptop computers to class. Although you might feel a desire to show off your high-tech toy, laptops are often poor tools for note-taking. Computer screens are not conducive for making marginal notes, circling important items, or copying diagrams. And although most students can scribble coherently without looking, few are really good touch typists. Finally, notes on a computer are often harder to access or scan when it comes time to review.

Entering notes onto a computer can provide an opportunity to review and reflect on your notes. On the other hand, if you enter them verbatim, you may be simply wasting time that could be spent more productively.

EXERCISE 6.2

Using Critical Thinking to Determine Main Ideas and Major Details

Divide a piece of paper as shown in Figure 6.2. Read the following excerpt from a psychology lecture on memory. Take notes on the right side of the paper, leaving the recall column blank. When you are done, use the critical thinking process to abstract the main ideas and write them in the recall column. Think about those ideas and jot down in the same recall column any thoughts, or possibilities, that occur to you. For example, your possibilities may include, "I wonder what I can attach this information about memory to so I can recall it later?" Or, "Maybe if I break my American lit notes into small chunks, I'll recall them easier."

Today we will continue our discussion of memory and treat the idea of distributed practice—an important aspect of memory. This is the practice of learning a little bit at a time, as opposed to a lot at a time. Cramming for a

Figure 6.2 Sample Page for Note-Taking

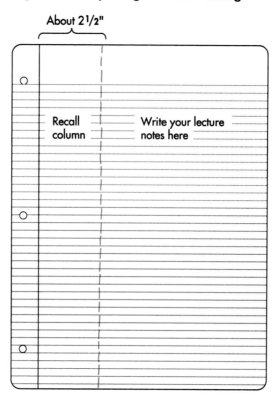

About 2½"

Recall
column

Write your lecture
notes here

test is an example of the opposite kind of practice known as massed practice. Distributed practice is what you need to develop as you study for your classes.

Further, what you learn tends to be remembered easily if you can attach it to similar knowledge. This is the third term I want to discuss today—the depth-of-processing principle. That is, information is stored in the brain on various levels. If it is stored superficially, the material cannot attach itself to rich associations. If it is stored deeply, the knowledge finds a series of associations to attach itself to. Storing material deeply allows for retention of it, while, as you would guess, storing superficially tends to lead to forgetting.

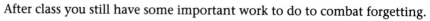

After the Lecture: Filling in the Recall Column, Reciting, and Reviewing

After class you still have some important work to do to combat forgetting.

1. **Write the Main Ideas in the Recall Column.** This is where the blank recall column becomes important. For 5 or 10 minutes, quickly review your notes and select key words or phrases (or make up some) that will act as labels or tags for main ideas and key information covered in the notes. Highlight the main ideas, and write them in the recall column beside the material they represent.

2. **Use the Recall Column to Recite Your Notes.** Now cover the notes on the right and use the tags in the recall column to help you recite out loud a brief version of what you understand from the class you have just participated in. If you do not have 5 or 10 minutes after class to review your notes, find some time during the day to review what you have written. You might also want to ask your instructor to glance at your recall column to see if you have noted the main ideas.

3. **Review the Previous Day's Notes Before the Next Class Session.** As you sit in class the following day waiting for the lecture to begin, use the time to review quickly the notes from the previous day. This will put you in tune with the lecture that is about to begin and will also prompt you to ask questions about material from the previous lecture that may not have been clear to you. These "engagements" with the material will pay off later, when you begin to study for your exam.

WHY IS THIS PROCESS SO POWERFUL? The key to this system is the fact that you are encountering the same material in three different ways: (1) active listening and writing, (2) reading and summarizing in the recall column, and finally (3) saying aloud what you understand from class. Your whole person—mind and body—is involved. All of these actions promote learning.

Recitation is a particularly effective guard against forgetting. The very act of verbalizing concepts gives your memory sufficient time to grasp them. That is, you move material from short-term memory to long-term memory, where you can call on it as needed. Strictly speaking, we never really forget anything; we just lose control of it somewhere in our minds. Having a good memory really means having an organized method of capturing and recalling whatever our mind encounters, and recitation bolsters this practice.*

Now you may object, "I have three classes in a row and no time for recall columns or recitation between them. What can I do?" Well, recall and recite as soon after class as possible. In the case of successive classes, review the most recent class first. Never delay recall and recitation longer than one day because by then you will have forgotten too much material. It will take you much longer to review, make a recall column, and recite. With practice you can fill in recall columns in 5 or 10 minutes when material is still fresh. Recitation need only take a few more minutes. Done faithfully, these two activities are great aids to understanding and remembering.

EXERCISE 6.3 Using a Recall Column

Suppose the information in this chapter had been presented to you as a lecture rather than a reading. Using the system described previously, your lecture notes might look like those in Figure 6.3. Cover the right-hand column. Using the recall column, try reciting in your own words the main ideas from this chapter. Uncover the right-hand column when you need to refer to it. If you can phrase the main ideas from the recall column in your own words, you are well on your way to mastering this note-taking system for dealing with lectures. Does this system seem to work? If not, why not?

---

*In addition to recitation's power to combat forgetting, it also has value in preparation for the actual writing of a test or exam. (See Chapter 8.)

Figure 6.3 Sample Lecture Notes

Sept 21 How to take notes

Problems with lectures	Lecture _not_ best way to teach. Problems: Short attention span (may be only 15 minutes!). Teacher dominates. Most info is forgotten. "Stenographer" role interferes with thinking, understanding, learning.
Forgetting curves	Forgetting curves critical period: over ½ of lecture forgotten in 24 hours.
Solution: Active listening	Answer: Active listening, really understanding during lecture. Aims— (1) immediate understanding (2) longer attention (3) better retention (4) notes for study later
Before: Read Warm up	BEFORE: Always prepare. Read: Readings parallel lectures & make them meaningful. Warm up: Review last lecture notes & readings right before class.
During: main ideas	DURING: Write main ideas & some detail. No stems. What clues does prof. give about what's most important? Ask. Ask other questions. Leave blank column about 2½" on left of page. Use only front side of paper.
After: Review Recall Recite	AFTER: Left column for key recall words, "tags." Cover right side & recite what tags mean. Review/Recall/Recite

EXERCISE 6.4 — Comparing Notes

A Pair up with another student and compare your class notes for several classes. Take a few minutes to explain to each other your note-taking system. Based on this discussion what improvements would you like to make in your note-taking method?

_____

_____

_____

B Use recall columns and make other improvements in your note-taking in several future classes. Use the recall column each time for recitation after class. Show your new notes to your partner and talk about any problems and improvements.

LEARNING: A COMPLEMENTARY PROCESS

Now that you know what to do to make the lecture system work as well as possible on your end, let's examine four things your instructors can do to make their lectures clearer and to help you listen actively. Ideally, where feasible, your instructors will follow these practices. Whether they do these things or not, remember the things you can do to maximize your learning:

1. **They:** Always refer specifically to any reading that relates to a forthcoming lecture; pose specific questions in advance to help you read well.
   You: Always read in preparation for class.
2. **They:** Always begin with an outline and/or a statement of purpose that helps you know what is important.
   You: Always search for important ideas.
3. **They:** Plan pauses in every lecture at 10- to 15-minute intervals for questions, illustrations, and learning activities; this helps rein in wandering minds.
   You: Use active listening and note-taking activities to keep your attention level high.
4. **They:** Stop lecturing with 5 or 10 minutes left in class to let you make recall columns, recite, or discuss for better retention and understanding.
   You: Review, recall, and recite as soon after class as possible, and review again just prior to the next class.

Following the "before/during/after" system will maximize learning even when the teaching is not ideal. If you use this three-phase method for each day's classes, you will be actively learning on a daily basis and preparing for effective study later.

TAKING NOTES IN NONLECTURE COURSES

Of course, you must be flexible in how you apply the system. When you encounter nonlecture styles (question–answer sessions, group discussions, workshops, seminars, and so on), always be ready to adapt your note-taking methods. In fact, group discussion is becoming a popular way to structure college learning, often replacing the traditional lecture format. In these discussion groups, you must still keep in mind the two basic types of information—general and specific.

Assume, for example, that you are taking notes in a problem-solving roundtable of four classmates. You would begin your notes by asking yourself, "What is the problem?" As the roundtable progresses, you would list the views or solutions offered. These would be the main ideas. The major details would include the pros and cons of each view.

The important thing to remember when taking notes in nonlecture classes is that you need to record the information presented by your classmates as well as that of the instructor. You must be sure to consider all reasonable ideas, even those that may be different from your own.

Suppose you are taking notes on a class discussion concerning a controversial subject such as euthanasia (mercy killing). You would begin your notes by stating the aspect of the issue being addressed. For example, the class might be focusing on whether mercy killing is moral or whether mercy killing should be limited in a particular way. Your notes would then be divided into arguments "for" and arguments "against." The details would include the reasons given to support each argument. It is important that you record *all* reasonable arguments, even if you do not agree with them, because your instructor may ask you to defend your own opinion in light of the others.

EXERCISE 6.5

Applying an Active
Listening and Learning System

Examine Carmen's study schedule on page 52 in Chapter 4, and then answer the following questions:

1. Where do you see evidence of plans to use the recall column?

_____

_____

_____

2. What problems will Carmen have in performing review/recall/recite as soon after class as possible?

_____

_____

_____

3. How can these problems be solved?

_____

_____

_____

Share your answers with other students in a small group.

Participating in Classroom Thinking

How much do your classes require or encourage you to develop the four general critical thinking skills? The answer will vary with the teaching ability of your instructor and with how much preparation you yourself bring to class. It may also vary according to the size and format of the class. Yet even in a lecture with many students, a talented teacher can stimulate your ability to form abstractions, think creatively, think systematically, and communicate well.

Consider several courses you are taking now. In a group, discuss the following issues.

A Compare your classroom experiences with different instructors.

Forming Abstractions

Do they expect or encourage students to raise questions?

Do they present evidence and challenge you to interpret it?

Do they challenge class members to restate or paraphrase the main idea of a lecture?

Creative Thinking

Do they help you practice looking at several sides of an issue?

Do they ask for your ideas on an issue?

Do they ask you to keep an open mind on a question that you at first think has an obvious right answer?

Do they use brainstorming strategies in which ideas can be generated without being prejudged?

Systematic Thinking

Do they give you practice in following a careful line of reasoning?

Do they ask you to fill in the missing steps in an argument?

Do they ask you to judge whether an idea is adequately supported by logic or data?

Communication

Do they have a process for encouraging students to speak—even shy students?

Do they ask a member of the class to clarify a point for the benefit of other students?

B Compare your own participation in classes with that of other students.

Forming Abstractions

Have you asked an instructor to clarify the main idea of a lecture or discussion?

Have you asked other questions about a lecture or the reading?

Have you volunteered to answer a question posed by the instructor?

Have you gotten lost or confused in a lecture? What did you do to get back on track?

Creative Thinking

Have you volunteered an idea?

Have you made an effort to keep an open mind about something about which you already had a strong opinion?

Have you participated in a group or classroom brainstorming effort?

Systematic Thinking

Have you outlined in your notes the general argument that an instructor is making in class?

Have you asked a question when you were uncertain about the reasoning behind an argument that is being made in the lecture or in the reading?

Communication

Have you talked with the instructor before or after class or during office hours?

Have you discussed ideas from the course or asked questions of other students in the class?

C Use the goal-setting process in Chapter 1 to expand your critical thinking participation in at least one of your classes. If something makes it hard for you to participate in class, make an office appointment to talk with your instructor or a counselor about the problem.

JOURNAL

Compare and contrast your present style of lecture note-taking with the approach suggested in this chapter. Consider a course in which you are experiencing difficulty taking what you consider satisfactory notes. List what you consider to be the "problems" you are encountering. How might the approach offered in this chapter help? Which particular strategies do you need to implement immediately? Consider sharing this information with the instructor of a course that is difficult for you. Ask for feedback on your choice of learning strategies.

SUGGESTIONS FOR FURTHER READING

Pauk, Walter. *How to Study in College,* 4th ed. Boston: Houghton Mifflin, 1989. See Chapter 5, "Forgetting and Remembering."

Sotiriou, Peter Elias. *Integrating College Study Skills: Reasoning in Reading, Listening, and Writing,* 4th ed. Belmont, Calif.: Wadsworth, 1996. See Part 3, "Taking Lecture and Study Notes."

A Sound Approach to Textbooks

Kenneth F. Long
University of Windsor

Mary-Jane McCarthy
Middlesex Community College

I've read this paragraph five times and I still don't understand it. How am I supposed to be ready to discuss this chapter tomorrow when I can't even get through the first page? There's gotta be a better way. Can't someone just drill a hole in my head and pour it in?

Chapter Goals

This chapter presents a method for reading textbooks and other course materials that is different from the method you use when reading for pleasure. After completing the chapter, you should know how to use a flexible, time-saving system for learning that combines planned reading, annotation, recitation, and writing.

What typically happens when you start to read those four chapters assigned for class two days away? At 7:00 P.M. you intend to start reading, but first you visit the bathroom (5 minutes), make a quick call to a friend (6 minutes), go get an apple (4 minutes), and then sit down to read, but only after clearing your desk, sharpening pencils, and arranging some notes (5 minutes). It is almost 7:30 and you haven't read a word yet! You continue to read, but your mind is wandering. Each time you catch yourself drifting off, you have to flip back a page or two to find where to start reading again.

This situation reflects two common problems students encounter when reading: procrastination and short attention span. The result is not only unfinished work but a feeling that reading for study is something they *cannot* do. When this happens over and over, it's no wonder students come to dislike reading.

Studies have shown that if you are a typical first-year student, your attention span for college material is only about 5 minutes. That's not long enough! You need to be able to focus on your reading for at least 15 minutes at a stretch for immediate academic survival—and even more as you progress.

Where to begin? Perhaps we should start by considering how reading for study differs from reading for pleasure. Reading a newspaper or favorite magazine for news or entertainment is generally easy because what you actually learn from the newspaper or magazine is often of secondary importance. Similarly most novels are devoted to providing pleasure and entertainment. In short the best-selling novel is written with you in mind, and its ultimate message is "Relax, enjoy."

The well-written textbook is also crafted with you in mind, but its appeal is almost purely to the intellect, and its message is "Wake up!" This is why it's so demanding, and also why your professor has assigned it. If you are going to learn from your academic reading, you must assume a great deal of responsibility.

Don't despair. You can learn how to take advantage of procrastination, dramatically lengthen your attention span, and hence improve your reading skill. If you apply a system like the one suggested for dealing with lectures in Chapter 6, it can become (and must become) a very manageable task.

It's a lot like jogging. At first you may not be able to run a mile. However, with planning and perseverance, a mile soon becomes only a warmup, and running, which was once boring and frustrating, becomes enjoyable and exhilarating.

EXERCISE 7.1 — What's Your Current Reading Attention Span?

Select a textbook from one of your courses. Begin reading a portion of it, timing yourself with a clock or stopwatch. Determine your attention span (the number of minutes you read before your mind begins to wander) and the number of words read. Don't prepare to read by skimming or using other techniques; just read. Try this activity three separate times for the same chapter. Report your scores here:

Attention span (minutes):   1. _____   2. _____   3. _____

Total number of words: 1. _____   2. _____   3. _____

We'll be referring back to these figures shortly.

■ A PLAN FOR READING TEXTBOOKS

The following planned approach to reading will increase your reading speed, promote understanding, and help you study for tests and exams. This system is based on two basic principles: (1) planning before reading and (2) marking, reviewing, and reciting.

Planning and Reading

Planning to read is an undemanding but important activity. The purpose is to create "advance organizers" in your mind by quickly surveying the pages to be read and looking for headings or key words or sentences that suggest what the reading is about. Sometimes chapters conclude with lists of main points, summary paragraphs, or questions. These are particularly useful in creating advance organizers, so read them as part of your planning.

If your instructor specifically mentions connections between readings and classroom instruction, reconsider these clues before you read and make note of them for upcoming tests. Use any or all of this to warm up your mind and create a general plan for reading. Ask yourself "Why am I reading this?" and "What do I want to know?"

EXERCISE 7.2 Creating Advance Organizers

Quickly survey the rest of this chapter by reading each heading and phrase in bold print. Then answer these questions:

1. How many pages does this chapter have? _____

2. What are the five major topics or skills covered?

a. _____

b. _____

c. _____

d. _____

e. _____

1. **Measure the Reading Assignment.** Measure the assignment and divide it up according to your own attention span and reading speed. Recall that a first-year student's attention span for reading textbooks is typically as short as 5 minutes, at a rate of far less than one page per minute. So let's say you can read about one or two pages in 5 minutes. Accept your current attention span as measured in Exercise 7.1. Measure the assignment, warm up with some planning activities, and then read.

2. **Read a Specific Amount in a Short Period, and Know What You Have Read.** Try to read a page or two in 5 minutes, increasing the rate as you become more comfortable with the system. An effective warmup alone will lengthen your attention span and boost your reading speed. Practice will increase them even further. Some students report a doubling of capacity very quickly. Surprisingly, faster reading speed can also aid concentration and comprehension. Soon you should be able to divide a fifteen-page textbook reading assignment into four intense sessions of 10 minutes each.

EXERCISE 7.3 Planned Reading

A Take up the same textbook you used in Exercise 7.1. Read the next portion of the chapter, timing yourself with a clock or stopwatch. This time, before you read, survey the chapter for advance organizers. Again, read until your attention begins to wander, and then record the results at the top of page 105.

Attention span (minutes): _____

Total number of words: _____

How do these scores compare with the scores in Exercise 7.1? How much improvement was there?

B Now read another portion of the same text. Before reading, measure out the number of pages you should be able to read attentively and increase the amount slightly. Repeat this process one more time.

Marking, Reviewing, and Reciting

The more actively you participate in the reading process, the more readily you will comprehend and retain the material. Therefore, during your intense reading sessions use the following procedures.

1. **Use Your Pencil as You Read.** During the actual reading, underline, circle, or draw arrows to important material and/or write notes in the margin. This is a part of active reading. Use your markings to point out key ideas and connections. Doing this will force you to concentrate as you seek out important ideas and supporting details. See how main ideas and supporting details inform what you read.

   Don't be afraid to mark up your textbooks. Sure, they cost a lot, but it's a foolish economy to keep them clean and neat for resale. If you read a chapter one week without marking it, you'll find you've all but forgotten it a few weeks later. The only alternative to marking is taking notes, but that is quite time consuming. Read well, mark well, and transform your text on a regular basis into a study device that facilitates review.

   The sample pages in Figure 7.1 discuss some ideas about improving memory. See how the reader marked the pages with underlinings and marginalia. Note that the underlining is selective and that much material is passed over. This shows that the reader consciously searched for what was important—the main ideas of the excerpt and the key supporting details. Note also that the marginalia state connections between important ideas. The marginalia serve as the recall column while the underlined text provides supporting detail. The reader has created a means to review the text quickly and efficiently before an examination.

EXERCISE 7.4 The Well-Marked Page

Photocopy Figure 7.2, which shows the next two pages of the book that was reproduced (and marked) in Figure 7.1. Then read and mark the two pages using your own underlinings and marginalia.

Compare your underlinings with those of your classmates. Are you picking out the main ideas? Are you noting connections? Should you be underlining less or more for effective later review? Pointed, serious discussion with willing, equally serious partners is a great way to practice using a well-marked-up textbook. It lightens the work load, too.

Write as you read. Taking notes on your reading helps you focus on the key ideas and summarize as you go. You take in and digest the material rather than skim it.

Tom Jorgenson/photo courtesy of The University of Iowa

2. **Review and Recite.** At the end of each 10 minutes of reading, use the markings to review and recite what you have learned. It will keep your concentration level high through a long assignment. Review and recitation for three or four pages should take only 2 or 3 minutes. For the fifteen-page assignment you should spend about 40 minutes actually reading (and marking) and about 8 minutes reviewing, for a total of 48 minutes.

Add 8 minutes for final review and recitation of the total assignment, reconnecting it to the purpose you established in your original warmup. Finish by answering aloud the questions "What did I learn, and how does it fit into the course?" You now have completed 56 minutes of highly concentrated reading—a demanding, rigorous, and rewarding intellectual exercise.

Not even most instructors read textbook-type material at a high level of understanding for much longer than an hour at a time. It's simply too fatiguing. All good readers punctuate bouts of reading with little pauses, or "breathers" for the mind. By planning these pauses and using them for review, you continually reinforce what you are learning, and you avoid becoming lost and feeling defeated. Certainly, you will be tired at the end of a reading session, so take a break, or study something else.

EXERCISE 7.5   Reviewing and Reciting

Using the sample markings in Figure 7.1 as well as your own markings in Figure 7.2, practice the review and recite process. The four pages should take about 5 minutes—10 minutes if you choose to work with a partner.

Figure 7.1 Sample Marked Pages

IMPROVEMENT, LOSS, AND DISTORTION OF MEMORY

How improve memory?

How can we improve memory?
Why do we sometimes forget?
Why do we sometimes think we remember something, when in fact we are wrong?

At one point while I was doing the research for this book, I went to find an article that I remembered reading, which I thought would very nicely illustrate a particular point I wanted to make. I was pretty sure I remembered the author, the name of the journal, and the date of the article within a year. So I was certain it would not take me long to find the article.

About four hours later I finally located it. I was right about the author, but I was wrong about the journal and the year. Worst of all, I discovered that the results the article reported were quite different from what I remembered. (The way I *remembered* the results made a lot more sense than the *actual* results!)

Why does my memory—and probably yours as well—make mistakes like this? And is there any way to improve memory?

IMPROVING MEMORY BY IMPROVING LEARNING

"I'm sorry. I don't remember your name. I just don't have a good memory for names." "I went to class regularly and did all the reading, but I couldn't remember all those facts when it came time for the test."

When people cannot remember names or facts, the reason is generally that they did not learn them very well in the first place. To improve your ability to remember something, be very careful about how you learn it.

Distribution of Practice

Distribution – over time

You want to memorize a part for a play. Should you sit down and study your lines in one long marathon session until you know them? Or should you spread your study sessions over several days? Research indicates that **distributed practice**—that is, a little at a time over many days—is generally better than **massed practice**, the same number of repetitions over a short time. One reason is that it is hard to maintain full attention when you repeat the same thing over and over at one sitting. Another is that studying something at different times links it to a wider variety of associations.

Depth of Processing

Depth – associations

Once again, how well you will remember something depends on how well you understood it when

"Alas! poor Yorick. I knew him, Horatio." Hamlet delivers some two dozen soliloquies (solo speeches) of hundreds of words each. (In comparison, the Gettysburg Address is 266 words.) Actors generally use distribution of practice to learn their parts, memorizing a little daily over weeks. They also associate their lines with emotional motivations, physical movements, cues from other actors, and their own memories to help them remember.

SOURCE: Pages reproduced with permission from James W. Kalat, Introduction to Psychology, *2nd ed. Belmont, Calif.: Wadsworth, 1990.*

Figure 7.1 *(continued)*

you learned it and how much you thought about it at the time. According to the **depth-of-processing principle** (Craik & Lockhart, 1972), information may be stored at various levels, either superficially or deeply, depending on the number and type of associations formed with it.

(margin note: Repetitions -shallow)

At the most superficial level, a person merely focuses on the words and how they sound. If you try to memorize a list by simply repeating it over and over, you may recognize it when you see or hear it again, but you may have trouble recalling it (Greene, 1987). Actors and public speakers who have to memorize lengthy passages soon discover that mere repetition is an inefficient method.

(margin note: Associations)

A more efficient way to memorize is to deal actively with the material and to form associations with it. For example, you read a list of 20 words. At a slightly deeper level of processing than mere repetition, you might count the number of letters in each word, think of a rhyming word, or note whether the word contains the letter *e.* Such activities require a more active involvement on your part and estab-

(margin note: Deeper associations → meaning)

lish more connections among the words on the list and other items in your experience. At a still deeper level of processing, you might consider the meaning of each word and try to think of a synonym for it. According to this theory (and according to many experimental results), the deeper the level of processing, the more you will remember. *(How can you use this principle to develop good study habits?)*

The depth-of-processing principle resembles what happens when a librarian files a new book in the library. Simply to place the book somewhere on the shelves without recording its location would be a very low level of processing, and the librarian's chances of ever finding it again would be slight. So the librarian fills out file cards for the book and puts them into the card catalog. To fill out just a title card for the book would be an intermediate level of processing. To fill out several cards—one for title, one for author, and one or more for subject matter—would be a deeper level of processing. Someone who came to the library later looking for that book would have an excellent chance of finding it. Similarly, when you are trying to memorize something, the more "cards" you fill out (that is, the more ways you link it to other information), the greater your chances of finding the memory when you want it.

(margin note: Association like multiple listings)

You can improve your memorization of a list by attending to two types of processing that are largely independent of each other (Einstein & Hunt, 1980; McDaniel, Einstein, & Lollis, 1988). First, you can go through the list thinking about how much you like or dislike each item or trying to recall the

(margin note: Remembering lists: two types of processing ① Each item)

last time you had a personal experience with it. That will enhance your processing of *individual items.* Second, you can go through the list and look for relationships among the items. That will enhance your processing of the *organization* of the list. You might notice, for example, that the list you are trying to memorize consists of five animals, six foods, four methods of transportation, and five objects made of wood. Even sorting items into such simple categories as "words that apply to me" and "words that do not apply to me" will enhance your sense of how the list is organized and therefore your ability to recall it (Klein & Kihlstrom, 1986).

*(margin note: ② Relationships *organization)*

Concept Check

4. Here are two arrangements of the same words:
a. Be a room age to the attend ball will over party across be there 18 you after wild in the class must.
b. There will be a wild party in the room across the hall after class; you must be over age 18 to attend. Why is it easier to remember b than a—because of processing of individual items or because of processing of organization? (Check your answer on page 312.)

Self-Monitoring of Reading Comprehension

What is the difference between good readers (those who remember what they read) and poor readers (those who do not)? One difference is that good readers process what they read more deeply. But how do readers know when they have processed deeply enough? How do they know whether they need to slow down and read more carefully?

Good readers monitor their own reading comprehension; that is, they keep track of whether or not they understand what they are reading. Occasionally in reading, you come across a sentence that is complicated, confusing, or just badly written. Here is an example from the student newspaper at North Carolina State University:

(margin note: Keep track of understanding)

He said Harris told him she and Brothers told French that grades had been changed.

What do you do when you come across a sentence like that? If you are monitoring your own understanding, you notice that you are confused. Good readers generally stop and reread the confusing sentence or, if necessary, the whole paragraph. As a result, they improve their understanding and their ability to remember the material. When poor readers come to something they do not understand, they generally just keep on reading. Either they do not notice their lack of understanding or they do not care.

296   CHAPTER 8: MEMORY

Figure 7.2 Sample Unmarked Pages

The same is true for whole sections of a book. A student who is studying a textbook should read quickly when he or she understands a section well but should slow down when the text is more complicated. To do so, the student has to monitor his or her own understanding. Above-average students can generally identify which sections they understand best; they single out the sections they need to reread. Below-average students have more trouble picking out which sections they understand well and which ones they understand poorly (Maki & Berry, 1984).

Actually, most people—including bright college students who get good grades—could improve their comprehension through better self-monitoring (Glenberg, Sanocki, Epstein, & Morris, 1987; Zabrucky, Moore, & Schultz, 1987). Many educators recommend that a reader pause at regular intervals to check his or her understanding. The Concept Checks in this text are intended to encourage you to pause and check your understanding from time to time.

A self-monitoring system you can use with any text is the **SQ3R method**: Survey, Question, Read, Recite, and Review.

- *Survey.* Read the outline of a new chapter and skim through the chapter itself to get a feeling for what the chapter covers. (Skimming a mystery novel would ruin the suspense. Textbooks, however, are not meant to create suspense.)

- *Question.* Write a list of what you expect to learn from the chapter. You might include the review questions in the chapter, questions from the Study Guide, or questions of your own.

- *Read.* Study the text carefully, take brief notes, and stop to think about key points. (The more you stop and think, the more retrieval cues you form.)

- *Recite.* Reciting does not mean simply repeating without thinking. It means producing correct answers. Use what you have read to answer the questions you listed.

- *Review.* Read the chapter summary, skim through the chapter again, and look over your notes.

A similar system is the **SPAR method**: Survey, Process meaningfully, Ask questions, and Review and test yourself. Both SQ3R and SPAR rest on the principle that readers should pause periodically to check their understanding. Start with an overview of what a

passage is about, read it, and then see whether you can answer questions about the passage or explain it to others. If not, go back and reread.

Encoding Specificity

A new book titled *Brain Mechanisms in Mental Retardation* arrives in the library. The librarian places it on the appropriate shelf and fills out three cards for the card catalog: one for the author, one for the title, and one for the subject, *mental retardation.* I happen to read a section in this book on the physiological basis of learning. Three years later I want to find the book again, but I cannot remember the author or title. I go to the card catalog and look under the subject headings *physiology* and *learning.* But the book I want is not listed. Why not? Simply because the librarian filed the book under a different heading. Unless I use the same subject heading the librarian used, I cannot find the book. (Had the librarian filled out several subject cards instead of just one, I would have had a better chance of finding it.)

A similar principle applies to human memory. (Note that I say *similar.* Your brain does not actually store each memory in a separate place, as a librarian stores books.) When you store a memory, you attach to it certain retrieval cues, like file cards. These retrieval cues are the associations you use both when you store a memory and when you try to recall it. Depending on your depth of processing, you may set up many retrieval cues or only one or two. No matter how many cues you set up, however, it helps if you use those same cues when you try to find the memory again.

The **encoding specificity principle** states that your memory will be more reliable if you use the same cue when you try to retrieve a memory as you used when you stored it (Tulving & Thomson, 1973). Although cues that were not present when you stored the memory may help somewhat to evoke the memory (Newman et al., 1982), they are less effective than cues that were present at the time of storage.

Here is an example of encoding specificity (modified from Thieman, 1984). First, read the list of paired associates in Table 8.3. Then turn to Table 8.5 on page 301. For each of the words on the list there, try to recall a related word on the list you just read. *Do this now.*

The answers are on page 313, answer C. Most people find this task difficult and make only a few of the correct pairings. Because they initially coded the word *cardinal* as a type of clergyman, for example, the retrieval cue *bird* does not remind them of the word *cardinal.* The cue *bird* is effective only if

SOURCE: Pages reproduced with permission from James W. Kalat, Introduction to Psychology, *2nd ed.* Belmont, Calif.: Wadsworth, 1990.

Figure 7.2 *(continued)*

TABLE 8.3		
Clergyman	—	Cardinal
Trinket	—	Charm
Social event	—	Ball
Shrubbery	—	Bush
Inches	—	Feet
Take a test	—	Pass
Baseball	—	Pitcher
Geometry	—	Plane
Tennis	—	Racket
Stone	—	Rock
Magic	—	Spell
Envelope	—	Seal
Cashiers	—	Checkers

cardinal is somehow associated with that cue at the time of storage. In short, you can improve your memory by storing information in terms of retrieval cues and by using the same retrieval cues when you try to recall the information.

Encoding Specificity: Context-Dependent and State-Dependent Memory

Almost anything that happens during an experience may serve as a retrieval cue for that memory. The environment at the time is likely to be associated with the experience and thus to become a retrieval cue. It may then be easier to remember the event in the same environment than in some other environment—an instance of **context-dependent memory**. For example, Duncan Godden and Alan Baddeley (1975) found that divers who learn a word list while 4.5 meters underwater remember the list much better when they are tested at the same depth underwater than when they are tested on the beach.

One's physiological condition at the time can also serve as a potent retrieval cue. A **state-dependent memory** is a memory that is easier to recall if a person is in the same physiological state he or she was in when the event occurred. Someone who has an experience while under the influence of alcohol, nicotine, or some other drug will remember that event more easily when under the influence of the same drug again (Lowe, 1986; Warburton, Wesnes, Shergold, & James, 1986).

All sorts of influence may lead to state-depen-dent memories. For example, the physiological condition of your body is different at different times of day. Other things being equal, your memory is slightly better when you try to recall an event at the same time of day at which it occurred (Infurna, 1981). (You may have noticed that when you wake up in the morning you sometimes start to think about the same thing you were thinking about the morning before.)

A person's mood may also contribute to state-dependent memory, although the evidence for mood-dependent memory is weak. Evidence is stronger for a related phenomenon: When someone is happy, he or she is more likely to think of happy events and words associated with happiness; a person who is sad is more likely to think of unhappy events and words associated with sadness (Blaney, 1986).

When you are trying to recall an event that happened first thing in the morning or when you were sick or when you were in some other distinct physiological state, trying to reconstruct how you felt at the time may strengthen your memory by opening up your access to state-dependent memories.

Mnemonic Devices

When you know that you will have to remember certain information at a future time—such as tasks you must tend to on Thursday or items you need to buy at the grocery store—what can you do to make sure you will remember?

One strategy is to repeat the list over and over again. That is the way Ebbinghaus memorized his lists of nonsense syllables. It may work fairly well for you, though you will probably forget at least part of the list.

A better strategy is to write out the list. Unless you lose the list, you need not worry about forgetting any of the items. Even if you do lose the list, you are likely to remember more items than if you had never written it out (Intons-Peterson & Fournier, 1986). (This is one reason it pays to take notes during a lecture.)

But what if you have no pencil and paper handy? Someone says, "Quick, we need supplies for the party. Go to the store and bring back ginger ale, ice, cups, instant coffee, napkins, hot dogs, paper plates, and nacho chips." One way to remember is to take the initials of those items—GICINHPN—and rearrange them into the word PINCHING. Now you just have to remember PINCHING and each letter will remind you of one item you need to get.

Any memory aid that is based on encoding each item in some special way is known as a **mnemonic device**; the word *mnemonic* ("nee-MAHN-ik") comes

Analyzing and Thinking Critically About Texts

When we analyze an argument we have read, we first must understand its parts and then see how they combine. Is the argument a good one? Suppose someone alleges that *the rise in the number of violent crimes is caused by the increase in violence on television*. Although it may at first appear easy to agree or disagree with this idea, the following analysis makes us think more carefully about it:

1. **Define the terms.** Which crimes are considered violent? Is destruction of property a violent crime, or do people have to be physically harmed? Under one definition, graffiti might be a violent crime but not armed robbery. What does violence consist of on television? Are the NBA playoffs an example of violence on TV? Is a horror movie that terrifies viewers but contains no physical violence okay?

2. **Examine the premises (the assumptions).** Has the number of violent crimes actually risen, or are they simply reported more frequently? Has there actually been an increase in violence on television (as you defined it), or have viewers been more sensitive to violence on television recently?

3. **Examine the logic.** If those who commit violent acts also watch violence on television, can we conclude without seeking further evidence that watching violence causes their violent acts? More data will be needed to rule out the possibility that people who are already violent simply tend to watch violent television. Certainly there are those who watch violent programs who do not become violent. Perhaps we need to find evidence showing that the more violence an individual watches, the more likely he or she is to become violent.

Try applying these critical thinking strategies when you read.

■MAINTAINING FLEXIBILITY

With effort you can improve your reading dramatically, but remember to be flexible. How you read should depend on the material. Assess the relative importance of assigned readings, and adjust your reading style accordingly. Connect the whole to another important idea by asking yourself, "Why am I reading this? Where does this fit in?" When textbook reading is virtually identical to lecture material, you can save time by concentrating mainly on one or the other.

Remember that reading serious material with sound understanding and good recall requires a planned approach. So always keep in mind the following rules for textbook reading:

1. Plan to read in your prime study time.

2. Use warmup time to prepare to read.

3. Set a specific number of pages to read within a specific amount of time.

4. Organize your work into short tasks for high concentration.

5. Underline, review, and recite for each section of reading.

6. Review and recite again for the whole reading.

7. Reward yourself.

How to Read Fifteen Pages of Textbook in Less Than an Hour

It takes practice—but it can be done!

Pages 1–3	Read and mark	10 minutes
	Review and recite	2 minutes
Pages 4–7	Read and mark	10 minutes
	Review and recite	2 minutes
Pages 8–12	Read and mark	10 minutes
	Review and recite	2 minutes
Pages 13–15	Read and mark	10 minutes
	Review and recite	2 minutes
Review and recite for all fifteen pages. Answer aloud the questions "What did I learn? How does it relate to the course?"		8 minutes
	Total	56 minutes

Done. Take a break—you've earned it!

EXERCISE 7.6 Play It Again, Sam

Did you mark this chapter as you read it? If not, read it again, making notes in the margins and underlining as you go. Share your underlinings and notes with your peers and instructor.

MASTERING THE PRÉCIS: A CRITICAL THINKING PROCESS

Another technique for increasing comprehension and recall is writing the précis. A précis (pray-see) is a written summary of the main ideas in a longer document. This skill will be valuable to you not only in college but also in business, research, administration, journalism, and other lines of work.

Using the critical thinking process in Chapter 1 as a guide, you will be able to read a variety of materials on one subject and compare their main points. Outside of college, you will find this skill invaluable in communicating information to business associates, clients, or the general public.

A précis must be short, covering only the main ideas of each document and transitions to show how those ideas are related. Here is the process:

1. **Read the article.** Underline and mark main ideas as you go.

2. **Analyze and abstract.** What are the main ideas? Does the article attempt to define a concept, compare points of view, or prove an idea? (See the "key task words" in Chapter 8, beginning on page 123).

3. **Find new possibilities.** Mark connections between main ideas. What is the single main point of the article? What secondary ideas support the main point? Does the article make its point well or not? If the writer shows a bias, what is it? What might the author be trying to say? What other ideas do the words suggest to you about the topic?

4. **Select, condense, order.** Review underlined material and begin putting the ideas into your own words. Perhaps numbering your underlinings in a logical order will help. Does the evidence actually support the main points as the author claims? Note any weaknesses. What other ideas does the article contain, apart from those you underlined? Jot some notes on these connections.

5. **Communicate your ideas precisely in a draft.** Begin with one sentence that states the author's purpose or main point. Subsequent sentences should summarize ideas that support that purpose or point.

6. **Rewrite.** Read it over, adding missing transitions. Look back at the article to see if you have left out any main ideas. Rewrite the précis so it will be easier to read the next time you look at it. Head it with the author's name, title, source, and date of the article, and any other information you may need later.

EXERCISE 7.7 **Writing a Précis**

Using the underlining and margin notes you have made for this chapter, write a précis of this chapter (or some other material) following the directions in the preceding section. Exchange your précis with that of another student and discuss how effectively each précis summarizes the information.

JOURNAL

What do you think of the planned approach to textbook reading in this chapter? Which aspect of the approach is most appealing to you? Which aspect is least appealing? With which aspect were you most successful as you worked through the exercises? Which aspects will you have to work the hardest at? What problems do you foresee in using the entire plan? How might you overcome these problems?

SUGGESTIONS FOR FURTHER READING

Gross, Ronald. "Improving Your Learning, Reading, and Memory Skills." Chapter 6 in *Peak Learning.* Los Angeles: Jeremy R. Tarcher, 1991.

Phillips, Anne Dye, and Peter Elias Sotiriou. *Steps to Reading Proficiency,* 4th ed. Belmont, Calif.: Wadsworth, 1996.

Smith, Richard Manning. *Mastering Mathematics: How to Be a Great Math Student,* 2nd ed. Belmont, Calif.: Wadsworth, 1994.

Sotiriou, Peter Elias. *Integrating College Study Skills: Reasoning in Reading, Listening, and Writing,* 4th ed. Belmont, Calif.: Wadsworth, 1996. See Chapters 3–8.

CHAPTER

Making the Grade

Kenneth F. Long
University of Windsor

Debora Ritter-Williams
South Carolina Educational TV Network

Mary-Jane McCarthy
Middlesex Community College

*T*hree tests in the next two days! I am never going to live through this week. I mean, I did everything they said about how to read and how to take notes. I even studied all the homework I got back. I should be ready, but I'm freaking out. My nails are gone, I can't sleep. Help!

Chapter Goals

This chapter will help you perform well on tests. It also covers a problem-solving method that is useful in many situations. In addition, it will help you avoid being accused of academic misconduct.

Although test grades do not necessarily reflect what you really know, they are the common method by which learning is evaluated.

There are two basic types of tests: the essay and the objective. The objective test may take a number of forms such as multiple-choice, true-false, matching, or identification. Each type is quite different in terms of preparation, planning, and execution.

You will benefit most from this chapter if you have already read the preceding chapters on time management, note-taking in the classroom, and textbook reading.

■ TO KNOW AND DO BEFOREHAND

The days and hours immediately prior to a test are critical. How much time do you need to prepare? The answer varies, but it is always important to set aside enough time to study for the test and to know how to get the most out of that time. Good communication with your instructor, purposeful notes, well-reviewed texts, exam information, and refined time management all support your best efforts.

EXERCISE 8.1 Test-Taking Inventory

Place a check mark in front of the sentence in each pair that best describes you.

_____ 1a. I always study for essay tests by developing questions and outlines.

_____ 1b. I rarely study for essay tests by developing questions and outlines.

_____ 2a. I always begin studying for an exam at least a week in advance.

_____ 2b. I rarely begin studying for an exam a week in advance.

_____ 3a. I usually study for an exam with at least one other person.

_____ 3b. I rarely study for an exam with another person.

_____ 4a. I usually know what to expect on a test before I go into the exam.

_____ 4b. I rarely know what to expect on a test before I go into the exam.

_____ 5a. I usually finish an exam early or on time.

_____ 5b. I sometimes do not have enough time to finish an exam.

_____ 6a. I usually know that I have done well on an exam when I finish

_____ 6b. I rarely know whether I have done well on an exam when I finish.

_____ 7a. I usually perform better on essay tests than on objective tests.

_____ 7b. I usually perform better on objective tests than on essay tests.

Write a paragraph about yourself as a test-taker based on your answers to the inventory and your feelings about test-taking in general.

Find Out About the Test

In order to use the right test-taking strategies, find out several days in advance what type of test it will be and what kinds of questions will appear on it. It is at least inefficient, and possibly disastrous in terms of grades, to study for an essay exam when the format is multiple-choice or a mix of styles.

Find out how long the exam will last and how it will be graded. If you don't know, ask your instructor. Suppose a 1-hour test will include a short-essay question worth 25 out of a possible 100 points. Knowing that, you should plan to devote about one-quarter of your preparation time to the short essay and to spend about 15 minutes on it during the exam. If you enter the exam without such a plan and find you can answer the short-essay question better than you can the other questions, you may be tempted to spend 25 or 30 minutes on it. The result may be that you leave too little time for the rest of the test and end up with a lower grade than you deserved.

Also obtain copies of old test questions if they are available and only if your instructor allows it. Some teachers will provide you with sample questions that will help you focus on the central ideas.

EXERCISE 8.2 ## On-Line Exam Schedules

Find out whether your school publishes examination schedules on-line as a World Wide Web page or in some other electronic form. If it does, get access to the schedule for the next examination period on your own computer or on a campus computer. Record the information for your exams on your calendar.

Study Throughout the Course

If you study strategically and manage your time throughout the course, you will be able to make the best use of the critical time just before an exam. You won't have to complete other assignments and fulfill other commitments when you need to be preparing for the test. You'll avoid overload and panic.

If you have taken an organized approach to classroom learning and reading from the first week of classes, you won't be faced with pages and pages of unsummarized notes or chapters and chapters of unmarked text. Your materials will be in order. Through the steady use of recall columns and the review-and-recite process, you will already have digested and learned most of what you need to know. From annotating and writing about your reading, you will already have absorbed that information, too.

The result will be a lean body of concepts and information. While other students may be dealing with the material as though it were still all brand-new, for you it will be quite familiar. Now you can practice recalling information and refamiliarizing yourself with detail.

Develop a Study Group

Calculus professor Philip Uri Treisman is a prominent figure in the development of collaborative learning strategies to help African American and Hispanic students succeed academically. In the 1970s he began to question why Chinese students at UC–Berkeley outperformed African American students in freshman calculus. He discovered that one very important factor was the Chinese students' reliance on study groups. When Treisman proceeded to organize African American students into groups, they too succeeded at calculus.

Research has indicated that studying in groups can raise your chances of success in other subjects as well, because as you share notes and ideas about your courses with other students, you gain:

- Clarification of classroom notes
- Different views regarding instructors' goals and objectives
- Partners to quiz on the facts, concepts, and so on
- The enthusiasm of others to help sustain your own attention to and enthusiasm for the task

Study groups work as follows: The group meets a week or so before the exam and before each of you has studied alone. During that time the group members share notes and ideas. Together you devise a list of potential questions for review. Then each of you spends time studying alone, developing answers, outlines, and mind maps. The group then meets again shortly before the test to share answers and prep one another for the exam.

EXERCISE 8.3 Forming a Study Group

Use the goal-setting process from Chapter 1 to form a study group for at least one of your courses this term. As you do this, think about your strengths and weaknesses in a learning or studying situation. For instance, do you excel at memorizing facts but find it difficult to comprehend theories? Do you learn best by repeatedly reading the information or by applying the knowledge to a real situation? Do you prefer to learn by processing information in your head or by participating in a "hands-on" demonstration? Make some notes about your learning and studying strengths and weaknesses here.

Strengths: _____

_____

Weaknesses: _____

_____

_____

In a study group how will your strengths help others? What strengths will you look for in others that will help you?

How you can help others: _____

_____

_____

How others can help you: _____

_____

_____

In your first study group session, suggest that each person share his or her strengths and weaknesses and talk about how abilities might be shared for everyone's maximum benefit.

■THE ESSAY EXAM

An essay exam requires focused, detailed study on selected topics that you think are likely to appear on the exam. As you prepare for an essay exam, concentrate mainly on key ideas, the evidence supporting these ideas, and their relationship to other key ideas. Essay exam questions generally focus on broad questions rather than on details. The grade is generally based in part on how well organized your answer is.

The Basic System for Studying for Essay Exams

First select several pages of notes covering a body of information that you regard as a likely essay topic. Lay out your pages of notes on your desk with each page covering two-thirds of the one before so that only recall columns show. (This is why we recommended in Chapter 6 that you write on only one side of the piece of paper.) Let the recall columns prompt you through a paraphrased recitation of the material at hand. When you get stuck, consult the supporting details to "boost" the recall column and then continue to recite. Work through the text chapters in similar fashion by using your markings to prompt recitation. When you can recite, you can feel confident you know the material.

This method of study trains your mind to respond to the test situation. The words in the test questions act like the words in the recall columns to prompt your thoughts and your written answer. This is exactly what you have been practicing all along in looking for and marking important material and reciting. So the essay exam situation is really nothing new. This system works for almost any kind of review.

You can refine the process by organizing the information you have studied into potential questions for the exam. Familiarize yourself with the common task words used in essay questions (see pages 123–126) and determine which would best organize the material you have learned. As you work through the material, create outlines of the answers using the information in your recall columns. Composing and answering questions increases your understanding.

EXERCISE 8.4 Essay Exam Strategies

Working with a partner, use the information already presented in this section to develop and then answer two essay questions dealing with different material in this section or in a previous chapter. Share your questions and responses with your classmates and instructor.

Improving on the System: Super Recall Columns and Mind Maps

You can refine the basic system even further, especially for an exam covering large amounts of material. Let's say you have selected 100 pages of notes and supporting text. Divide these materials into ten more or less equal logical units or questions. As you work through each unit, continue to reduce each ten-page unit to one page as a *super recall column* or *mind map*.

The best way to conceive a super recall column is to imagine that you were allowed to bring one page of notes into the exam with you. What would you put on that page? You would probably want it to contain recall information that surveys the course—a "super" recall column. A mind map is essentially a super recall column with pictorial elements added. Its words and visual patterns provide you with highly charged cues to "jog" your memory. The task of making the super recall column or mind map is itself a form of concentrated study. Practicing responses to the cues in the mind map is like responding to the word cues in the questions on the exam. You may even see exactly the same words on the exam that you have used in your mind maps. Even if they aren't the same, your study method represents an accurate rehearsal of the kind of thinking you'll have to do in the exam.

Figure 8.1 shows what a mind map might look like for Chapter 6, "Listening and Learning in the Classroom." Note the use of lists, arrows, and circles, all powerful aids to memory. When something can be visualized, it is easier to remember, and mind maps are highly visual. Visualizing the mind map during the test will help to release the flow of words you will need to answer the question, as will your previous recitation of the material.

Super recall columns and mind maps are particularly useful in the last hour, right before the start of the exam. Whereas notes and texts are too unwieldy to be of much use at this point, mind maps allow for quick, effective review.

Consistent daily study and the right exam strategy are the surest means to real learning and strong performance. Note that the strategies recommended here are not those of memorization. Too often memorization reflects only shallow understanding, although it can be useful in remembering lists of items (see the box on pages 130–131). The mechanics of our in-depth system

Figure 8.1 Sample Mind Map on Listening and Learning in the Classroom

require you to apply yourself repeatedly and attentively to the material, focusing always on *understanding* the significant points in large amounts of written material. How else could you make recall columns or mind maps?

EXERCISE 8.5   The Power of the Mind Map

Working with your partner, review the mind map in Figure 8.1. Create a mind map for each of the essay questions you developed in Exercise 8.4. Use them to prompt a recitation of the material needed to answer each question. Put the mind maps away for a day. The next day, try to re-create the mind maps from memory. You should find your retention of the material has increased. Share these maps with your classmates and instructor, and see how theirs differ.

Three Principles for Taking Essay Exams

Following all of the previous suggestions won't be enough if you don't then perform well on the exam itself. Here are three principles for taking essay exams and ways to implement them.

1. **Use Exam Time Well.** Quickly survey the entire exam and note the questions that are easiest for you. To build confidence and start the recall process, answer these questions first. But be careful. Knowing certain material very well may tempt you to write brilliantly for 30 minutes on a question worth only 10 points, leaving little time for a harder question worth 30 points. This is how to get a C when you are quite capable of achieving a B or an A. Avoid this costly error by knowing ahead of time the basic exam structure, the point allotments, and the types of questions. Then govern yourself during the exam according to a plan for choosing questions and allocating the right amount of time for each. Also be sure to wear a watch to the exam. If you forget to do so, ask the instructor to call out periodically or write the time or the time remaining on the board.

2. **Write Focused, Organized Answers.** Many well-prepared students write fine answers to questions that have not been asked. This problem stems either from not reading a question carefully or from hastily writing down everything you know on a topic in the hope that somehow the question will be answered. This is like shooting at a target with a shotgun, never completely missing, perhaps, but rarely hitting the bull's-eye. Instructors agree that shotgun answers are frustrating to read because of their lack of focus and organization. A simple seven-point critical thinking strategy will help you stay focused and organized:

    1. *Read the entire question carefully.*
    2. *Take the time to read it again and underline keywords.* This forces you to read the question accurately. The underlined words will stimulate recall of relevant information.
    3. *Brainstorm.* Write down all the ideas you can think of in response to what the question asks. Then read over your notes, underline the most important points, and use them in your answer. If you do this extra writing on the exam paper, be sure to cross it out if you do not want it counted for credit.

4. *Use the underlined words in the question and in your written brainstorming to construct a brief outline.* This ensures good organization.

5. *Begin your answer by rewriting the question or problem.* This reinforces your focus.

6. *Write the rest of the answer according to your outline.* For each major idea try to write at least one paragraph and give at least one supporting example. If new ideas come to mind as you write, add them at the end.

7. *Make sure each answer begins with an introduction and ends with a conclusion.*

Here is a sample question from a psychology test, selectively underlined to focus the question.

Modern educational psychology has discovered a great deal about <u>how students learn,</u> and this has led to the development of several powerful study techniques. <u>Identify three such techniques and explain how and why they work.</u>

Figure 8.2 shows how an outline for answering the question might be written during the actual exam. Commentary is provided on the right. While writing the essay our hypothetical test-taker remembers an additional important idea—visualization and mind maps—and adds that at the end of the essay.

3. **Know the Key Task Words in Essay Questions.** Essay questions often use certain task words such as *discuss* or *define.* Help yourself to focus more quickly and avoid misinterpretation by becoming familiar with them now. Don't feel you must memorize the exact definitions of these terms, and don't "lock up" on the exam if you can't define them precisely. A general familiarity will do. Perhaps your instructor will tell you which of these terms (what kinds of tasks) will appear on the test. Why not ask? Here are some of the most frequently used terms and their meanings.

Key Task Words

Analyze: to divide something into its parts in order to understand it better, then to see how the parts work together to produce the overall pattern. Analyzing a problem may require you to identify a number of smaller problems that are related to the overall problem.

Compare: to look at the characteristics or qualities of several things and identify their similarities. Instructions to compare things often are intended to imply that you may also contrast them.

Contrast: to identify the differences between things.

Criticize/Critique: to analyze and judge something. Criticism can be either positive or negative, as the case warrants. A criticism should generally contain your own judgments (supported by evidence) in addition to whatever authorities you might invoke.

Define: to give the meaning of a word or expression. Definitions should generally be clear and concise and conform with other people's understanding of the terms. Giving an example of something sometimes helps to clarify a definition, but giving an example is not in itself a definition.

Describe: to give a general verbal sketch or account of something, in narrative or other form.

Figure 8.2 Sample Essay Exam Outline

Introduction	Brief statement of topic or question and the approach.
Modern educational psychology has a lot to offer the student who wants to learn how to study more efficiently.	A simple direct restatement begins the answer with a focus on *how*.
Define efficiency. Describe forgetting as the problem.	The answer will build on two key concepts: efficiency and the problem of forgetting.
4 Advance organizers (conclusion) *3 Recitation* *1 Recall columns* *2 Super recall columns* *5 Multiple-choice strategies (conclusion)*	The techniques are first listed without numbers, in the order remembered. Then the techniques are numbered in the order that seems most logical for presenting them in the written answer. The first three techniques will appear in the body of the answer. The last two will be mentioned in a concluding paragraph, just to show that there are more than three.
Conclusion	Brief summary—final thoughts and perspectives.

Diagram: to show the parts of something and their relationships in pictorial form, such as a chart. You are usually expected to label the diagram, and you may be asked to explain it in words as well.

Discuss: to examine or analyze something in a broad and detailed way. Discussion often includes identifying the important questions related to an issue and attempting to answer these questions. Where there are several sides to an issue, a discussion involves presenting this variety of sides.

Be sure you're answering the question that was asked. Before you start writing an essay, analyze the question and make notes that will collect your ideas and organize your response.

Photo by David Gonzales

A good discussion explores as much of the relevant evidence and information on a topic as it can.

Enumerate: to respond in the form of a concise list or outline rather than in great detail.

Evaluate: to judge the worth or truthfulness of something. Evaluation is similar to criticism, but the word *evaluate* places more stress on the idea of making some ultimate judgment about how well something meets a certain standard or fulfills some specific purpose. Evaluation involves discussing strengths and weaknesses.

Explain: to clarify or interpret something. Explanations generally focus on *why* or *how* something has come about. Explanations often require you to discuss evidence that may seem contradictory and to tell how apparent differences in evidence can be reconciled.

Illustrate: on an essay examination, to give one or more examples of something. Examples help to relate abstract ideas to concrete experience. Examples may show how something works in practice. Providing a good example is a way of showing you know your course material in detail. Sometimes the instruction to illustrate may be asking you to literally draw a diagram or picture. If you're uncertain of the intention, ask the instructor.

Interpret: to explain the meaning of something. For instance, in science you may be asked to interpret the evidence of an experiment, that is, to explain what the evidence shows and what conclusions can be drawn from it. In a literature course you may be asked to interpret a poem, that is, to explain what a specific passage or the poem as a whole means beyond the literal meaning of the words.

Justify: to argue in support of some decision or conclusion, to show sufficient evidence or reason in favor of something. Whenever possible, try to support your argument with both logical reasoning and concrete examples.

*If you've set realistic goals
and used good study tech-
niques, chances are you'll
make high marks.*

Photo by Lynn Howlett Photography

Label: to point to and name specific parts of a figure or illustration.

List: to present information in a series of short, discrete points. See also *enumerate.*

Narrate: to tell a story, that is, a series of events in the order in which they occurred. Generally, when you are asked to narrate events, you are also asked to interpret or explain something about the events you are narrating.

Outline: to present a series of main points in appropriate order, omitting lesser details. Also, to present some information in the form of a series of short headings in which each major idea is followed by headings for smaller points or examples that fall under it. An outline shows the correct order and grouping of ideas.

Prove: to give a convincing logical argument and evidence in support of the truth of some statement. Note, however, that academic disciplines differ in their methods of inquiry and therefore also differ in what they require in statements of proof.

Relate: to show the relationship between things. This can mean showing how they influence each other or how a change in one thing seems to depend on or accompany a change in the other. In showing how things relate, it's often a good idea to provide an example.

Review: to summarize and comment on the main parts of a problem or a series of statements or events in order. A review question usually also asks you to evaluate or criticize some aspect of the material.

Summarize: to give information in brief form, omitting examples and details. A summary should be short yet cover all of the most important points.

Trace: to narrate a course of events. Where possible, you should show connections from one event to the next. Tracing a sequence of events often points to gaps in the sequence that you may need to fill in by logical suppositions about what might link one event to the next.

EXERCISE 8.6 | **Key on Task Words**

Essay questions may require quite different responses, depending on their key task words. Discuss the following in class. In your discussion, include what each task word is asking you to do, and how it differs from the other two listed here.

1. How would you define the purposes of this course, chapter, or book?

_____

_____

_____

_____

2. How would you evaluate the purposes of this course, chapter, or book?

_____

_____

_____

_____

3. How would you justify the purposes of this course, chapter, or book?

_____

_____

_____

_____

Summary Time Management Plan for Essay Exams

1. Study your notes using the recall column throughout the term.
2. Set aside time for study in your weekly planner a week or two before the exam.
3. Find out from the instructor the basic exam structure, the point allotments, and the types of questions.
4. Allot an appropriate percentage of study time for each potential exam section.
5. Set aside time just before the exam to review notes and jog memory.
6. Use exam time well. Quickly preview the entire exam to determine the value of each section, and then allot time accordingly. Answer the questions you are sure of first. Try to allow time for a quick review at the end. And wear a watch!

EXERCISE 8.7 | **An Essay Exam**

Treat the following as an essay exam question. Use techniques (such as mind maps or outlines) and information from this section and previous chapters to organize and write your answer:

How soon is a student likely to forget lecture material even when full notes are taken? How much is likely to be forgotten? How can this problem be alleviated? Based on your own experience and your reading here, what is your opinion of recitation as a study technique?

Share your response with your classmates and instructor.

THE MULTIPLE-CHOICE EXAM

Studying for multiple-choice exams is different from studying for essay exams. However, preparing for multiple-choice exams still requires purposeful notes, well-reviewed texts, and active daily learning. Whereas an essay exam requires focused, detailed study on selected topics (excluding a lot of material altogether), the multiple-choice exam requires a light review of nearly everything covered. Thus you should plan to review the material several times before the exam. Use your notes and text markings, aided by regular recitation, to quickly review large amounts of material.

Take advantage of the many cues that multiple-choice questions contain. With careful reading you will find that the right answer is frequently apparent. Two suggestions will be helpful here. First, question those choices that use absolute words such as *always, never,* and *only.* These choices are often incorrect. Second, read carefully for terms such as *not, except,* and *but,* which may come before the choices. Look at the following sample multiple-choice question on writing an essay exam:

> 1. *In answering an essay question it is wise to do all of the following except:*
>   a. *review your notes before the exam*
>   b. *write out study maps to synthesize the material*
>   c. *always memorize specific details at the expense of main ideas*
>   d. *both a and b*

Do you see how choice *d* would seem to be acceptable if you had not read the "except"? Also, did you notice the use of the qualifier "always" in choice *c*?

Some questions will be puzzlers. Skip over these questions as you first work quickly through the exam, but mark them so that you can find them easily later. When you have finished answering all of the obvious questions, return to the puzzlers. You will discover that you now know the answers to some of them. Why? Because a multiple-choice exam is a review of interrelated material, and information given in question 46 may contain or suggest the answer to question 10. This technique lets the nature of the exam work in your favor.

For the few puzzlers that remain, try another strategy. Since you can't find the right answer, try eliminating those that are clearly wrong. Usually at least one of the choices is far-fetched, another unlikely, and a third a "maybe." Eliminate as many choices as you can so as to increase the odds in your favor, and then make the best guess possible. You can often reduce your choices to two, so that your odds for correctly answering the question are 1 out of 2 rather than 1 out of 4 or 5.

Following these strategies can often mean a difference of 5 or 6 percentage points, which in turn can be the difference between a B and a C. Light, quick review of material (several times if necessary) and good exam room strategy make multiple-choice exams that much easier.

A word of caution: Make sure you know the scoring system. If, for exam-

Personal Emergency? Your Instructor Needs to Know

Emergencies do happen. Even though your instructor may have warned you that there is no excuse for missing a quiz or turning in a paper beyond the deadline, he or she may bend the rules if it's a true emergency. Here are some things you can do to soften the consequences of missing class:

1. *For a recurring medical condition that you know may keep you home unexpectedly on some days:* Let the instructor know about it early in the term. Schedule a meeting during office hours and make it clear you are not asking for relief from required work, but for some allowance for turning in work late if you are unable to attend on an important day.

2. *For an emergency:* Get phone numbers and/or e-mail addresses in advance. If possible, leave word. Many faculty have answering machines and will get your message even if they're not in the office when you call. Leave a number where you can be reached. If you don't know where you'll be, leave the number of a friend or relative who could relay the message to you.

   At some colleges your academic advisor or counselor or the student services office can distribute a memo to all of your instructors to in-

form them of an emergency, especially if you will be missing classes for a week or more.

3. *For a situation when you know in advance you can't make a class:* Tell the instructor as soon as you know. Even if the excuse seems unimportant to everyone but you, it's always worth asking; do it early so there's more of a possibility that arrangements can be made for you to turn in work early or make up work when you return.

   Even if you missed an important quiz or deadline for dubious reasons, let your instructor know anyway. It's better to make a fool of yourself by admitting you overslept or even forgot a paper was due or left the essay at home than to get a zero. Instructors forget or leave things at home, too, and may give you the benefit of the doubt. If you are polite and reasonable in your approach, you may be surprised how willing your instructor is to help you in your dilemma.

ple, there is a built-in factor to penalize you for guessing (number right minus a percentage of number wrong), it is not wise to guess. When in doubt, ask the instructor what the scoring procedure will be.

THE TRUE-FALSE EXAM

You will find that true-false questions are often used in examinations. True-false questions contain only two choices, rather than the four or five you often

Hard to Remember?
Tips on Memory

Thirty days hath September, April, June, and November. . . .
Doe a deer, a female deer. Ray, a drop of golden sun. . . .
A pint's a pound, the world around.

Out of desperation and amusement, the human mind has discovered ingenious ways to remember vital information. Here are some methods that may be useful to you when you're nailing down the causes of the Civil War, trying to remember the steps in a physics problem, or absorbing a mathematical formula for tomorrow's quiz.

1. **Use mnemonics.** Create rhymes, jingles, sayings, or nonsense phrases that repeat or codify information. "Homes" is a mnemonic word for remembering the five Great Lakes: Huron, Ontario, Michigan, Erie, and Superior. "Spring forward, fall back" tells many Americans how to set their clocks.

   "Every Good Boy Does Fine" is a mnemonic sentence: The first letter of each word is the letter of a line of the music staff, bottom to top. Setting a rhyme to music is one of the most powerful ways to make words memorable.

2. **Associate.** Relate the idea to something you already know. Make the association as personal as possible. If you're reading a chapter on laws regarding free speech, pretend your right to speak out on a subject that's important to you may be affected by those laws. In remembering the spelling difference between *through* and *threw,* think of walking through something "rough," and that "threw" comes from "throw."

3. **Peg.** Visualize in order a number of locations or objects in your home. To remember a list of things, associate each item in the list with one of the locations or objects. For example, let's memorize three classic appeals of advertising (appetite, fear, and sexual attraction):

   - *Appetite:* The first peg is the corner countertop. Visualize some creature devouring your favorite chocolate cake.

   - *Fear:* The second peg is the coat rack. Visualize a menacing coat rack running after you.

   - *Sexual attraction:* The third peg is a sofa. Use your imagination.

find in a multiple-choice question, so your chances for selecting a correct answer are better. Like the multiple-choice question, the true-false question tests your understanding of detail more than your mastery of general concepts.

Here are some hints for answering the true-false question:

1. Be sure that every part of the question is correct. For the question to be true, every detail within it must also be true.

2. Check to see how qualifiers are used. As with multiple-choice questions, true-false questions containing words such as *always, never,* and *only* are usually false. Conversely, less definite terms such as *often* and *frequently* suggest that the statement may be true. Note how the use of *always* makes the following statement false, while the use of *often* makes it true:

   _____ 1. *True-false questions always test specific information.*

   _____ 2. *True-false questions often test specific information.*

The first statement is suspect, because if you can think of even one example to counter the claim, the statement is automatically false. By contrast

4. **Visualize.** Make yourself see the things that you've associated with important concepts. Concentrate on the images so they'll become firmly planted in your memory.

5. **Overlearn.** Even after you "know" the material, go over it again to make sure you'll retain it for a long time.

6. **Use flashcards.** Use index cards. Write the word or information to be learned on one side and the definition or explanation on the other. Review the cards often; carry them with you. Prepare them well in advance of the day of the test and spend more time on the hard ones.

7. **Categorize.** Even if the information seems to lack an inherent organization, try to impose one. Most information can be organized in some way, even if only by the look or sound of the words.

8. **Draw a mind map.** (See the previous discussion in this chapter.) Some speakers claim they can prepare an hour-long talk simply by arranging the main topics on a single sheet of paper and connecting the points in logical fashion by arrows, dots, and so forth. Large points are written in large boxes or circles, smaller points in smaller ones. Subgroups are placed under major headings. Drawing relationships on paper—even faces, objects, or stick figures—can help you visualize them later.

9. **Surprise yourself.** Math professor John Horton Conway and his wife have memorized 1,000 digits of the value of pi. It begins 3.14159265358793238462 . . . In a group or by yourself, create a method to remember pi's first seven digits. (That's only one telephone number.) Expand the technique to memorize pi to twenty-one places. (That's only three phone numbers!)

the second statement allows for a few exceptions and is thus more likely to be true.

3. As with the multiple-choice question, read through the entire exam to see if information in one question will help you answer a question whose answer you are unsure of.

■THE MATCHING EXAM

Matching questions are still used on objective exams, particularly those that use a combination of objective questions: multiple-choice, true-false, and matching. Unlike these other two types of objective questions, the matching question is the hardest to answer by guessing. With the matching question, you need to know your stuff. Often matching questions test your knowledge of definitions as well as names and events. In one column you will find the term, in the other the description of it.

Before answering the matching-question part of the exam, review all of the terms and descriptions. See if a pattern emerges—perhaps terms on one side and definitions on the other, people in one column and descriptions of them in the other, or a combination of both. Match up those terms you are sure of first. As you answer each question, cross out both the term and its description. This will enable you to see more clearly which choices remain.

Here is an example of part of a matching test on this chapter:

_____ 1. *essay question*   a. *often the most difficult objective question to answer*

_____ 2. *multiple-choice question*   b. *requires knowledge of general concepts*

_____ 3. *true-false question*   c. *provides only two choices*

_____ 4. *matching question*   d. *usually presents four or five choices per question*

Do you see how this set of matching questions asks you to match up a term with a description of it? Now go back to these four questions and answer them, crossing out each correct match that you determine.

EXERCISE 8.8   Designing an Exam Plan

A Use the following guidelines to design an exam plan for one of your courses:

1. Find out what the characteristics of the exam are: What material will be covered? What type of questions will it contain? How long will it be? How many questions will there be? What is the grading system?

2. Based on these characteristics, determine what type of studying is necessary.

3. Establish how much time and how many study sessions you will need to complete your studying.

4. Create a study schedule starting one week before the test. Indicate the length of each study session, the material to be covered, and the study techniques to be used. Arrange with family or roommates to assure quiet time for your study needs.

Share your responses with other students and with your instructor. See how their responses are similar to or different from yours.

B Create a study group of three or four others in the class. Review the material in this chapter. Create a hypothetical exam containing both essay and objective questions. Share it with the class, modifying it as needed. Then, after studying the material individually, come together as a group to share the answers.

■ACADEMIC HONESTY

Higher education evolved in America with a strong commitment to the "search for truth," uncovering new knowledge and solving problems to benefit society. The commitment to truth was accompanied by the concept of academic freedom, which is the freedom of faculty and students to pursue whatever inquiry they believe is important and to speak about it in classrooms without fear of censorship.

Honesty and integrity are crucial to the search for truth and academic freedom. Imagine where our society would be if researchers reported fraudulent results that were then used to develop new machines or medical treatments. The integrity of knowledge is a cornerstone of higher education, and activities that compromise that integrity damage everyone.

Most colleges and universities have academic integrity policies or honor codes that clearly define cheating, lying, plagiarism, and other forms of dishonest conduct, but it is often difficult to know how those rules apply to specific situations. For example, is it really lying to tell an instructor you missed class because you were "not feeling well" (whatever "well" means) or because you were experiencing that conveniently vague and all-encompassing malady "car trouble"? Some people would argue that car trouble includes anything from a flat tire to difficulty finding a parking spot!

Types of Misconduct

Institutions vary widely in how specifically they define broad terms such as *lying* or *cheating*. For instance, one university's code of student academic integrity defines cheating as "intentionally using or attempting to use unauthorized materials, information, notes, study aids or other devices . . . [including] unauthorized communication of information during an academic exercise." This would apply to all of these:

- Looking over a classmate's shoulder for an answer
- Using a calculator when it is not authorized
- Procuring or discussing an exam without permission
- Copying lab notes
- Duplicating computer files

Plagiarism is especially intolerable in the academic culture. *Plagiarism* means taking another person's ideas or work and presenting them as your own. Just as taking someone else's property constitutes physical theft, taking credit for someone else's ideas constitutes "intellectual theft."

Rules for referencing (or "citing") another's ideas apply more strictly to the papers you write than to your responses on a test. On tests you do not have to credit specific individuals for their ideas. On written reports and papers, however, you must give credit any time you use (1) another person's actual words, (2) another person's ideas or theories—even if you don't quote them directly—and (3) any other information not considered common knowledge. Chapter 10 provides more about how to properly quote and cite others' writing in your own. Check with your instructors about how to cite material they've covered in classroom lectures. Usually you do not need to provide a reference for this, but it is always better to ask first.

Many schools prohibit other activities besides lying, cheating, and plagiarism. For instance, the University of Delaware prohibits fabrication (intentionally inventing information or results); the University of North Carolina outlaws multiple submission (earning credit more than once for the same piece of academic work without permission); Eastern Illinois University rules out tendering of information (giving your work or exam answer to another student to copy during the actual exam or before the exam is given to another section); and the University of South Carolina prohibits bribery (trading something of value in exchange for any kind of academic advantage). Most schools also outlaw helping or attempting to help another student commit a dishonest act.

Does Cheating Hurt Anyone?

WHAT ABOUT THE INDIVIDUAL?

- **Cheating sabotages academic growth.** Cheating confuses and weakens the process by which students demonstrate understanding of course content. Because the grade and the instructor's comments apply to someone else's work, cheating prevents accurate feedback, thus hindering academic growth.

- **Cheating sabotages personal growth.** Educational accomplishments inspire pride and confidence. What confidence in their ability will individuals have whose work is not their own?

- **Cheating may have long-term effects.** Taking the "easy way" in college may become a habit that can spill over into graduate school, jobs, and relationships. And consider this: Would you want a doctor, lawyer, or accountant who had cheated on exams handling your affairs?

WHAT ABOUT THE COMMUNITY?

- **Cheating jeopardizes the basic fairness of the grading process.** Widespread cheating causes honest students to become cynical and resentful. This is especially true when grades are curved and the cheating directly affects other students.

- **Widespread cheating devalues the college's degree.** Alumni, potential students, graduate schools, and employers learn to distrust degrees from schools where cheating is widespread.

Some outlawed behaviors do not seem to fall within any clear category. Understanding the mission and values of higher education will help you make better decisions about those behaviors that "fall through the cracks."

Reducing the Likelihood of Problems

In order to avoid becoming intentionally or unintentionally involved in academic misconduct, consider the reasons it *could* happen.

Ignorance is one reason. In a survey at the University of South Carolina, 20 percent of students incorrectly thought that buying a term paper wasn't cheat-

"The Only A"

As a student at a large, predominantly white university, I enrolled in an advanced composition course. The class of twenty-five or so was all white with the exception of me and another black student. As part of the writing process, the instructor required the class to read each other's papers. After the first peer critiquing session, the other black student and I compared notes and thought we saw a pattern. Not only did our student critics seem to be critical of our writing, but their comments carried what we perceived as racial overtones. Needless to say we were both bothered by this, but decided to dismiss it as oversensitivity on our part—until we encountered the same sort of comments on our drafts the next week. The other student decided that our classmates were racially biased and dropped the class. I searched for a different approach, especially since I needed the course to complete my degree requirements in time.

I carefully considered the comments my classmates were making and decided that some of them were unfounded and probably motivated by personal bias. Many of their comments, however, were based upon instructions from the professor and appeared to be valid. I then sifted through their comments, discarding the obvious personal ones and paying attention to those that seemed justified. And each time the peer critique session was held, I wrote and rewrote my papers, basing many of my changes on the comments of my peer critics.

When grades were posted that semester, I made the traditional trek to the professor's office door, where he had promised to post the final grades. When I arrived, four or five of my classmates were perusing the grade roster, and I could tell that they were trying to decipher who had made what grade. Since only Social Security numbers appeared on the sheet, figuring out who was who was a little difficult. I approached the grade roster and looked for my grade. When I saw what it was, I placed my finger at the top of the list and ever so gently let it slide down the page, where, residing beside my Social Security number, was the only A in the class. The other students at the professor's door congratulated me, and I thanked them—both for their kind comments and for their help in netting me that A.

So what was an unbearable situation for one student became a success story for another, all because the two of us chose to react to a negative situation differently. Yes, I still think that some of the comments my classmates made on my papers were unnecessarily personal and harsh, but I also recognized the worthwhile comments. This approach allowed me to glean from a negative situation the positive elements that I used to my advantage.

—John Slade, coordinator of Summer School and co-director of the Freshman Seminar Program, Winston-Salem State University

ing. Forty percent thought using a test file (a collection of actual tests from previous terms, usually kept by an organization such as a fraternity or sorority) was fair behavior. Sixty percent thought it was all right to get answers from someone who had taken an exam earlier in the same or in a prior semester.

This may not be so unusual in light of the fact that in some countries students are encouraged to review past exams as practice exercises. In other countries, it is also acceptable to share answers and information for homework and other types of assignments with friends. In some countries, these behaviors are not only acceptable, they are considered acts of generosity and courtesy.

Instructors also may vary in their acceptance of such behaviors. Because there is no universal code that dictates such behaviors, you should ask your instructors for clarification. When a student is caught violating the academic code of a particular school or teacher, pleading ignorance of the rules is a weak defense.

A second reason some people cheat is that they overestimate the importance of grades, apart from actual learning, and fall into thinking they must "succeed" at any cost. This may reflect our society's competitive atmosphere. It also may be the result of pressure from parents, peers, or teachers. The desire for "success at any cost" is often accompanied by a strong fear of failure that is hard to confront and deal with.

A third common cause of cheating is a student's own lack of preparation or inability to manage time and activities. The problem is made worse if he or she is unwilling to ask an instructor to extend a deadline so that a project can be done well.

Here are some steps you can take to reduce the likelihood of problems:

1. **Know the Rules.** Learn the academic code for your school. If a teacher does not clarify his or her standards and expectations, ask exactly what the rules are.

2. **Set Clear Boundaries.** Work with a partner or study group to prepare for a test, but refrain from discussing past exams with others unless it is specifically permitted. Tell friends exactly what is acceptable or unacceptable if you lend them a term paper. Refuse to "help" others who ask you to help them cheat. In test settings, keep your answers covered and your eyes down, and put all extraneous materials away. Help friends to resist temptation. Make sure your typist understands that he or she may not make any changes in your work.

3. **Improve Self-Management.** Be well prepared for all quizzes, exams, projects, and papers. This may mean *un*learning some bad habits (such as procrastination) and building better time management and study skills. Keep your own long-term goals in mind.

4. **Seek Help.** Find out what is available for assistance with study skills, time management, and test-taking—and take advantage of it. If your methods are in good shape but the content of the course is too difficult, consult with your instructor.

5. **Withdraw from the Course.** Consider cutting your losses before it's too late. Your school has a policy about dropping courses and a "last day to drop without penalty" (drop date). You may choose this route and plan to retake the course later. Some students may choose to withdraw from all their classes and take some time off before returning to school. This may be an option if you find yourself in over your head, or if some unplanned event (a long illness, a family crisis) has caused you to fall behind with little hope of catching up.

6. **Reexamine Goals.** You need to stick to your own realistic goals instead of giving in to pressure from family or friends to achieve impossibly high standards. What grades do you *need,* and what grades do you have the potential to earn? You may also feel pressure to enter a particular career or profession. If this isn't what you want, your frustration is likely to appear in your lack of preparation and your grades. It may be time to sit down with others—perhaps professionals in your career and counseling centers—and tell them you need to choose your own career.

JOURNAL

If you have already taken at least one exam in college, reflect on how it went. What strategies did you use to prepare? How well did they work? Did you get the results you were aiming for? If not, why not? What specific strategies from this chapter might you want to apply on your next round of exams?

Are you facing any issues related to academic honesty? What are they? What are you doing about them? How are your actions serving your own best interests and the best interests of your institution?

SUGGESTIONS FOR FURTHER READING

Adams, James L. *Conceptual Blockbusting: A Guide to Better Ideas,* 3rd ed. Reading, Mass.:Addison-Wesley, 1986.

Buzan, Tony. *Use Both Sides of Your Brain.* New York: Dutton, 1974.

Cahn, S. M. *Saints and Scamps: Ethics in Academia.* Totowa, N.J.: Rowman & Littlefield, 1986.

McKowen, Clark. *Get Your A out of College: Mastering the Hidden Rules of the Game.* Los Altos, Calif.: Crisp Publications, 1979.

Smith, Richard Manning. *Mastering Mathematics: How to Be a Great Math Student,* 2nd ed. Belmont, Calif.: Wadsworth, 1994.

Thriving in the Information Environment: Your Campus Library

Marilee Birchfield
University of South Carolina

Faye A. Chadwell
University of Oregon

I've heard about people who've been lost for years in the New York City Public Library. They just go in and never come out. They fall asleep and die, or else they get slimed like those guys did in Ghostbusters. . . . Actually, I kind of like the long, tall rows of books. They seem to absorb all human sound, like snow. I don't mind libraries. I just never seem to know what I'm looking for or how to find it.

Chapter Goals

This chapter will help you feel at home in the library and strengthen your information-gathering skills. It will also show you how to do library research better and more quickly.

The Information Age is no longer encroaching on us—we are of and in it. What makes this age exciting and potentially empowering for millions of people is not that information has just been invented or that people are just beginning to look for it. Rather, it's the amount and diversity of information that is available through innumerable sources, the ease and speed with which you can obtain this information, and the incredible possibilities for applying it to everyday situations.

Just imagine:

- By means of fiber optics, AT&T transmits information from Chicago to the East Coast at 6.6 gigabits per second—equivalent to the information contained in 1,000 books. At this rate the entire book holdings of the Library of Congress, totaling 23 million volumes, could be dispatched in 24 hours. On the computers of yesterday, this process would have taken 2,000 years (Wriston, 1992).
- One CD-ROM (Compact Disc Read-Only-Memory) can store as much as 1,000 standard floppy disks used by regular personal computers (Tehranian, 1990).
- The Internet, or the information superhighway, allows users to send electronic mail messages across the world, connect to hundreds of databases and library catalogs worldwide, participate in on-line discussion groups on topics of personal or professional interest, and review news and weather updates. As of 1993, an estimated 5,000 individual networks connecting 2 million computers and 15 million people made up the Net, as it is known by its travelers (Gaffin, 1994).

The growth of computer technology has had a tremendous impact on campus. Nowhere is this more evident than in the library, a central information resource. Most campus libraries now are using computerized library catalogs or networks rather than the traditional card catalog. Many libraries also provide access to resources like Internet, on-line computer databases, and CD-ROMs, in addition to the library's typical printed sources. Overall, the changes brought on by the Information Age make the library an excellent place for experiencing the transformation from print technology to computer technology.

The growth of your critical thinking skills in college will depend a great deal on how much and how well you learn to use your campus library.

Abundant information is the starting point for thinking effectively in any academic field. The power of your arguments will depend on how well you can support them with facts and data. Hearing or reading numerous competing arguments about a question is a great way to stimulate your mind to create sound arguments of your own.

Unfortunately, students often share several common misconceptions and even fears about their campus library, particularly those who are intimidated by computers. Your concerns about using the library are certainly warranted, especially when a lack of good information-gathering skills may adversely affect you not only in the classroom but in other areas. Poor performance in class can lead to inadequate preparation for your first job, unfulfilled career and personal goals, and a mediocre return on your investment in college.

EXERCISE 9.1 **Power and Information**

- Pat's local newspaper publishes an ad for what appears to be a terrific job with a company for which he would really like to work. Pat interviews with the company and takes the offered position. Within six months, to his surprise and dismay, the company closes its door, leaving him without a job. As it turns out, according to the same local newspaper, the company had been in financial trouble for some time.

- Laura has been dating Chris for several months. Chris tells her that he has been sexually active in the past year with another person, but that there is no need to use a condom when they decide to have sex, since his sexual activity was limited to just one person. Laura wants to believe Chris; however, having read a free pamphlet from the college health center, she knows that having unprotected sex with Chris is risky because every one of his previous partners, and each of their partners, may not have always practiced safer sex.

1. It's been said that "Power resides with the information holder." How does that idea apply to each of the stories above? In each case, what is the information problem and how might it be handled?

2. Have you ever been in a position of power because you were able to withhold information? Have you ever been in the opposite situation in which information was withheld from you or only grudgingly offered?

3. Think about your own experiences using libraries—both the rewarding and the challenging or frustrating ones. What are some of your concerns or feelings? Discuss them with others in a group.

4. Suggest and discuss some ways that a lack of computer skills or an inability to use the Internet might limit a person's power.

GET A GRIP ON THE LIBRARY

The first step is to familiarize yourself with your library system *before* you have to use it. Is there more than one library on campus? If so, is one geared toward helping undergraduates? Does your library offer tours? (Your class may be able to schedule one.) Try taking a tour to discover what some of the services and various departments offer you. Maybe your library offers an orientation via a computer system.

Look over the following list of common concerns and misconceptions about libraries and librarians:

- I should automatically know how to use the library.
- The library is too big, and I never find what I need.
- Librarians speak a language that only they understand.
- Librarians look too busy to help me.
- I don't know how to use the library's materials; its computers just make it more complicated.
- Librarians in the past haven't helped me.
- I hate doing research and writing papers.
- Doing research usually requires having to talk to someone and ask for help, which can be tough.

Think about you own experiences using libraries—both the rewarding and the challenging or frustrating ones. What are some of your concerns or feelings? Discuss them with others in a group. Of the items listed above, are there any that you would not consider misconceptions?

Does your library have handouts describing various services and different library departments and their hours? Get these handouts. Note the different library departments that might interest you—for example, government documents, reserve, interlibrary loan, or a special collection devoted to one subject area.

Selecting and Surveying a Topic

Usually before you go to the library, you will have selected a topic or your instructor will have provided an assignment for you to complete. (In the exercise at the end of this chapter, you will be asked to select a topic.) This is not always an easy task. If you find it difficult, focus on selecting something in which you are genuinely interested. Browse through recent newspapers and news magazines for ideas. Also, talk to your instructor or your peers about possible ideas. Some libraries have books listing possible research topics, or you may consult a librarian.

If you already have a general topic but have not focused on one specific area, remember that defining and refining your topic is a natural process and one of the objectives of doing research. During your first visit in the library, your goal should be to survey the topic and obtain ideas on how you might want to develop it. When you don't have a clear sense of what you are looking for, give yourself time to reflect before trying to find information.

When surveying the topic, ask, "Does there seem to be enough information? Is there too much?" If there is not enough information, you may want to try a broader approach. If there is too much information, you may want to zero in on one aspect of a more general topic. Instead of looking for information on crime, you might want to focus on a particular crime, like carjacking, and examine how the police are responding to it.

Libraries everywhere have
been computerizing their
catalogs. In many cases,
however, not all resources
are listed yet in the computer. Ask a librarian about
sources that may not show
up on the screen.

Photo by David Gonzales

Defining Your Need for Information

You can begin to gather information by asking yourself several questions
even before you physically or electronically enter the library. The following
questions will give you ideas on how to think about your topic before actually searching for information. Carefully thinking through your topic will
not only help you focus but also help you communicate your needs to a librarian. Sometimes these questions may be difficult to answer when you are
starting out. Don't worry. Try talking through your topic with a friend or
consulting a librarian or your instructor.

1. **What Do You Already Know About Your Topic?** Consider names,
   events, dates, places, terms, and relationships to other topics. Clarifying
   your topic in this way may give you leads on how to look for more information. And have confidence: You will know something about your
   topic.

2. **Who Would Be Writing About Your Topic?** For example, what
   scholars, researchers, professionals in specific fields, or other groups of
   people might be interested? Asking this question helps you to see your
   topic more fully and identify new aspects of it. This basic question will
   also help you relate your topic to a major way libraries and information
   resources are organized—by discipline, or field of study. Disciplines are
   broadly classified as the *arts* (performing and fine arts such as music,
   painting, and architecture), *humanities* (religion, philosophy, literature),
   social sciences (psychology, sociology, communications, education, anthropology, law, political science, criminology, economics), and *natural
   sciences* (biology, chemistry, mathematics, engineering, physics, computer science).

3. **What Do You Want to Know About This Topic?** Asking these
   questions further focuses your research or your assignment. Sometimes
   your first question may be too general and not easily answered. For instance, your original question may be "Is the increasing amount of violence on television ruining society?" There isn't one answer to this
   question. It isn't a factual question; it is a research question that leads
   you to additional questions you might need answered in order to answer

Research Tips

WRITING THE "WRITE" WAY

1. Come prepared with the necessary supplies: paper, notecards, pen or pencil, computer disks for downloading, your college ID, and cash for photocopying.

2. Be clear in your notes if you are taking down information verbatim (direct quotes) or if you are paraphrasing. Be wary of plagiarizing. Plagiarism is using someone else's work without giving that person credit.

3. Write down all the appropriate information about sources to avoid unnecessary and frustrating backtracking when it comes time to write up your bibliography or cite your sources.

AVOIDING FRUSTRATION

1. If the necessary sources are not on the shelf, ask for help. They may be misshelved, checked out, or available in another library through interlibrary loan, a service that finds the material in another library and then borrows it for you.

2. Start early. Allow yourself the time it will take to gather sources before you have to write the paper.

the original question. For example: Are there measures of the amount and type of violence portrayed on television, and have these measures changed over time? Is there research linking viewing to actual behavior or changes in attitude toward violence? Does violence on television affect different populations differently—children, teenagers, adults, males, females? Are particular types of television broadcasting becoming more violent—children's shows, news, primetime dramas, commercials? What arguments can be made for government regulation versus personal responsibility in determining what is viewed?

4. **What Is the Vocabulary of Your Topic?** What words describe it? Are there specialized terms? Some words are what you might call context-sensitive. For example, the word *dating* means one thing to a sociologist and another to an archaeologist. Also, if you are using a specialized database or index focusing on, say, biology, you probably would not use the term *biology* as a vocabulary term because the whole database or index covers biology. For more in-depth discussion of what vocabulary to use, see the section "Looking for Books on a Subject."

5. **What Do You Want to Do with This Information?** Are you writing a research paper, giving a speech, preparing for a debate or an interview, looking for a single fact or statistic, satisfying your curiosity about the nature of something, persuading someone to believe your ideas or someone else's, explaining a phenomenon, informing others, or telling a story? Although these examples are not comprehensive, they will help you determine how much information you need and where to look.

6. **What Are the Characteristics of the Information You Need to Find?** Characteristics or qualities of information don't necessarily fall into discrete categories, but can occur in combinations or along a continuum:

- **Introductory:** general information on a topic; written for an audience without prior or special knowledge in an area
- **In-depth:** specialized and detailed information on a topic; written for an audience with prior or special knowledge in an area
- **Biographical:** about someone but by another person
- **Autobiographical:** about someone and by that same person
- **Current:** about an event or idea that just occurred
- **Contemporary:** a perspective at the time an event occurred
- **Retrospective:** written by someone reflecting on a topic
- **Summative:** summarizing or giving an overview of a topic
- **Argumentative or persuasive:** expressing a strong point of view
- **Analytical:** breaking an idea down into its components

Answering these six questions will help you to clarify the information you want and to explain your needs to a librarian.

Tips on Talking to Librarians

"A problem without a solution is usually a problem that is put the wrong way."

1. Recognize that librarians are usually more than willing to help you and that they can save you time and effort.

2. Don't feel you have to know everything about a topic, every aspect of using the library, or any specialized language or jargon. When a librarian uses a term you do not know, ask for clarification.

3. Accept responsibility for your work. Librarians will expect you to know what your assignment is; to bring relevant assignment sheets, class notes, textbooks, and so on; to make decisions about the usefulness of sources; to ask questions; and to discuss what steps you have already taken.

4. Not all librarians are alike. Different librarians have different communication styles and areas of expertise. If you are not satisfied after talking to one librarian, seek another.

5. Ask as many questions as you need to. Librarians do not have a quota for the number of questions you may ask.

6. Word your requests carefully to a librarian just as you would to describe symptoms to a doctor. For various reasons, students may often not ask for what they want. For example, one student may ask where the science books are when actually he is looking for information on rain forests. Another student may need to locate research on memory studies in psychology journals, but she asks instead where the psychology journals are. Ask for what you want and be descriptive. You may think you're saving the librarian and yourself time, but more often than not, shortcuts waste time. In most cases the librarian will interview you to determine how to meet your needs.

7. Don't worry if your topic is of a controversial or personal nature. Librarians have a professional responsibility to treat your request confidentially.

■FINDING YOUR WAY

"Cheshire-Puss," she began rather timidly. "Would you tell me, please, which way I ought to go from here?"

"That depends a good deal on where you want to get to," said the cat.

"I don't much care where—" said Alice.

"Then it doesn't matter which way you go," said the cat.

Lewis Carroll, *Alice in Wonderland*

Sometimes just exploring is fun, but unlike Alice, usually you will care where you get to so it will matter which way you go. Knowing the general pathways to information is an important step in learning to find and use information wisely. Typical information sources include almanacs, bibliographies, catalogs, dictionaries, directories, encyclopedias, and indexes.

General Encyclopedias

The word *encyclopedia* comes from the Greek meaning "instruction in the circle of knowledge." Encyclopedias, especially general ones that attempt to cover the world of information, are often good starting places because they can (1) give you some background on a subject, (2) provide you with an overview on a broad topic and suggest possible ways to narrow it, (3) recommend other reading to you, and (4) give clues on how to search the topic in other sources by giving you terminology, key personalities, or events. A major disadvantage of encyclopedias, however, is that they become outdated. It generally takes seven years for an encyclopedia to be published, and not all of the articles are updated when a new edition is issued. If your topic is current, an encyclopedia may not help much.

Although encyclopedias are useful tools for getting you started, instructors will not want you to rely on them as the major source for the papers you submit. Using an encyclopedia as a starting point, you should make an effort to find information in other sources.

Following are some sample titles that may be available in your library. Encyclopedias are not all equal, and which is best will depend on your topic. (Use the checklist in Exercise 9.4, part A, to evaluate an encyclopedia.) When looking for information, you may want to compare several encyclopedias or ask a librarian to recommend one. See a reference librarian if at least one of these is not in your library.

Encyclopedia Americana
World Book Encyclopedia
Collier's Encyclopedia
Compton's Encyclopedia
Encyclopaedia Britannica

Grolier's (on compact disc; need a computer to search)
Information Finder (on compact disc)

Subject Encyclopedias

Subject encyclopedias are constructed the same way as general encyclopedias, but they are more specialized. They concentrate on a narrower field of knowledge and cover it in greater depth. (Use the checklist in Exercise 9.4, part B, to evaluate an encyclopedia.)

The subject encyclopedias listed here are grouped by general areas. This is not a comprehensive list. If you cannot find a title that fits your area of interest, ask a librarian to suggest one.

Arts

The New Grove Dictionary of Music and Musicians

Encyclopedia of World Art

McGraw-Hill Encyclopedia of World Drama

Humanities

Encyclopedia of Philosophy

Encyclopedia of Bioethics

Encyclopedia of Religion

Handbook of American Popular Culture

History

Encyclopedia of American Social History

The African American Encyclopedia

Dictionary of American History

Social Sciences

International Encyclopedia of the Social Sciences

Encyclopedia of Educational Research

International Encyclopedia of Communications

Encyclopedia of American Economic History

Encyclopedia of American Foreign Policy

Encyclopedia of Psychology

Encyclopedia of Sociology

Guide to American Law

Natural Sciences

McGraw-Hill Encyclopedia of Science and Technology

Encyclopedia of Computer Science

Catalogs

A catalog is a list of books and periodicals (magazines, newspapers, or journals) owned by the library. The catalog may also list other materials such as films, videos, audiotapes, manuscripts, and government documents. Your library's catalog may be the traditional card catalog; it may be computerized ("on-line" as librarians say); it could be a combination of cards and computers; or it could even be available on microform (microfiche or microfilm) or in another format. Nowadays, you also may be able to gain electronic access or "log on" to your catalog without even going to the library. Whatever the format, it is important to familiarize yourself with the library's catalog and the particulars of looking for a book or other materials by its author, title, or subject.

LOOKING FOR BOOKS ON A SUBJECT

You generally will begin to look for information by using books. Often, finding books on a subject is difficult or tricky for several reasons:

- You may not know the subject well.
- The terminology or vocabulary may be unfamiliar.
- Your term may not exactly match the catalog's. For example, the catalog may list *modern history* as *history, modern*, or it may list *light bulbs* under the heading *electric lamps, incandescent*.
- Your term may be so new that a subject heading has not been created for it. For example, before the AIDS epidemic, the disease's now familiar acronym was not used as a subject heading.

- Your topic is so narrow you need to rely on a broader heading instead to gather additional information. For example, you may find some information under *hate crimes,* but to find more you might need to look under *racism* or *bigotry.*

Most of the materials in libraries are located using what are called "subject headings," "descriptors," or "index terms." Indexers, catalogers, and researchers select the terms in order to organize information; however, sometimes these professionals select terms that you or your instructor may not have thought to use. Your job is to match your own language with that used in catalogs or indexes. For example, a library source may describe cars using the subject heading or descriptor *cars, automobiles,* or *motor vehicles.* Often, when you look up a term, you will be referred to the preferred subject heading or term.

KEYWORD SEARCHING

Most computerized sources also provide searching by "keyword." Here, the computer searches the entire record of an item for the words or phrases you entered. The word you entered might appear somewhere in the title, might be a subject term, or might be in another part of the description of the item. When you search by keyword, you can specify how to combine the terms you want it to search, how to position a word in relation to other words, and where to look for a word in the record (for example, only in the title).

There are advantages and disadvantages to searching either by subject heading or by keyword. What's most important is that you think about the vocabulary of your topic beforehand and use both subject headings and keywords for the best results.

Indexes

Indexes identify articles in periodicals, which may be published daily, weekly, monthly, bimonthly, or quarterly. The most common periodicals you will use are newspapers, magazines, and journals. Because articles are published more frequently and more quickly than books, they often contain more current information. When you look in an index, you do not actually find the article itself. You find a citation listing the author(s), title of the article, title of the magazine or journal, date of the issue, and volume and page numbers. Some indexes, called abstracts, also provide a short summary of the article's content, which can tell you if the article is relevant.

Using an index to locate articles saves time. You could browse through journals for information, but for more thorough coverage, use an index. Some indexes also list materials published in books, usually in collections of essays. Your library may also have a computerized version of a particular index. If you want to use a computerized version or an index on CD-ROM, ask a librarian what your library offers.

Some indexes may include both magazines and journals, so be wary if you plan to focus on one type of periodical. Magazines provide important information, but generally they do not cover topics in depth. Some well-known magazines are *Time, Newsweek, Ebony, U.S. News & World Report,* and *Science.* Scholars usually do not write magazine articles. If they do, they write the article to address a broader audience who may not understand technical terms. To distinguish between magazines and journals, you can (1) look for titles containing the word *journal*; (2) look at the length of the article, because

Library of Congress Subject Headings

If you have trouble finding the right subject headings, you may want to consult an official list, such as that found in the set of volumes entitled the *Library of Congress Subject Heading,* or *LCSH.* If your term is not a preferred subject heading, *LCSH* will refer you to appropriate terms. For instance, if you look up the term *College life, LCSH* will tell you to use *College students. LCSH* will also offer related terms and even subheadings or subject divisions once you have located the preferred subject heading. Below is one *LCSH* entry:

College students (*May Subd Geog*)

UF	College life
	Counterculture
	Undergraduates
	Universities and colleges—Students
	University students
BT	Students
NT	College freshmen
	College seniors
	Graduate students
	Junior college students
	Minority college students
	Talented students
	Teachers college students
	Vocational school students
	Wages—College students
	Women college students

—Attitudes
—Library orientation
—Sexual behavior
—Social conditions

UF	College students' socioeconomic status

This entry tells you that *College students* is the authorized term. The comment (*May Subd Geog*) tells you that the term *College students* may be subdivided geographically. That is, you may be able to locate information on college students in your state—for example, *College students—North Carolina.* The *UF* means "used for." The term *College students* is used for the terms listed after *UF.* You may have *University students* as a term, but in this case *LCSH* is telling you that the authorized term *College students* is used for *University students. BT* means "broader term." If you do not find enough information using the term *College students,* you may want to use the authorized term *Students. NT* means "narrower term." If you are finding too much information using *College students,* you may want to use one of the authorized terms following *NT* to help focus your search. *RT* (not shown in this example) means "related term" or a synonymous term. If the term *College students* is not exactly the term you want to use, one of the terms following *RT* might provide more useful information. The boldfaced terms following dashes (**—Attitudes** and so on) are examples of subject divisions. Subject divisions help you focus your search if your first topic is too broad.

journal articles are usually longer; (3) look for titles that use technical or specialized vocabulary, a good indication of a journal article; or (4) ask a librarian for help.

Different kinds of indexes cover various types of publications. In addition to newspaper, magazine, and journal (or specialized subject) indexes, there are indexes to types of material. For example, the Speech Index identifies speeches published in books; Granger's Index to Poetry indexes poems published in collections of poetry; Book Review Index lists reviews of books published in periodicals.

MAGAZINE INDEXES

Magazine indexes list articles in magazines on a wide variety of topics. Some frequently used magazine indexes include the following:

Readers' Guide to Periodical Literature   *Academic Index* (computerized)
Infotrac (computerized)   *Periodical Abstracts* (computerized)
Magazine Index (computerized)

SUBJECT OR SPECIALIZED INDEXES

Specialized subject indexes list articles in journals that cover a narrow subject field. Instructors may specifically request that you look for journal articles rather than magazine articles. Below is a useful, but not comprehensive list of subject indexes. Ask a librarian to suggest other indexes.

Humanities

Humanities Index

Philosopher's Index

Music Index

Religion Index One

Art Index

MLA International Bibliography (literature, linguistics)

Natural Sciences

General Sciences Index

Applied Science and Technology Index (engineering)

Life Sciences Collection (biology, botany, zoology)

Cumulative Index to Nursing & Allied Health Literature

Index Medicus (medicine)

ACM Guide to Computing Literature

Social Sciences

Social Sciences Index

Education Index

ERIC (computerized; education)

Psychological Abstracts

PsycLit (computerized version of *Psychological Abstracts*)

PAIS International (government, social issues, political science)

Sociological Abstracts

Business Periodicals Index

ABI-Inform (computerized; business)

Finding Periodicals in Your Library

Once you have chosen your articles of interest, you will have to locate the actual magazines, newspapers, or journals. Usually you will consult the library's catalog to see if the library has the title you need. Some libraries keep a separate list of their journals and magazines. However, the library's catalog may not indicate which specific issues of a periodical the library actually contains. Ask a librarian for help.

Periodicals may be shelved by call number with the books, or they may be organized alphabetically. If they are shelved by call number, you will have to look in the catalog, or possibly another list, to discover what the correct call number is. Most libraries will have the back issues of these periodicals bound into hardcover volumes by year. The more current issues are usually not bound until a volume is complete. Some periodicals are available on microform. Newspapers are almost always kept on microfilm, except for the most recent issues.

CRITICAL THINKING ABOUT SOURCES

Successfully gathering information involves more than just locating enough sources. It also involves critically evaluating articles, books, and other materials once you have found them. Particularly in the Information Age, as the volume of available information increases daily, you should not settle for the first available sources. These sources may not be as relevant as others; they may be dated; or they may be inaccurate. To evaluate a source you might ask these questions:

1. **Is the source relevant to your information needs?** You can begin by looking at the title of the book or article, its length, the type of source you need, and the type that is available or that you have at hand.

2. **Is the information in the source accurate?** If your topic is controversial, if you are relying on just a few sources, or if you are using a questionable fact, you might want to find some reviews or additional commentary to check how accurate the information is. Compare other sources to see what they say.

3. **Does the author or the source show bias?** Consider why material was written or for whom it was written. When might you need to seek a different opinion?

4. **Is the author credible or reliable?** What are the author's credentials? If you have trouble answering this question, see a reference librarian.

5. **Is the information timely?** That is, is it the most up-to-date information you could locate? You might consider this question when using statistics or when you are in a fast-paced field constantly undergoing change (for example, computer science, medicine, economics).

Use the questions throughout this chapter and the procedures suggested by the exercises for future research projects you undertake during college and after.

EXPLORING DATABASES

The World Wide Web is rapidly becoming a resource of choice for students doing research for class papers. For many kinds of information, this can be a productive approach. However, the information available on the Internet may not have the authority or authenticity of material available in the library or from databases such as Lexis/Nexis, Data-Star, and Dialog.

EXERCISE 9.3 Library Databases

At your campus library or at a computer that is linked to the library, find out what databases are available on-line or on CD-ROM at the library. For each, make a list of (1) the name of the database, (2) how to reach it, (3) the material it includes, and (4) the nature of its output (for example, citations only, on-screen text, or downloadable computer files). If your campus has more than ten databases or CD-ROMs, pick the ten that would be most useful to you. Keep the list where you can use it in your future research for writing a paper.

Internet Resources

Finding information on the Internet depends on knowing where to look for it. It helps to know the existence and uses of a number of electronic resources—both in general and in your field of interest:

Databases (both public and commercial)

Abstract services (which provide summaries of journal articles or other information)

Specialized on-line library collections

Professional associations

State and government agencies

Nonprofit organizations

Usenet newsgroups and Listserver discussion groups

Anonymous software archives, known as FTP (File Transfer Protocol) archives.

You also need to know how to gain access to the above resources by using various other services and programs. Each service accesses different resources. Depending on what you are looking for, you select the appropriate service:

E-mail: for contacting specific people, or posting a message to a discussion group or newsgroup.

Listserv/Discussion Groups: for locating and communicating with individuals as representatives of an organization or sharing a specific interest.

Newsgroups: for discussion of a particular topic or issue, or to identify individuals with a specific interest.

FTP/Archie: for sending or receiving specific computer files, especially programs related to the Internet. If you are not sure where to find specific files, the associated search program, Archie, is a useful tool.

Gopher/Veronica: for locating documents, files, information, or data from or about a specific education, governmental, or nonprofit organization or association. The search program Veronica can be of service here.

WAIS: for specific documents or to search the content of a certain type of document or database.

World Wide Web: for locating documents, files, information, or data from or about a specific commercial enterprise or other institution. The same is true for product information and technical assistance. The Web is the choice for most multimedia presentations, whether sound, movies, or simply graphics, as well as for the site of homepages for popular issues and concerns.

The World Wide Web is an easy place to start, because many World Wide Web search programs include references to other services of the Internet and often provide direct links to them.

To use the Internet—and your own time—effectively, be careful to distinguish between active discovery and idle diversion, between productive research and sheer busywork.

SOURCE: Adapted with permission from Daniel J. Kurland, *The 'Net, the Web, and You: All You Really Need to Know About the Internet and a Little Bit More.* Belmont, CA: Wadsworth, 1996.

Finding Information in the Library

Choose a topic that interests you. If you have trouble choosing, consider a subject you have discussed in class, or your current major study or career interest. What is your topic?

_____

What are some related vocabulary words that might help you find your topic in an index?

_____

_____

A General Encyclopedias

Choose and locate one general encyclopedia in your library from the list in the text. Which one did you choose?

_____

1. Is there an index? If so, does it list other related terms or topics to look under? What are several of them?

   _____

   _____

2. Find several articles in the encyclopedia related to your topic. If you did not find entries on your topic, what seems to be the problem?

   _____ Topic is too current; encyclopedia is too old.

   _____ Topic is too specific; need to look in the index to see if information is contained in an article on a broader topic.

   _____ Encyclopedia uses different language than I'm using; need to think of other terms to look for in the index.

   _____ Topic is too specialized for a general encyclopedia.

   _____ Other reasons (List them here):

   _____

3. Choose one article on your topic or on another topic that interests you. Does the article list other terms or topics to look under? If so, record several of them.

   _____

   _____

4. Does the end of the article list other sources or references? List several that look useful.

   _____

   _____

B Subject Encyclopedias

Choose and locate one subject encyclopedia in your library from the list in the text. In deciding which to choose, think back to the process of determining your information need, especially the question, Who could be interested in my topic?

To locate the subject encyclopedia, you may need to look it up by title in your catalog. If you have trouble, ask a librarian. Which one did you choose?

_____

1. Look for several articles related to your topic. (Use the index if there is one.) If you did not find entries on your topic, what seems to be the problem?

    _____ Topic is too current; encyclopedia is too old.

    _____ Topic is too specific; need to look in the index to see if information is contained in an article on a broader topic.

    _____ Encyclopedia uses different language than I'm using; need to think of other terms to look for.

    _____ Topic is not covered adequately by any of the subject encyclopedias.

    _____ Other reasons (List them here):

    _____

2. What similarities and differences do you notice between general and subject encyclopedias?

    _____

    _____

    _____

C Library Catalogs: Looking for Books on a Topic

1. Refer back to the section "Catalogs." What type of catalog is yours? If your catalog is computerized, does it have a special name? What is it? Does your library catalog provide access to libraries at other locations? List one or two. If your catalog is half card and half on-line, what date divides the two parts?

    _____

    _____

    _____

2. Using your same topic of interest, consult the *Library of Congress Subject Heading* list. Ask your librarian if you do not see this set of volumes. Is your term an appropriate subject heading or does *LCSH* tell you to use another term instead? If so, what is the appropriate search term?

    _____

3. List any related terms, broader terms, or narrower terms, and explain why you think these could be helpful.

    _____

    _____

    Now locate the titles of books on your topic using the subject heading you found in *LCSH*. Pick one specific book.

4. List the author, title, date of publication, publisher, call number, and location for the book.

    _____

    _____

    _____

5. How could you find other books by this book's author?

_____

6. Does your library contain other books by this author? If so, list a title.

_____

7. Besides subject searching, what are other ways to locate books using the catalog? (For instance, what if you knew the title or the author? What if you are using a computerized catalog?)

_____

_____

8. What can you do if your library does not have a copy of the book you need?

_____

D Magazine Indexes: Looking for Articles in Magazines

Choose one of the magazine indexes listed in the text to complete the following questions.

1. What index did you choose?

_____

2. How is it arranged? If you are using a computerized index, describe instead some of the ways you can search.

_____

_____

Look under your topic.

3. What can you do if your exact topic or term is not listed in the index or if using your term yields no results in the computerized index?

_____

4. Find a citation. If you don't understand how to read a citation, where can you find an explanation? Does the computerized version have help screens?

_____

5. List the author, title, complete magazine title, volume, date, and page numbers.

_____

_____

_____

6. Is the magazine title abbreviated? If so, where do you find the complete title?

_____

7. To what in the citation should you pay attention to determine relevancy?

_____

E Specialized Subject Indexes: Looking for Articles in Journals

Choose one subject index to complete the following questions.

1. What index did you choose? What discipline(s) does this index cover? Check the preface of the print index or available help screens on the computer. Look under a topic of your choice.

© 1997 Wadsworth Publishing Company

_____

_____

2. Are there related terms or subject headings? If you are using a computerized index, does it have a list of preferred subject terms, also known as a thesaurus? (Hint: The thesaurus may be available in print format or on the computer.)

_____

3. Find a citation. If you don't understand how to read a citation, where can you find an explanation? Does the computerized version have help screens?

_____

4. List the author, title, complete magazine title, volume, date, page numbers.

_____

_____

_____

5. If journal title is abbreviated, where did you find the complete title?

_____

F Finding Magazines or Journals in Your Library

Select either the magazine or journal citation that you have already written down above.

1. What is the journal or magazine title?

_____

2. Does your library have this journal or magazine? Does it have the volume you need? How did you find this out?

_____

_____

3. How are the journals and magazines shelved in your library—in one place (perhaps alphabetically by title) or arranged by call numbers like the books? Are any kept on microfilm? If your library does have the journal or magazine listed in your citation, find the volume with your article and photocopy the first page of the article.

_____

_____

G Finding Databases

Look over the list of databases in your campus library that you developed in Exercise 9.3. Explore several databases to find one that contains information related to your topic.

1. Which database did you select?

_____

2. Does it provide only citations to other sources, or does it also provide actual text? How useful does the information appear to be in relation to your topic?

_____

_____

© 1997 Wadsworth Publishing Company

In its quiet way, having explored the "stacks" of the library may become one of your fondest memories of college. But you'll get the most out of your exploration if you've prepared well beforehand by exploring catalogs and indexes.

Photo courtesy of University of Connecticut

■LIBRARY LANGUAGE

Abstract: a summary of an article or book.

Almanac: a compilation of useful but skeletal information and statistics on countries, people, events, and subjects. Often filled with fascinating bits of information over a wide range of subjects.

Annotation: a description of an article or book. An annotated bibliography is especially useful to locate because it includes a brief summary that can help you determine if something is relevant. You may have an assignment to annotate a source. That means you would write a description of the reading.

Bibliography: a list of materials (books, articles, videos, and so on) on one subject or by one author. Bibliographies can be helpful because they gather and identify materials on a common theme. Be wary of outdated bibliographies, however.

Bound periodical: issues of magazines or journals arranged together under one hard cover.

Call number: a unique combination of letters and numbers used to identify items in a library. Materials are arranged on the shelves in call number order. A call number is given to an item on the basis of subject so that materials on a similar subject will be shelved together.

Catalog: a listing of what a library contains.

Citation: the written information that identifies a book or article. A citation is the information you will need to locate the item or to include as a reference in your paper. It usually includes information such as author, title, pages, and date.

Database: an organized collection of records having a standardized format and content. For example, a cookbook is a database of recipes. Computerized indexes and catalogs are two of the most common types of databases in libraries.

Directory: something that gives contact information (address, phone, titles of officers) and perhaps a brief description. Helpful for locating other people, experts, organizations, agencies, businesses, and so on.

Gopher: a computer program that uses simple menus to allow searchers to reach a large variety of information resources and services on the Internet.

Index: (1) in a book, an alphabetical list of names and subjects in the book along with the corresponding page number(s); (2) as a type of reference source, a systematic guide to the contents of a discrete set of materials. For example, periodical indexes allow you to search for articles published in particular magazines or journals. These indexes cover a specific time period and may be searched by subject and often by author.

Interlibrary loan (ILL): the service, and often library department, that gets materials from other libraries.

Microform: general term used for printed materials that have been reduced in size and are read using special machines. Microforms include microfilm (on a roll) and microfiche (small sheets).

Noncirculating: materials that can be used only within the library and cannot be checked out.

Periodical: a magazine, journal, or newspaper that is published at regular time periods, or periodically. A periodical is a type of serial.

Record: used most often in the context of computerized sources, refers to all the information given about a particular item. A record typically includes the citation information, an abstract, and other information such as language.

Reference: (1) another term for citation; (2) a service, and usually a department, provided by the library to help people find the information they need.

Reserve: a service, and most often a department in a library, whereby heavily used items are placed by instructors to allow access by a greater number of students. Materials on reserve can be checked out for a much shorter period of time so that they will be available for more people to use.

Serial: a publication that comes out in parts. Serials include newspapers, journals, magazines, annual reports, and yearbooks.

JOURNAL

How have your feelings or concerns about using the library changed as a result of this chapter? What do you need to do at this point to improve your general library skills? What else might you do now to learn more about the libraries and other information resources on your campus that might be useful to you?

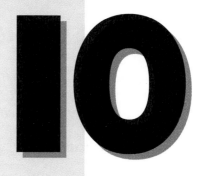
Writing and Speaking for Success

Carolyn Matalene
University of South Carolina

Constance Courtney Staley
University of Colorado-Colorado Springs

Robert Stephens Staley III
Colorado Technical University

I get writer's block when I'm even in the same room with a sheet of paper. It's even worse when I know I have to present a paper in front of the class. What do I have to say, anyway? Why can't I just tape record my ideas and hand them in? That way, if I sound stupid, I won't be around to hear myself.

Chapter Goals

This chapter should help you feel more comfortable about the writing and speaking you will be asked to do throughout college and your career. It should also help you integrate writing into your critical thinking process. After completing this chapter, you will have the foundation for effective public speaking and writing.

As a first-year student, you are almost certainly required to take a course in writing. Why, then, a chapter here devoted in part to writing? College composition courses usually focus mainly on techniques for writing essays and term papers assigned in class. The purpose of this chapter is to encourage you to take a broader, more integrated view of writing as an active tool of learning, useful not only in demonstrating what you know—the fourth step in the critical thinking process, but in actually learning in the first place.

We'd like you to come to embrace writing as a constant activity in your personal and academic life and as an ingredient in all four phases of the critical thinking process outlined in Chapter 1.

■ FROM PRIVATE TO PUBLIC WRITING

One of the most effective ways of becoming a learner is to become a writer. Because writing is a process uniquely suited to learning, the more you use writing as a way of studying, the more you will learn. Start with some *private writing*. Private writing means writing that you undertake as a way of learning, writing that you practice as a technique for studying, writing that only *you* see because it is not intended to communicate knowledge or information to anyone but yourself.

Private writing works as a medium for you to communicate with yourself as a learner, asking your own questions about what you read and hear, questioning your own answers, and eventually becoming fluent in the language of a discipline. Of course, you will also have to produce *public writing:* the essays, exams, research papers, and critical analyses for your courses. In public writing you must go through the process of revision and editing; your writing must be finished and polished. By contrast, private writing can remain unfinished, exploratory, inconclusive—a way of remembering facts and terms even if their meaning is not yet clear to you.

In order to become an active participant in any field of learning, you have to master the language of that field. In any course you take, you need

Like most complex undertakings, strong writing begins with exploring one's own awareness. That begins with private writing.

Zimble/Monkmeyer Press Photo

to write as well as read, speak as well as listen. Some students start out thinking that reading is enough. And certainly readers can be active learners if they engage with the text, ask questions, make connections and comparisons, evaluate—if, in a word, they think. In order to really learn something, either in class or from a textbook, you need to combine listening and reading with a faithful system of taking and reviewing notes.

Try this: For each of your courses, use one section of your course notebook for *reading notes*. Take your sociology text, for example, and read a portion, perhaps a chapter. Don't underline or highlight every sentence. Instead, read thoughtfully and then close the book. Now, in your reading notebook, write a brief summary in your own words of what you read: What is the chapter really about? Next, write some of your own reactions, comments, and thoughts: What does this chapter make you think of? What can you relate it to? What examples from your own experience can you think of that would prove the major points? Or what examples can you think of that would disprove those points? What questions do you have? What seems strange? What seems unclear or hard to understand? If you could ask your instructor some questions about this material, what would they be?

As you write, you will have more ideas. By writing, you increase your chances of remembering the material because you are involved in it. You are also becoming literate in the field you are reading about; you are making the language of the subject your own. You are engaged. And that is the essence of what any teacher wants from any student—not agreement, but engagement with the subject.

As you write privately about your studies, you will be engaging with ideas more deeply and more personally. The difference between success and failure in college is *engagement*. Successful students don't end their studies in the classroom or with their homework assignments. They carry what they are learning into their private lives, their social lives, their family lives. They integrate what they are learning with who they are. You can too—by putting pen to paper.

EXERCISE 10.1 **Engage by Writing**

A Sit down with a reading assignment you have recently completed in one of your courses. Write a summary of what you read. Write down any questions that the reading raised for you. Write about why you think you were asked to read the material and what reading it accomplished for you. Finally, write down any additional personal responses you may have had to the material. (This is private writing in the sense that it is for your personal benefit. However, your instructor may ask you to turn it in so that he or she can respond.)

B Look back over what you've written. In what ways does the thinking you did in the course of that writing reflect the first three phases of critical thinking (abstract, creative, and systematic thinking)?

Procedures of Thought

When you write in response to what you read or observe, you learn a lot more. Research shows that students who engage in extended writing about a topic are capable of more complex thoughts and are better able to see relationships among concepts. When you write in response to a text or a topic, your mind inevitably performs the mental procedures that all humans use to analyze experience and to learn systematically. You try different ways of looking; you practice *procedural* knowledge.

There are a number of common *procedures of thought* you can use as you respond to reading by writing. The first and most important is simply to read for the main idea: What is the main, central, or most important idea presented in this section or chapter? Once you have answered that question, you can choose from a number of analytical strategies to organize your thoughts and your writing.

If the following list looks familiar to you, it is probably because these are forms of thinking (and writing) that are practiced in most first-year college composition courses. For now, however, try to think of them not simply as ways in which you may need to organize an essay, but as frameworks for focusing your writing—even private writing or public writing that requires no particular form.

- **Narration.** Perhaps the simplest and most obvious way to organize is to express a series of events in the order in which they occurred. This happened, then that happened, and so on. Turning events or procedures into a story may help you remember them and sort out connections. One strength of narrative is that it is often entertaining and easy to follow. A weakness is that it may distract you and readers from deeper abstract and analytical thinking.

- **Comparison and Contrast.** One common way to explore the meaning or value of something is to compare it thoroughly with something else. Do you really want to become a lawyer? How does that choice compare with some alternatives in terms of the actual work, the pay, the amount of preparation it will take to enter the profession? Examining similarities and differences between two ideas illuminates them both.

- **Cause and Effect.** In some courses, especially history and the sciences, thinking of the cause or effect of something is important. What has caused the United States to have such high levels of interpersonal violence? What effects can we predict from global warming? What caused you to decide to go to college? What's the likely effect of that decision?

- **Theories and Opinion.** Theories represent abstract thinking—large ideas based on the synthesis of smaller ideas and supporting information. What was Adam Smith's theory of the "invisible hand" in economics? What was Mary Daly's feminist philosophy? Does your history instructor disagree with the textbook on some broad issue? How? Why? Have you begun to regard life in general or certain values differently than your parents? Writing about theory begins by laying out the main ideas of a viewpoint and examining the assumptions behind them.

- **Explanation and Argument.** Explaining or arguing means building a convincing, systematic case in support of an idea. You may believe you have the best solution to a campus or national problem, but what evidence and logic can you muster to convince others that your position is correct? What counterarguments will people make against it? How can you respond to these challenges?

Choosing a suitable procedure of thought is a good way to organize your writing and to find out what you know and don't know. It is also a good way to narrow down a writing assignment topic to a manageable size and to begin to plan how to research and arrange your information and ideas.

EXERCISE 10.2 Procedures and Structures

A What relation do you see between each of the five procedures of thought and the first three steps of critical thinking described in Chapter 1?

B Are there other procedures of thought—ways of organizing or structuring your thinking and writing—you would consider adding to the list?

C If you are currently enrolled in a composition course, look at the syllabus to see whether the course involves practicing any of the five procedures described above. If it does, does it emphasize some procedures more than others? Ask your composition instructor how he or she went about designing the course and what different types of learning he or she expects you to gain from completing the various assignments.

Going Public

Once you've acquired some specific analytical skills and practiced using them in your private writing, you're ready to apply them to your public writing—essays, reports, exams, and so on. The transition from private writing to public writing terrifies many students, but the more you practice private

Stop, Read, and Listen!

How well informed are you about what's happening in the world?

1. Do you listen to National Public Radio? When you're getting dressed in the morning, do you tune in to "Morning Edition"? When you're exercising after class, do you listen to "All Things Considered" on your headset? Do you listen to your campus station? What other good local or national radio information programs do you listen to regularly?

2. Do you read your campus newspaper? Do you read the local paper every day? On Sunday do you set aside some time to read a good national paper, such as *The New York Times, The Washington Post,* or the *Los Angeles Times?*

3. Do you read a magazine or two every week? Along with *Time* or *Newsweek,* do you read *Rolling Stone, The New Yorker, Sports Illustrated, Harper's, Vogue, Vanity Fair, Esquire,* or *The Atlantic Monthly?* Do you read any of the many specialized magazines on computers, sports, cars, boats, and so on? Do you go to the open periodical room in your library and let yourself do some random reading every now and then?

4. Do you ever read some good current nonfiction? Have you ever tapped the wealth of living writers helping us make sense of our world—among them John McPhee, Joan Didion, Jane Kramer, Tracy Kidder, Garry Wills, Mark Singer, Lewis Thomas, Roger Angell, Alice Walker, Tom Wolfe, Michael Herr, Annie Dillard, Paul Theroux, Russell Baker, and Frances Fitzgerald?

The more you know about what's going on, the more you'll have to say, both in and outside class. The more you read, listen, and inform yourself in general, the better you'll write.

writing, the less you will need to worry about exams and papers. You will gain confidence as a writer because you will be developing a composing process that works for you.

The composing process refers to the stages a writer goes through in order to achieve results that are worth being read. Private writing can just flow as a stream of consciousness, wandering out of the main channel, stopping and starting. In private writing, the focus is on the first stage of the composing process, *invention*. During the invention stage (some call it prewriting), writers concentrate on thinking, questioning, connecting, generating, gathering, analyzing, and evaluating. The drafting is fast and free, with little concern for grammar, syntax, sentence structure, and so on. When you engage in public writing, however, the drafting must yield more structured discourse; somewhere along the way, either on paper or in your head, planning must take place.

Moving from private to public writing requires you to focus on structure. If you have been studying all along—and studying, you should realize by now, means reading *and* writing—then you have been practicing invention all along. When exam time comes or when the paper assignment is given, you have available an abundance of content that you must now shape into the proper *form*. A successful piece of public writing will be based on a plan, an organizational principle, a structure so clear that a reader could outline it if need be.

ESTABLISHING STRUCTURE

Figuring out what you are going to say and how you are going to say it—that is, establishing your structure—is hard, essential work.

Some writers just plunge into writing—the same way you do in private writing. Their writing "grows from the top." The problem with this approach is that, if an idea or plan or project fails, a huge amount of time and labor can be lost. It's much easier to discard a plan—a page with some words and arrows and circles on it—than to throw away an entire draft of hard-won sentences. Writers who do not plan, who write by drafting (and some excellent writers do proceed this way), often insist they don't really throw away sentences; it only looks that way for a while. Eventually, everything gets used, but maybe in a different place. On balance, that approach will almost certainly be less efficient for you than doing some prior planning. But whether you plan before you write or plan while you write doesn't matter in the long run if your writing is effective. What does matter is that the writing you hand in goes through the transformation from private to public and has a clear structure.

WHAT IS STRUCTURE?

When applied to writing, structure means the conceptual "skeleton" that holds the writing together. In carefully structured discourse, each sentence relates to the main idea of the paragraph, each paragraph relates to the idea of that section, and each section relates to the plan of the whole. As you might suspect, each of the procedures of thought introduced above lends itself to structuring a piece of writing in a somewhat different way. However, behind all effective structures is an outline or framework of some sort that has to do with the relation between broad generalities (main points or abstractions) and lesser points or supporting evidence and examples.

In fact, levels of generality is what the outline is all about. An outline is a diagram that shows hierarchical structure; the main points (I, II, III, and so on) are general or abstract. They are supported or proved by less general or more specific statements (A, B, C, and so on). These in turn are supported by even more specific information (1, 2, 3, and so on). Even further down the abstraction ladder are the specifics or the details (a, b, c, and so on) that make writing believable and colorful and memorable. Try to keep an outline structure in your mind's eye as you write. Remember that good writing does not stay at the same level of generality or abstraction all of the time. Hearing only about the decisions of the generals during a battle won't tell us everything about what happened; we need information from the front as well as from headquarters. This is a metaphoric way of saying that good writing offers us information from a variety of levels; good writing "moves" between the abstract and the concrete, between the general and the specific, between assertions and proof. Readers find such writing both readable and convincing.

MAKING CONNECTIONS

Sometimes writers do a good job of including the concrete information necessary to support their assertions, but don't do a good job of showing their readers how the information and the assertions connect. Readers want to know exactly how the pieces of information in the text they are reading fit together. They want not only good organization but also signs telling them what the organizing principle is, how the writer is proceeding, why this piece of data leads to this conclusion.

Readers like to know what's coming: "In this paper, I will analyze *x* in terms of *y* and *z*," or "First, I will present findings, then I will explain their relevance." They also like signpost words along the way: *therefore, thus, however, because, in conclusion,* and the like.

EXERCISE 10.3 Being Specific

A Make up a generalization about the students at your school, such as "The problem with students here is apathy," "The students here are high achievers," or "Students here have great school spirit." Now provide a number of specifics to prove or support your statement. What does it take to convince your classmates that your generalization is accurate?

B Before you hand in your next piece of academic writing, read it one more time to see if you have provided your reader with enough signposts, enough instructions for reading your text. (And if they seem scarce, think about adding some.)

DRAFTING

Drafting (that is, writing it down) may be the stage in the composing process that holds the greatest terror. Those of us who plan before we write do so not because we are virtuous but because planning makes us feel braver as we face a blank page or an empty screen. Panic, it seems, is part of the process for most writers. As with the fear you feel at the top of the ski run or on the high dive or at center stage, you have to learn to deal with it. Many would-be writers intensify their own panic by trying to do two tasks at once, two tasks that can only be achieved separately. They try to get it down and get it right at the same time. Thus, for every thought the right brain sends out, the left brain pounces on it and says, "That's stupid! You dummy! Nobody would want to read that!" The writer writes a word, crosses it out, writes a sentence, and then crumples the page. It's called writer's block. The internal editor functions as a nagging and judgmental critic. It is a visitor from the third (systematic) stage of the critical thinking process that has forgotten about the second (creative) stage.

That editor must be told to be quiet for a while. Speak to your negative critic firmly: "Shut up! I don't have to listen to you. I will call on you later. Right now I need to take some risks, and I am too inspired to worry about your misplaced concerns."

As John McPhee, a talented professional writer, says, "You've got to put bad words down. And then massage them." What he means is his first draft, and your first draft, will probably be terrible, but only after you have something on paper can you work out the kinks. Perfectionism applied too early in the process prevents many intelligent people with interesting things to

In many ways, the personal computer has revolutionized the act of writing. Above all, it has made the process of revising a number of drafts easier. Random thoughts can be easily grouped and related into a coherent discussion. When you make minor changes, you do not have to retype the complete manuscript; you simply insert the corrections and print. And you can disseminate your thoughts to a worldwide audience in seconds via an Internet discussion group.

Photo by David Gonzales

say from ever becoming capable or competent writers. In fact, an important reason for engaging in private writing is that writing for yourself, quickly and furiously, will make you feel more confident about drafting. You will not be embarrassed to express outlandish ideas on paper; you will be comfortable with sloppy phrasing. Messy prose can always be tidied up, revised, and edited. Blank pages can't be turned into anything.

REVISING AND EDITING

After you have completed the first sloppy draft, it's time to move to the third critical thinking stage and unleash your internal editor. Try to read what you have written as a reader rather than as the writer. Of course, if you are writing within the time constraints of an examination, you must speed up the entire composing process. You can't revise your answer; there isn't time. (That's why the planning matters so much.) The best you can do is to proofread carefully, add a few words, correct the obvious errors, and turn it in. But essay exams are only one kind of public writing—a special, hurried kind that *requires* you to turn in first drafts. Many college students don't seem to understand this and turn in first drafts as final versions for all of their writing assignments. Not surprisingly, they tend to get C's—or worse.

If you want to get A's on your papers, you have to hand in final versions, not first drafts. That means putting your rough first draft through the process of revision, making it clearer, better organized, more tightly focused, more interesting, and livelier. Some professors will offer to read a draft of your paper and make suggestions before the final version is due. *Always* take them up on this. Their criticisms and suggestions are the blueprints for your A.

Revising (getting the big plan right) and *editing* (tinkering with the words and sentences to make them say what you want them to say) are essential el-

Giving Credit

As Chapter 8 points out, most colleges have strict rules against using another person's words or ideas without giving proper credit for them. Whenever you use other people's words, ideas, or special information in your public writing, you must give them credit and clearly separate their actual words from your own. If you are quoting more than a few lines, set them off from your own writing by indenting the excerpt in a paragraph of its own. For example:

> This is the lesson of all great television commercials: They provide a slogan, a symbol or a focus that creates for viewers a comprehensive and compelling image of themselves. . . . We are not permitted to know who is best at being President . . . , but whose image is best in touching and soothing the deep reaches of our discontent. We look at the television screen and ask, in the same voracious way as the Queen in *Snow White and The Seven Dwarfs*, "Mirror, mirror on the wall, who is the fairest one of all?" We are inclined to vote for those whose personality, family life, and style . . . give back a better answer than the Queen received. As Xenophanes remarked twenty-five centuries ago, men always make their gods in their own image. But to this, television politics has added a new wrinkle: Those who would be gods refashion themselves into images the viewers would have them be.[1]

Note the numbered footnote at the bottom of this box. In the example above, we have inserted ellipses (. . .) in several places to show that we took out a few words to shorten the quote.

When you want to quote a few words or phrases, embed them in your own writing, but separate the words from your own by putting them in quotation marks. Again, give credit in a footnote. For example:

> How do TV advertisements work? Perhaps they present "a slogan [or] a symbol . . . that creates for viewers a comprehensive and compelling image of themselves."[1] If this is so, then television commercials are not truly informative about the products that they sell.

Note how we have added a word of our own in brackets [or] so that the quote will read smoothly in the context when we take out a few of Postman's words. Of course, we were careful not to change his meaning.

You can also paraphrase writers, putting their ideas in your own words. When you do this, be sure that your words really are your own, and again give credit for the ideas:

> As Neil Postman writes, television is not nearly as truthful as the magic mirror in the tale of *Snow White*. The magic mirror told the Queen the truth that Snow White was more beautiful than she. By contrast, television tends to flatter us and hide the sometimes painful differences between ourselves and the politicians we elect.[1]

[1]Postman, Neil. *Amusing Ourselves to Death: Public Discourse in the Age of Show Business*. New York: Penguin Books, 1986, p. 135.

ements of the writing process. Professional writers invest extraordinary amounts of time and energy in revising and editing. So, as an amateur, you should certainly invest some. Actually, revising can be rewarding; turning an ordinary paper into a highly respectable one feels good—though it usually feels best after you are done. And editing—searching for just the right word and changing weak sentences into powerful ones—offers pleasures too.

Some writers give their first drafts to someone else to read. The truth is, everybody needs an editor. Professional writers have professional editors. Finding a good editor for your own writing, though, can be tricky. You need an editor who reads well and who has the courage to say to you—in a kindly way and only when asked—"No, I can't follow your argument. No, it doesn't make sense." You want an editor who doesn't gush or flatter but who can be an honest critic, someone who wants you to succeed but who knows clarity from chaos, good writing from bad. Writing is one of the most complex mental tasks we try. Not surprisingly, we aren't always good at judging our own creations. The editor who didn't experience the sweat you invested in your draft may be a better judge of its worth than you are.

When you think your draft is as good as you can make it in the time available, check for punctuation and spelling. If you are writing on a word processor—and you certainly should be—run the spelling check to catch the typos.

There is no use in pretending that revising and editing your own work is fun or easy or simple. Almost all writers find it worrisome, hard, and complicated—but, alas, necessary. Use the following checklist to get started. Remember, always start with the big issues; there is no point in polishing a paper that doesn't have anything interesting or insightful to say.

Revision and Editing Checklist

1. Does this draft fulfill the assignment? Is its central purpose clear?
2. Does the paper meet the needs of your audience? This is a tricky question when you are writing an academic paper. You are trying to write like an expert for an expert. Sometimes students go wrong by assuming that their reader knows it all already; if you aren't sure about how much explaining to do, talk with your instructor about just what kind of audience you should be writing for—*before* you turn in your paper.
3. Do you give your reader adequate organizational signposts? Do the paragraphs follow logically?
4. How does the paper sound? Do the sentences make sense? One of the best ways to catch problems is to read your paper out loud.
5. How does the paper look? Run a spell-check and a grammar-check one more time.

When at last you hand in your great work, you probably will feel it still isn't perfect. That's okay—nothing is. The ultimate point is not the *product* anyway, but the *process:* What has this piece of writing done for you as a learner? How have you changed because you wrote it?

Writing, private or public, is finally not about grade points. Writing is really about you, about the richness of your life lived in language, about the fullness of your participation in your community and in your culture, about the effectiveness of your efforts to achieve change. The person attuned to the infinite creativity of language leads a richer life. So can you.

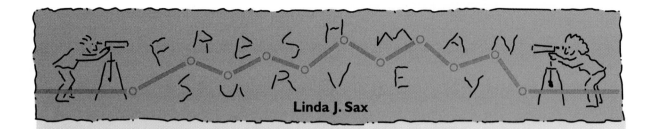

Linda J. Sax

Public Speaking

The graph shows the percentage of first-year students who rate themselves as "above average" or "top 10 percent" in four areas of ability: academics, leadership, writing, and public speaking. Contrast the level of confidence in academics and leadership with the much lower level in public speaking! If you feel anxious about speaking in public, take comfort in the fact that the person sitting next to you probably feels the same.

SOURCE: Higher Education Research Institute, UCLA

Self-Rated Abilities, 1995

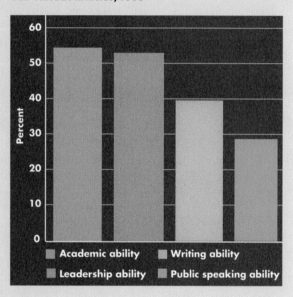

■ SUCCESSFUL SPEAKING

The human brain is a wonderful organ.
It starts to work as soon as you are born
and doesn't stop until you get up to deliver
a speech.

George Jessel

Most of us think we communicate fairly well—after all, we've been at it all our lives, right? But some types of communication situations are downright threatening to many of us—giving speeches, for example. Having all those people staring at us suddenly can be unnerving even to those of us (like teachers) who communicate for a living.

The *Book of Lists* reports that speaking in front of others is the number one fear of Americans. It's more frightening for most of us than death, sickness, deep water, financial problems, insects, or high places. Isn't it sad to realize that what humans fear most is each other?

EXERCISE 10.4 Introduce Yourself

To try your hand at speaking in front of the class, prepare a 3-minute presentation introducing yourself to your classmates. Bring or wear a "prop" that characterizes or caricatures you. For example, if you like to ski, wear your goggles; if you flip burgers on the weekends, wear your apron and carry a spatula. You can talk about your hometown, your high school days, your family, your reasons for going to college, or some other topic your instructor suggests.

Basics of Public Speaking

Speaking in front of others may be our most prevalent fear, but it doesn't have to be. Here are some essentials you may not have considered:

- **Once you begin speaking, your anxiety is likely to decrease.** Anxiety is highest right before or during the first 2 minutes of a presentation.
- **Your listeners will generally be unaware of your anxiety.** Although your heart *sounds* as if it were pounding audibly or your knees *feel* as if they were knocking visibly, rarely is this the case.
- **Having some anxiety is beneficial.** Anxiety indicates that your presentation is important to you. Think of your nervousness as *energy*, and harness it to propel you before and during your talk. The more opportunities you accept to speak, the more this principle will become second nature.
- **Practice is the best preventive.** The best way to reduce your fears is to prepare and rehearse *thoroughly*. World-famous violinist Isaac Stern is rumored to have once said, "I practice 8 hours a day for 40 years, and they call me a genius?!"

Six Steps to Success

If you're assigned a speaking task in class, how should you proceed? Successful speaking involves six fundamental steps:

- **Step 1:** Clarifying your objective
- **Step 2:** Analyzing your audience
- **Step 3:** Collecting and organizing your information
- **Step 4:** Choosing your visual aids
- **Step 5:** Preparing your notes
- **Step 6:** Practicing your delivery

Step 1: Clarifying Your Objective

You need to identify what you are trying to accomplish. To *persuade* your listeners that your campus needs additional student parking? To *inform* your listeners about student government's accomplishments? *What* do you want your listeners to know, believe, or do when you are finished?

When it comes to holding forth in public, a few of us seem blessed with a wonderful sense of freedom. Most are more hesitant. Fortunately, your anxiety can help release the energy it takes to speak well to a group.

© 1992 Chuck Savage/photo courtesy of Beloit College

Step 2: Analyzing Your Audience

You need to understand the people you'll be talking to. Ask yourself:

1. What do they already know about my topic?
2. What do they want or need to know?
3. What are their attitudes toward me, my ideas, and my topic?

In other words, consider the audience members in terms of their *knowledge, interest,* and *attitudes.*

KNOWLEDGE

During your preliminary analysis, discover how much your audience knows about your topic. If you're going to give a presentation on the health risks of fast food, you'll want to know how much your listeners already know about fast food so you don't risk boring them or wasting their time.

INTEREST

How much interest do your classmates have in nutrition? Would they be more interested in some other aspect of college life?

ATTITUDES

Recognize that your listeners will respond with both head and heart (and in this case, stomachs) to your message. How are they likely to feel about the

Figure 10.1 The GUIDE Checklist

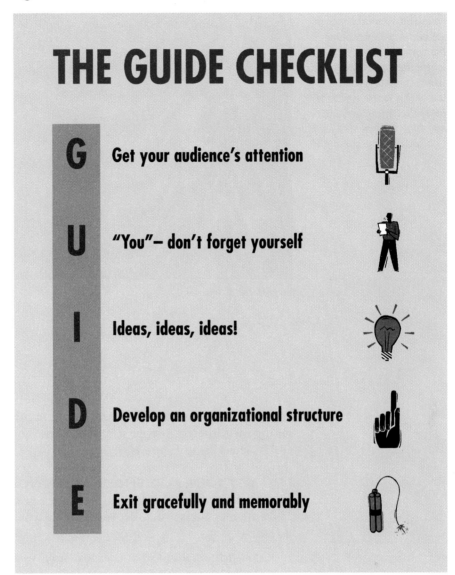

THE GUIDE CHECKLIST

G Get your audience's attention

U "You"– don't forget yourself

I Ideas, ideas, ideas!

D Develop an organizational structure

E Exit gracefully and memorably

ideas you are presenting? What attitudes have they themselves cultivated about fast food?

Step 3: Collecting and Organizing Your Information

Now comes the critical part of the process: "building" your presentation by selecting and arranging "blocks" of information. One useful approach is to choose from the same kinds of procedures suggested earlier for structuring a piece of writing (narration, comparison, cause and effect, and so on).

Another useful analogy for this step is to think of yourself as *guiding* your listeners through the ideas they already have to the new knowledge, attitudes, and beliefs you would like them to have.

Imagine you've been selected as a guide for next year's prospective first-year students and their parents visiting campus. Picture yourself in front of the administration building with a group of people assembled around you.

Think of a speech as a guided tour, with things you want your audience to see and experience along the way. Let them know where the tour is going and what you hope they'll get out of it. Choose a path of ideas that stimulates interest along the way and leads to a satisfying destination.

Photo by David Gonzales

You want to get their attention and keep it in order to achieve your *objective:* raising their interest in your school. Let's be more specific by discussing the GUIDE checklist in Figure 10.1.

[G] GET YOUR AUDIENCE'S ATTENTION

In order to guide your audience, you must get their attention right away. There are many ways to do so. For example, you can relate the topic to your listeners:

> *"Let me tell you about what to expect during your college years here—at the best school in the state."*

Or you can state the significance of the topic:

> *"Deciding on which college to attend is one of the most important decisions you'll ever make."*

Or you can arouse their curiosity:

> *"Do you know the three most important factors students and their families consider when choosing a college?"*

Or you can begin with a compelling quotation or paraphrase:

> *"Alexander Pope once said, 'A little learning is a dangerous thing; Drink deep or taste not the Pierian spring.' That's what a college education is all about."*

You can also tell a joke, startle the audience, question them, tell a story, or ask a rhetorical question. Regardless of which method you select, remember that a well-designed introduction must do more than simply get the audience's attention. You must also develop rapport with your audience, motivate them to continue listening, and preview what you are going to say in the rest of your speech.

EXERCISE 10.5 Writing an Opening

Assume you've been assigned to give a speech at another college or university on the value of your first-year seminar class. Write an introductory paragraph using one of the methods outlined above.

[U] "YOU"—DON'T FORGET YOURSELF

In all this talk of objectives, audience analysis, and "guides," we must not exclude the most important source of your presentation—YOU. You might think that speaking in front of others means assuming a role, being someone other than who you really are. Even in a formal business or professional presentation, you will be most successful if you develop a comfortable style that's easy to listen to. The presentation represents you and your thinking. Don't play a role. Let your wit and personality shine through.

[I] IDEAS, IDEAS, IDEAS!

This brings us to the "meat" of your presentation. Create a list of all the possible points you might want to make. Then write them out as conclusions you want your listeners to accept. For example, let's imagine that in your campus tour for prospective new students and their parents you want to make the following points:

1. Tuition is reasonable.
2. The faculty is composed of good teachers.
3. The school is committed to student success.
4. College can prepare you to get a good job.
5. Student life is a blast.
6. The library has adequate resources.
7. The campus is attractive.
8. The campus is safe.
9. Faculty members conduct prestigious research.
10. Our college is the best choice.

For the typical presentation, five main points are the most that listeners can process. After considering your list for some time, you decide that the following five points are critical:

1. Tuition is reasonable.
2. The faculty is composed of good teachers.
3. The school is committed to student success.
4. The campus is attractive.
5. The campus is safe.

Try to generate more ideas than you think you'll need so that you can select the best ones. Don't be critical at first. Then, from the many ideas you come up with, decide what is relevant and critical to your objective.

As you formulate your main ideas, keep these guidelines in mind:

Main points should be parallel, if possible. Each main point should be a full sentence with a construction similar to the others. A non-parallel structure might look like this:

1. Tuition. (*a one-word main point*)
2. Student life is a blast. (*a full-sentence main point*)

Main points should each include a separate, single idea. Don't crowd main points with multiple messages, as in the following:

1. Tuition is reasonable and the campus is safe.
2. Faculty are good teachers and researchers.

Main points should cover relatively equal amounts of time in your presentation. If you find enough material to devote 3 minutes to point 1 above, but only 10 seconds to point 2, you'd better rethink your approach.

Ideas rarely stand on their own merit. To ensure that your main ideas work, use a variety of supporting materials. The three most widely used forms of supporting materials are *examples, statistics,* and *testimony.*

Examples include *stories* and *illustrations, hypothetical events,* and *specific cases.* They can be powerful, compelling ways to dramatize and clarify main ideas, but make sure they're relevant, representative, and reasonable.

Statistics are widely used as evidence in speeches. Of course, numbers can be manipulated, and unscrupulous speakers sometimes lie with statistics. If you use statistics, make sure they are clear, concise, accurate, and comprehensible to your listeners.

Testimony includes quoting outside experts, paraphrasing reliable sources, and generally demonstrating the quality of individuals who agree with your main points. When you use testimony, make sure that it is accurate, qualified, and unbiased.

Finally, since your audience members are each unique individuals, you are most likely to add interest, clarity, and credibility to your presentation by varying the types of support you provide.

[D]   DEVELOP AN ORGANIZATIONAL STRUCTURE

Now that you've decided on the main points you want to make in your presentation, you must decide how to arrange your ideas. You'll be able to choose from a variety of structural formats, depending on the nature and objective of your presentation. For example, you may decide to use a *chronological narrative* approach by discussing the history of the college from its early years to the present or you may already have chosen some other procedure. Or you might wish to use a *problem–solution* format in which you describe a problem (such as choosing a school), present the pros and cons of several solutions (or other schools), and finally identify your school as the best solution.

Begin with your most important ideas. Writing an outline might be one of the most useful ways to spend your preparation time. List each main point and subpoint separately on a 3 × 5 or 4 × 6 notecard. This allows you to work on a large surface (such as the floor) arranging, rearranging, adding, and deleting cards until you find the most effective format. Then simply number the cards, pick them up, and use them to prepare your final outline.

As you organize your presentation, remember that your overall purpose is to **GUIDE** your listeners. That means you must not neglect connectors between your main points. For example:

Now that we've looked at the library . . .

The first half of my presentation has identified our recreational facilities. *Now let's look* at the academic hubs on campus.

So much for the academic buildings on campus. *What about* the campus social scene?

In speaking as in writing, transitions make the difference between keeping your audience "with" you and losing them at an important juncture.

[E]   EXIT GRACEFULLY AND MEMORABLY

Someone once commented that "a speech is like a love affair. Any fool can start it, but to end it requires considerable skill." Most of the suggestions for introductions also apply to conclusions; that is, you can effectively conclude your speech by relating the topic to your listeners, stating the significance of the topic, ending with a quotation or paraphrase, telling an anecdote, making a startling statement, asking a question, telling a story, referring back to your introduction, or issuing a challenge.

Whatever else you do, go out with style, impact, and dignity. Don't leave your listeners asking, "So that's it?" Subtly signal that the end is in sight (without the overused "So in conclusion"), summarize your major points, and then conclude.

Step 4: Choosing Your Visual Aids

When visual aids are added to presentations, listeners can absorb 35 percent more information—and over time they can recall 55 percent more. Should you prepare a chart? Show a videotape clip? Write on the blackboard? Distribute handouts? You can also make excellent overhead transparencies on the computer using large and legible typefaces. As you select and use your visual aids, consider these rules of thumb:

1. Make visuals clear and easy to follow—use readable lettering and don't crowd information.
2. Introduce each visual before displaying and explaining it.
3. Allow your listeners enough time to process visuals.
4. Proofread carefully—misspelled words hurt your credibility as a speaker.
5. Maintain eye contact with your listeners while you discuss visuals.

Step 5: Preparing Your Notes

If you are like most speakers, you will find having an entire text before you to be an irresistible temptation and end up reading much more of your presentation than you had planned. A second temptation to avoid is memorizing your presentation and eliminating notes altogether. Your memory may fail you. And even if it doesn't, your presentation could sound "canned." A better strategy is to memorize only the introduction and conclusion so that you can maintain eye contact and therefore build rapport with your listeners as you speak.

The best notes are a minimal outline from which you can speak extemporaneously. You will rehearse thoroughly in advance, but since you are speaking from brief notes, each time you give your presentation, your choice of

Rehearse your talk with a friend. Ask for feedback about your words, your posture, your gestures, and anything else that contributes to the total effect of your presentation. Practicing erect and out loud will help you much more than memorizing with your head bowed.

Photo by Hilary Smith

words will be slightly different, causing you to sound prepared but natural in your delivery. You may wish to use 3 × 5 or 4 × 6 notecards, since they are small and unobtrusive. (Make sure you number them just in case you accidentally drop the stack on your way to the front of the room.)

After you have become more experienced, experiment with other methods of preparing notes. Eventually, you may want to let your visuals serve that purpose. A handout listing key points may also serve as your basic outline. As you become even more proficient, you may find you no longer need notes.

Step 6: Practicing Your Delivery

As you rehearse, form an image of success rather than failure. Practice your presentation aloud several times beforehand—harnessing that energy-producing anxiety we've been talking about.

Begin a few days before your target date, and continue until you're about to go "on stage." Make sure you rehearse aloud; *thinking* through your speech and *talking* through your speech have very different results. Practice before an "audience"—your roommate, a friend, your dog, even the mirror. Talking to something or someone helps simulate the distraction listeners cause. Consider audiotaping or videotaping yourself, to pinpoint your own mistakes and to reinforce your strengths. If you ask your "audience" to critique you, you'll have some idea of what those changes should be. Beginning this process early leaves enough time to make changes if something isn't working.

Listening to Your Voice and Body Language

Many speakers seem to need to occupy their hands when speaking when they should allow hands to hang comfortably at the sides, reserving them for natural, spontaneous gestures. Avoid overgesturing or undergesturing.

Don't lean over the lectern, if there is one. Plan to move comfortably about the room, without pacing nervously. Some experts suggest changing positions between major points, in order to punctuate your presentation. The unconscious message is "I've finished with that point; let's shift topics." Face your audience as much as possible, and don't be afraid to move toward them while you're speaking. That communicates your interest in their needs.

Eye contact is even more important. Make contact with as many listeners as you can by looking at individuals as directly and engagingly as possible. This also helps you read their reactions and establish speaker command.

A smile helps to warm up your listeners, although you should avoid smiling excessively or inappropriately. Smiling through a presentation on "World Hunger" would send your listeners a mixed message.

As you practice, also pay attention to the pitch of your voice, your rate of speech, and your volume. Project confidence and enthusiasm by varying your pitch within your natural range. Speak at a rate that mirrors normal conversation—not too fast and not too slow. Consider varying your volume for the same reasons you vary pitch and rate—to engage your listeners and to produce special effects.

Pronunciation and word choice are important, too. A poorly articulated word (such as "gonna" for "going to"), a mispronounced word (such as "nucular" for "nuclear"), or even a misused word can quickly erode credibility. Check meanings and pronunciations in the dictionary if you're not sure, and use a thesaurus for word variety. Fillers such as "uhm," "uh," "like," and "you know," are distracting, too. If your practice audience hears you overusing these fillers, then, uh, like, cut them out, you know?

Finally, consider your appearance. Convey a look of competence, preparedness, and success. As Lawrence J. Peter, author of *The Peter Principle,* says, "Competence, like truth, beauty, and a contact lens, is in the eye of the beholder."

EXERCISE 10.6 Thoughts on Delivery

Think about your teachers this term or in the past; your rabbi, pastor or priest, television speakers; and so on. What aspects of their deliveries impressed or bothered you?

▮SPEAKING ON THE SPOT

Most of the speaking you will do in college and after will be impromptu mini-speeches; that is, they will be given on the spot with little or no preparation. When your instructor asks your opinion on last night's reading, when a classmate stops you in the hall to find out your position on an issue, or when your best friend asks you to defend your views, you give impromptu speeches. Of course, because this kind of speaking is what you do most, it also shapes your image as a successful communicator. For this reason you need to think about how you can prepare for impromptu speaking.

EXERCISE 10.7 **Speaking on the Spot**

A To practice becoming a dynamic speaker, come to class prepared to give a 1-minute speech on your worst pet peeve—something that *really* annoys you. Your instructor will give you a rolled newspaper. Use it to accentuate your main points and emphasize your feelings by hitting the lectern or desk with the newspaper. *OR:*

B For this exercise your instructor will bring a shopping bag filled with common objects to class. Each class member will have an opportunity to draw out an item and give the class a 1-minute sales pitch. The catch, however, is that you must find a new use for the item. (For example, if you draw an egg slicer, you could sell it as a "pocket guitar.") *OR:*

C Select two students to go to the front of the classroom for a "speak down." Your instructor will assign a controversial impromptu topic (for example, "the worst thing about the opposite sex"), and both students will begin speaking on the subject at the same time, each trying to capture the audience's attention and steal attention from the other speaker. After 2 minutes the instructor will call time, and class members will vote on which speaker they listened to most and discuss why.

When you must speak on the spot, it helps to use a framework that allows you to sound organized and competent. There are many ways to arrange your thoughts, but one of the most popular ways is called the PREP formula (Wydro, 1981). Short for *preparation,* this plan requires you to give the following:

[P] **Point of view:** Provide an overview—a clear, direct statement or generalization.

[R] **Reasons:** Give the reasons you hold this point of view, broadly stated.

[E] **Evidence or examples:** Present specific facts or data supporting your point of view.

[P] **Point of view restated:** To make sure you are understood clearly, end with a restatement of your position.

Let's look at an example of how you might use the PREP formula to answer a question in class:

Professor Snodgrass: Do you think the world's governments are working together effectively to ensure a healthy environment?

You: [P] After listening to yesterday's lecture, yes, I do.

[R] I was surprised at the efforts the United Nations General Assembly has focused on the environment.

[E] For example, the industrialized nations have set stringent goals on air pollution and greenhouse gases for the year 2010.

[P]   So yes, the world's governments seem to be concerned and working to improve the situation.

Using a device like the PREP formula, you sound logical, organized, and competent—whether you're communicating with other students in a discussion group, talking to an instructor during office hours, or answering a question in class.

EXERCISE 10.8 Using PREP

Bring five notecards to class with each one listing a question on which your classmates would have an opinion (for example, "Should the first-year seminar be a required course at all universities?" or "Should students have a say in the hiring and firing of college faculty?"). Your instructor will collect the cards and place one card face down on each student's desk. One at a time, each student will turn over his or her card and answer whatever question is written there using the PREP formula. You may not turn your card over until the person before you begins to speak.

■ "YES, BUT . . . "

What if you plan, organize, prepare, and rehearse, but calamity strikes anyway? What if your mind goes completely blank, you drop your notecards, or say something totally embarrassing?

For the most part, we're sure you'll find that things will go smoothly and your preparation will pay off. If you make a mistake, the most important factor is not *that* the mistake occurred, but rather that you as the speaker *handled* and *minimized* the problem. Don't forget, your audience has been in your position and probably empathizes with you. Accentuate the positive; rely on your wit; use the opportunity to emphasize that you're not perfect. Your recovery is what they are most likely to recognize; your success is what they are most likely to remember.

JOURNAL

Write about yourself as a writer. How do you proceed when given a writing assignment? How well does your method work? What are your strengths and weaknesses as a writer? What suggestions have instructors made to you about your writing? Now think of yourself as a speaker and answer the same questions. Do you consider yourself a better writer or speaker? Explain why.

SUGGESTIONS FOR FURTHER READING

Burk, Carol, and Molly Best Tinsley. *The Creative Process.* New York: St. Martin's Press, 1993.

Goldberg, Natalie. *Living the Writer's Life.* New York: Bantam New Age, 1990.

Stone, Janet, and Jane Bachner. *Speaking Up: A Book for Every Woman Who Wants to Speak Effectively.* New York: McGraw-Hill, 1977.

Williams, Joseph M. *Style: Ten Lessons in Clarity and Grace,* 3rd ed. Glenview, Ill.: Scott, Foresman, 1989.

Woolever, Kristin R. *About Writing: A Rhetoric for Advanced Writers.* Belmont, Calif.: Wadsworth, 1991.

Wydro, Kenneth. *Thinking on Your Feet: The Art of Thinking and Speaking Under Pressure.* Englewood Cliffs, N.J.: Prentice-Hall, 1981, pp. 64–69.

Zinsser, William. *On Writing Well: An Informal Guide to Writing Nonfiction,* 4th ed. New York: Harper & Row, 1990.

———. *Writing to Learn: How to Write and Think Clearly.* New York: Harper & Row, 1988.

Problem-Solving and Success in Math and the Sciences

Mary Ellen O'Leary
University of South Carolina

D id someone say "word problems"? Ouch! I've never liked those things! First, they're hokey. Second, they're confusing and they always depend on some new twist. Sometimes I can't even get started on the solution. Trying to make the biggest box possible by cutting the corners out of a rectangle and turning up the flaps—who has a "problem" like that anyway?

Chapter Goals

After reading this chapter, you will find that, by following a carefully structured plan, you can improve your problem-solving skills in mathematics and the sciences. Even though you may not be a math or science major, you will also learn to appreciate these skills as they apply to other academic pursuits and to life itself.

Consider these real-life problems:

In your history class you will have four equally weighted tests, and it takes a 90 average to get an A. Your scores on the first three tests were 87, 92, and 94. What must you score on the fourth test to get an A for the course?

What will you wear to go out tonight, since it's been two weeks since you've done any laundry?

If you need to finish your paper for psychology, study for the Spanish quiz, put in 4 hours at your job, and work out a dozen bugs in your computer program that's due tomorrow, how many people do you have to be?

Would you be able to solve them? How would you go about it?

In the past, you may have encountered "problem-solving" as a kind of enrichment activity in math and other courses, added on after basic techniques and computational skills were mastered. Problems were neatly organized by type, and often only one "correct" solution was allowed for each. In a calculus class, the solution likely had to display the use of differential or integral calculus, while in algebra the solution involved an equation or system of equations. Each of the natural sciences also had its own techniques and prescribed formats for solving problems. The problems themselves were often contrived and artificial, and the answers tended to "come out even"—the computations were "clean" and nothing like real life.

Today, problem-solving is the central focus of science, mathematics, and engineering courses. Modern technology allows students to undertake "messy" computations that would be difficult or impossible to perform by hand. Textbooks can now include more authentic problems with data from the real world. Students are encouraged to tackle a problem in a variety of ways, to experiment with methods of solution, or to start out with a trial-and-error approach. In this chapter, you'll learn how to apply a simple four-step strategy to problems across the natural sciences.

Almost any problem can be solved more quickly and more pleasingly when people work together. Start by talking about ways that the problem could be defined. Listen for different perspectives that suggest different ways of resolving it.

Photo courtesy of Earlham College

CRITICAL THINKING AND PROBLEM-SOLVING

One important milestone in our understanding of the universal nature of problem-solving was the publication of *How to Solve It* in 1945. Although this classic work was written by the distinguished mathematician G. Polya, it really is a book on how to think straight in any field. Polya endorses a method that emphasizes experimentation, discovery, and invention in training students to find things out for themselves. His approach involves inductive reasoning, in which the problem solver starts with particular facts and circumstances and works toward a general conclusion. Polya shows that solutions are found through questioning and guided discovery. He explains that the basic processes of problem-solving are the same whether the problem comes up in an academic setting or in everyday life.

How to Solve It describes the four stages of all successful problem-solving. Perhaps we want to plan the menu and quantities needed for a group outing, determine the surface area of a kidney-shaped swimming pool, or assess the effectiveness of a new medication for Alzheimer's disease. Whatever kind of problem we are tackling, we need to do four things:

- **Step 1:** Understand the problem.
- **Step 2:** Devise a plan.
- **Step 3:** Carry out the plan.
- **Step 4:** Look back.

Polya's steps seem simple and obvious, but they embody powerful notions. As a problem solver, you must first take time to fully understand the problem. Read the problem at least two times, and then reread the last sentence. It often tells you what you are trying to find. Then ask yourself, What information is given? Is it enough to solve the problem? Is there some unnecessary information that can be ignored? Ferreting out the "givens" and the "to find" is a large part of Polya's first step. Often students overlook obvious information that is important for the solution. When a student has missed an important fact, some instructors will ask a mock question such as

"What color is my white horse?!" You can use this question on yourself when you think you may be overlooking something essential.

The second step—"Devise a plan"—is the hardest one for most problem solvers. Looking back at similar problems that you have solved in the past is a time-honored approach, but other strategies will be given below.

The third step may be routine or challenging. Whether it requires simple calculations, sophisticated computer technology, or just basic logic, it should be done carefully. Check and verify the accuracy of each stage as you work out your solution.

In the satisfying glow that comes with solving a challenging problem, the fourth step is often neglected. Real growth in problem-solving is achieved by looking back, reflecting on the problem and the method that led to success. Can you think of other problems that you could solve with the same approach? If you solved the problem for a particular value of a variable, can you generalize your result for other values? Can you extend your solution to a closely related but more complicated problem?

Polya's four steps carry you successfully through a wide variety of problems—from mathematical ones such as the test score needed to get an A average in history, which has a single correct answer, to ones from everyday life such as the laundry dilemma, which may have several appropriate solutions.

■SOME PROBLEM-SOLVING STRATEGIES

Here are nine practical strategies that will help you implement Polya's approach to problem-solving. The first four—*draw a picture, experiment and act out, find a pattern,* and *make a table*—may be especially useful in understanding a problem. The rest of the strategies—*guess and check, solve a simpler problem, use logic, work backward,* and *use mathematical methods*—may apply more to devising a solution.

1. Draw a Picture

Often, drawing a picture can help you better understand the problem and devise a plan. Imagine how hard it would be to tell someone how to drive from a house in Seattle to a house in Miami without a map that showed how various highways are connected. A map or picture can show how things are related to each other, and therefore how to go from one point or step to another.

Make your map or diagram big enough to label clearly. You may lay out or label yours differently from the next person, or you may introduce a coordinate system that is oriented in an unusual way. Don't worry. An individualized approach is fine—as long as it is consistent with the facts of the problem.

EXERCISE 11.1 **The Horse Race**

Note: Read through Exercises 11.1–11.9 as you read the chapter, but wait until you are in a group in class before you actually try to solve them. In the group, share ideas about how to solve the problems. Make sure that each person fully understands the problem. Then work together in devising a plan, carrying out the solution, and looking back on the problem.

In a make-believe horse race between five famous horses, Citation finished one length ahead of Seattle Slew, Spectacular Bid finished ahead of Citation but behind Secretariat, and Man-O-War finished four lengths ahead of Seattle Slew and one length behind Spectacular Bid. What was the finish place of each horse?

2. Experiment, Act Out, and Manipulate

Do anything you can to bring the problem to life: Move pennies around, cut corners out of a piece of cardboard and turn up the flaps, make a three-dimensional model, and so on.

EXERCISE 11.2 **The Intelligent Pinsetter**

The bowling pins shown below have been arranged incorrectly, with the triangle pointing away from the bowler. Can you make the triangle point toward the bowler by repositioning just three pins?

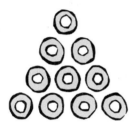

3. Find a Pattern

The better you become at recognizing patterns, the better problem solver you will be.

EXERCISE 11.3 **Looking for Patterns**

Fill in the following missing entries:

1. 21, 32, 43, 54, _____, _____, _____

2. A1, B2, D4, Z26, J10, C_____, _____7, N_____, M13,

   E _____, _____16

3. 1, 1, 2, 3, 5, 8, 13, _____ , _____

4. A, E, F, H, I, K, L, M, N, _____

5. 77, 49, 36, 18, _____

4. Make a Table

Many types of problems can be better understood if the information is laid out in some kind of rectangular chart, grid, or table.

EXERCISE 11.4 ## Which Is Whose?

Ina, Jill, Louis, and Miguel each have a different favorite color among red, blue, green, and orange. No person's name contains the same number of letters as her or his favorite color. Louis and the boy who likes blue live in different parts of town. Red is the favorite color of one of the girls. What is each person's favorite color?

5. Guess and Check

Once discouraged in favor of algebraic or other formal mathematical methods, the guess-and-check technique now is recognized as integral to the way people really solve problems in everyday life.

EXERCISE 11.5 ## Circle Madness

Place the numbers 1 through 7 in the circles below so that the sum of the numbers along each line is 10.

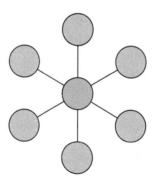

6. Solve a Simpler Problem

Often you can split the problem into smaller subproblems.

How many squares are there in the checkerboard figure below?

7. Use Logic

The basic principles of reasoning are at the heart of most problem solutions.

EXERCISE 11.7 **Three Men and a Wall**

Three men are wearing blindfolds and standing in a line perpendicular to a wall. From a bin containing three tan hats and two black hats, three hats are selected and placed on their heads. Then the blindfolds are removed. Each man is asked to determine what color hat he is wearing. The man farthest from the wall, who sees the two men and their hats in front of him, says, "I do not know which color hat I am wearing." The man second from the wall, who hears the reply and sees the man and the hat ahead of him, says the same thing. The third man, who sees only the wall but has heard the two replies, says, "I know which color hat I am wearing."

Which color is he wearing, and how does he know?

8. Work Backward

Try beginning at the end.

EXERCISE 11.8 The Shopper

You enter a store and spend half your money and then $20 more. Then you enter a second store and spend half your remaining money and then $20 more. Now you have no money left. How much money did you have when you went into the first store?

9. Use Algebra, Calculus, or Other Mathematical Tools

The strategies listed above will lead to complete solutions for some of the problems you encounter in your course work. At the very least, they will help you get started on problems that will eventually require algebra, calculus, or some other specific mathematical method.

EXERCISE 11.9 The Squirrel

A squirrel runs spirally up a cylindrical post, making one circuit for each vertical rise of 4 feet. How many feet does the squirrel travel if the post is 16 feet tall and 3 feet in circumference? (*Hint:* You may not need as much mathematics to solve this as you think at first.)

EXERCISE 11.10 Applying Polya's Method

Think of several problems in your own everyday life. In a small group, explore which of these might lend itself to Polya's problem-solving steps. Then choose one of these everyday problems and write an outline of how your solution could follow the four-step process outlined here.

■ SUCCEEDING IN COLLEGE-LEVEL MATH AND SCIENCE COURSES

Polya's process for problem-solving can be applied to any situation or discipline. At the same time, certain problem-solving skills are developed in very specific ways in mathematics and science classes. As you choose courses to meet general education requirements or as electives, don't avoid mathematics and science. Even outside an increasingly complex and technical workplace, you need scientific literacy in order to vote intelligently and to understand ethical and environmental concerns. You need "numeracy"—

quantitative insights, estimation skills, a basic understanding of probability—to evaluate the statistical claims in advertisements and news reports; not all such claims represent valid applications of scientific and mathematical principles.

A New World of Math and Science

As you move from high school mathematics and science courses to college-level work, you will encounter familiar concepts but at more advanced levels. Here are other differences you may notice:

- The pace will be faster and the material more compressed. The topics covered in 180 days in high school may be presented in forty-two class meetings in college. It is likely that a new textbook section will be covered each day.

- Your instructor may consider your doing the assignments as essential to the course but actually collect your work only rarely or not at all. It will be your responsibility to keep up with the material regardless of whether your work is monitored.

- Theory—mathematical or scientific—may be the central focus. Lectures may be devoted to deriving formulas or to proving theorems. Smaller amounts of class time may be allowed for examples and problems.

- The classes may be larger—perhaps much larger—and the format quite different from anything you have experienced before. Classes may be organized in lecture sections, accompanied by recitations (problem sessions, often led by teaching assistants, where the lecture class is broken into smaller groups).

- Expectations may be different. There may be a greater emphasis on understanding concepts and applying principles than on developing manipulative skills and memorizing facts.

- You may be expected to use your campus computer network to access problem sets, to post your answers or check your results, to use demonstrations, or to access data for analysis. You may learn how to use computer statistical packages or other specialized software.

A Chance to Put Aside Some Myths

It is important to consider how science and math can be different at the college level, especially if your confidence is low in these areas. In high school, you may have yielded to a myth such as "Girls can't do math" or "Minorities don't succeed in science" or "Physics is for an elite few." With such negative attitudes, you may not have performed to the true level of your abilities. You may have been in classes where "the brains" dazzled everyone with their quick answers and perfect test scores. You may have felt inadequate by comparison and decided that you were not a math person or that science wasn't your thing.

Later in the chapter, we will look further at stereotyping in math and science fields. Here, just consider that it's time to abandon such unfortunate and unfounded attitudes. As you embark on your college career, previous failures and frustrations can be put behind you. You are in a different setting with instructors who have little or no knowledge of past performance. This is your opportunity to begin with a more determined and confident approach.

"Congratulations! Yours Is the First Generation . . . "

A widely used precalculus textbook contains a startling statement that goes something like this: "Congratulations! Yours is the first generation not to suffer through long, tedious problems involving the computational uses of base-ten logarithms." This is an encouraging thought, indeed. But on the next page, the text continues, "So now we are going to show you what you missed," and proceeds to give several pages of long, tedious computational log problems requiring "characteristics," "mantissas," "antilogs," and "interpolation"!

If these terms are foreign to you, be thankful that you are a student in this era of supercalculators and computers. This technology frees you to pursue interesting problems, look for underlying principles, and focus on the big picture in your mathematics and science course work. Thus, the textbook exercises on logarithms seem like an April Fool's joke—they should have disappeared along with the slide rule.

Today, logarithms are studied as a profoundly important family of functions, but logs are no longer needed to simplify arithmetic operations. Your calculator handles those operations immediately, with as many as thirteen decimal places of accuracy. But that is only the beginning of the power at your fingertips. You can produce an instant picture of a function with your graphing calculator and analyze its properties. With symbolic algebra capability on a computer or calculator, you can apply powerful mathematical methods with ease. Programming techniques allow you to customize solutions to an unlimited array of problems.

The pace of technological improvement has been breathtaking, as capability and cost have moved in opposite directions. One can only speculate on the wonders to come as multimedia approaches are tapped in education, as the

communications superhighway is opened to all citizens, and as palm-top computers become as essential as textbooks for college students. The promises of tomorrow are intriguing, but the technology of today has already significantly enhanced the study of mathematics and science. Your generation does have cause for celebration—not just because you are the first to escape tedious exercises with logarithms, but, more significantly, because you can apply the power of technology to delve deeply into real problems.

EXERCISE 11.11 — Replacing Myths

As you think back on your high school experience, describe yourself as a math/science student. Have you been influenced by a particular negative myth? Explain. Now write a short paragraph describing the positive attitude that can replace the myth in your mind.

Strategies for Success in Math and Science Courses

Here are some simple but important strategies for handling any math or science course.

1. **Make Full Use of Placement Tests and Advisors.** Most colleges will help you begin where you have the greatest likelihood of success.

2. **Wherever Possible, Choose Your Instructors with Care.** Follow the advice of those you trust who have gone before you. Remember, though, that your learning style may differ from your friend's. Also, there is much to be gained from taking a course with a demanding instructor who evokes your best efforts, even though other students may advise against it.

3. **After the First Meeting in a New Class, Reflect and Plan.** Write out specific goals for that course, along with a game plan for achieving them. Your goals will probably start with a desired letter grade but should also include a statement of what you hope to gain from the course. Reflect on why you are taking the class and write a paragraph for yourself on why success in this particular course is important to you and to your future. Your game plan expresses in detail your commitment to succeed. Here are some commonsense suggestions that you can incorporate in your plan to help you achieve your goals.

   1. *Sit front and center.* Look alive and interested—it will help you to *feel* alive and interested.

   2. *Attend every class.* Getting the notes from a friend is not the same as being there yourself. Don't get behind. In mathematics, and sometimes in science and engineering, concepts "stack up" vertically. Missing any portion undermines the whole structure.

   3. *Expect to spend the time.* Unlike high school, in college you master the material on your own outside of class. Although it's generally accepted that you need to devote 2 hours out of class for every hour in class, for some courses you will need to devote more than 2 hours, particularly when the material is dense and complicated.

   4. *Be neat and organized.* Diagrams drawn with rulers, correctly labeled functions and expressions, clearly presented and legible solutions—all convey a positive impact, much like a word-processed and laser-printed term paper.

   5. *Use all available resources.* Get to know the instructor and stop in during office hours. One-to-one help is even more valuable if you come prepared for the meeting—that is, if you have already worked hard on the problems and have marked questions in your notebook. Use the Math Lab if your school has one and attend review sessions when

they are offered. Take advantage of technology—calculators and computers—as allowed and available.

6. *Keep track of how you are doing.* Record your scores in a specific place in your notes. Hang onto all tests, quizzes, and solution sheets, and use them to study for the final exam. Be serious about the final. Cumulative 2- or 3-hour exams that cover the entire content of the course require advance planning and intense, focused effort.

4. **Think About the Bigger Picture.** In addition to the practical strategies just described, try to reflect on the nature of the learning in the particular discipline covered in the course.

For example, physics may require mastery of dozens of formulas but contain only a few basic concepts. What are these essential ideas? In biology, in what ways are organisms or systems all more or less alike? In what ways are they different? How much does the discipline rely on quantitative methods? What are some of the applications? What is the role of the discipline in the economic and environmental challenges facing society?

EXERCISE 11.12 Planning for Success

Choose part A or part B.

A *If you are currently taking math or science courses:* List each science and/or each math course that you are taking. For each course, write a statement of your goals for the class including what you expect/hope to learn and your plan for achieving those goals.

From the courses you have listed, choose the one that you expect to find most challenging. Then review Exercise 8.3 on forming study groups. Write out a plan for organizing a study group in that course. Are there people in that class that you already know? Are there people you know who are in the same course but in other sections? Can you ask the instructor for help in setting up a group? Plan how you can best handle the logistics: time, place, and commitments to meet regularly.

B *If you are not taking math or science courses now but plan to do so in the future:* Consult your course catalog. List a science and/or math course that you plan to take. Write a statement of your goals for the course including what you expect or hope to learn and your plan for achieving those goals.

Ask at least three people who have taught or taken the course what the course is like. Find out more about the purpose and requirements of the course. Find out which instructors are most likely to be right for you. Plan to do your best to take the course with one of them.

■ MAJORING IN MATH OR SCIENCE OR ENGINEERING

Perhaps the choice seems obvious for you. As a child you had a fascination with nature and an overflowing curiosity about how the universe works. You asked questions about clouds, you wondered how airplanes got off the ground, and you took a seed pod apart to study all the intricate detail inside. You pondered the geometric patterns in snowflakes, and you learned how to build a homemade battery.

How to Do Your Math— or Chemistry, Biology, Electromagnetics, or Statistics—Homework

No matter what the science or math course, the following five-step process can help ensure that you successfully complete homework assignments.

1. **Take 10 minutes to review.** Don't let your notes get cold. As soon as possible after class, skim through them. Put a question mark next to anything you don't understand at first reading. Put stars next to topics that warrant special emphasis. Try to place the material in context. What has been going on in the course for the last few weeks? How does today's class fit in?

2. **Warm up.** When you are ready to sit down and do the assignment, look through your notes again. But this time, use pencil and paper to *rework all the example problems*. Compare your solutions to the ones in your notes. Now read through the related material in the text. Go back to the examples, one at a time. Cover the solution, and *attempt to do each problem on your own*. Look at the author's work only after a serious personal effort.

3. **Do the assigned problems.** Now you can start on the homework itself. As you read each problem, ask, What is the given? What needs to be found? Of the given information, what is essential and what is extraneous? Read the problem several times and state it in your own words. The last sentence may provide a starting point; it usually spells out what you are trying to find.

4. **Persevere.** When you hit a problem you cannot readily solve, move on after a reasonable effort. After you've worked on the entire assignment, come back to those that stumped you. Try once more, and then take a break or work on another subject. You may have to mull over a particularly difficult problem for several days. Think about the problem at odd moments. Inspiration may come when you are waiting for a stoplight or just before you fall asleep.

5. **Wrap up.** When you complete an assignment, look back and reflect on the experience. Talk to yourself about what you learned from this particular problem set. Generalize about how the problems differed, which strategies were successful, and what form the answers took. Think about variations and extensions of the problems where appropriate.

You may be thinking, "The 10-minute review and the warm up are well and good, but who has time to do all that extra work? I'm lucky to get the assigned problems done." In reality, the approach does work and it actually saves time. Try it for a few weeks. The frustration that comes when you tackle your homework problems cold will disappear. The hours you devote to assignments will be more productive, and you will become more comfortable and confident in the subject area.

The science that you studied in prior schooling answered many of your questions and raised others. Now, as a new college student, you are considering a major in the natural sciences, engineering, or mathematics.

Or perhaps the choice was not so certain. Sometimes well-intentioned parents direct a son or daughter to a field such as engineering or computer science *only* because they foresee a good job with a secure future. Students themselves may base the major decision on a romanticized view of the life of, say, a marine biologist or an aeronautical engineer. Television has imprinted appealing images on all of us, and students may envision themselves swimming with dolphins or gazing from a spaceship back toward Earth.

The truth is, choosing a major should not *begin* with an analysis of the job market or with the question "What can I do with it?" Instead, you should search for a field that you enjoy *for its own sake*. Parental advice and employment prospects will ultimately influence your choice, of course. But the process should begin with an awareness of your talents and interests, and the choice should comprise a "good fit" with the discipline itself.

Leaving Options Open

Whatever forces influence your choice of major, leave your options open as much as possible. As you start out, explore different disciplines and possible majors by taking as wide a variety of courses as you can. And even if your school requires an early declaration of major, this is not an irrevocable decision. Admittedly, a tightly packed curriculum—such as that of engineering or pharmacology—will make exploring more difficult. But wherever possible you should choose courses that will apply in more than one program, and devote your first terms in college to discovering what you enjoy and where you are motivated to excel.

EXERCISE 11.13 ## Exploring Your Options

Consider the major you are in or are planning to pursue. Explore your college catalog. Find at least two other mathematical or science-related majors that you might consider. What makes your current major better for you than the others? Discuss your choice with a group of students in other majors. Explain why your present choice is number one and why the other possibilities also make sense. Plan to explore (and possibly enroll in) at least one course related to each of those majors.

Fighting Common Misconceptions and Deterrents

Perhaps you are drawn to a major in a scientific field or to a particular career involving mathematics or science, but something is holding you back. Behind your lack of confidence lies a myth or deterrent that you can recognize and overcome.

SCIENCE BELONGS TO THE "ELITE"
You may accept this common notion that science, mathematics, and engineering belong to an elite few, to exceptional individuals with special aptitudes whose genius was apparent to all at a very early age.

SCIENTISTS ARE NERDS
Your mental picture of a scientist might be a person with hair slicked down and parted in the middle who wears heavy dark-rimmed glasses and a plastic

Born in the U.S.A.

The question "Why do men do better than women on SAT mathematics tests?" has led some people to jump to the conclusion that there might be a possible physiological basis for this difference.

An equally interesting fact is that the number of successful women in science and mathematics who were born outside the United States is very much higher than the number of successful American-born women. A typical example is a woman physicist who emigrated from Europe to New York as a high school student and found she was considered peculiar because in America "girls were not supposed to be smart." She had not encountered this pressure in Europe.

The top women who have had successful careers in America in my own field of nuclear physics have nearly all been born outside the United States. In many countries, such as France and Italy, the number of women in science is incomparably greater than in the United States. In my recent contacts with Soviet Jewish immigrants to Israel and the United States, I have been impressed by the large number of women mathematicians, physicists, and engineers. One of these women was the only woman with a tenured position in a leading American university mathematics department for several years. Recently they hired another woman as a full professor—she was born in China.[*]

Does this professor's information cast doubt on the idea that men are somehow more suited

Mathilde Krim (Ph.D., genetics), founding co-chair of the American Foundation for AIDS Research. Nationality? Swiss. What explains the relative strength of European and Asian-born women in mathematics and the sciences?

physiologically to mathematics than are women? Why do you suppose men do better than women in math on the SAT? How could you test your explanation?

*Adapted, with permission, from Harry J. Lipkin, "Women in Math and Science," *UME Trends* (American Mathematical Society, October 1990).

pocket protector filled with pens. You think of someone who virtually lives in his laboratory and has no social life. Because of movie stereotypes and the scarcity of role models, you may not picture a woman or a member of a racial or ethnic minority when you think of "scientist" or "mathematician" or "engineer."

In the past, scientists may have come from a select and rather narrow band of the population. That is much less so today. Today we recognize that women and minorities can "do science"—indeed that they *must* do it if we are to stay competitive in a global economy.

SCIENCE MAJORS ARE PREPARING FOR A NARROW LINE OF WORK

Perhaps you find science fascinating but believe that all scientists work in isolation and fear that you will not find a career that suits your personality.

Science is a collaborative field. If you're thinking about a major or career in science, begin now to get to know your science teachers. Find out about their research or other science interests outside class. See where your interests match.

Photo by David Gonzales

In truth there are all kinds of jobs available to those with an undergraduate or a graduate degree in a scientific field. Some involve a great deal of interaction with people; others are based in pure research. The possibilities for the kinds of work that you can do with a science background, and the kinds of ways that scientists now go about solving problems, are much broader and less compartmentalized than formerly.

Careers in medicine are the goal for many life science majors, and many possible careers exist within the health care field. But that is only one large professional area open to people with science degrees. Your campus career center can outline the opportunities, and your advisor may be able to tell you about the various kinds of careers that recent graduates have entered.

Remember, the kind of work you end up doing is the result of a complex web of personal circumstances. The choice of undergraduate major is only one factor.

SCIENCE IS JUST TOO HARD

People often believe that the more math involved in a subject, the more difficult it is. The quantitative skills required for most of the sciences and for engineering present a hurdle for many students. The compression of the material—the sheer volume of information and the rapid pace of coverage—in many science courses is a challenge. The technical vocabulary and the required level of precision add to the perception of difficulty. A significant challenge to science majors is the difficult schedule. With the extra hours required for laboratory courses, students in scientific fields have very full programs.

Of course the work will be challenging, but that is a major reason why it will also be rewarding. If you are fascinated with how the universe works, or appreciate the creative process of formulating a hypothesis and designing a test for its validity, or enjoy pursuing a complicated problem to a successful conclusion, you can be successful in a scientific major and find great personal satisfaction in your chosen field.

■PLANNING FOR SUCCESS

Communication and Support

Some students believe that if they go through all the right motions, make good progress, and systematically check off all requirements, they will become scientists, mathematicians, or engineers. But there are less tangible elements that play perhaps an even more important role. You need to find a "home" within your chosen discipline. The personal connections and out-of-class interactions that you have with faculty and fellow students will add depth to your developing insight into the true nature of your chosen field. Through outside discussions and topics investigated simply for curiosity's sake, you will reinforce and extend the knowledge you are gaining in the classroom. A growing sense of identification with the field will help you persevere and excel in a scientific major, even in the face of mathematical hurdles, demanding class and lab schedules, and compressed course curricula.

The Key Role of Study Groups

One important study at Harvard investigated the factors affecting perseverance in science of undergraduate women who had started college as science majors. Similar research has looked at the forces affecting retention rates in scientific fields for other categories of students. These studies have yielded a common and somewhat surprising result: the crucial role played by study groups. Evidence is mounting that, from kindergarten through college, students learn best when they struggle together, when they learn from and teach each other.

The study group not only promotes higher achievement in a particular course, but serves other functions as well. It becomes one of the social circles of the college experience—a group of friends in which the common thread is interest in science or mathematics or engineering. The study group promotes personal identification and a sense of belonging within the discipline. It provides support and encouragement when things aren't going well. It often acts as a reality check, giving you a better sense of how much time is actually required to succeed in certain courses as well as a context within which to assess your progress.

Take a leadership role in organizing a study group if necessary. Start with a group of three to five students in one course, and progress to a second course after your first group is well established and meeting regularly. Some of the most effective groups include students from a particular major who work together through several terms and various courses.

The Wide Range of Opportunities

As your undergraduate years progress, you will want to expand your contact with other students, faculty members, and other professionals in your field, both at your school and in outside employment. In a co-op position or summer internship, you can experience the professional life of an engineer or scientist and make contacts that will be invaluable when you are looking for a permanent job. Through on-campus opportunities—as a research assistant in a faculty member's lab, for instance—you can receive formal or informal mentoring, gain specialized technical knowledge, and experience significant personal growth. All these factors enhance your course learning and nurture your development as a scientist.

 **EXERCISE 11.14**   ## Creating a Major Plan

If you are considering a major in a math- or science-related discipline, write out a plan of courses that could carry you to graduation. Study your school's catalog and consult with your advisor to be sure that your list meets all requirements. If your class will also be reading Chapter 15 on choosing a major, talk with your instructor about how to coordinate this exercise with your work in that chapter.

JOURNAL

Find a "hero" in science or mathematics. The person may or may not be living today. Read a few articles about the work and personal qualities of your hero or heroine. Explore why you find this person inspiring.

SUGGESTIONS FOR FURTHER READING

Adams, James L. *Conceptual Blockbusting: A Guide to Better Ideas,* 3rd ed. Reading, Mass.: Addison-Wesley, 1986.

Paulos, John Allen. *Innumeracy: Mathematical Illiteracy and Its Consequences.* New York: Hill & Wang, 1988.

Polya, G. *How to Solve It: A New Aspect of Mathematical Method,* 2nd ed. Princeton, N.J.: Princeton University Press, 1955.

Rosser, Sue. *Female Friendly Science.* Elmsford, N.Y.: Pergamon Press, 1990.

Smith, Richard Manning. *Mastering Mathematics: How to Be a Great Math Student,* 2nd ed. Belmont, Calif.: Wadsworth, 1994.

Tobias, Sheila. *Succeed with Math: Every Student's Guide to Conquering Math Anxiety.* New York: College Entrance Examination Board, 1987.

Computing for College Success: Technology on Campus

Steven W. Gilbert
American Association for Higher Education

Kenneth C. Green
Claremont Graduate School

People keep telling me that it's getting easier to use computers. I'm glad to hear that. How about if I just put off learning how until they're so easy to use that I don't even know I'm using one?

Chapter Goals

If you've already had some experience using computers, this chapter will help you explore more ways that you can use them in college and benefit from information technology. If computers are new to you, that's okay too—this chapter will get you started. If you're already completely at home with computers or maybe even a techno-wizard, the chapter may reveal some unique aspects of computing on your campus.

As recently as five years ago, students planning nontechnical majors could, with some effort, avoid computers and information technology. This no longer is possible. Regardless of your major or career plans, computers and information technology will be important tools and resources during your college years—and beyond. Indeed, even if your major or career seems to have little to do with technology, you're probably better off starting to master computers now than letting them master you.

By the time you graduate from college, there will be new ways to use information technology that are difficult to imagine today. The World Wide Web already provides electronic access to books, newspapers and magazines, scientific and commercial data, pictures, audio and video recording snips, and other text and graphics. Soon, movies, interactive entertainment, and more may begin to enter our homes, schools, and offices via the "information superhighway." This could provide tremendous benefits (or distractions!) for students at every level of education.

Here we offer an introduction to some of the most obvious and accessible applications of information technology in the late 1990s. This will give you a good start if you have had little or no prior experience with computers and information technology. As you become more confident with and knowledgeable about the tools available today, you will also be better prepared to take advantage of future options and new technologies.

■ WHAT YOU NEED TO KNOW

If you had a class on computing in high school, you probably learned something about *bits, bytes, RAM, ROM,* and other technical terms that help explain how a computer works. The traditional way of learning about computers emphasizes the *technical aspects* rather than the *applications* (how it works rather

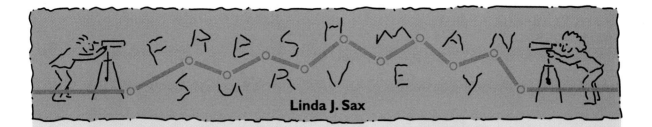

Linda J. Sax

Computers on the Rise

Not too long ago, the average college student relied on a typewriter or a pen and paper to complete assignments. These days, increasing numbers of students are using computers to write, compute, compose, design, explore, and communicate.

As the accompanying figure shows, students today are coming to college with much more computer experience than their counterparts did a few years ago. How do you think the rise in computer usage has affected student performance? Study habits? Class assignments? Instructors' expectations? How do you think computers will change the college classroom into the twenty-first century?

Percentage of Freshmen Using a Personal Computer "Frequently" in High School, 1985–1995

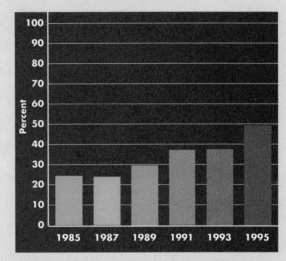

SOURCE: *Higher Education Research Institute, UCLA*

than what you can do with it). For most people, however, using a computer has become like driving a car: You don't really need to know what's under the hood. Rather, you need a general sense of how the car works—and how to make it work well for you. You also must know what to do if the computer won't do what you need it to do.

In many ways, computers are still young, "immature" technologies that are evolving very quickly. Information technology still is not standardized enough to let us give you specific instructions that will work for most combinations of computers, software, printers, and telecommunication setups. Instead, we'll try to point you in the right direction, describing the skills you need to acquire and identifying where you might find help and training on your campus.

One reassurance and a caution: In normal use, it is almost impossible for you to damage a computer—unless, of course, you spill a drink on the keyboard or hit the machine angrily because it "ate" or "destroyed" some of your work. Although you cannot break a computer through normal use, you should understand that a computer can do major damage to your work: For example, it can quickly (and completely) erase the term paper you labored on late at night and through several weekends.

Ask for help. Good helpers will know what to do but will show you how rather than doing it themselves. They will also know how to explain things to you in a way that you can understand. If they don't, ask questions. If questions don't get through, look for a different helper.

Photo courtesy of Grinnell College

■ COMPUTERS (AND PEOPLE) AT YOUR SERVICE

Engineers and scientists created computers to serve people—to help them work more quickly, efficiently, and productively. If you have an experience with computers (or computer "experts") in which this doesn't seem to be true, then something is wrong with the situation, not with you. Don't be reluctant to ask questions or to ask for help. Approach technology with the assumption that you are going to use it as necessary for your purposes, whether those purposes lead you to need information technology rarely or almost constantly.

Don't be intimidated by machines—or by computer "experts." Do the "experts" give you the impression that you aren't up to their standards or that you'll never master the technology? *They are wrong!* The problem is their attitude, not your ability to understand and use the technology.

It's always best if you can find another student or a computer technology staff person who knows how to do most of the things you need to do with a computer and who is able and willing to explain things to you while treating you like a competent person. Best of all is someone who will let you do the work instead of taking over and turning you into an observer.

■ A COMPUTING STRATEGY

What Are Your Options?

You need a *computing strategy* or plan, similar to the plan or strategy your college or any business has developed for computing. You have essentially the same three choices. You may have already chosen one of them, perhaps unconsciously, based on your prior experience. But note that your first year of college is a great time to make *conscious* choices and to change. Think a little about which of the following is the strategy you really want to be using and try it on for size for a while. If it doesn't fit well, try another.

- **Option 1: Extended Avoidance.** Try to avoid computers completely. Eventually, you will encounter some situation in which it will be nearly impossible to proceed without computing skills. For most students, a long term paper provides that occasion. Writing instructors will tell you that good writing is really good *re*writing; word processing makes it easier to change, correct, modify, and amend your work. Additionally, once you become comfortable with word processing software, you'll probably find it easier to learn other computer applications. Extended avoidance involves major risks. First, growing numbers of faculty are using computers and information technology resources in their classes: sending students to computer labs to use various kinds of simulation software, assigning students to find resources on World Wide Web sites as part of the reading materials for a class, or using electronic mail to communicate with students outside class sessions. In sum, technology today involves much more than word processing. If you consciously choose to avoid technology, you may lose out on some important aspects of your college learning.

- **Option 2: The "Everybody's Doing It" Strategy.** Pay attention to what your peers are doing with computers and information technology. Look around you at other students who have career goals similar to yours and are majoring in the same field. Are 20 percent or 25 percent (or more) of them using computers for term papers and other class work? If so, perhaps you should begin to do the same. Having the same computer tools as many of your peers means that you are likely to have several people you can ask for help when you're having trouble.

- **Option 3: Leader of the Pack.** Become a technology "expert." Your career goals or your personal interest in technology may prompt you to be among the first of your friends and peers to exploit the power of information technology. You might decide that you definitely need great information technology skills as you compete for jobs or academic opportunities. When asked, "Why should we hire you?" you can answer, in part, "Because of my excellent technology and information management skills." Indeed, you might also enjoy being one of the people that other students (and even some faculty) turn to for help with their computer questions. Find out if your institution has a formal program for training and managing student assistants who can help their peers and even faculty learn to use information technology.

Each strategy clearly leads to different decisions and activities. Each approach depends both on you (your skills, talents, and interests in computers) and on your campus computing resources.

What If You Really Hate Computers?

If you really hate computers (or feel intimidated by computer people), you could try to pick a major, specific classes, and even a way of life to help you avoid today's technology. However, these choices are getting more and more limited—and could have unfortunate consequences. Face the facts—technology skills will play a significant role in the twenty-first-century job market.

So meet this issue head on. You might begin with one of the more recent books about computers intended for people who are not interested in technology and would rather avoid it. The books assume you don't have a natural enthusiasm for playing with machines or learning new technical terms. You might also look into workshops for beginners where you will learn with others who might share your concerns. You also could make a pact with a friend who shares your attitudes about computers. Agree that you will help each other. Attend the same training class, review the class activities and exercises, work together after your classes, and push (and pull) each other along. Or approach someone who is just a few months ahead of you who still remembers how painful the first steps were.

A growing number of colleges provide computer instruction and give computer-based assignments in first-year courses, especially writing classes. Often, lab sessions for these classes take you into a computer classroom to learn the basics: how to use a computer and to develop word processing skills. Sometimes these classes also teach you how to use the computer to explore the library card catalog and other kinds of on-line information resources. Many residence halls or libraries have computer labs staffed with troubleshooters who can help you with your learning.

If possible, develop your basic word processing skills several weeks before your first paper is due. Use the preparation of that paper as a practical objective to focus your efforts and distract you from your fears and discomfort. Look forward to the reward of a professional-looking paper.

EXERCISE 12.1 Choosing a Strategy

In a small group, talk about your reactions to computers and the options described above. Ask what options others might choose and why. Compare your situations, your prior experience, and your concerns. Move to another group if no one in yours seems to favor your strategy. Try to find at least one other person in your class whose choice or experience is fairly similar to yours. Then talk about what you want to do.

EXERCISE 12.2 Rating Your Computer Skills

A Rate your current computer skills from 1 (low) to 5 (high) for each of the following:

_____ 1. Keyboarding or typing

_____ 2. Word processing

_____ 3. Electronic mail

_____ 4. The Internet and the World Wide Web

_____ 5. Computerized library/card catalog search

_____ 6. Spreadsheets/budgeting software

_____ 7. Presentation graphics

_____ 8. Computer programming

Where do your answers cluster? Mostly 3's, 4's, or 5's suggest you have some advanced skills. Mostly 1's or 2's suggest you're just getting started and should think carefully about ways to acquire skills that will help you during and after college.

B Next, identify the technology skills that are important for students in your major. Which skills are important for people in the career field you intend to pursue? If you don't know, find out. Ask an academic advisor, a faculty member, or a career counselor about the key technology skills for your major and intended career. Match their answers about key skills against your self-assessment of your skills. Taken together, this will help you set priorities and map a strategy for developing and enhancing your technology skills.

My Current Skills	My Planned Major	My Intended Career	
_____	_____	_____	Keyboarding or typing
_____	_____	_____	Word processing
_____	_____	_____	Electronic mail
_____	_____	_____	The Internet and the World Wide Web
_____	_____	_____	Computerized library/ card catalog search
_____	_____	_____	Spreadsheets/ budgeting software
_____	_____	_____	Presentation graphics
_____	_____	_____	Computer programming
_____	_____	_____	Other: _____
_____	_____	_____	Other: _____

C Use the goal-setting process from Chapter 1 to address any needs suggested by step B.

GETTING STARTED

Keyboarding

Alas, cheap and highly efficient systems for converting speech to print are not yet available and are not expected in the next few years. And machines that recognize your handwriting and convert your written notes into computer text are still primitive. Consequently, keyboarding still remains the core skill for using a computer. If you can type, you're in good shape for working with a computer. If you can't type, you need to learn. Find a keyboarding course that fits into your schedule, or learn on your own with an inexpensive "typing tutor" software package. (To find the right one, look at ads in a computer magazine or ask someone in a computer store or your campus bookstore for suggestions.)

Accessing Computers

Does your college sell computers through the bookstore? Will you have to pay a lab fee for computer time and access for some of your classes? Will you be charged printing fees? The answers to these questions may depend on your major or your courses.

Different campuses have different policies and procedures for providing access to computing resources for students. A small number of schools require (or strongly encourage) all students to own computers. These institutions have committed themselves to bringing information technology into nearly every aspect of academic life—from wiring residence halls into a campus network to including the cost of a computer as part of total college costs.

Many campuses encourage computer use in other ways: selling computers in the bookstore, providing campus labs for student use, offering e-mail accounts to students, establishing a campus "home page" on the World Wide Web, allowing students to set up their own home pages, and offering various support services such as training classes and computer consultants to help solve specific problems.

EXERCISE 12.3 Campus Strategies and Access

A As a class find out what steps your school has taken to make information technology available to students and faculty. What seems to be its overall plan, if any? Be sure to check for any booklets and guides, intended for students and faculty, that describe services and resources.

B Place a check mark next to each of the following that is available on your campus.

_____ 1. "Intro to Computers" classes

_____ 2. Training seminars/workshops on specific computer applications such as word processing, graphics, e-mail, and Internet/World Wide Web

_____ 3. A computer support center for assistance

_____ 4. A call-in phone number for computer assistance

_____ 5. Computers for sale in the bookstore

_____ 6. Dial-up access to the campus network from a computer in campus living quarters or at off-campus locations such as your home or place of work

_____ 7. Resources to help you construct your own home page on the campus World Wide Web site

_____ 8. Something else: _____

_____

Finding the Right Kind of Help

Even as you become comfortable doing routine computing tasks, you'll still have occasional problems or questions. Most often, you'll want to ask questions such as "Now that I'm doing X, how can I get the computer to do Y?" Some questions may concern the kinds of information sources and services available through your computer and telecommunications options. Here are some sources of help:

- **FAQs.** When you're getting started using computers, most of the help you will need will be what insiders call "frequently asked questions," or FAQs. Your campus may have a source of FAQs and answers "on-line." ("On-line" means that you can locate answers via the computer itself. See the section "On-Line Services, the World Wide Web, and the Internet" later in the chapter.)

- **Support for academic computing.** Many campuses have a group or department responsible for *academic computing*—the use of computing and information technology for instruction and research. This unit often includes a "user support service" that can help you. Academic computing is usually not the same as the department of computer science or whatever academic department is responsible for teaching computer courses for credit, but if you have trouble finding the right place, someone in the computer science department can probably tell you where it is.

- **A few good souls.** Find a few people with whom you feel comfortable asking questions about computing. First, identify one or two who can answer questions that you think may be "dumb." They should be people who know enough about computing and who are especially likely to treat you nicely no matter how basic the question may sound. Second, identify one or two others you want to reserve for questions that you think are more sophisticated. Here you need someone who has some expertise—even if he or she doesn't have such a great "bedside manner." Any of these "help" people might be students; if so, be sure that they know what they are talking about and are not overconfident. Also, try to find at least one librarian who is able and willing to answer questions about computer-related information resources in the library and through your campus network (if you have one) and the Internet and World Wide Web (if you have access to it).

- **A few good notes.** Don't be reluctant to make notes about the steps necessary to perform a task that is likely to be important to you. Computers are still so new that the sequence of steps required to do some of the things you will want and need to do may not make much sense. Don't be surprised or upset when this happens. Don't assume that you will automatically be able to remember the magic words and motions next time. Write down the steps on these pages or in a special notebook. Keep handouts or "cheat sheets" where the information will be handy when you need it again.

- **A few good books.** In almost any bookstore, you will find dozens of books about computing, information technology, and computer software.

EXERCISE 12.4 **Help at Hand**

1. Locate the user support services part of the academic computing office (it may have some other name). Fill in the following:

   Office name: _____

   Location: _____

   User support phone: _____

   User support hours: _____

2. Ask academic computing or others whether there is a list of FAQs and answers and how to get it.

3. Names, addresses, phone numbers, and hours of availability of people who are good for basic questions:

_____

_____

_____

_____

4. Names, addresses, phone numbers, and hours of availability of people who are good for advanced questions:

_____

_____

_____

_____

Preventing Disaster

Whether you're using your own computer or another one, take precautions to avoid the most serious catastrophes.

1. **Don't do anything silly to a computer.** Don't spill things on it. Don't drop it. Don't hit it. However, yelling and screaming are okay and often fairly common and acceptable behaviors.

2. **Learn how to start, stop, and restart the computer you are using.** Two common problems are (1) a computer gets "hung up" so that no matter what you do, absolutely nothing changes on the screen, and (2) you get "lost" in an application program and suddenly don't know what you're doing and can't figure out how to move back to doing something that was making sense. In both cases, the last (and very desperate) option is to turn the computer off and then restart it. Usually, you will lose whatever work you had done since the last time you saved or filed your work. But at least you will be back in operation.

3. **Learn how to make "backups."** Be sure you understand the different ways to make backup copies and know where you can save and store copies of your computer work (your computer files). Learn what *diskettes, hard disks, internal memory,* and *network server shared storage* are and whether each is available to you. Learn how to use them. Always think about how serious a problem it would be for you to re-create (from notes and memory) your current work. If it's no big deal, then don't worry about it. However, for your most important projects, you should probably:

   a. *Save* the document at least every 5 or 10 minutes while you work on it. Give the file or document a name that you can easily recognize and remember. Use numbers to help identify the version number of the document. (Is it your first draft or your fourth rewrite?)

   b. *Make a backup copy.* Desktop computers such as an IBM-compatible (sometimes called a Windows computer) or a Macintosh allow you to copy documents (*files*) from the computer to a diskette (and vice versa). Be sure you save your work on the document frequently and also at the end of a work session. If what you're working on is extremely important, keep the diskette in a different room or building than the computer.

c. *Print a "hard" (paper) copy* of the most up-to-date version at the end of each work session and keep it in a safe place. Use it to make corrections for future revisions.

EXERCISE 12.5 **Preventing Disaster**

For any of the following information that you don't already know, ask someone and record enough notes here to remind yourself what to do.

1. To start your computer:

_____

_____

_____

_____

2. To turn off and restart your computer (be sure that this procedure is considered safe by your "expert"):

_____

_____

_____

_____

3. To file or save a document on the computer:

_____

_____

_____

_____

While you're at it, check to see if there's a way to set the computer to file or save automatically every 15 minutes; if so, do so.

4. To file or save a document from the computer onto a diskette and to "format" or "initialize" a diskette (only format or initialize a diskette if you must and if you are ready to have any existing data on the disk erased—forever):

_____

_____

_____

5. To print a document from the computer onto paper:

_____

_____

_____

_____

Computer graphics aren't only for art and video commercials. They are also revolutionizing how computers help us see, share, and analyze complex information.

Photo courtesy of University of Utah

■APPLICATIONS

The kinds of software used for college work are generally the same as or similar to those used in the business and professional world. Word processing is the most widely used, and we'll talk about it in the next section. We'll also talk in detail about electronic mail and World Wide Web browsers, two forms of telecommunication software that let you communicate from your desktop computer with other computers, large and small, across the campus or across the country. Through these, you can find and retrieve all sorts of information.

Spreadsheets

A spreadsheet program divides the computer screen into "cells" arranged in rows and columns. In each cell, you can type a number, a short bit of text, or a formula that performs some calculation on the contents of other cells. Spreadsheets are most widely used for budgeting and financial analysis. They are also useful wherever there is a need to experiment and calculate with numerical data. One great advantage of a spreadsheet over old-fashioned pencil-and-paper methods is that, once you have typed in the data, the computer does all the calculations, such as finding the total of a column of numbers. Spreadsheets are better than calculators in that the spreadsheet stores the data so that it never has to be retyped. One way to learn about spreadsheets is to use one to work out your personal budget.

Databases

A database can be used to manage, sort, summarize, and print out large amounts of systematic alphabetic or numerical data. Businesses use databases to keep records of things such as inventory, customers, and transactions. The electronic catalog in your campus library is a database. Researchers use databases to record and manipulate research data, such as survey results. One way to get started with a database is to use it in place of an old-fashioned personal address book.

Graphics and Presentation Software

Graphics and presentation software lets you capture, create, and display words and visual images, maps, and other graphic data on the computer monitor, on projection screens, and in printed form. Computer graphics are everywhere you look today in art and advertising. They also have many uses on campus. For example, medical schools are now creating and using graphics software to teach human anatomy and medical diagnosis.

Personal Productivity Software

Personal productivity software includes personal information managers (PIMs) such as electronic phone books, calendars, and other tools that help you manage information about your activities and contacts. Sometimes these come as bonus products when you buy computers.

EXERCISE 12.6 Knowing What Can Be Done

Review the software descriptions you've just read. If you're already familiar enough with an application to know how it might be useful to you, place a check mark by it. For the rest, consult someone else or a magazine or other source for some fairly simple explanations and write them down. Exchange your explanations with others in your class until each of you understands these terms. Add more of your favorite new applications, if any (or ones you are curious about), and do the same thing.

■WRITING PAPERS WITH WORD PROCESSING

For most first-year students, word processing is by far the most important application of information technology. No longer is there any excuse for spelling errors in written work. Learning to use word processing with a spelling checker is essential. It is equally important to learn the limitations of most word processing software: It cannot help you pick the right word, cannot supply the ideas, and cannot do the research for you. But if you learn to use a reasonably powerful word processor, your papers will look better and require less effort to write and revise. Some word processing packages can even take care of the placement and numbering of footnotes for you.

Word processing involves some risks and costs. If you are careless, you can lose the results of your work just at the wrong time. It may be addictive: You can find yourself exploring too many features that you don't really need yet, getting too fancy with choosing type fonts (sizes and styles), and changing the appearance of your documents instead of working on the content. Finally, access to a good word processing program may increase your tendency to procrastinate. If you can produce a nice-looking paper in a few hours and can make changes right up until you are ready to print, you may be inclined to put off starting, and the quality of your writing may suffer.

When you use a spelling checker, keep in mind that such programs don't end the need for your own intelligent proofreading. For example, spelling checkers won't pick up errors such as typing "there" for "their" or "too" for "to." Thus you will need to continue to proof your own work.

The main advantage of word processing over other forms of writing is that you can revise with much less effort. With practice, you can find your own most effective techniques and "rhythm" of writing—but this will work only if you also learn how to plan your time to let yourself do more than one draft before the final version. "Sleeping on it" is one of the best things you can do between drafts.

EXERCISE 12.7 Word Processing—Beginning and Advanced

A *For those not already using word processing:* Learn by doing a real task. Pick an assignment in one of your courses in which you must produce a paper, preferably not too long and due somewhere between one and five weeks from now.

If your campus offers some sort of noncredit or nominal credit workshops to introduce word processing, sign up and go. If you can find a tutorial disk or video, try it.

Use the computer to write, save, revise, and print your paper. Remember that famous computer advice "If all else fails, try reading the manual." If the manual is impenetrable, buy another, easier book about your particular software package. Learn the basics of how to make your report look nice, but don't try to get too fancy this time. Keep your design simple.

B *For those already using word processing:* Mark each of the following either T (true) or F (false).

1. When I use the computer to prepare a paper, I routinely use a spell-checking program.

2. I never turn in work that I have done on a computer that has spelling errors.

3. I know how to use advanced features of my word processing program such as headers, footers, and footnotes, and I actually use them fairly often.

4. I always save my work regularly and never lose long or important pieces of my work.

5. From session to session, I back up my work on disk.

6. I rarely waste much time getting fancy with fonts, paragraph formats, and other superficial stuff.

7. When I write a paper, I always go through a stage in which I focus hard on deciding what I want to say and how I plan to organize my thoughts (perhaps more than once).

8. I don't procrastinate. Whenever possible, I start writing a paper early and leave time to think about it between drafts. I always plan time to revise.

9. I always proofread work before I turn it in or share it with others.

Do your answers suggest any need for improvement? Discuss this in a group.

ON-LINE SERVICES, THE WORLD WIDE WEB, AND THE INTERNET

The Internet

Ten years ago, comparatively few people knew—or cared—about the Internet. It was a technical resource that largely involved engineers, scientists, and computer tekkies. In the mid-1990s, public awareness of and interest in the Internet exploded. Newspaper and magazines started covering the Internet; bookstores began to sell new titles intended to help nontechnical computer users—people interested in doing things with computers, rather than how computers work—make sense of the Internet and, by extension, the World Wide Web.

What is the Internet? At its simplest level, the *Internet* is many thousands of computers connected by telephone lines used to exchange messages and find or offer other forms of information. There is no recognized governing body, just widespread agreement among users on some standard ways of packaging and sending information.

Although the number of people using the Internet and the amount and variety of information available through it are growing rapidly, it has been difficult for analysts to get an accurate count of the number of users. For example, in summer 1995, one research report suggested that there were 27 million Internet users in the United States. A second report issued in January 1996 suggested the number was 9 million. And a third report, focused just on the use of the Internet in higher education, estimated some 7 million Internet users among the 16 million students, faculty, and staff of colleges and universities in the United States.

A second measure widely used to estimate the growth of the Internet is the number of home pages on the World Wide Web. At the end of 1993, there were fewer than 400 home pages; by summer 1995, analysts counted more than 28,000 and estimated that the number of World Wide Web home pages was doubling every 108 days. By March 1996, the "doubling period" was down to 90 or maybe 75 days, depending on which report you reviewed.

If the numbers about the Internet seem confusing, they all point in the same direction—explosive growth for a worldwide information resource that has growing importance for students and faculty. The Internet and the World Wide Web are also widely used in business, industry, and government. In sum, it is no longer the domain of the tekkies.

Most colleges and universities have computer networks of their own and access to the Internet. The personal computer that you now own or may soon own can be hooked up to the Internet through a direct connection to your campus network or through a *modem*, a small device that lets your computer communicate with other computers via telephone lines. If your institution has a Campus Wide Information System (CWIS), you may, through a microcomputer, find information about course offerings, campus policies and regulations governing students and faculty (perhaps including an "acceptable use" policy or guidelines suggesting appropriate on-line behavior), phone numbers, faculty ratings, course schedules, other institutional publications, and the campus events calendar.

Consider learning more about the Internet and the World Wide Web, just as you are learning about how to use your college libraries. It is a *major* resource for finding information in a variety of forms for you to use as background information or for research required for term papers. Although your initial contact with the Internet and the World Wide Web may be prompted by a class assignment, you may return to the Internet and the World Wide Web for fun or for personal reasons. Once on the Internet, watch out for the day that you get sucked into "browsing the Web" or "surfing the Internet" and look up from your computer 5 hours later having missed a meal!

EXERCISE 12.8 Learning to Use the Internet

A Go to your list of "help" people and ask if it's possible to use the Internet from your campus system. Find out whether you are charged for using it. Learn how to get started.

Note: There is a difference between using a microcomputer or terminal that is connected directly to the Internet via a campus network and connecting to the Internet via a modem and telephone line. Be sure that you get the instructions that best match your situation.

B Learn how to connect to your college library catalog (if available) and search for a book. See if you can figure out if the library has a copy of the book available to borrow right now. Find out whether other libraries have interlibrary loan agreements with yours and catalogs accessible through the Internet. From them, you can request a book that your library doesn't have, at little or no cost and with little effort.

The World Wide Web

The World Wide Web is simply the most recent, exciting, powerful way of linking information within the Internet. What makes it different is both the kind of information that can be packed together and how it can be linked.

The Web permits packaging information on individual computers in a way that allows the inclusion of pictures, sounds, and other formats as well as text. Individuals can set up their own personal sets of information—home pages—once they have learned a little about the language of the Web (Hyper Text Mark-up Language, or "HTML"). Watch for new kinds of word processing software that make it easier and easier to create Web pages without having to learn very much at all about the actual HTML language.

Most important, the Web enables people to build "hot links" into their home pages. Usually, these appear as buttons or words underlined in color. When you are "browsing" someone's home page, you may "click" on any hot link and immediately find that you are reading a different section or a completely different home page or Web site. The person who built the home page you were reading first had selected another place that seemed relevant and made the arrangements that permitted you to hop to it.

What is so different about "browsing" the Web from previous uses of the Internet is both the variety of media formats you will find and the fact that you never need to know which computer you're looking at or even to think about what path your hops are taking. The Web links and your browsing software do that work for you.

The good news is that you can keep hopping from site to site until you find what you are looking for. Hundreds of thousands of people (at least!) have made information available in this way. The bad news is that there is no mechanism for policing these folks, for determining who among them is well intended or competent, for confirming which sites are full of accurate information, and for detecting which are pure garbage.

Right now, the World Wide Web is a little like an old-fashioned library card catalog in which someone dumped all the cards on the floor, and then thousands of individuals strung threads between those cards that they personally believe should be connected. But no one is in charge of the overall arrangement of all those strings. And these same individuals can change their minds any time and remove or change the connections of the threads—with no notice to anyone. You can't be sure that what you find today will be in the same place or at the end of the same links tomorrow.

EXERCISE 12.9 Learning About the World Wide Web

A Find out whether your college or university offers some form of access to the World Wide Web.

Are there publicly accessible workstations with direct connections to the Internet and Web browser software? Where are they located, and what are the rules governing your use of them?

_____

_____

_____

If you have your own computer, does your campus offer a way of dialing in to a modem that will enable you to connect to the Internet? If so, what software is recommended to permit you to explore the Web from your home or anywhere else? What fees are involved?

_____

_____

_____

Note: The most popular software for Web use is available free on the Web. Get some help from the computing people on your campus on how to obtain the Web browser they recommend.

If you work at a company that has Internet access, find out if you are permitted to use the machines to get on the Web—and what sort of software they provide.

B Once you figure out how to get on the World Wide Web, "browse"! You'll probably need to figure out how to use one of the "search" tools. (See the box on page 152 in Chapter 9.) Ask for some help. Find out if your library has someone on staff who helps students learn to use the Web and to find things on it. See if you can find a home page for your own college.

C Try to use the Web for your next research paper. See how quickly you can find sources relevant to your topic. Ask for a model of the format for citing references found on the Web.

Electronic Mail—Some Basics

Like many business networks, your campus network may have a system of electronic mail (e-mail) that lets you send and receive messages via computer. These messages may be local—on your campus to other students and to faculty—and they also may be sent out on the Internet to people at other campuses and to off-campus organizations and firms.

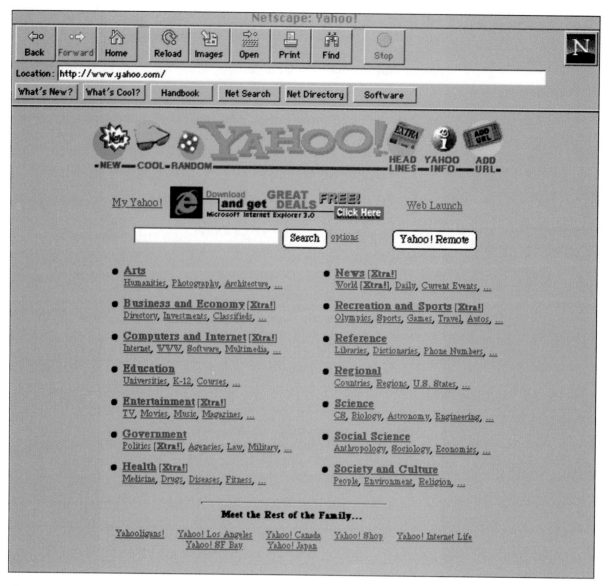

Shown here is the WWW home page for YAHOO (www.yahoo.com), one of several WWW "search engines" that provide an index to Web resources.

Perhaps the main advantage of e-mail is that it is asynchronous—you and the other person do not have to be using it at the same time. Each computer has a brief *address* (a sort of "mailbox") on the system. You can send a message that will travel almost instantly to someone else, and you then will wait until he or she sits down at the computer, reads it, and sends an answer back.

More and more faculty members are using e-mail to communicate with their students. It may be easier for you to get a faculty member to answer a question via e-mail than to wait in line after a class to try to schedule time during office hours. Indeed, you might well view e-mail as just another way to communicate with your teachers.

COMPOSING, EDITING, AND SENDING E-MAIL

Most people compose e-mail by typing directly; generally e-mail involves very little editing or rewriting. Spelling, capitalization, and grammar errors are usually considered okay—and even add a touch of personality—to informal e-mail communications, but if you have too many errors they become distracting to the reader.

✓ ℋ   ✓ ⊞   ✓ ⇥   ▯   ✓ QP   [Send]

```
          To: Steve Gilbert
        From: cgreen@mail.earthlink.net (Casey Green)
     Subject: Computer Chapter
          Cc:
         Bcc:
 Attachments: :Casey:2:Computing/Draft 2:
```

Steve:

Attached is the revised draft of the FYE chapter on computing. I think
the new material looks good and reads well. Clearly many things have changed
since the first edition of the book; the role of the WWW -- barely out of the
research labs when we drafted this for the first edition -- being a good example.

The attached document is a MS Word file. Please get back to me in the next day
or two with your comments.

Casey

A sample e-mail screen. The message also includes an attached word processing file.

When sending longer or more formal e-mail messages—for example, a comment to one of your instructors—it is a good idea to compose and edit the message using your usual word processing package and then send it via e-mail or "upload" it to the e-mail system. (*Uploading* means launching a file of electronic information onto a network or into a larger system; *downloading* means taking a file out of the system for your own use.)

Ask if your campus supports e-mail packages that make it easy to upload a document or simply to send it to someone else via e-mail. If you cannot avoid using one of the more complex e-mail systems, once you find out how to upload, make some notes and put them and any available written instructions where you will be able to find them the next time you need to upload or download.

COMPUTER ETIQUETTE: REPLYING, PAUSING, AND FLAMING

One nice feature of most e-mail systems is that you don't have to look up someone's e-mail address every time. Usually, there is an easy way to reply to an incoming message. Unfortunately, people often use the "reply" feature too quickly or without thinking carefully. Thus, be sure that you understand how your "reply" option works in general and that each time you use it you know where your reply will *really* go.

One common mistake occurs when you reply to a message that came from a "Listserv"—a kind of on-line information service that relays messages provided by one person to all others on the service. When you respond to a message forwarded from a Listserv, it is easy to think you are replying to the original author. However, the local e-mail system may send your message to the address that sent it to you—which may be someone other than the author and may even be a list of hundreds of people. It's usually easy to find out how your "reply" feature works and easy to check that your outgoing reply is going where you intend, to one or two or three people, rather than to ten or fifty or hundreds.

Flaming refers to sending highly emotional, highly critical messages via e-mail. Sometimes this is exactly what you want and need to do, but most "flames" result from someone having an immediate strong emotional reaction to a message just received, writing an almost stream-of-consciousness response, and sending it without thinking about the consequences. The problem is that with most e-mail systems, once you have sent a message you cannot "unsend" it. Unfortunately, an apology offered afterward rarely undoes the harm or takes away the hurt.

The real solution to the "reply" problem and to the risk of inadvertent "flaming" is to pause and take a deep breath before you send any e-mail message. Take a few seconds to review what you have written and to ask yourself if what you intended to say will be clear from what you have typed. If you aren't sure, fix it! Remember that e-mail makes it very difficult for the reader to know when you are joking or when you are extremely serious. Even typing a sideways smile— :) —doesn't always work to convey humor. AND IF YOU TYPE ANYTHING IN ALL CAPS, IT HAS THE EFFECT OF MAKING IT SEEM LIKE YOU ARE YELLING AT THE RECIPIENT! Use these techniques sparingly.

Here is a short list of common e-mail codes called "Smileys."

:-)	Smile
:-}	Grin
;-)	Wink
:-]	Smirk
:-x	Kiss
:-*	Ooops
:^D	Great
I-{	Good grief!
8-)	Wide-eyed
:-D	Laughing out loud
:-(	Frown
:-/	Chagrin

Try to avoid flaming. Especially if you are communicating via e-mail as part of your course work, make sure that your e-mail message is something you will be proud to have others read. Also, when you communicate with your instructors, don't waste their time with unnecessary questions or comments. People are already beginning to resent junk e-mail just as they do conventional junk mail.

One last reminder about e-mail: It is usually easy to "forward" e-mail—to send a copy of a message you receive to someone else or to a list of e-mail addresses. Technically, this process usually can be done without permission from the original author and without the author knowing that the item has been sent to others. The ease and speed with which a message or document can spread through the Internet is truly amazing. This has two consequences for you.

- The possibility always exists that an e-mail message that you send to one person will be seen by others. Pause and think about that before you send it.

- It not only reflects common courtesy but may be a legal requirement that you get permission from the author (or copyright holder) before forwarding a message or document. Pause before sending it, and consider the likely wishes of the author or publisher.

Be careful to avoid publicizing what was intended as a private message. If you have any doubt about the author's wishes (or any doubt about maintaining a friendship), check with the author before sending a copy to someone else.

EXERCISE 12.10 Learning to Use E-Mail

A Is e-mail available to students on your campus? If so, learn how to use it. Find out if and how you will be charged for using e-mail. If possible, get an account and an e-mail address. Write your e-mail address here:

_____

Write your password, if any, somewhere else where you won't lose it.

B Exchange e-mail addresses with another student enrolled in this course and also with the faculty member teaching this course. Write in the e-mail addresses below:

Teacher name _____ E-mail address _____

Student name _____ E-mail address _____

Student name _____ E-mail address _____

Send some messages to each other. Learn how to use the "reply" and "forward" features and practice them together.

1. Learn how to use your e-mail system in conjunction with your word processing package. (If the process is too difficult, save it for special occasions that involve very long messages.)

2. Try exchanging messages with someone else on your campus and with someone at another campus who also has an e-mail account.

C Find out if any faculty members on your campus are using e-mail. Find out if any of your own teachers are using e-mail, and make a point of asking an intelligent question via e-mail and making use of the answer.

D Send an e-mail message to the publishers of this book. Tell them how you like the book and how you think it could be improved for future first-year students. Address your message over the Internet to the editor:

chaun_hightower@wadsworth.com

E Use e-mail to speak out on an issue that is important to you. Send a letter, via e-mail, to any of the following:

NBC's *Dateline* news program, in response to a story:
dateline@nbc.news.com

The White House: *president@whitehouse.gov*

Newsweek magazine in response to a recent article: *letters@Newsweek.com*

F Subscribe to a Listserv. Consult your library for advice about finding a Listserv that discusses some topic of interest or use to you. Find out whether it is "open" (permits anyone to subscribe himself or herself) or "closed" (requires the permission and intervention of the list "owner" to subscribe). Find out whether it is "unmoderated" (anyone can send a message that will be automatically and immediately distributed to everyone who has already subscribed) or "moderated" (messages submitted are reviewed and edited by a human "moderator" before they are distributed to the full list). Get an estimate of the daily level of messages and how much it varies.

Once you have gotten the name and e-mail address of the Listserv, make sure you understand how to "unsubscribe" before you subscribe! To subscribe, the usual arrangement is simply to send an e-mail message to an address associated with the Listserv. This message should usually have the subject or header section blank. The body of the message should say "SUBSCRIBE nameofListserv yourfirstname yourlastname" and nothing more. For example, to subscribe to the list that discusses issues of teaching, learning, and technology for higher education, send a message to

LISTPROC@LIST.CREN.NET

saying

SUBSCRIBE AAHESGIT JOHN DOE

and then wait for the messages you will begin receiving.

■ETHICAL AND LEGAL ISSUES

Your campus may have materials or courses explaining local policy and relevant law. In any event, you are responsible as an individual for knowing enough to avoid breaking the law. With the ongoing development of so many new technologies, the environment in which you work as a student has become much more complex. You are likely to face many of the same dilemmas now facing faculty and businesspeople. Old laws don't quite address all the new situations, at least not in obvious ways. You are likely to be tempted to do things with computers that would seem clearly wrong in other situations.

The best advice is, first, don't "disconnect" your ethical principles just because you're working with computers. Second, learn enough of the relevant law to be comfortable; at least learn whom you can go to on campus for reliable advice about what is and is not permitted. The library and the computing center are good places to start.

EXERCISE 12.11 **Computer Ethics**

Find out if your college or university has adopted a policy or guidelines for ethical and legal use of computers and telecommunications. (This may be called an "acceptable use" policy. Ask people in the academic computing office, the computer science department, or the library.) If it has, get a copy. Be sure you understand the policy. Are there any aspects of the policy that seem unclear or difficult to follow? Be prepared to discuss your thoughts in class.

JOURNAL

If you have been writing your journal assignments on a computer, what barriers, if any, stand in the way of your taking full advantage of the new information technology? What might you do to break through? If you haven't been using a computer, what might you gain from doing so?

SUGGESTIONS FOR FURTHER READING

Things change so fast in this field that it is almost impossible to recommend books that won't be outdated by the time you read this. If you need to read something to help you get started or to use as a reference, ask your computer resource people what to read. Try skimming some computer magazines, especially if you're trying to make a decision about buying a computer. If your campus computing organization has some pamphlets, "cheat sheets," or training materials such as videocassettes, those may be very useful to you. Consider taking (even noncredit) workshops offered by your campus computing organization or your library.

The Liberal Arts: Foundation for Lifelong Learning

H. Thorne Compton
University of South Carolina

A rt, history, music, English, psychology! I came here to major in (put your major here), so why do they insist I take courses in some subjects I could care less about? My buddy's a biology major who wants to go into medicine. What the heck is he going to do with those courses in sociology and English lit they're making him take?

Chapter Goals

After reading this chapter, you should understand more clearly why a strong education in the liberal arts is a "must" for success in life. No matter what your major is, this chapter reminds you that part of every career involves the human factor, from how we think and from what sources we draw our ideas and opinions, to how we interpret the behavior of others and arrive at solutions to problems large and small, personal or professional.

When I started college, I had a clear idea of what I wanted to *be,* but very little idea of what I wanted to *study.* I wanted to be a journalist, and I imagined that I would take a lot of courses that would teach me to write exciting, perceptive, investigative essays for newspapers, and that would be my college education. Instead, after my first advisement session, I found myself taking required courses in European history, logic, French, biology, and English—none of which was even *distantly* related to what I wanted to do. I was frustrated, even angry, but when I confronted my advisor about this, he had no sympathy. "How are you going to be a writer," he said, "when you don't know anything to write *about?*" When I questioned him about how French and biology would help me to be a journalist, he told me to come to see him at the end of the year if I still felt they were irrelevant. He ended the interview by telling me, "If you want to write about insects, you study insects; if you want to write about human beings, you study the human species. That's what the liberal arts are all about."

That was the first time I had really paid attention to the phrase *liberal arts,* and I had no idea what it meant. By the end of the year, I wasn't so sure what was "irrelevant" anymore, and the more I explored in the liberal arts, the less sure I became of who I was and what I wanted.

At the same time that I was learning what to think *about,* I was learning *how* to think in a very different way. Some of my teachers seemed to challenge everything I had been taught. With others, I found it impossible to take notes—the whole class was spent in a dialogue and the instructor never said which answers were the right ones. It took almost three years to see the relationship between *what* I was learning and *how* I was learning to think about it.

Although I eventually changed my career goal several times, I never gave up needing to understand the human species. Today, as a teacher of theater history, an academic advisor, and an administrator, I spend a lot of time talking to students about this important part of their college education. The liberal arts are for some students a part of their professional training; for others they are the focus of their education. For all, the liberal arts are the firm foundation for the rest of learning.

Studies in the liberal arts help to maintain the connection between our collective past accomplishments and the resources we need to succeed in present and future challenges.

Photo by David Gonzales

■ THINKING ABOUT THE LIBERAL ARTS

Most of us have heard the phrase *liberal arts college* or know someone who majored in the liberal arts. Many colleges and universities require a set of liberal arts courses for everyone. What are these liberal arts? Where do they come from? Why are they called "liberal"? And what makes them important in a time of increasing technological complexity and specialization?

The *liberal* in *liberal arts* has nothing to do with politics. It comes from a Latin root word *liber*, which means to free. (*Liberate* comes from the same root.) An art (from the Latin root *ars*) is a skill, an ability to do something. So the liberal arts are the skills and abilities, or understandings, that set us free. The liberal arts focus heavily (though not exclusively) on how human beings think, behave, and express themselves within their cultures and their broader world environment. Among other subjects, they include such things as language, history, geography, and the arts—in essence, the culture of human beings. These studies liberate us by helping us to understand ourselves, our culture, and our world.

How does studying such subjects make one free? A broad definition of freedom is the ability to act independently. Imagine that you win an all-expenses-paid trip to Paris. Your friend, who speaks French and has traveled all over Europe, agrees to meet you at the Paris airport. Somehow you end up on a plane that lands near a small town in Germany. You have very little money (you weren't supposed to need any) and speak no German. Through a fellow passenger who speaks a little English, you discover that no plane will leave this airport for the next three days. What do you do? Your companion agrees to help you briefly, but you find that you are absolutely dependent on her to be able to do the simplest thing (even find the rest room), and you are ready to panic when she leaves. It is as if you had become a child again. You can't make decisions by yourself because you don't understand anything about where you are or how to get what you need. You have lost your independence, your real freedom to act because you cannot understand the culture you are in or manipulate your world. It is not simply a question of not knowing German (though that would surely help). It is also a question of knowing how the German culture that surrounds you works.

Like the traveler into another culture, a person without the background of a liberal arts education is likely to lack an understanding of much that goes on in life around him or her. The liberal arts allow you to understand not only where you are, but how the people there think, communicate, and survive. With this knowledge, you can take control of yourself and your environment. You can really be free.

EXERCISE 13.1 Your Institution's Ideal Graduate

In your college catalog, find the "mission statement." It is usually on the first few pages and should be prominent. What language do you find there about the liberal arts? What does it say about the type of college graduate the institution wishes to produce? Write a brief paper that compares the mission statement to the concept of liberal arts discussed in this chapter. If asked, present your paper to the class.

The Liberal Arts Tradition

The liberal arts are certainly not a new idea in higher education. The liberal arts college is the ancestor of all modern colleges, universities, and professional training programs. Only in recent times has training in law, medicine, engineering, and business administration been separated from a broad liberal arts environment. The liberal arts core provides the context for all other kinds of education because it gives us an understanding of ourselves, our culture, and our physical environment.

A liberal arts program is normally organized around several groups of disciplines that integrate knowledge from a variety of perspectives. These groups usually include:

- **The arts,** which study human thought and behavior through the creative works of people from the earliest appearance of humans until today. Creating works of art is a way of both understanding and expressing ideas and feelings.

The Arts and Technology

It is important to dispel the myth of conflict between technology and the liberal arts. In earlier years, computers were primarily tools of the sciences. With the development of the personal computer, computers have become a major tool for research and communication in the liberal arts.

Word processing has, of course, virtually replaced the typewriter. Students now find it far easier to edit and revise their papers.

The Internet has become the medium of choice for academic communication, both for private and collective discussions. Electronic document archives, databases, and journals in the humanities and social sciences constantly appear on the Internet, initially on "gopher" sites and more recently on the World Wide Web.

Computers not only make a diverse range of material readily accessible but also provide it in a form conducive for analysis and excerpting. The complete texts of literary masterpieces and legislation at all levels of government are now available on-line. Computer literacy is no longer solely for geeks; it is an important tool for a liberal education.

- **The humanities,** which study human thought and experience through the written record of what people have thought, felt, or experienced in a variety of cultures. Some of the subject areas included are language, literature, philosophy, history, and religious studies.
- **The social sciences,** which study human beings and their behavior from a variety of perspectives: as individuals (psychology), within social groups (sociology), within cultures (anthropology), or as economic or political entities (economics and political science).
- **Quantitative studies,** which create systems for describing the physical world or human behavior in abstract or mathematical terms, as in mathematics, statistics, computer science, and similar fields.
- **The natural sciences,** which study the physical world, its inhabitants, and the symbolic relationships within it as in physics, biology, chemistry, geology, astronomy, and other sciences.

Although colleges and universities are normally divided into separate departments, such as History, Management Studies, and Music, the knowledge that each department seeks to explore or teach is often closely interrelated with the knowledge explored in other departments. Psychology is the study of human behavior, but in order to understand human behavior, it is useful to understand the human mind as it is revealed in its creations—literature, images, music, or drama. We must also understand something about human biology, about the social systems that regulate human behavior and how those systems come to be. A liberal arts program implies study that integrates a wide variety of disciplines, most of which have applications to professional programs such as mass communications, business, law, nursing, criminal justice, and education.

The Liberal Arts at Your Institution

Use your college bulletin and class discussions to discover how the liberal arts are organized at your institution. Apply your critical thinking strategies of *systematic* thinking to answer the following:

1. Which departments can be labeled as part of the liberal arts? Which cannot, and why?

2. How many liberal arts courses are you presently taking? How many of these are in your major? What applications do the others have to your major?

3. Are you taking any liberal arts courses that are required by your major? If you feel that some of these do not really apply to your major, why do you think that you are required to take them?

Try thinking broadly about these questions. Think about what the lifelong consequences of each course might be for you. Take notes on your thinking. Your instructor may ask you to respond in writing.

Why Integration of the Liberal Arts Is Important

The integrated nature of the liberal arts is a result of the enormous complexity of studying the human species. To understand literature, it is as essential to know something of astronomy and theology as it is to know psychology and literary theory. Historical events are often as influenced by scientific phenomena as by political conspiracy.

For example, several hundred years ago, the Black Plague radically changed the population centers of Europe, destroyed the power to make war in some nations, and inflicted psychological scars on whole cultures. On this basis, one might argue that the flea (which carried this disease) was a more significant factor in European history than any dynasty of kings. Currently, in parts of central Africa, HIV has been spreading similar devastation. Our past and future histories hinge on biology. By focusing on the *integration* of all of these studies, we can begin to get an understanding of our history, our world, and ourselves.

Because so much of what we learn in any one field is dependent on a broader understanding of the human context, most schools require a core of liberal arts courses during the freshman and sophomore years. This core provides foundational knowledge and strengthens certain essential communication, thinking, and research skills, which are the tools for learning in these areas.

For similar reasons, even the so-called "professional" degree programs— business administration, law, medicine, mass communication, engineering, nursing, and so on—often require a broad liberal arts background and have started to include more liberal arts courses in their programs. Even "professionals" ultimately have to live as social beings in their culture. They must strive to understand and get along with others. Perhaps even more than others, they must communicate effectively with other people and be able to respond to change. Employers know this and seek professionals who are able to think analytically and independently, communicate effectively, and understand an increasingly complex world.

The Liberal Arts Beyond College

Most jobs in our economy require working with other people and depend on people as consumers or clients. As the president of a large bank told me, "Banking is not a money business; it's a people business. Banks don't create money—bankers must persuade people to put money into the bank." Knowing how the society works, knowing the cultural conceptions of the people with whom you work, and knowing how to communicate effectively make it possible for you to work successfully in any job.

In the last decade, the high-tech occupations have become very glamorous. In fact, several years ago, *Time* magazine featured the computer as its "Man of the Year." At that time, it was predicted that the home computer would become as ubiquitous and as essential as the dishwasher. A number of huge companies, with fantastic technology and extensive market research, sank billions of dollars into the home computer market. The product was truly remarkable and could be produced at a reasonable price, yet within two years, many of the companies were either out of the home computer market or out of business entirely. The difficulty was not with the product; rather, it was that the attention to the human dimension had not kept up with the technological innovations.

Although the computer was a remarkable machine, it didn't do anything in the home that most people needed to be done or couldn't do more easily themselves. The decision that most people had to make was not whether they *wanted* a computer, but whether buying a computer was more important than buying snow tires or getting the heater fixed. The surviving companies were the ones that hired people (most often with liberal arts backgrounds) who figured out how to sell the product and to use it in new ways that appealed to the great majority of nontechnical humans. The key was to redefine some things that people already liked to do—such as communicate with each other, shop, and explore new things—and could do using a computer. The result was the development of e-mail, games, and references on CD-ROM and other multimedia, and the World Wide Web.

EXERCISE 13.3 How Do We Know Whether "Newer" Is "Better"?

Anytime we introduce something new into our lives or into our society, we have to find out how it fits into the way we live. In a small group, use the four aspects of critical thinking to develop an idea for a new product or choose an existing product. (You may want to focus on something that could be of use to people on your campus.) Present the class with answers to these and other relevant questions:

1. What is the product?

2. Why would anyone want to buy it? Specifically, what type of person might be strongly attracted to your product? (Besides the obvious characteristics of age, gender, income, and so on, think in terms of the kinds of interests and values this person might have that could make this product especially appealing.)

3. What might be some barriers to your product's success? (Think beyond competing products. What other things might the person do with the money, time, and energy needed to use your product?)

4. How might your product be changed to make it even more appealing, either to the individual you have chosen or to other types of people?

5. How many of the liberal arts have you employed in coming up with your answers to the first four questions?

Creating a Self to Be

Most of us think that when we finish college we will find a job that will be challenging and satisfying. We hope to work with interesting, creative people and to make a significant contribution. Although that may happen to some degree, a large part of our working lives is going to be spent in the routine, repetitive, and sometimes frustrating tasks that are a part of every job. We will also spend a lot of time worrying about making mortgage payments, getting teeth straightened, and generally carrying out the sometimes dull responsibilities that are the stuff of long-term success. When this happens, it is important to have something in your head besides what you *do*—a sense of who and what you *are*.

In the last few years, the FAX machine has become an essential part of business life. This technological marvel has only one function: It takes text and pictures that have been created in one place and transmits them to another place. It goes to work for you in the morning and lapses into "sleep mode" when a busy day is done. It works and does no more. You may know people who are like that—who seem to function only for work and have no identity or ideas outside work. Most of us don't want to end up that way. Your college education, especially in the liberal arts, should help you develop a self that transcends your job skills and allows you to be a thoughtful, creative, and fulfilled person outside work.

A social worker friend of mine was an undergraduate history major. I asked her once if history was a good major for social workers, and she replied that it was "because it gives me something to think about when I'm going crazy." That may seem like a very limited "use" for your major, but it could take on real meaning for you.

The World Beyond the Workplace

Just as the workplace has grown more complex and demanding, so has living outside the workplace. As a parent, as a citizen, and as a person, you will be faced with a number of hard decisions when you leave college. As a citizen, you may be asked to vote on issues such as the location of toxic waste disposal facilities in your community. A bad decision may be catastrophic. To make a good decision, you must synthesize a lot of often contradictory information from scientists and "experts" on both sides of the question.

As a parent, you may face more complex choices about your children's educations than your parents had to face about yours. At some point, other parents may come to you with strong feelings about sharing a classroom with children or teachers who carry HIV. You will have to separate the hysteria from the real information and come to your own conclusions. Such issues can be extremely complex because they involve not only scientific and technical questions, but also many political and social issues. You *will* have to make these decisions. If you have had the broad education that helps you to understand a problem, you will have at least a foundation on which to base your choices.

Thinking About the Unthinkable, Expressing the Inexpressible

Just as we should expect hard choices, so we should also be ready for failures and tragedies that may seem both overpowering and inexplicable. There is much about ourselves and our lives that we will spend a lifetime trying to understand.

Being able to put these problems into a context, knowing that people over the centuries have endured the same tragedies and uncertainties, being able to experience these feelings through the arts or see them examined by thinkers in psychology, philosophy, or theology—these abilities connect us to other people, to our culture, and to our species. They remove the sense of isolation and empower us to "take arms against a sea of troubles," as Hamlet said when he was home on vacation from college. Although this prince of Denmark may not have been too successful at resolving *his* conflicts, his eventual willingness to confront them made him, in the end, a hero. Experiencing a work like Shakespeare's *Hamlet* can make our dilemmas a bit more comprehensible.

■ THINKING IN THE LIBERAL ARTS

The liberal arts not only give you "something to think about" but also help you with the process of thinking—especially the kind of thinking you are often asked to do in college.

As suggested in Chapter 2, "Exploring the Student–Teacher Connection," one of the differences between high school and college that some students find especially difficult involves the expectations of teachers. One of my students put it this way:

> *In high school, when the teacher asked you a question, he knew the answer and wanted to see if you knew it too. In college, they ask you questions that* no one *knows the answer to, just to see what you will say.*

Although that may be a slight exaggeration, it is essentially true.

In grades 1–12, we were building a knowledge base. It was important to learn facts and concepts and their applications. To make sure we were learning the "facts," we were most often tested on *what* we knew and almost never on *how* we knew it. Unfortunately, this process also implied that there were always "right" and "wrong" answers, and that being wrong was bad. When in doubt about an answer, we learned that it was best just to keep quiet.

In college, we assume that the fundamental knowledge base and the tools for learning are there. There may be a lot more facts to learn, but much more emphasis is placed on using knowledge as a foundation for new ideas and concepts. That's why teachers ask questions "no one knows the answer to." They are more interested in students' learning the process of generating new ideas than in rehashing old ones.

The Courage to Think

The problem for many students when they begin college is that they have been trained not to be "wrong" and are afraid to take risks in learning. The psychologist and philosopher Rollo May tells us in *The Courage to Create* that creating anything new implies risk and destruction. Just as a bird must painfully tear its way out of the egg and destroy what has been its security and protection, just as it must emerge completely vulnerable in order to continue living, so we must be willing to give up our old, familiar protections and ideas in order to continue growing. That can be frightening, especially in the pressure cooker of college.

When I went to college, I felt lucky thinking that at least I knew who I was and what I wanted to do with my life. Within a year, I found I no longer had clear ideas about either. The process of leaving that security was frightening and painful. In retrospect, some of the ideas and identities I tried on in my search seem ridiculous now, but they were an integral part of my growth to adulthood.

EXERCISE 13.4   ## The Courage to Create

Consider Rollo May's idea that we must be willing to give up the security of what we know in order to grow. Does it seem appropriate now as you experience the challenges of college. Write a statement exploring how you prepared yourself for these challenges. Having some taste now of the realities of college, what ideas, securities, or plans must you be willing to abandon or change? What might make those changes difficult?

Integrating What We Know

The risks we take to grow are many and frightening. In the classroom, we may fear failure so much that at times we cannot think or learn at all. We can combat these fears by acknowledging what we do know and learning to use it, integrating what we have learned from all of our courses and experiences.

The liberal arts encourage you to think beyond "facts." History is not a list of dates and kings. Those dates and kings are just markers within a complex and dynamic pattern of ideas and events. A recent study by two economic historians explored the economic efficiency of slavery in America by examining certain economic data and statistical models (Robert W. Fogel and Stanley L. Engerman, *Time on the Cross: The Economics of American Negro Slavery.* Boston: Little, Brown, 1974). Their conclusion was that slavery was often economically successful. Do the data and models prove that slavery was a good system? Of course not. The study of just these specific facts ignores both the human and moral consequences of the system. By any measure that honestly reflects our basic values, slavery was a disaster—and not only for the slaves. We must integrate what we know of human beings and our own value and moral system with our learning of "facts" if we are to make informed choices and decide on some truth.

If we let our learning of mathematics simply become a memorization of formulas, then we will never be able to proceed beyond the last formula we learned. For most of us, symbolic systems like the ones we find in math or logic only have much meaning when we can see them as tools for solving problems. In studying math, it is important to work on making this connection rather than trying to master information that we do not see as useful.

Photo by David Miller/courtesy of Skidmore College

Thinking and Feeling

In creating or appreciating the arts, students sometimes feel totally at a loss because the process of creative thinking seems so subjective or abstract. Poems (and other artistic expressions) often work at a "superrational" level at which ideas and feelings come together in ways that are hard to define or formulate. What guidelines can there be for creating or finding deep meaning in a work of art? How can a poem "mean" something beyond what is obvious?

In his poem "Meditation at Oyster River," the American poet Theodore Roethke begins his description of a tidal river with the words "Over the low, slow, elephant-colored rocks . . ." Perhaps we can consider not only that the rocks are the color of elephants (grayish-brown), but that the words mean to suggest the elephant's large, roundish *shape* as well. We may notice that rocks may well be "low" but wonder how they can be called "slow." Does the word *slow* remind us of the ponderous movement of elephants? In this fine piece of art, we tend to "feel" the image before we analyze it, and then perhaps discover that the words do "say" what we feel.

We may wonder how an abstract painting or piece of music can *mean* anything at all. In a poem or a novel, it may seem fairly easy to analyze the work and find words or phrases that give us certain ideas. In a work of abstract painting or music, it may be much more difficult to describe where our ideas come from. When we talk about an artistic experience, we are usually talking about something that is on the border between "reason" and "feeling."

Suppose you are driving with a friend and a song comes on the radio that suddenly evokes vivid feelings and memories. As you try to explain this to your friend, you may find that there is no logical link between what the song "says" and what you are thinking. Music, poetry, painting, dance, and the other arts seem to have the power to touch us in ways that are completely beyond logic. When we try to explain a work of art, we are most often talking about how we respond to it, what ideas it gives us, and how it does that.

Just because it is difficult or seems irrational doesn't mean that an idea is any less real or important. If I were to ask you why you fell in love with a particular person, you could probably give me a number of "reasons," but if you tried to show by analysis why these reasons applied only to this person, you would soon find yourself giving up pure logic in favor of describing your emotions. Studying the arts tells us a great deal about ourselves, especially those aspects that seem so powerful and yet so mysterious.

EXERCISE 13.5 Creating and Explaining Art

A Write a short essay on a poem, a piece of art, or a song that is meaningful to you. Try to explain why it gives you ideas or feelings. Once you have finished creating your piece, use the four-part critical thinking framework to help create your explanation.

or

B With a small group, create an object that expresses your ideas or feelings about your first-year experience to this point.

Your liberal arts courses offer you an opportunity to study people and the world from many perspectives. From your understanding of the human species comes your understanding of yourself and your world. That is the beginning of real freedom. Your diploma is not a certification that you know all you will ever need to, but an indication that you have the tools and knowledge to continuing learning, growing, and creating.

JOURNAL

Think about the wide range of subjects that are included under the liberal arts. How do these courses establish a foundation for a professional education? How do they relate to the kinds of situations encountered by citizens on a daily basis? Are there particular areas within the liberal arts that particularly interest you? Explain your interest.

SUGGESTIONS FOR FURTHER READING

Boyer, Ernest. *College: The Undergraduate Experience in America.* Princeton, N.J.: Carnegie Foundation for Advancement of Teaching, 1987.

Figler, Howard E. *Liberal Education and Careers Today.* Garrett Park, Md.: Garret Park Press, 1989.

Levine, Arthur, ed. *Higher Learning in America, 1980–2000.* Baltimore: Johns Hopkins University Press, 1993.

Mason, Jeff, and Peter Washington. *The Future of Thinking: Rhetoric and Liberal Arts Teaching.* London/New York: Routledge, 1992.

Mitlas, Michael H., ed. *Moral Education and the Liberal Arts*. New York: Greenwood Press, 1992.

Oakley, Francis. *Community of Learning: The American College and the Liberal Arts Tradition*. New York: Oxford University Press, 1992.

Odom, Keith C. *Jane Austen: Rebel of Time and Place*. Arlington, Tex.: Liberal Arts Press, 1991.

Scott, Barbara Ann (ed.), with Richard P. Sloan. *The Liberal Arts in a Time of Crisis*. New York: Praeger, 1991.

Sykes, Charles, and Brad Miner, eds. *The National Review College Guide: America's 50 Top Liberal Arts Schools*. New York: National Review Books, 1991.

Woodruff, Cheryl. *150 Best Companies for Liberal Arts Graduates: Where to Get a Winning Job in Tough Times*. New York: Wiley, 1992.

Finding Answers: Your College Catalog and Academic Advisor or Counselor

A. Jerome Jewler
University of South Carolina

John N. Gardner
University of South Carolina

Mary Stuart Hunter
University of South Carolina

I don't know how to choose my courses. Do I need computer science? Have I taken all the math I need? Someone said to look in the catalog to find out the requirements. Maybe I can just get my advisor to explain it to me. I wish I knew what I was doing.

Chapter Goals

After reading this chapter, you should understand the importance of reading your college catalog for information on curriculum requirements, academic regulations, important dates, and course descriptions. You should also learn how to develop a productive relationship with your academic advisor, who can help you with important decisions regarding your college experience.

College catalogs and bulletins were probably an excellent resource for you when you were choosing which college to attend. Now that the decision has been made, you may be inclined to leave your institution's catalog on a shelf to gather dust or even toss it in the trash, thinking it's no longer needed. Don't. College is complex and expensive, and the college catalog is a sort of user's manual for your institution. Learn what's in your catalog—it should be a valuable resource throughout your college years.

Much of the information once found only in college handbooks is now available on-line. Campus computer bulletin boards and Internet home pages are especially useful for information that is in constant flux or that has changed recently. In addition to lists of classes and prerequisites, office hours, and student services, you can often search listings of job opportunities, scholarships, schedules, and departmental telephone numbers and e-mail addresses.

EXERCISE 14.1   Finding Your Catalog and Starting a File

A If you haven't already received your catalog, check with your advisor or counselor. If your advisor does not have a copy for you, contact the admissions office, the registration office, the departmental office of your academic major, or your campus bookstore. Make sure you have the catalog that is dated the year you matriculated, or entered a program of study, at your institution, not the year you applied for admission and were accepted.

B Start a file for your catalog and other documents such as your grade reports, advisement forms, fee payment receipts, schedule change forms, and other proof of financial and academic dealings with your institution. Plan to keep all these things until your diploma is in your hands.

C If it is likely that you may transfer to another college to complete an associate or bachelor's degree, also obtain a copy of the catalog for that school. It will be useful when you meet with your advisor to plan your courses.

HOW TO READ YOUR COLLEGE CATALOG

Does the previous exercise sound obsessive? It isn't. The reason that you should keep not only your catalog but all those forms and receipts is that when you apply for graduation, your department may conduct what is called a *degree audit, senior audit,* or *graduation check.* This process will compare your transcript with the academic requirements for the certificate or degree you are seeking. Any discrepancy between what you present as your academic record and the requirements in the catalog must be reconciled. Should the school's records be incomplete or inaccurate, your own file might make a difference in your favor.

What's in the Catalog?

First and foremost, the catalog is the official publication of your institution and contains valuable information about it: regulations, requirements, procedures, and opportunities for your development as a student. Although the catalog doesn't contain *everything* students need to know, it does provide an excellent summary of critical information available in greater detail elsewhere on your campus. The style of catalogs varies, but most provide you with the following information.

PUBLICATION DATE

Most college catalogs are published annually or every two years; a few are published twice a year. The publication date is generally shown on the cover. It is important for you to know which catalog was in effect when you matriculated (that is, enrolled for the first time) rather than when you applied for admission, because you are subject to the rules and regulations that were in effect when you matriculated.

Colleges and universities are constantly changing admissions standards, degree requirements, academic calendars, and so on. But the catalog in use at the time of your matriculation will generally stand as your individual "contract" with the institution. This constancy is to your benefit. Imagine the chaos if you had to adjust to a new set of degree requirements with each newly published catalog! The catalog in effect at your matriculation is the one that defines the requirements for your degree, unless it states a time limit to complete the degree under those requirements.

EXERCISE 14.2   Finding Some Key Dates

Look through your college catalog. Find and record the following important dates:

Publication date of the catalog: _____

	This Term	Next Term
First day of classes	_____	_____
Last day to add a class	_____	_____
Last day (if any) to drop a class without penalty	_____	_____
Midpoint in the term	_____	_____

	This Term	**Next Term**
Last day of classes	———	———
Final exam period (first day)	———	———
Final exam period (last day)	———	———
Official last day of term	———	———
Holidays (no classes held):		
_____	———	———
_____	———	———
_____	———	———
_____	———	———
_____	———	———

If your campus has a Campus Wide Information System or a home page on the Internet, see how many of the items are available on-line.

NOTE: If not in your catalog, this information should be available in the master schedule of classes for the current term.

GENERAL INFORMATION

The introductory information in the catalog usually stresses an institution's unique characteristics, mission, and educational philosophy. While philosophies and mission statements are sometimes discounted as unimportant, in reality they may determine whether or not you will find a good "fit" at the institution. For example, if you are interested in a broad liberal arts education, you might think twice about enrolling in a school that stresses business and engineering. Likewise, if engineering or computer technology are your areas, you may want to think again about the fit of a small liberal arts college.

Opening sections of the catalog frequently also list the governing officers and officials, describe the physical plant and facilities, recount a brief history of the school, and state its current accreditations (accredited institutions and programs are those that have met specific national standards). Accreditation is important because it assures you that a program is of an acceptable quality. Future employers and graduate school admissions officers pay special attention to the accreditation status of undergraduate schools.

ADMISSIONS INFORMATION

College catalogs serve many purposes, including student recruitment. So there is almost always admissions information in the catalog. This section will list the various categories of admissions and specify admissions procedures, application deadlines, and criteria for admissions decisions.

GENERAL ACADEMIC REGULATIONS

General academic regulations include requirements, procedures, and policies that are applicable to all students regardless of individual majors or student classifications. Fully understanding and complying with these rules will help you progress through your academic years without running into roadblocks.

Students often distort or misinterpret academic regulations. To be fully and accurately informed, don't rely on secondhand, "grapevine" information. Become familiar with these rules directly from the catalog. If you don't understand something in the catalog, seek clarification from an official source. Your academic advisor or counselor may be able to connect you with such sources.

The regulations section outlines the institution's enrollment and registration procedures. It also explains the grading system, course credit options, grade point average calculation, and academic suspension system, and describes academic honors and graduation requirements as they apply to students throughout the school. It may also detail students' rights, including the confidentiality of student records and the right to appeal or petition for relief from certain academic regulations.

FINANCIAL INFORMATION

Your catalog may also outline the current costs of attending your institution: academic fee schedules, costs of various housing options, prices of meal plans, and schedule of fines, refund policies, and payment options. Government-assisted schools also include rules for resident and nonresident status and resulting fee differentials.

The high cost of a college education concerns most students, as it does most college administrators. Not only may cost have affected your choice of a school, but costs will probably continue to rise throughout your years in college. But the financial section may have good news for you: detailed information on financial aid, scholarships, loans, and work opportunities. Study this section for sources of financial help.

ACADEMIC CALENDAR

Most college catalogs include a current academic calendar, which states the beginning and ending dates of the academic terms as well as dates of holidays and other events within each term. Being familiar with the calendar in advance will help you make sound decisions. For example, if you are not doing well in a particular class, you may want to drop the course rather than receive a failing grade, but you must do so before the deadline for withdrawal. To facilitate general planning, some catalogs give the academic calendars for several years in advance.

ACADEMIC PROGRAM

By far the lengthiest part of most catalogs is the section on academic programs. This summarizes the various degrees offered, the majors within each department, and the requirements for studying in each discipline. The departmental outlines include most of the information that is unique to each department, supplementing any institution-wide rules and regulations. They also list any special admissions criteria for special programs, as well as the progression, curriculum, and degree requirements.

The academic program section also describes the individual courses offered at your institution. Basic information usually includes course number, course title, units of credit, prerequisites for taking the course, and a brief statement of the course content.

Remember, the catalog is only a *summary* of information. Individual department offices frequently offer more detailed information in the form of course descriptions, curriculum checklists, departmental advisement guidelines, and so on. Your academic advisor or counselor may also have such supplemental information.

If you are planning to transfer to another school, be sure you also have a catalog from that school. Consult both catalogs about any articulation agreements between the schools, which will state what courses are necessary for transfer and what courses will receive transferable credit at your new school.

Scoping Out the Catalog

Bring your catalog to class. Form a small group with several other students who plan to follow a program or enroll in a major similar to your own. Do the following as a group.

1. From information in the catalog, answer the following questions about the program or major:

   a. What are the core requirements of the program?

   b. What prerequisites (if any) are there for the program?

   c. Is there a sequence that must be followed when taking specific courses? (For example, are there some courses that must be taken in order but are taught only in certain semesters?)

   d. What courses will each person in the group need or plan to take next semester?

   If your campus has a Campus Wide Information System or a home page on the Internet, also look for this information.

2. Find at least one specific piece of information that might be useful or surprising to other members of the class. Prepare to report on that information.

■ YOUR ACADEMIC ADVISOR OR COUNSELOR

The idea of academic advising or counseling is certainly not new, but never before has it been regarded as so essential. There's good reason for this; with so many programs and so many choices, even experienced faculty and staff must check and double-check academic requirements and regulations to be certain students are making the right choices. Because so many students today are the first in their families to attend college, it is even more important that there be someone to advise them. In broader terms, if faculty and staff believe that college should help students develop holistically—that is, vocationally, emotionally, physically, spiritually, culturally, and socially as well as intellectually—the academic advisor can be the focal point for such development.

We already know that when a student has one person on campus who cares about his or her survival, that student stands a better chance of succeeding than the student who lacks a relationship with a significant other person. A mounting body of evidence has convinced colleges and universities that poor academic advising is one major reason students drop out of college. Thus academic advising has become one of the most important ingredients for student success. Although your "significant other" person may be an instructor, a staff member, an upper-class student, or a counselor, it might also be none other than your academic advisor.

What Is Academic Advising?

Academic advising is a dynamic process for obtaining the critical information you need to make the most important decisions about college, decisions affecting

What Are You Looking for in Your Academic Advisor?

This graph from a study of students at Harvard shows that men and women tend to seek different qualities in advisors.

When asked about advising, men want an advisor who "knows the facts." Or "if he doesn't know the data, he knows where to get it or to send me to get it." Or one who "makes concrete and directive suggestions, which I'm then free to accept or reject."

Women more often want an advisor who "will take the time to get to know me personally." Or who "is a good listener and can read between the lines if I am hesitant to express a concern." Or who "shares my interests so that we will have something in common." The women's responses focus far more on a personal relationship.*

What do you plan to look for in your advisor? What can you do to ensure that you get the advisor who is best for you?

*Richard J. Light. The Harvard Assessment Seminars, First Report (Cambridge, Mass.: Harvard University Graduate School of Education and Kennedy School of Government, 1990).

What Students Want from Academic Advisors
(percentage indicating "very important")

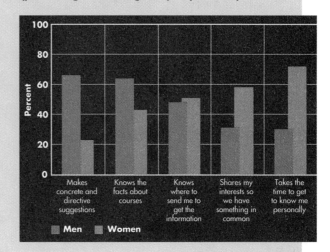

your academic major, career goals, elective courses, secondary fields of study, and co-curricular activities. Academic advising is also a one-to-one, highly personal, out-of-class form of learning. Academic advising includes periodic assistance in scheduling courses that you will take the following term and is inextricably related to the process of career planning and decision making. But beyond decision-making and scheduling considerations, it represents a relationship between two human beings who care about, understand, and respect each other and share a common goal: the student's education.

Some schools may practice a more holistic view of academic advising, in which the advisor serves as a personal counselor to whom you can turn for any sort of problem, especially if the problem is affecting your ability to complete course work successfully. Such problems might include a learning disability; a personal problem that causes stress, insomnia, or anxiety; perceived unfair treatment by a teacher; indecision about choice of major, career, or transfer to another school; an ethical or moral dilemma; inability to keep up with course work due to any number of reasons, including excessive employment hours; or poor grades that may lead to suspension.

The best academic advisor is someone who really wants to get to know you and welcomes your questions and concerns. If these qualities seem to be missing, think about whether there is something you can do to improve communication. Or consider looking for an advisor with whom you feel more at home.

© Brian Smith/Stock Boston

Even if you have no serious problems, you may want to talk with your advisor for any number of reasons: to get advice on applying for a job, to get a reaction to a piece of writing or a project, to ask for the names of books in a given field that might be helpful to you, to share some good news about grades or job interviews, or to check on academic rules and regulations.

At most schools, academic advising is less comprehensive, and you may need to ask about separate counseling services for nonacademic personal issues. At a minimum, your academic advisor informs you about your program requirements and options and gives you approval to register for courses each term. Ideally, academic advisors also help you explore life goals and vocational goals, select academic programs, and choose and schedule courses.

Academic advising should be a process whereby you communicate regularly with someone you respect about a broad range of concerns. The process should be linked to career planning and may include personal counseling. It may also include an "early warning system" through which the college monitors your academic progress and sends frequent grade reports during your first term to your advisor. He or she then contacts you and refers you, as needed, to other counseling and support resources to assist you with academic difficulties. The purpose is not to criticize you but to help you cope with the academic problems you may be experiencing.

Academic advising may also include a process that monitors your class attendance during your first term and alerts you if you miss too many classes.

Later the process will include your advisor making sure that you have met all the requirements for graduation and certifying that you are eligible to receive your diploma.

EXERCISE 14.4   Academic Advising at Your School

Explore the academic advising or counseling process at your institution. To find out about it, you may have to contact your advisor, the advisement center, your department head, or another campus resource. Knowing how to locate resources is an important skill to develop in college!

Try to answer these questions and others you may have:

1. Who are the advisors?

    _____ Teachers

    _____ Counselors

    _____ Professional advisors

    _____ Other: _____

2. What services do they offer?

    _____

    _____

    _____

    _____

3. How does a student get assigned to a particular advisor? Does a student normally have the same advisor throughout college? How can a student go about arranging for a different advisor if necessary?

4. What other counseling and advising services can your academic advisor help you find when you need them?

5. Are there specific counselors for transfer purposes?

Who Are Academic Advisors?

At many colleges, academic advisors are full-time faculty. At some schools they may be educators whose sole professional responsibility is advising. At other schools, you'll find a combination of faculty and professional staff members as advisors.

In many community colleges, academic advising is done by counselors in the college counseling/advising center. These counselors are trained in and responsible for assisting students with both academic and personal issues. If you haven't declared a major, you may be assigned to an advisor who specializes in dealing with undecided students. You may be attending an institution that, as a matter of policy, does not initially assign new students to advisors in their intended major field, but does so later on. Even if you are not assigned a faculty member from your special area of interest, your advisor is usually expected to be familiar with the requirements of your program. If your advisor is not familiar with them, there may be a center on campus where a staff advisor can give specific program information.

EXERCISE 14.5 — Who's Your Academic Advisor?

Find out and record the name of your academic advisor, along with his or her office location, phone number, and normal advising hours. If you have not already done so, arrange to meet this person.

Name: _____

Office location: _____

Phone(s): _____

_____

Hours: _____

Where and When Is Academic Advising Conducted?

One of the many differences between high school and college is that most college faculty have private offices where they can meet with you during their posted office hours. At many institutions, academic advising takes place in advisement centers. These centers may also include offices for personal counseling, career planning and placement, financial aid, and study skills.

Ideally, academic advising is a process that involves more frequent interaction between you and your advisor. The nature and frequency of this relationship depend on how you and your advisor choose to pursue this opportunity. Like virtually everything in college, academic advising will be what you make of it.

Generally, at least once a term, students are notified to sign up for appointments with their advisors to discuss the selection and scheduling of courses for the next term. This advising period may last up to two weeks and is usually widely publicized on campus. It is very important that you be aware of these periods and schedule a conference to discuss your course selections for the coming term.

EXERCISE 14.6 — Advising Process and Schedules

To prepare for your basic academic advising sessions, do the following:

1. Find out when the course selection and scheduling process for next term

   begins, and record the date here: _____

2. Record what you need to do to prepare for this process (include any important dates):

   _____

   _____

   _____

   _____

   _____

Don't forget to transfer the important dates to your calendar so you'll be prepared!

RELATING TO YOUR ADVISOR

Advising is likely to be much more successful for you if you take the relationship seriously and work hard to make it meaningful. Take responsibility for keeping your advisor informed of your progress or problems. At the very minimum, make an appointment to meet at least once a term to discuss plans for the next term. Ask for advice on course prerequisites, interesting courses to take, good teachers to study under, or other options.

Discuss any major decisions—such as adding or dropping a course, changing your major, or transferring or withdrawing from school—*before* making them. You may also need to discuss personal problems with your advisor. If he or she can't help you with a certain problem, ask for referral to a professional on campus who can. Your advisor should be someone you can always turn to. Even if he or she doesn't know the answer immediately, the advisor should know who to call to get you the help you need. Will your advisor respect your request for confidentiality on such matters? That's something you will need to clarify.

Your advising sessions will be more productive if you are already familiar with your college catalog. Make up a list of questions before your appointment and also arrive with a tentative schedule of courses and alternate choices for the coming term. At many colleges, your entire academic record will be stored in an on-line database that your advisor can access on a personal computer during your advising sessions. At others, the department office will have your academic records on file for use in the advising session.

EXERCISE 14.7   Questions to Ask Advisors

Read the following description of Frank, a first-year student:

> Frank has had an average first term. He excelled in English Composition and Western History but was disappointed with his performance in biology and math. He was a good student in all subjects in high school, so he's somewhat baffled by his performance. He thinks it may be because his job keeps him up late at night, so he's not alert for his morning classes, which happen to be math and biology. Or it may be the way those classes are taught—lots of students, lots of lectures, little personal attention. Whatever it is, he's decided to switch his course-work focus from the biosciences to philosophy. He's not sure how to tell his family about this—they think he wants to work in science. He also wonders what kind of job he'll get if he eventually gets his B.A. in philosophy. One thing he does know is that the philosophy courses a friend of his is taking sound a lot more interesting than his science classes! Actually his friend's whole life sounds a lot more interesting. How does he have time to get involved in so many things when all Frank can manage to do is study, work, and make it to class?

1. Frank has an appointment with his academic advisor tomorrow. What questions would you suggest Frank ask?

_____

_____

_____

Compare your suggestions with those of other students in your class.

2. Now spend some time reviewing your school term so far. Jot down some of the issues you're experiencing, or questions you have, so you'll remember to speak with your advisor about them.

_____

_____

_____

_____

Is Your Advisor Right for You?

The key word here is _trust._ You will know you have the right academic advisor if you establish good rapport with this person. Do you feel comfortable with him or her? Does your academic advisor seem to take a personal interest in you? Does the advisor listen actively? Does the advisor provide enough time for you to accomplish what needs to be done? Does he or she either make an effort to get you the information you request or tell you where you can find it yourself?

If your advisor isn't right for you, you could discuss your lack of satisfaction with him or her as tactfully as possible. But since this may be awkward, a better approach might be to ask for another advisor. To find a better advisor, you might consider asking one of your instructors, perhaps one with whom you have developed a personal rapport or whom you respect. Get his or her agreement, or check with your departmental advising coordinators about other possibilities for advisors. Then make the change officially. _Never_ stay in an advising relationship that isn't working for you.

Colleges and universities have made enormous strides since the mid-1970s in improving the condition of academic advising, and it is now being taken very seriously at many schools. A number of advisors are now being trained, evaluated, and rewarded. The process of personalizing academic advising will more than likely continue, and more and more students like you will have the opportunity to benefit from it. Be certain that you do.

EXERCISE 14.8 Preparing to Meet with Your Advisor

Think ahead to your next appointment with your advisor. What questions do you have in each of the following areas? Record those questions here. (You may be able to answer some of these questions yourself by consulting your catalog.)

1. Your major and potential career:

_____

_____

_____

2. Alternate majors and potential careers:

_____

_____

_____

3. Classes you need next term:

_____

_____

_____

4. Proper sequencing of classes you need to take:

_____

_____

_____

5. Difficulty level of classes you may be taking next term:

_____

_____

_____

6. Good balance in the combination of class work loads and types of classes you have chosen:

_____

_____

_____

7. Electives you might be interested in:

_____

_____

_____

8. Schedule problems:

_____

_____

_____

9. Teaching styles of specific instructors:

_____

_____

_____

10. General campus information:

_____

_____

_____

11. Information about scholarships, internships, cooperative education, or other opportunities:

_____

_____

12. Other questions or issues including change of major (don't forget the notes you recorded for Exercise 14.7):

_____

_____

_____

Throughout the rest of this term, use this worksheet to record other questions for your advisor as you think of them. The night before your appointment, review the list for any additions or deletions. To make good use of your appointment time and not forget anything, take this list and your catalog with you. If you're considering transferring, also bring the catalog from the school to which you may want to transfer.

JOURNAL

What has your academic advising experience been like to date? Describe your satisfaction or your lack thereof with the academic advising you have received. Comment on the characteristics and personality of your academic advisor. Also describe what attempts you have made to develop a relationship with him or her and how successful they have been.

SUGGESTIONS FOR FURTHER READING

Your college catalog

Your student handbook

Current schedule of classes

CHAPTER 15

Choosing a Major and Planning a Career

Linda B. Salane
Columbia College

My career inventory results said I should go into the funeral business. I'm a marketing major. Does that mean I'll be selling to the dead!? My counselor said it all made sense because funeral parlors have to sell their services to the survivors. Still, it was enough to make me think of changing majors again. Maybe I should do a little more than think.

Chapter Goals

After reading this chapter, you should have a clearer understanding of the connection between the courses you are taking and the types of careers they may lead to. You will also take a number of inventories and complete additional exercises designed to help you focus your career search on manageable and achievable goals.

■ MAJORS = CAREERS? NOT ALWAYS

For some students, choosing a major is a simple decision, but most students who enter college straight out of high school (and even some who've worked a while) don't know which major to select or which career they may be best suited for.

Before you actively begin planning your major or career, consider several truths about majors and their effect on careers. First, the relationship of college majors to careers varies. Obviously, if you want to be a nurse, you must major in nursing. Engineers major in engineering. Pharmacists major in pharmacology. There's no other way to be certified as a nurse, engineer, or pharmacist. However, most career fields don't require a specific major, and people with specific majors don't have to use them in usual ways. For example, if you major in nursing, history, engineering, or English, you might still choose to become a bank manager, sales representative, career counselor, production manager, or any number of other things.

Second, in most cases a college major alone is not enough to land you a job. There is tremendous competition for good jobs, and you need experience and competencies related to your chosen field. Internships, part-time jobs, and co-curricular activities provide opportunities to gain experience and develop these competencies.

The most common question college students ask is, "What can I do with my major?" Career planning helps you focus on a more important question: "What do I *want* to do?" This question leads you to explore yourself and fields where you can achieve what you want.

As you attempt to determine what you want to do, the choice of an academic major will take on new meaning. You'll no longer be so concerned with what the prescribed route of certain majors allows you to do. Instead you'll use your career goals as a basis for academic decisions about your major, your minor, elective courses, internships, and co-curricular activities. Consider these goals when you select part-time and summer jobs. Don't confine yourself to a short list of jobs directly related to your major; think more broadly about your goals.

Write a brief answer to each of the following questions. Try to answer each question even though you may feel uncertain about it.

1. In general, what kind of work do you want to do after finishing your education?

   _____

   _____

2. What career fields or industries offer opportunities for this kind of work?

   _____

   _____

3. What role will college play in preparing you for this work?

   _____

   _____

4. What specific things do you plan to do to enhance your chances of getting a job when you graduate?

   _____

   _____

   _____

5. Do your career goals seem compatible with your other life goals and values?

   _____

   _____

6. Is it likely that you will need to transfer to another college in order to get the education you need for your career?

   _____

   _____

FACTORS IN YOUR CAREER PLANNING

Some people have a very definite self-image when they enter college, but most of us are still in the process of defining (or redefining) ourselves when we enter college and even long after. There are several useful ways to look at ourselves in relation to possible careers:

- **Interests.** Interests develop from your experiences and beliefs and can continue to develop and change throughout life. For example, you may be interested in writing for the college newspaper because you wrote for your high school paper, or because you'd like to try something new. Involvement in different courses may lead you to drop old interests and cultivate new ones. It's not unusual for a student to enter Psych 101 with a great interest in psychology and realize halfway

*Biology . . . evolution . . . history . . . literature . . . ?
Start your search for your major with some wide-ranging thought about your major interests.*

© Rogers/Monkmeyer Press Photo

through the course that psychology is not what he or she imagined or wants to pursue.

- **Skills.** Skills are measured by past performance and are almost always improvable with practice.
- **Aptitudes.** These are inherent strengths, often part of your biological heritage or the result of early training. Aptitudes are the foundation for skills. We all have aptitudes we can build on. Build on *your* strengths.
- **Personality.** The personality you've developed over the years makes you *you,* and can't be ignored when you make career decisions. The quiet, orderly, calm, detail-oriented person probably will and should make a different work choice than the aggressive, outgoing, argumentative person.
- **Life Goals and Work Values.** Each of us defines success and satisfaction in our own way. The process is complex and very personal. Two factors influence our conclusions about success and happiness: (1) knowing that we are achieving the life goals we've set for ourselves and (2) finding that we value what we're receiving from our work.

Dr. John Holland, a psychologist at Johns Hopkins University, has developed a number of tools and concepts that can help you organize these various dimensions of yourself so that you can identify potential career choices. For example, Exercise 15.2 is based on his work.

EXERCISE 15.2 What Are Your Life Goals?

The following list includes life goals some people set for themselves. This list can help you begin to think about the kinds of goals you may want to set. Place a check mark next to the goals you would like to achieve in your life. Next, review the goals you have checked and circle the five you want most. Finally, review your list of five goals and rank them by priority (1 for most important, 5 for least important).

_____ the love and admiration of friends

_____ good health

_____ lifetime financial security

_____ a lovely home

_____ international fame

_____ freedom within my work setting

_____ a good love relationship

_____ a satisfying religious faith

_____ recognition as the most attractive person in the world

_____ an understanding of the meaning of life

_____ success in my profession

_____ a personal contribution to the elimination of poverty and sickness

_____ a chance to direct the destiny of a nation

_____ freedom to do what I want

_____ a satisfying and fulfilling marriage

_____ a happy family relationship

_____ complete self-confidence

_____ other: _____

NOTE: Adapted from Human Potential Seminar by James D. McHolland, Evanston, Ill., 1975. Used by permission of the author.

Holland separates people into six general categories based on differences in their interests, skills, values, and personality characteristics—in short, their preferred approaches to life:*

R ● Realistic. These people describe themselves as concrete, down-to-earth, and practical—as doers. They exhibit competitive/assertive behavior and show interest in activities that require motor coordination, skill, and physical strength. They prefer situations involving "action solutions" rather than tasks involving verbal or interpersonal skills, and they like to take a concrete approach to problem solving rather than rely on abstract theory. They tend to be interested in scientific or mechanical areas rather than cultural and aesthetic fields.

I ● Investigative. These people describe themselves as analytical, rational, and logical—as problem solvers. They value intellectual stimulation and intellectual achievement and prefer to think rather than to act, to organize and understand rather than to persuade. They usually have a strong interest in physical, biological, or social sciences. They are less apt to be "people-oriented."

A ● Artistic. These people describe themselves as creative, innovative, and independent. They value self-expression and relations with others through artistic expression and are also emotionally expressive. They dislike structure, preferring tasks involving personal or physical skills. They resemble investigative people but are more interested in the cultural-aesthetic than the scientific.

S ● Social. These people describe themselves as kind, caring, helpful, and understanding of others. They value helping and making a contribution. They satisfy their needs in one-to-one or small group interaction using strong verbal skills to teach, counsel, or advise. They are drawn to close interpersonal relationships and are less apt to engage in intellectual or extensive physical activity.

E ● Enterprising. These people describe themselves as assertive, risk-taking, and persuasive. They value prestige, power, and status and are more inclined than other types to pursue it. They use verbal skills to

*Adapted from John L. Holland, *Self-Directed Search Manual* (Psychological Assessment Resources: 1985). Copyright © 1985 by PAR, Inc. Reprinted with permission.

supervise, lead, direct, and persuade rather than to support or guide. They are interested in people and in achieving organizational goals.

C • **Conventional.** These people describe themselves as neat, orderly, detail-oriented, and persistent. They value order, structure, prestige, and status and possess a high degree of self-control. They are not opposed to rules and regulations. They are skilled in organizing, planning, and scheduling and are interested in data and people.

Exercise 15.3 provides a means of seeing (roughly) how you yourself relate to Holland's categories.

EXERCISE 15.3 Personality Mosaic

Circle the numbers of the statements that clearly feel like something you might say or do or think—something that feels like you. When you have finished, circle the same number on the answer grid on page 262.

1. It's important for me to have a strong, agile body.

2. I need to understand things thoroughly.

3. Music, color, beauty of any kind can really affect my moods.

4. People enrich my life and give it meaning.

5. I have confidence in myself that I can make things happen.

6. I appreciate clear directions so I know exactly what I can do.

7. I can usually carry/build/fix things myself.

8. I can get absorbed for hours in thinking something out.

9. I appreciate beautiful surroundings; color and design mean a lot to me.

10. I love company.

11. I enjoy competing.

12. I need to get my surroundings in order before I start a project.

13. I enjoy making things with my hands.

14. It's satisfying to explore new ideas.

15. I always seem to be looking for new ways to express my creativity.

16. I value being able to share personal concerns with people.

17. Being a key person in a group is very satisfying to me.

18. I take pride in being careful about all the details of my work.

19. I don't mind getting my hands dirty.

20. I see education as a lifelong process of developing and sharpening my mind.

21. I love to dress in unusual ways, to try new colors and styles.

22. I can often sense when a person needs to talk to someone.

23. I enjoy getting people organized and on the move.

24. A good routine helps me get the job done.

25. I like to buy sensible things that I can make or work on myself.

26. Sometimes I can sit for hours and work on puzzles or read or just think about life.

27. I have a great imagination.

28. It makes me feel good to take care of people.

29. I like to have people rely on me to get the job done.

30. I'm satisfied knowing that I've done an assignment carefully and completely.

31. I'd rather be on my own doing practical, hands-on activities.

32. I'm eager to read about any subject that arouses my curiosity.

33. I love to try creative new ideas.

34. If I have a problem with someone, I prefer to talk it out and resolve it.

NOTE: From Betty Neville Michelozzi, *Coming Alive from Nine to Five*, 4th ed. Mountain View, Calif.: Mayfield Publishing Co., © 1980, 1984, 1988, 1992. Used by permission of the publisher.

35. To be successful, it's important to aim high.

36. I prefer being in a position where I don't have to take responsibility for decisions.

37. I don't enjoy spending a lot of time discussing things. What's right is right.

38. I need to analyze a problem pretty thoroughly before I act on it.

39. I like to rearrange my surroundings to make them unique and different.

40. When I feel down, I find a friend to talk to.

41. After I suggest a plan, I prefer to let others take care of the details.

42. I'm usually content where I am.

43. It's invigorating to do things outdoors.

44. I keep asking "why."

45. I like my work to be an expression of my moods and feelings.

46. I like to find ways to help people care more for each other.

47. It's exciting to take part in important decisions.

48. I'm always glad to have someone else take charge.

49. I like my surroundings to be plain and practical.

50. I need to stay with a problem until I figure out an answer.

51. The beauty of nature touches something deep inside me.

52. Close relationships are important to me.

53. Promotion and advancement are important to me.

54. Efficiency, for me, means doing a set amount carefully each day.

55. A strong system of law and order is important to prevent chaos.

56. Thought-provoking books always broaden my perspective.

57. I look forward to seeing art shows, plays, and good films.

58. I haven't seen you for so long. I'd love to know what you're doing.

59. It's exciting to be able to influence people.

60. Good, hard physical work never hurt anyone.

61. When I say I'll do it, I follow through on every detail.

62. I'd like to learn all there is to know about subjects that interest me.

63. I don't want to be like everyone else. I like to do things differently.

64. Tell me how I can help you.

65. I'm willing to take some risks to get ahead.

66. I like exact directions and clear rules when I start something new.

67. The first thing I look for in a car is a well-built engine.

68. Those people are intellectually stimulating.

69. When I'm creating, I tend to let everything else go.

70. I feel concerned that so many people in our society need help.

71. It's fun to get ideas across to people.

72. I hate it when they keep changing the system just when I get it down.

73. I usually know how to take care of things in an emergency.

74. Just reading about new discoveries is exciting.

75. I like to create happenings.

76. I often go out of my way to pay attention to people who seem lonely and friendless.

77. I love to bargain.

78. I don't like to do things unless I'm sure they're approved.

79. Sports are important in building strong bodies.

80. I've always been curious about the way nature works.

81. It's fun to be in a mood to try to do something unusual.

82. I believe that people are basically good.

83. If I don't make it the first time, I usually bounce back with energy and enthusiasm.

84. I appreciate knowing exactly what people expect of me.

85. I like to take things apart to see if I can fix them.

86. Don't get excited. We can think it out and plan the right move logically.

87. It would be hard to imagine my life without beauty around me.

88. People often seem to tell me their problems.

89. I can usually connect with people who get me in touch with a network of resources.

90. I don't need much to be happy.

Now circle the same numbers below that you circled above.

R	I	A	S	E	C
1	2	3	4	5	6
7	8	9	10	11	12
13	14	15	16	17	18
19	20	21	22	23	24
25	26	27	28	29	30
31	32	33	34	35	36
37	38	39	40	41	42
43	44	45	46	47	48
49	50	51	52	53	54
55	56	57	58	59	60
61	62	63	64	65	66
67	68	69	70	71	72
73	74	75	76	77	78
79	80	81	82	83	84
85	86	87	88	89	90

Now add up the number of circles in each column.

R ———— I ———— A ———— S ———— E ———— C ————

Which are your three highest scores?

1st ———— 2nd ———— 3rd ————

Now go back and reread the descriptions of these three types and see how accurately they describe you!

Holland's system organizes career fields into the same six categories. Career fields are grouped according to what a particular career field requires of a person (skills and personality characteristics most commonly associated with success in those fields) and what rewards particular career fields provide for people (interests and values most commonly associated with satisfaction). As you read the following examples, see how your career interests match the category as described by Holland.

R ● **Realistic.** Agricultural engineer, barber, dairy farmer, electrical contractor, ferryboat captain, gem cutter, heavy equipment operator, industrial arts teacher, jeweler, navy officer, health and safety specialist, radio repairer, sheet metal worker, tailor, fitness director, package engineer, electronics technician, computer graphics technician, coach, PE teacher

I ● **Investigative.** Urban planner, chemical engineer, bacteriologist, cattle-breeding technician, ecologist, flight engineer, genealogist, hand-writing analyst, laboratory technician, marine scientist, nuclear medical technologist, obstetrician, quality control technician, sanitation scientist, TV repairer, balloon pilot, computer programmer, robotics engineer, environmentalist, physician, college professor

A ● **Artistic.** Architect, film editor/director, actor, cartoonist, interior decorator, fashion model, furrier, graphic communications specialist, jewelry designer, journalist, medical illustrator, editor, orchestra leader, public relations specialist, sculptor, telecommunications coordinator, media specialist, librarian, reporter

S ● Social. Nurse, teacher, caterer, social worker, genetic counselor, home economist, job analyst, marriage counselor, parole officer, rehabilitation counselor, school superintendent, theater manager, production expediter, geriatric specialist, insurance claims specialist, minister, travel agent, guidance counselor, convention planner, career specialist

E ● Enterprising. Banker, city manager, employment interviewer, FBI agent, health administrator, industrial relations director, judge, labor arbitrator, personnel assistant, TV announcer, salary and wage administrator, insurance salesperson, sales engineer, lawyer, sales representative, marketing specialist, promoter

C ● Conventional. Accountant, statistician, census enumerator, data processor, hospital administrator, instrument assembler, insurance administrator, legal secretary, library assistant, office manager, reservation agent, information consultant, underwriter, auditor, personnel specialist, database manager, abstractor/indexer

At first glance, Holland's model may seem to be a simple method for matching people to career fields, but it was never meant to oversimplify the process. Your career choices ultimately will involve a complex assessment of the factors that are most important to you. To display the relationship between career fields and the potential conflicts people face as they consider them, Holland's model is commonly presented in a hexagonal shape (see Figure 15.1). The closer the types, the closer the relationships among the career fields; the farther apart the types, the more conflict between the career fields.

Figure 15.1 Holland's Hexagonal Model of Career Fields

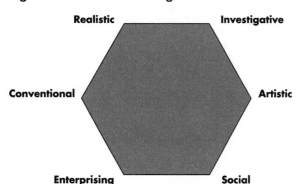

Realistic   Investigative

Conventional   Artistic

Enterprising   Social

EXERCISE 15.4 **The Holland Hexagon**

A Go back to Exercise 15.3 and look at your three categories. Based on the list of careers on pages 262–263, how well do the three categories match your career interests?

B Now look at the Holland hexagon. See where your first, second, and third choices in Exercise 15.3 are located on the hexagon. Are they close together or far apart? If far apart, do you feel they reflect a conflict in your goals or interests? Write a brief statement about how the conflict has affected you so far.

C Look back at your responses to Exercises 15.2 and 15.3. Discuss your responses and your writing in parts A and B of this exercise with a classmate.

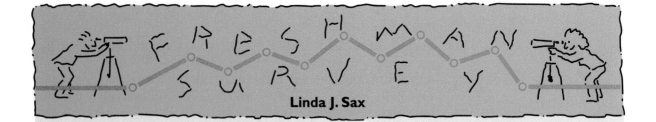

Linda J. Sax

Changing Interest in Business and Health-Related Majors

Between 1966 and 1987, the proportion of first-year students interested in business careers doubled, as the first graph shows. Although interest in business careers has declined steadily since 1987, it is still the most popular college major and career choice. The percentage of first-year students planning to major in business increased from 14.3 percent in 1966 to 24.6 percent in 1987, and then dropped to 16.3 percent in 1995.

Women's interest in business careers has grown dramatically. Between 1966 and 1985, the proportion of women planning business careers increased sixfold. Indeed, in some business specializations, women now outnumber men. For several years more women than men have stated a preference for accounting majors and careers.

The second graph shows how sharply the declining interest in business in recent years contrasts with the rising interest in health-related majors. Why do you think the health professions have become so popular?

Freshman Interest in Business Careers, by Sex, 1966–1995

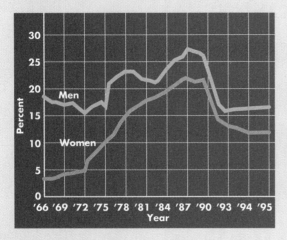

SOURCE: *Higher Education Research Institute, UCLA*

Freshman Interest in Business and Health-Related Majors, 1966–1995

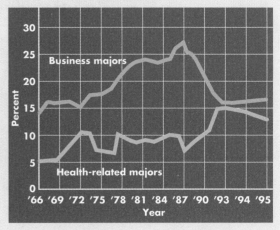

SOURCE: *Higher Education Research Institute, UCLA*

Holland's model can help you address the problem of career choice in two ways. First, you can begin to identify many career fields that are consistent with what you know about yourself. Once you've identified potential fields, you can use the career library at your college to get more information about those fields. Find out the following information:

- Daily activities for specific jobs
- Interests and abilities required

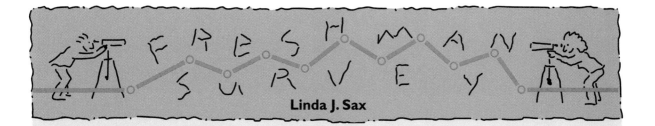
Engineering and Computer Science

Freshman interest in engineering careers and majors fell sharply in the early 1970s, just after the first Apollo moon walk and the termination of funding for the American supersonic transport airplane project and other large government contracts. Potential engineering students saw televised coverage of unemployed engineers in Seattle, Long Beach, and St. Louis, cities where aerospace and defense contractors had large plants, and chose other fields and careers.

Interest in engineering careers rose again after 1975. This increase reflected a return of men into engineering as well as a growing (if still small) number of women. Later in the 1970s, rising interest in technical careers such as engineering and computing was further stimulated by declines elsewhere in the economy; science and technology were the only "hot spots" in an otherwise slow job market.

In the last decade, however, student interest in engineering dropped surprisingly, nearly one-half, from a peak of 12 percent in 1982 to 6.4 percent in 1995. The proportion of freshmen planning careers as computer programmers fell even more.

Why the apparent declining interest in technical careers? Recent years have shown us that the market for jobs in engineering and computing is extremely sensitive to changes in the economy. Defense cuts and fewer government

Freshman Interest in Technology Careers, 1966–1995

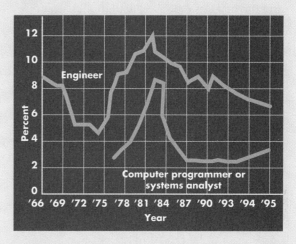

SOURCE: Higher Education Research Institute, UCLA

contracts have reduced the demand for new technical workers.

However, the growing trend in telecommunications and information systems, as well as the widening of international markets, may raise the need for engineers and computer programmers in the coming years. Can you think of other fields that are this responsive to changes in the economy?

- Preparation required for entry
- Working conditions
- Salary and benefits
- Employment outlook

Second, you can begin to identify the harmony or conflicts in your career choices. This will help you analyze the reasons for your career decisions and be more confident as you make choices.

College students often view the choice of a career as a monumental and irreversible decision. Some feel haunted by the choice as they decide on a

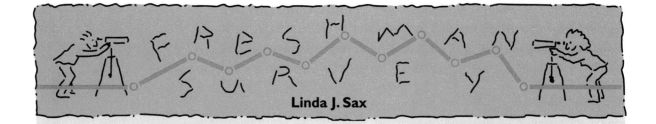

Linda J. Sax

Declining Majors in the Humanities

The humanities have declined in freshman popularity over the past two decades, with English and the fine arts especially hard hit. For example, between 1966 and 1995 the proportion of freshmen planning to major in English fell from 4.4 to 1.4 percent. (English actually dropped as low as 0.8 percent in 1982!)

Although many students indicate that they would prefer to major in literature, they also feel they need to study business to be competitive in the job market. However, some corporations prefer liberal arts majors to business students as management trainees, even though the former group may have comparatively little formal training in "business skills." You may be sur-

prised to learn that in some organizations, liberal arts majors actually have a better track record for performance and promotion than their peers who majored in business as undergraduates. For example, a twenty-year study of AT&T employees reveals that liberal arts majors advanced faster than other, nontechnical managers (that is, individuals who were not initially hired as engineers or researchers).

What advantages or disadvantages do you see in these fewer numbers for those who major in English and other liberal arts fields? Why do you think some corporations would prefer to hire liberal arts graduates over business majors?

college major. Others panic about it as they approach graduation and begin to look for a job. They falsely assume that "the decision" will make all the difference in their lives. In its broadest sense a career is the sum of the decisions you make over a lifetime. There is no "right occupation" just waiting to be discovered. Rather, there are many career choices you may find fulfilling and satisfying. The question to consider is, "What is the *best* choice for me *now*?"

EXERCISE 15.5 Exploring New Fields

Do you already have some career experience? (If you are a returning student who's chosen college as a path to a new career, the following exercise may be especially helpful in sorting out your options.)

1. What interests have you developed from life and work that might be part of your future career planning?

   _____

   _____

   _____

2. What skills do you bring from life and work that might be assets in other careers?

   _____

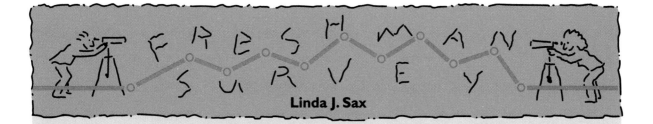

Linda J. Sax

Shifting Interest in Science

Of all the traditional liberal arts fields, the sciences have shown the most severe decline in student popularity. Between 1966 and 1995, the proportion of first-year students planning to major in mathematics dropped by nearly 90 percent, while interest in physical sciences majors (for example, chemistry and physics) fell by nearly 50 percent, as shown in the accompanying figure.

Although there has been an overall decline in the proportion of freshmen pursuing science majors, the CIRP Freshmen Survey data indicate that whereas men's interest in science has dropped by 35 percent since 1966, women's interest in science has *risen* by 7 percent. In fact, women's interest in science is currently higher than men's. How would you explain these trends?

Interestingly, the biological sciences have experienced dramatic fluctuations in student interest. Although interest in biological science majors reached a low of 3.7 percent in 1990, these majors have gained popularity in recent years, reaching 6.9 percent among 1995 fresh-

Freshman Interest in Science Majors, 1966–1995

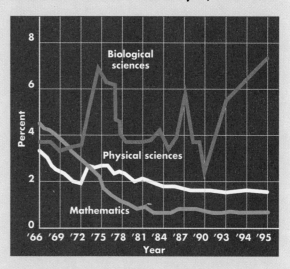

SOURCE: *Higher Education Research Institute, UCLA*

men. Why do you think there has been a sudden interest in the life sciences? What careers are biological science majors preparing for?

_____

_____

3. What things do you most enjoy about your present or most recent work?

_____

_____

_____

4. What things do you least enjoy about your present or most recent work?

_____

_____

_____

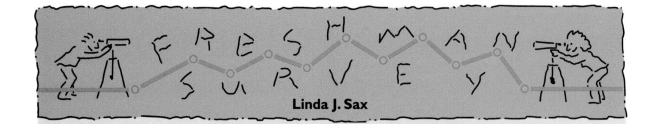

Linda J. Sax

A Teacher's Market

Talk has increased in recent years about the critical role of education in the nation's future, and students are once again thinking about teaching careers.

As the graph shows, teaching was an extremely popular career choice among young women in the late 1960s. But its popularity fell dramatically in the 1970s and the first part of the 1980s. Yet in recent years student interest in teaching careers has been rising. Why do you think freshman interest in teaching careers has been on the rise since 1985?

Although the numbers are up, current levels of interest in teaching are still far below those of the mid- to late-1960s—and well below the numbers required to meet future needs. Even though teaching is becoming a popular career choice again, we may not have enough new teachers to replace the many who will retire in the next ten to fifteen years. What effect do you think this may have on our educational system? What might be some of the attractions of a career in teaching?

Freshman Interest in Teaching Careers, by Sex, 1966–1995

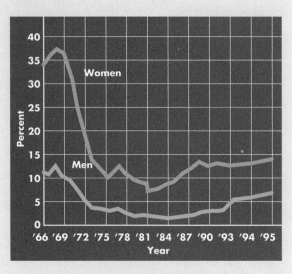

SOURCE: Higher Education Research Institute, UCLA

5. Go through your college catalog and list any majors that interest you. At this point, don't worry too much about whether the subject seems unfamiliar or too difficult. List the majors below, along with the reasons they appeal to you. As much as possible, try to link the reasons to your comments in the first four items of this exercise.

Major: _____ Reasons: _____

_____

Major: _____ Reasons: _____

_____

Major: _____ Reasons: _____

_____

Major: _____ Reasons: _____

_____

Looking for an unusual major? Try bagpiping at Carnegie-Mellon University. Requirements include bagpipe instruction and music theory, composition, and history, as well as a good set of lungs. Aerobic exercise may be recommended.

Photo by Ken Andreyo/courtesy of Carnegie-Mellon University

6. Discuss your responses in class, with your academic advisor, and/or with a career counselor. Rethink your choices in light of these discussions.

■ TIME FOR ACTION

In selecting a major, ask yourself these questions:

1. Am I interested in learning about the field?
2. Do I have the skills necessary for success?
3. Am I gaining skills, information, and perspectives that will be helpful in my career choices?

After choosing a major, begin to learn about other academic opportunities in your department. Talk with your advisor about minors, internships, independent study, study abroad, exchange programs, and other options that might broaden your academic experience.

As we said earlier, for some people there is a direct correlation between the major and the career; for others the choice of a major is best based on subject interest, not career considerations. If your major is not directly related to your career choices, plan to use work experience or campus activities to gain entry into your first job—many students are hired as bank management trainees or investment analysts based on their experience as treasurer of a student union committee rather than on their finance major.

Involvement in campus activities and part-time jobs are important in two ways. First, these experiences serve as the basis of a resume, which you will write to get your first job after college. Second, through these experiences you develop confidence in your career choice. It is better to discover that you hate inventory control *before* you graduate and accept a fabulous, high-paying job as an inventory control trainee.

Choosing a Major and Planning a Career   **269**

Throughout this section, you have done exercises aimed at gathering information about yourself and about the world of work and clarifying the most important issues involved in your choice of career and academic major. Here are a few other activities that may help:

- **Career exploration.** Once you've selected possible career fields, talk with people working in those fields and try to spend a day observing them at work to get a clear idea of what life is really like as a social worker or accountant or office manager. Read what people in this field read. Visit local professional association meetings.
- **Choice of major.** Talk with faculty members about the skills and areas of expertise you'll develop in studying the disciplines they're teaching. Ask if they're aware of careers or jobs in which the skills and knowledge they teach can be used.
- **Connection between major and career.** Ask employers if they look for graduates with certain majors or academic backgrounds for their entry-level positions.
- **Skill development.** Get involved in work experiences or campus activities that will allow you to develop skills and areas of expertise useful to your career plans. Find a summer job in that area, or volunteer as an intern. Keep a record of skills you have demonstrated.

By identifying and evaluating your interests and skills, obtaining career information, and assessing the role of goals and work values in your life, you turn career planning into an effective decision-making process. Career planning isn't a quick and easy way to find out what you want to do with your life, but it can point you to potentially satisfying jobs. Career planning can help you find your place in the world of work. Take advantage of it.

EXERCISE 15.6

Following Up on Careers

A Look back over your answers to the previous exercises. Which career possibilities seem to recur and to use the personal attributes summarized in Exercise 15.3? Choose two or three such career ideas. Find the *Occupational Outlook Handbook, Career Book,* or some other career reference work in your library or campus career center. Read more about these careers.

B Use the Internet to examine the home pages of professional societies or associations, Listserv discussion groups, or Usenet newsgroups in your field of interest. Are the issues more diverse than you had expected? More specialized? More technical? What can you learn from these sources about possible careers?

C Some campuses list current internship and employment opportunities on their local computer network or World Wide Web home page. If this service is available to you, access the service and look for positions that might offer an opportunity to evaluate your employment choice or to gain experience for future employment.

JOURNAL

Look back at your answers to Exercise 15.1. Have your thoughts changed about them? How? If you are still undecided about your major or career, that's fine. You probably still have quite a while to work on answering these questions.

SUGGESTIONS FOR FURTHER READING

Bolles, Richard N. *What Color Is Your Parachute? A Practical Manual for Job Hunters and Career Changers.* Berkeley, Calif.: Ten Speed Press, 1994.

Carney, Clarke G., and Cinda Field Wells. *Discover the Career Within You,* 3rd ed. Pacific Grove, Calif.: Brooks/Cole, 1991.

Carter, Carol. *Majoring in the Rest of Your Life.* New York: Noonday Press, 1990.

Dictionary of Occupational Titles (DOT). Washington, D.C.: Bureau of Labor Statistics.

Directory of Directories. Detroit: Gale Research. Published annually.

Encyclopedia of Associations. Detroit: Gale Research. Published annually.

Felderstein, Ken. *Never Buy a Hat If Your Feet Are Cold: Taking Charge of Your Career and Your Life.* El Segundo, Calif.: Serif, 1990.

Harbin, Carey E. *Your Transfer Planner: Strategic Goals and Guerrilla Tactics.* Belmont, Calif.: Wadsworth, 1995.

Holland, John. *The Self-Directed Search Professional Manual.* Gainesville, Fla.: Psychological Assessment Resources, 1985.

Jackson, Tom. *The Perfect Resume.* New York: Doubleday, 1990.

Lock, Robert D. *Taking Charge of Your Career Direction.* Pacific Grove, Calif.: Brooks/Cole, 1992.

Occupational Outlook Handbook. Washington, D.C.: U.S. Government Publication Staff. Published annually.

Salzman, Marian, and Nancy Marx Better. *Wanted: Liberal Arts Graduates.* New York: Doubleday, 1987.

Smith, Devon Coltrell, ed. *Great Careers: The Fourth of July Guide to Careers, Internships, and Volunteer Opportunities in the Non-Profit Sector.* Garrett Park, Md.: Garrett Park Press, 1990.

Stair, Lila B. *Careers in Business: Selecting and Planning Your Career Path.* Homewood, Ill.: Irwin, 1986.

Whitaker, Urban G. *Career Success Workbook: Five Essential Steps to Career and Job Satisfaction.* San Francisco: The San Francisco Learning Center, 1992.

16

A Personal System of Values

Richard L. Morrill
University of Richmond

I t amazes me to hear people talk about what's important to them. I mean, two of my friends think nothing of spending the night together three or four times a week. Someone else I know feels guilty if he misses church! I thought people here were going to feel more like I do.

Chapter Goals

After reading this chapter, you should understand the meaning and importance of values, and should be able to identify your own personal values and their sources. You should also be more aware of the possibility that your values may conflict with the values of others and some ways in which your own and others' values may change.

Discussions about values often generate more heat than light because the word *values* means different things to different people. For some the word refers to specific positions a person holds on controversial moral issues such as capital punishment. For others it refers to whatever might be most important to a person, such as a good job, a fancy car, or the welfare of the family. For still others it refers to abstractions such as truth, justice, or success. In this chapter, we offer a definition of values and explore ways to discover your values and apply them to the college experience.

■ DEFINING VALUES

Perhaps we can best define a *value* as an important attitude or belief that commits us to taking *action*, to doing something. We may not necessarily act in response to others' feelings, but when we truly hold a value we act on it. For instance, we might watch a television program showing starving people and feel sympathy or regret but take no action whatsoever. If our feelings of sympathy cause us to raise funds to help those suffering, then those feelings qualify as values. Action does not have to be overtly physical. Action may involve thinking and talking continually about a problem, trying to interest others in it, reading about it, or sending letters to officials regarding it. The basic point is that when we truly hold a value, it leads us to *do* something.

Let us also define values as beliefs that we accept *by choice*, with a sense of responsibility and ownership. Much of what we think is simply what others have taught us. Many things we have learned from our parents and others close to us will come to count fully as our values, but only once we fully embrace them for ourselves. One must personally accept or reject something before it can become a value.

Finally, let us make the idea of *affirmation* or *prizing* an essential part of values. We are proud of our values and the choices to which they lead. We also find ourselves ready to sacrifice for them and to establish our priorities around them. Our values draw forth our loyalties and commitment. In other words, a real aura of pressure or "oughtness" surrounds the values we have chosen.

In summary, then, *our values are those important attitudes or beliefs that we accept by choice, affirm with pride, and express in action.*

■DISCOVERING VALUES

You probably already have at least a fair sense of what your values are. Yet one of your key tasks in college is to more consciously define your own approach to life and articulate your values. College is an opportunity to locate and test those values by analyzing their full implications, comparing them with the values of others, and giving voice to your beliefs.

Identifying your values is at once simple and complex. One way to start is by asking yourself directly what your most important values are.

EXERCISE 16.1 **Prioritizing Your Values**

Consider the following list of twenty-five values. Rank-order these values (1 for the most important value, 2 for the second-most important value, and so on down to 25 for the least important one).

_____ 1. companionship

_____ 2. family life

_____ 3. security

_____ 4. being financially and materially successful

_____ 5. enjoying leisure time

_____ 6. work

_____ 7. learning and getting an education

_____ 8. appreciation of nature

_____ 9. competing and winning

_____ 10. loving others and being loved

_____ 11. a relationship with God

_____ 12. self-respect and pride

_____ 13. being productive and achieving

_____ 14. enjoying an intimate relationship

_____ 15. having solitude and private time to reflect

_____ 16. having a good time and being with others

_____ 17. laughter and a sense of humor

_____ 18. intelligence and a sense of curiosity

_____ 19. opening up to new experiences

_____ 20. risk taking and personal growth

_____ 21. being approved of and liked by others

_____ 22. being challenged and meeting challenges well

_____ 23. courage

_____ 24. compassion

_____ 25. being of service to others

Look at your top three choices on the list. What was the source for each of these values? We usually "learn" values from important people, peak events, or societal trends. List each value and try to indicate where you "learned" it.

NOTE: List used with permission from Gerald Corey and Marianne Schneider Corey, *I Never Knew I Had a Choice,* 5th ed. (Pacific Grove, Calif.: Brooks/Cole, 1993).

Value   **Source**

1. _____   _____

    _____

2. _____   _____

    _____

3. _____   _____

    _____

Review the values and their sources. Can you detect an overall pattern? If so, what does the pattern tell you about yourself? Were there any surprises?

EXERCISE 16.2   Evidence of Values

Another way to start discovering your values is by defining them in relation to some immediate evidence or circumstances. In the space below, list fifteen items in your room (or apartment or house) that are important or that symbolize something important to you.

_____   _____   _____

_____   _____   _____

_____   _____   _____

_____   _____   _____

_____   _____   _____

Now cross out the five items that are least important—the ones you could most easily live without. Of the remaining ten, cross out the three that are least important. Of the remaining seven, cross out two more. Of the remaining five, cross out two more. Rank-order the final three items from most to least important.

What has this exercise told you about what you value?

Another way to begin discovering your values is by looking at some choices you have already made in response to life's demands and opportunities. Many students will say that they chose a certain college because of its academic reputation. How much do you value your school's reputation? And more precisely, what does the word *reputation* mean to you? Are you interested in the

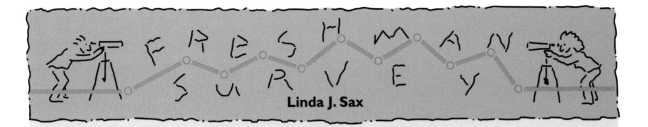

Linda J. Sax

What's Essential?

This graph shows dramatic shifts over the past two decades in the life goals of entering freshmen. Each year since 1967, the UCLA Freshman Survey has asked students to indicate the importance of "being very well-off financially" and "developing a meaningful philosophy of life." How would you interpret the results in the graph?

One striking aspect of these dramatic shifts in values during this period has been the changes in goals among first-year women. In 1967, first-year men were almost twice as likely as first-year women to identify "being very well-off financially" as an important life goal (54.2 percent for men, 30.0 percent for women). By 1995, the gap between men and women on this issue had narrowed from 24 to 3 percentage points (76.0 percent for men, 72.5 percent for women).

Changes in Freshman Life Goals, 1967–1995 (percentage indicating "essential" or "very important")

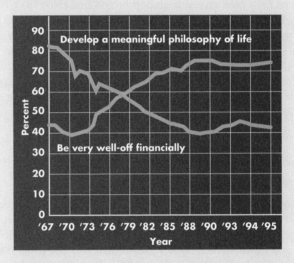

SOURCE: Higher Education Research Institute, UCLA

prestige that comes from enrolling in the college? Does this signify an interest in high achievement and in meeting demanding standards? Obviously, a value such as prestige can run in several directions, one being social, another intellectual. Finding the values that stand behind your choices requires continual exploration of the implications of those choices.

Many students say they have chosen a college because it offers the best opportunity for a good job in the future. Is this true for you? The choice to seek education in terms of your future career suggests any number of possible values. Does this mean that economic security is one of your top values, or does it suggest that you are defining personal success or power in terms of wealth? And once again, what are the implications of the choice? How much are you willing to sacrifice to achieve the goals connected with this economic value? How will your obligations to family and to society relate to this particular value?

EXERCISE 16.3 **Shared Values?**

List all the reasons you chose to attend college. Look back at your responses to Chapter 1, Exercises 1.1 and 1.2, regarding your reasons for attending college.

Share your reasons in a small group. Attempt to arrive at a consensus about the five most important reasons for people in general to choose college. Then rank the top five, from most important to least important.

Share your final rankings with other groups in the class. How similar were the results of the groups? How different? How easy or hard was it to reach a consensus in your group? In other groups? What does the exercise tell you about the consistency or inconsistency of values among members of the class?

In exploring your values, you may also ask how you became committed to this value in the first place and how it relates to other values. Conflict in values is a frequent, sometimes difficult problem. How far are you willing to go in service to this value? What sacrifices do you accept in its name? How do the values you have chosen provide you with a meaning for your future? Few of us ever stop trying to give a sharper and clearer account of exactly what our values mean and what implications they have for ourselves and those around us.

The previous exercises present ways to begin identifying values. Of course, this is not a one-time task—strongly held values may change with time and experience. Thus you should not only develop a sense of your present values but also gain some sense of how they are evolving in a variety of areas: personal, moral, political, economic, social, religious, and intellectual.

EXERCISE 16.4 Your Values and Your Family's Values

The process by which we assimilate values into our own value systems involves three steps: (1) choosing (selecting freely from alternatives after thoughtful consideration of the consequences), (2) prizing (cherishing the value and affirming it publicly), and (3) acting (consistently displaying this value in behavior and decisions). List three values your family has taught you are important. For each, document whether you have completed the three-step process to make their value yours.

Value	Choosing	Prizing	Acting
1. _____	_____	_____	_____
	_____	_____	_____
2. _____	_____	_____	_____
	_____	_____	_____
3. _____	_____	_____	_____
	_____	_____	_____

If you haven't completed the three steps, does it mean you have not chosen this value as your own? Explain your thoughts about this.

_____

_____

_____

_____

Choice shows value. What you choose to do with a few free minutes or hours of your time may say more about your values than what you spend long hours doing because you have to.

Photo courtesy of Earlham College

■COLLEGE CHALLENGES TO PERSONAL VALUES

Almost all students find that college life challenges their existing personal and moral values. The challenge typically comes through friendships and relationships with new people whose backgrounds, experiences, goals, and desires run counter to their own. This clash with diversity can be unsettling, threatening, exciting; it can also produce positive change.

Students differ from one another in everything from sleep and study habits to deep philosophical beliefs about the purposes of life. First-year students are often startled at the diversity of personal moralities to be found on any campus. For instance, some students have been taught at home or in church that it is wrong to drink alcohol. Yet they may find that friends whom they respect and care about see nothing wrong with drinking. Likewise, students from more liberal backgrounds may be astonished to discover themselves forming friendships with classmates whose personal values are very conservative.

How do you react when you do not approve of some aspects of a friend's way of life? Do you try to change his or her behavior, pass judgments on the person, or withdraw from the relationship? Often, part of the problem is that the friend demonstrates countless good qualities and values that make the conduct itself seem less significant. In the process, your own values may begin to change under the influence of a new kind of relativism: "I don't choose to do that, but I'm not going to make any judgments against those who do." A similar pattern often develops regarding sexual involvements. People become friends with others whose behavior and values differ from their own, and the result can be personal turmoil.

A Personal System of Values   **279**

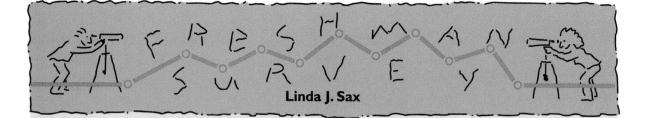

FRESHMAN SURVEY

Linda J. Sax

Social and Political Issues

How have the personal values of first-year students changed in the past seventeen years?

What does the first graph suggest about student attitudes on some key political and social issues? Although it suggests a movement toward more liberal positions in recent years, entering freshmen have also become increasingly conser-

vative on selected issues over the past seventeen years, as the second graph shows.

Do any of these percentages surprise you? In what respect? Do you think these numbers would hold for your campus? What is the mood on political issues on your campus? Among your friends?

Freshman Attitudes on Political and Social Issues, 1978, 1993, and 1995 (percentage who "agree" or "strongly agree")

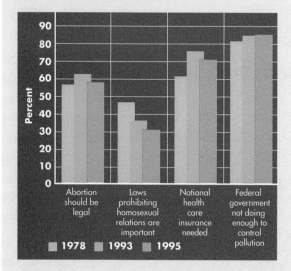

SOURCE: *Higher Education Research Institute, UCLA*

Freshman Attitudes on Crime-Related Issues, 1978, 1993, and 1995

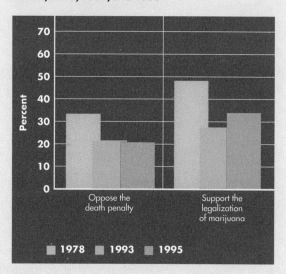

SOURCE: *Higher Education Research Institute, UCLA*

EXERCISE 16.5 Friends and Values

Consider several friends and think about their values. Pick one who really differs from you in some important value. In a small group, discuss this difference in values. Explore how it's possible to be friends with someone so different.

Photo by Hilary Smith

You probably get along most easily with people who dress and act like you do. You expect to have a lot in common. At the same time, you may find that you learn a lot from friends whose backgrounds and values are very different from yours.

In such cases, one can always recommend tolerance, since tolerance for others is a central value in our society and one that often grows during college. Yet it is easy to think of cases in which tolerance becomes indulgence of another's destructive tendencies. It is one thing to accept a friend's responsible use of alcohol at a party, and quite another to fail to challenge a drunk who plans to drive you home. Sexual intimacy in an enduring relationship may be one thing; a never-ending series of one-night stands is quite another. Remember, the failure to challenge destructive conduct is no sign of friendship.

EXERCISE 16.6 Values in Conflict

Choose part A or B. Read the situation and discuss your responses in a small group. Describe any similar situations you've experienced. How did you respond to the situation? Were you successful? How did you define success?

A You have become good friends with your roommate since the beginning of the term. You know he or she uses drugs once in a while, which usually results in some rowdy behavior you're not always comfortable with. He or she certainly doesn't use drugs every day, but you wonder if even occasional use is healthy. You've tried to discuss the topic with him or her and received very little response.

Last night, while under the influence of drugs, your roommate set fire to a number of flyers and posters on the hallway walls. Today, your resident assistant (or house supervisor or landlord) wants an explanation and demands to know who is responsible. Your roommate doesn't seem willing to come forward.

Which of your values may come into play here? Will any of your values conflict with one another? How might your values conflict with those of your roommate? Your resident assistant, supervisor, or landlord? How would you resolve the situation?

In addition to the questions above, discuss how changing one part of the scenario might change your response. (For instance, what if your friend burned *your* posters on the door to *your* room?)

B You get a ride to school fairly often with a person who happens to be in one of your classes. You haven't known this person long but do consider him or her a friend on campus. From your talk while you commute, you know that he or she lives a somewhat wilder life than you do and at least occasionally takes drugs as part of an outside social scene.

Yesterday, he or she was driving badly on the way to school and got into an argument with some other motorists at a stoplight. You had the feeling alcohol or some other drug was behind the problem.

It really is convenient to ride together. It saves you several hours a week in travel time. Also, you don't have a lot of friends on campus and would like to keep this friendship if you can. When you meet later in the day, you try to find out what was wrong that morning, but your friend denies that there was any problem.

In addition to the questions above, discuss how changing one part of the scenario might change your response. (For instance, what if you were driving and the person's behavior somehow interfered with your own safe driving?)

Are there better and worse ways to deal with these challenges to personal and moral values? As we saw earlier, true values must be freely chosen and cannot be accepted simply on the authority of another person. After all, the purpose of values is to give active meaning to our lives. Trying to make sense out of the complex circumstances of our own lives by using someone else's values simply doesn't work.

At the same time, it is appropriate to talk about values with those whose values seem to be in conflict with our own. What are the other person's true values (consciously identified, freely chosen, and actively expressed)? Do his or her current behaviors correspond to those values? Much can be learned on both sides.

Many people make the mistake of fleeing from the challenge of diversity and failing to confront conflicting value systems. The problem with this strategy is that at some time in their lives, often within a year or two, these people find themselves unable to cope with the next set of challenges to which they are exposed. They do not grow as persons because they do not prize their own values and their behaviors are not consistent with what they say they value. Although it's only a first step, you must work through challenges to your own personal values by finding answers that truly make sense to you and help you to move ahead with your life.

■CHANGING INTELLECTUAL VALUES

Intellectual values such as clarity, accuracy, rigor, and excellence cluster around the central value of truth. One of the most striking transitions that occurs during the college years has to do with the way in which a person's notion of truth changes.

Many students enter college assuming the process of education is one in which unquestioned authorities "pour" truth into the students' open ears. Some students believe that every problem has a single right answer and that the instructor or the textbook will always be the source of truth. However, most college instructors don't believe this, and their views on truth often initially shock these students.

Academics tend to see "truth" in a much more flexible way. It's not that the teacher is cynical about the possibility of truth, but rather that the scholar's role involves an ongoing, open-ended search. He or she is seeking as many valid interpretations of the information as can be found. College instructors continually ask for reasons, for arguments, for the assumptions on which a given position is based, and for the evidence that confirms or discounts it.

Just as with personal and moral values, college-level education involves the assumption that as a student you will become a maker of your own meaning, on your own, with the ultimate responsibility for judgments of truth and falseness resting in your hands. The whole system of a university's intellectual values—openness, freedom of inquiry, tolerance, rigor, and excellence—is based on this approach, and there is no escaping it.

EXERCISE 16.7   Applying Your Values in College

Although values are not always expressed openly, they are reflected in your college environment, for example in academic integrity policies and various individual behaviors. The variety of values, as we have discussed, can often lead to conflict.

A Academic integrity. Academic dishonesty often occurs when the intellectual values held in higher education (see Chapter 8)—honesty, freedom of inquiry, openness, and excellence—conflict with those of individual students. What values might lead students to commit an academically dishonest act? What can be done about it?

B Values and personal behavior. Recall Chapter 4 on time management, which discussed prioritizing activities by their importance to you. This is a way of expressing your values through actions. For the following two values, list a variety of actions that would express those values.

Achieving Excellence in College

1. Reading one book each week not required for class but related to my major

2. _____

3. _____

4. _____

5. _____

Maintaining a Great Social Life

1. Spending weekends out of town with friends

2. _____

3. _____

4. _____

5. _____

The Right to Vote

No matter what their political preference, college students have a poor record of showing up to vote. Government data suggest that voting in presidential elections among 18- to 21-year-olds has dropped steadily since 1972, the first year persons under 21 were allowed to vote. Americans ages 18–24 have the lowest levels of voter turnout of any age group.

How would you explain this apparent lack of interest in voting?

Although achieving excellence and maintaining a social life may not seem like conflicting values, the actions that express the values may cause conflict. In other words, acting on one value may prevent you from staying true to the other. Which of the actions you've listed in each column might conflict with one another? If you held these two values, how would you reconcile each of these conflicts?

▪CHOOSING VALUES

We have stressed that the essential first step in developing a value system is for you to become your own maker of meaning. But it is only a first step; you must be aware not only of making meaning but also of making a meaning that can lead to a coherent and fulfilling life. As crucial as it is to develop your own values, it is equally important that you find ethical values. Little is accomplished if you develop a genuine system of values that leads to egocentric, dishonest, cruel, and/or irresponsible conduct.

The question of what ethical values are cannot be answered simply. There are no automatic criteria (though perhaps the "Golden Rule" will serve as well as any). Yet clearly all of us who have accepted life in a democratic society and membership in an academic community such as a college or university are committed to many significant values. To participate in democratic institutions is to honor such values as respect for others, tolerance, equality, liberty, and fairness. Members of an academic community are usually passionate in their defense of academic freedom, the open search for truth, honesty, collegiality, civility, and tolerance for dissenting views.

Yet many issues relating to values are open for continuing and legitimate discussion and disagreement. For instance, to what extent should the college or university take it upon itself to ensure the success of each of its students? To what extent may it simply offer certain opportunities for learning and then let each student sink or swim?

Perhaps what college can do best with regard to values is teach a process for making value choices, for thinking seriously about values, just as a good education teaches us to think in other realms. That is, an education in values can teach us how to assess our values while leaving us to choose our own actual values. This might involve in part the posing of a series of overarching questions relating to values.

For example, are our values *consistent* with one another? Contradictions among values can be just as harmful and foolish as contradictions among ideas. Are our values sufficiently broad in *scope*—that is, do they provide us with a comprehensive outlook on life? We learn that our values may work very well within the small circle of our family but produce conflict with individuals from a different background. This presses us toward common ground, areas of agreement based on which we can overcome conflict. The pressure always to enlarge our circle of association, to move toward the universal sphere of the human family, beyond all divisions of race, sex, and the like—that is where we have to go to find our true and best selves.

Other tests can also measure the depth, the richness, and the adequacy of our values. We know that many of our choices fail to meet the test that *time* itself provides. Others fail to meet the test of *relative worth*. Life teaches us that transient satisfactions and pleasures leave us with little if they rob us of opportunities and accomplishments that may stay with us for a lifetime.

Life itself continually tests which of our values will create coherent, consistent, and enduring results, the greatest fulfillment of our potential. Just as we can be educated with regard to ways of thinking, so we can be educated with regard to our values and our choices. This too is what college is all about. The opportunity for growth is yours.

JOURNAL

This chapter suggests that any belief or behavior that is primarily a result of what someone else expects of us without our own active and free choice is not the expression of our own true values. It also suggests that for many students college is a time and an experience in which everyone's true values are tested. Describe your current system of "true values" (chosen, affirmed, and acted upon). In what ways has college already tested or changed those values?

SUGGESTIONS FOR FURTHER READING

Bellah, R., R. Madsen, W. M. Sullivan, A. Swidler, and S. M. Tipton. *Habits of the Heart.* Berkeley: University of California Press, 1985.

Corey, G., and M. S. Corey. *I Never Knew I Had a Choice,* 5th ed. Pacific Grove, Calif.: Brooks/Cole, 1993.

Kolak, Daniel, and Raymond Martin. *Wisdom Without Answers: A Guide to the Experience of Philosophy,* 3rd ed. Belmont, Calif.: Wadsworth, 1996.

Lewis, Hunter. *A Question of Values.* New York: Harper & Row, 1990.

Morrill, R. L. *Teaching Values in College.* San Francisco: Jossey-Bass, 1980.

Niebuhr, H. R. *Faith on Earth.* New Haven, Conn.: Yale University Press, 1989.

Pojman, Louis P. *Ethics: Discovering Right and Wrong,* 2nd ed. Belmont, Calif.: Wadsworth, 1995.

Rokeach, M. *The Nature of Human Values.* New York: Free Press, 1973.

Simon, S., L. Howe, and H. Kirschenbaum. *Values Clarification.* New York: Hart, 1972.

Diversity on Campus

Joan A. Rasool
Westfield State College

I *know "diversity" is in these days, but I'm not much into talking about it. I'm not even sure what it means. We had "diversity celebration days" in high school, but nobody took them very seriously. They seemed to separate us, not bring us together. I'm open to meeting other people but I don't want to force anything. Live and let live.*

Chapter Goals

This chapter explores the riches of diversity in all its dimensions, beginning with the most obvious: the realms of race, ethnic groups, and culture. It suggests methods of clear communication that can help break down barriers between you and others. It deals with the homophobia and hate speech prevalent on some campuses and offers suggestions for understanding the perspectives of others.

Ask almost any person in this country about his or her racial or ethnic background and you have the start of an interesting story:

My father is mostly Arab and part Kurdish. He always said that his strength and determination came from his Kurdish background. My mother's background is Scottish and English. She told me her mother's side of the family came over on the Mayflower. My parents met when my dad was a graduate student and my mother was an undergraduate. She was studying economics and he agreed to tutor her. I came to this country when I was 4 years old and I'm still figuring out what it means to be an Arab American.

—Baidah

My racial background is African American. The other thing I would add is that I see my background as black and working class. Those two things go together for me; they are a part of my roots. How I grew up was kind of varied. On one hand I was born in California and on the other hand I was raised in Texas during segregation. Part of me grew up in a strongly segregated part of the South, and another part of me, as an adolescent, grew up in integrated California.

—Terrell

I'm American. I don't feel like I have a strong attachment to any particular group. My family is Italian, Polish, Irish, and French. On St. Patrick's Day, I say I'm Irish. If I go to an Italian restaurant, I pretend I'm Italian! I call one grandmother "Bapshee," and that's about how bilingual I am. Maybe I'm not anything.

—Eric

I'm Filipino American, and like most Filipinos I am also Catholic. Family values are stressed in my home. Outsiders might say that my culture is very patriarchal, but I certainly grew up watching my parents share power equally. My mother was a very strong woman, and as I remember, the final decisions were always hers. I am the youngest of six children and am very

Figure 17.1 A Diversity Attitude Scale

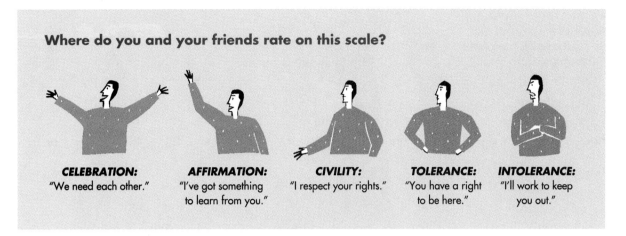

Where do you and your friends rate on this scale?

CELEBRATION: "We need each other."

AFFIRMATION: "I've got something to learn from you."

CIVILITY: "I respect your rights."

TOLERANCE: "You have a right to be here."

INTOLERANCE: "I'll work to keep you out."

opinionated so no decision is ever easy in my household. In addition to family, education is heavily stressed. Attaining a college degree is a must—no, not a must, it just should happen—like breathing.

—Cristina

Neither the United States nor Canada are as they used to appear on television—homogeneously white and more or less middle class. They never were. But now more than ever, our societies are multiracial and multicultural. A quick glance at official college calendars will give you a clue. The major holidays for members of the Buddhist, Baha'i, Christian, Hindu, Jewish, Muslim, and Sikh faiths may be listed!

You may also be aware of or have experienced the racial tensions on college campuses today. Racial harassment, the lack of greater numbers of students and faculty of color, and the need to pluralize the curriculum are some of the issues being discussed. These are serious issues that merit serious attention.

If you are like most students, you see college as the beginning of an exciting new stage in your life, a time when you can learn a lot about yourself and the world as well as prepare for the future. How can you be sure that you will feel comfortable here, that you can be yourself, and that you will have the opportunity to meet new people and have new experiences? What is your responsibility to help create a campus environment in which all students can pursue their goals? (See Figure 17.1.)

This chapter should increase your appreciation of your own and others' backgrounds. It will also show you how campus culture influences students' academic and personal lives and help you develop strategies for making the campus a more welcoming place for everyone.

RACE, ETHNIC GROUPS, AND CULTURE

The word *race* generally refers to a group of people who are distinct from other people in terms of certain very obvious inherited characteristics—skin color, hair color and degree of straightness, body build, proportions of facial and other body features. *Ethnic group* may refer to people of different races or

Most colleges make an effort to help students feel welcome, respected, and supported in every way that the students themselves feel is important.

Photo courtesy of Earlham College

to people of the same race who can be distinguished by language, national origin, religious tradition, and so on.

Culture refers to the material and nonmaterial products that people in a society create or acquire from other societies and pass on to future generations. Culture includes a society's intangible beliefs, values, norms, and language as well as tangible realities such as cellular telephones, futons, basketballs, and college yearbooks. Nonmaterial culture can't be touched, held, or transported, but it plays a major role in influencing how people define reality. Recall Cristina's statement about the high value her culture places on education. Many European Americans believe children should learn how to be independent and self-sufficient at an early age. Many Hispanic Americans place a high value on strong family ties.

You celebrate your background as easily as you breathe in air. From the moment you open your mouth and say "buenos dias," "good morning," or "magandang umaga," you affirm your cultural ties. The music you listen to, the food you eat, the clothes you wear, the holidays you celebrate, the "walk you walk" and the "talk you talk"—all make statements about the importance of culture.

EXERCISE 17.1   Sharing Your Background

In the beginning of this chapter, Baidah, Eric, Cristina, and Terrell start to tell "their stories." Now it's your turn. Write a two-part essay. In the first part, describe the racial or ethnic groups to which you belong. Can you belong to more than one? Absolutely. Think of your own background. Be sure to include some of the beliefs, values, and norms in your cultural background. In what ways do you celebrate your background? What if you are like Eric and don't feel a strong attachment to any group? Write what you know about your family history and speculate on why your ethnic identity isn't very strong.

In the second part of your essay, discuss a time when you realized that your racial or ethnic background was not the same as someone else's. For example, young children imagine that their experiences are mirrored in the lives of others.

If they are Jewish, everyone else must be too! If their family eats okra for breakfast, then all families do the same. Yet at some point they begin to realize that there are differences. When did you realize that you were African American or Hispanic American or European American or Korean American or biracial or whatever?

Share your essays with other members of the class. In what ways are your stories similar? In what ways are your stories different?

■ CULTURAL PLURALISM: REPLACING THE MELTING POT WITH VEGETABLE STEW

For years, students were taught that the immigration of different people to the United States created a "melting pot"—as diverse groups migrated to this land, their culture and customs mixed into this American pot to create a new society. The reality of what happened, however, is more complex. Instead of "melting" into the "pot," most immigrants were asked to become more like what was already here—an Anglo-European soup. For example, in order to get ahead, immigrants had to change their names to make them sound more Anglo-American; they had to make sure their children gave up their native language and learned English; and they had to do business the American way. Some groups could accomplish this more easily (for example, the Irish, French, and Germans), although not without experiencing some discrimination. Today, members of these groups may be more likely to see themselves as Eric does—as "just American." It is important to note, however, that many European Americans have retained strong ethnic ties. Equally important is the recognition that other non-European groups (for example, Africans, Japanese, and Chinese) found both laws and racial barriers impeding their integration into the culture at large.

As a result, many sociologists and educators have concluded that American society is less like a melting pot and more like vegetable stew. While each group has its own unique characteristics and flavor, all the groups together create a common broth. The dominant culture has begun to acknowledge and affirm the diversity of cultures within its borders. After years of stressing commonalities, we are now focusing on our differences.

Cultural pluralism has replaced the melting pot theory. Under cultural pluralism, each group is free to celebrate and practice its customs and traditions, and in return each group is expected to participate in the general mainstream culture and abide by its laws. "Unity in diversity" is the new rallying cry.

Whoever you are, in some ways you are part of the mainstream culture. In other ways, however, you probably feel that you are part of a smaller group, a microculture within society.

EXERCISE 17.2 · Creating Common Ground

Examine the items in the following chart. For each item, decide whether you would describe your preferences, habits, and customs as reflecting the mainstream or macroculture or a specific ethnic or microculture. Enter specific examples of your own preferences in the appropriate column (two examples are given). For a given item, you may enter examples under both Macroculture and Microculture, or you may leave one or the other blank. In filling out the chart, you may want to look back at the essay you wrote in Exercise 17.1.

Category	Macroculture	Microculture
Language		
Food	hamburgers	sushi (Japanese)
Music (for your peer group)		
Style of dress (for your peer group)		
Religion		
Holidays celebrated		
Heroes/role models		
Key values		cooperation (Native Amer.)
Lifestyle		
Personal goals		

Compare answers in a small group. Do most people in the group agree on what should be considered an example of the macroculture and what is an example of a microculture? Is there anyone who identifies completely with the macroculture? Is there anyone who feels completely outside it? What do you and others in your class regard as significant differences among you? In what areas do you share common ground?

Cultural pluralism doesn't mean groups must remain isolated. In fact, as you learn more about another ethnic group's heritage, there may be customs and traditions in which you would like to participate. Particular values stressed in one culture may better suit you. For example, you may prefer the punctuality emphasized in European American cultures or the more "relaxed" time schedule of Arab Americans. You may value the sense of duty and family obligation among Hispanic Americans or admire the sense of individual control and independence offered in the Anglo culture. Or your preferences may be directed toward language, music, food, dress, dance, architecture, or religion. The possibilities are endless.

■ UNDERSTANDING THE PERSPECTIVES OF OTHERS

Remember the children's story of the Three Little Pigs? The big bad wolf "huffs and puffs" and blows down the houses of the first two little pigs. He finally meets his downfall when he attempts to climb down the third little pig's brick chimney only to find himself landing in a pot of boiling water. All this is refuted in the recent publication of *The True Story of the 3 Little Pigs! by A. Wolf*:

Everybody knows the story of the Three Little Pigs. Or at least they think they do. But I'll let you in on a little secret. Nobody knows the real story, because

"That Corner in the Cafeteria"

When I think about my freshman year at a predominantly white university, these are the things I remember: " 'Negro' students who graduate from your high school tend not to do well at this university; therefore, we encourage you to attend a summer pre-college program," said a representative from the university. (I did.) "You'll do well here if you never take a math course," stated my advisor during the freshman orientation program. (I never did take a math course, and I paid for it!) Of the 300 students in Psychology 80, no one would sit next to me!

One day, by accident, I wandered into the commuter cafeteria, and there they were—black people! I was so glad to see them that I think I ran toward them. The group was composed primarily of upper-class students and two graduate students. "Hey, what's your aim in life?" hollered Jack, one of the graduate students, as I approached the group. I opened my mouth to respond, but I don't think anything coherent came out. Can you imagine how I felt when they told me that we were in a university of well over 20,000 students and that maybe, just maybe, there were a total of 50 black undergraduate

and graduate students? Later I found out that 15 out of the 50 black students were freshmen!

As the semester progressed, I spent a considerable amount of time in the cafeteria and became better adjusted to the university. That corner in the cafeteria was my home away from home. Those black students were my family and support system. They reprimanded me for cutting class and applauded me for my achievements. There were no black faculty, as far as I knew.

Interaction with white students was fairly minimal. They appeared not to know what to say to me, and vice versa. Communication with white faculty members was a little different. They had the information; therefore, I did talk to them. My grades were not that fantastic, though, and it wasn't until my junior year that I became a serious student.

SOURCE: Francine G. McNairy, vice president for academic affairs and provost, Millersville University of Pennsylvania. Reproduced, with permission, from *College Is Only the Beginning: A Student Guide to Higher Education*, 2nd ed., John N. Gardner and A. Jerome Jewler, eds. (Belmont, Calif.: Wadsworth, 1989).

nobody has ever heard my side of the story. . . . I don't know how this whole Big Bad Wolf thing got started, but it's all wrong. . . . The real story is about a sneeze and a cup of sugar.

The "real story," it turns out, is that Mr. A. Wolf had a cold the day he went to his neighbor's house to borrow a cup of sugar. Unfortunately, he sneezed so hard that the house fell down killing his good neighbor—the pig. He was then *forced* to eat him because he couldn't let a good meal go to waste!

All these years and no one thought to ask the wolf for his side of the story! And yet that is just the point. If we are going to accept and affirm the differences of other groups, then each group needs to be ready to listen to the other. This is not to say that "the other group" is the villain, but that groups tend to look at one another's perspective or side of the story as misguided, wrong, or backward.

EXERCISE 17.3   Hearing All Sides of a Story

This exercise involves forming caucus groups. A caucus group is defined as any group in which you feel you automatically belong. For example, you might form caucus groups under the following headings: commuters, learning-disabled students, Catholics, biracial students, gay and lesbian students, African American women, men, nontraditional students, and so on. First generate a list of possible caucus groups, and then decide if there are enough potential members in the class to form a group of three or more members.

Join a caucus group. Meet in your group to discuss the following questions: How does your group experience campus life? What are the major academic, residential, or social concerns of your group? How well does your college meet the needs of your group?

As a caucus group, report on your discussion while other class members just listen. Afterward, the listeners may comment or ask questions on what has been said, but they should refrain from challenging the *perceptions* of the group they are listening to.

■EXPANDING OUR VIEW OF DIVERSITY

In recent years, the concept of diversity has expanded to include sexual orientation. If our goal is to make all students feel welcome, then colleges and universities must consider the needs and concerns of gay, lesbian, and bisexual students.

Gary, a mass communications major in his junior year, decided to "come out" during this year's annual National Coming Out Day. He said:

I am tired of pretending I am someone I'm not. I need the community of other gay people to help me deal with the homophobia on campus, and I want to celebrate a part of me that I have come to accept and love. Believe me, my life would be a lot easier if I could accept the "normal" heterosexual lifestyle that society keeps shoving down my throat. What do I want from life? I want what most people want—the chance to go to school, have friends, get a job, and find someone to love.

In order to create a welcoming environment for gay and lesbian students, it is important to unlearn stereotypical ideas. For example, it is *not* possible to tell someone's sexual orientation just by looking at him or her. Both gay and straight people lose when society rigidly categorizes people based on a particular style of dress or haircut, or personal interest such as ballet or sports. Second, being gay or lesbian is not solely a choice. Each year, scientists find further evidence that suggests that sexual orientation may be influenced by genetic factors. Perhaps homosexuality is a combination of genetic material and environmental factors. Last, most child molesters are *not* homosexuals; most child molesters are white male heterosexuals.

■THE DIVERSITY OF CAMPUS CULTURE

How diverse is your campus? Are you aware of the diversity that does exist on your campus? In what ways does your school encourage all students to

A healthy diversity on campus depends on a general willingness to let social groups form in whatever patterns are helpful and constructive. It also depends on groups and individuals welcoming communication and exchange.

Photo by Hilary Smith

feel welcome? How easy is it for students to express their culture and to learn about their backgrounds or the backgrounds of others?

EXERCISE 17.4 ## Getting the Diversity Facts on Your Campus

Consider campus diversity in a broader context—among the student body, faculty, administrators, and staff; in the curriculum; in social and residential settings; and at the institutional level (that is, the overall policies and procedures followed by the college).

In a group with three or four other students in your class, investigate one of the areas in the following list. Use the questions under each heading to help guide your research. Your instructor may be able to offer suggestions on where to locate relevant materials or appropriate people to interview. Each group should report to the class their general findings in the various areas. Groups should focus on two questions: (1) How easy is it for students to express their culture and to learn about their backgrounds or the backgrounds of others on this campus? and (2) In what ways does our school try to make all students feel welcome?

A. Diversity in Numbers

1. In what ways are your student body, faculty, administrators, and staff diverse? What percentage of students, faculty, administrators, and staff come from different ethnic/racial groups?

2. What religious, linguistic, socioeconomic, gender, and geographic differences are there among students?

B. Diversity in the Curriculum

1. What are you learning about the contributions and concerns of people of color in any of your classes? Are you learning about different perspectives as a central focus of your courses, or are the views or contributions of "others" highlighted in special chapters or special sections of chapters? Give examples.

"I Knew I Was Gay When I Was 13"

I knew I was gay when I was 13 years old. My friends were falling in love with members of the Fairview Little League team, and I was daydreaming about Mary Sue Cook. Still, I didn't even know what a homosexual was until the AIDS virus hit. Kids in my middle school had cheerfully announced that some disease was killing all the fags, and I had said, "Good riddance!" No one had told me there was a word to describe me. Fags got AIDS, so I spent the rest of that year pretending to have crushes on the Little League boys.

By the time I was 15 I knew a whole lot about fags. I learned that faggots were actually pieces of kindling used to start a fire and that the term was transferred to homosexuals when they were burned at the stake for moral crimes. I learned about the National Gay Hotline and about the sodomy laws that still exist in most states. The Good Samaritan Church started a youth group for gay teens. Up until that point the word lesbian had been "the L word," because I had never heard it spoken in a positive way. Now it is a definitive term for everything I have been through.

We were a fairly insecure lot in those days. We fought against traditional values by coloring our half-shaved heads and dressing in black clothing. We spent our time crouching in mall emergency exits listening to Depeche Mode or Dead or Alive. We exchanged antique jewelry and jotted down poetry about an unjust world. We hid our faces behind heavy eyeliner and burgundy bangs. We were America's gay youth, and we had already learned that hiding was the easiest way to survive.

When I went away to college I was still a loathsome "closet case." My roommate and I seemed to hit it off, and I was afraid that my "news" might scare her away. God knows I didn't want her thinking I was interested in her. That may seem like a strange thing to say, but you would be surprised at the way the "straight" world views a friendship with a homosexual. I had known Wendy for almost three months, but I knew that everything would change when she found out. She would treat me like a different person, and yet I would be the same. I did finally confide in her after months of isolation and insecurity, and she stood by me despite her own fears. She even admitted that she would have blindly hated me if I had told her when we met. I guess I was supposed to be glad that I had lied.

After that, it was relatively easy to come out to my friends. One of the girls across the hall from me clipped out articles from the student newspaper about National Coming Out Day. She told me I should go to the Gay/Lesbian Student Association meetings to meet other people. There were hundreds of gay and lesbian students at the University of South Carolina, and perhaps thirty of them were comfortable enough to show their faces at the Gay/Lesbian Student Association.

I just knew that there would be a line of gay-bashers waiting to see just who went to those meetings. I finally worked up the nerve to walk over to Harper College one evening but quickly retreated when I realized that there were classes being held that I would have to walk in front of to get to the stairs. I skulked back to my room to tell my roommate of my misadventure. I really thought she'd pour out the sympathy over my pitiful condition. Instead, she got up, put her shoes on, and told me that the two of us were going to march right back over there and go to that meeting.

I have come a long way from my 13-year-old fears of getting AIDS. The "coming out" process is more than finding loopholes in society where you might feel safe. It's not just asking society to accept you, but learning to accept yourself.

SOURCE: Jen Bacon, *Portfolio* XI (no. 1), Fall 1990 (a University of South Carolina student publication). Used with permission.

2. What courses or workshops are available if you want to increase your racial awareness and understanding?

3. Are courses offered that include the contributions and perspectives of gays and lesbians?

C. Diversity in Social and Residential Settings

1. Who or what groups are reflected in the artwork, sculptures, and names of buildings on your campus?

2. Whose food preferences are served on a regular basis at the college dining facilities?

3. If your school has campus residences, does residential life staff schedule ongoing discussions on issues of sexual orientation, diversity, and tolerance? Who is in charge of these programs?

4. Do students from different ethnic groups have organizations and hold social events? Give some examples. How does school governance support a variety of diverse activities being brought to campus?

5. Do gay and lesbian students have organizations and hold social events? Give some examples. Are there gay and lesbian support groups on campus? Who is in charge of these groups?

6. Where does cross-racial interaction exist on your campus? Is the atmosphere one of peaceful coexistence and/or resegregation? Where do students find opportunities to work, study, and socialize across racial/ethnic lines?

D. Institutional Commitment to Diversity

1. How does the mission statement of your school address cultural pluralism? (Your college mission statement may be printed in the college catalog.)

2. What policies and procedures does your school have with regard to the recruitment and retention of students of color? (Contact your admissions office for information.)

3. What policies and procedures does your school have with regard to the recruitment and hiring of faculty and staff of color? (Contact your affirmative action/equal opportunity office for information.)

4. Does your school administration feel responsible for educating students about diversity, or does it assume that students and faculty of color will do this?

5. Does your school administration feel responsible for educating students about tolerance, or does it assume that gay and lesbian organizations will do this?

■DISCRIMINATION AND PREJUDICE ON COLLEGE CAMPUSES

Unfortunately, incidences of discrimination and acts of prejudice are rising on college campuses. Although some schools may not be experiencing overt racial conflict, tension may still exist; many students report having little contact with students from different racial or ethnic groups. Moreover, a recent national survey, "Taking America's Pulse," conducted for the National Conference of Christians and Jews, indicates that blacks, whites, Hispanics, and Asians hold many negative stereotypes about one another. The good news is that "nine out of 10 Americans nationwide claim they are willing to

The "New Majority"

Why are institutions of higher learning so concerned about diversity on their campuses? One reason has to do with population figures. In 1990, 48 million Americans (about one-fifth of the total population) were identified as "minorities." By the year 2020 they will make one-third of the population, and by the last quarter of the twenty-first century they will be the majority.[*]

As part of their mission, colleges and universities educate and train the nation's work force. College administrations realize that the "new majority" will be a major economic strength to the nation and will be responsible—through their taxes, Social Security payments, and other contributions—for helping to maintain *everyone's* standard of living.

The total U.S. population in 1990 was about 250 million according to the Bureau of the Census.[†] Here are some of the groups currently considered minorities in the United States, although in some areas of the country they are actually in the majority.

AFRICAN AMERICANS

African Americans make up about 12 percent (30 million) of the U.S. population. They come from diverse cultures and countries in Africa, the Caribbean, and Central and South America. Excluded from the mainstream white culture despite the end of slavery, they developed a system of historically black colleges and universities dating from the mid-nineteenth century. As of 1980, these schools still awarded nearly 70 percent of all bachelor's degrees received by African Americans.

ALASKAN NATIVE/AMERICAN INDIANS

About 2 million Americans identify themselves as (non-Hispanic) Eskimo, Aleut, and American Indian, from more than 300 tribes. Their heritage includes more than 120 separate languages.

ASIAN AMERICANS

Since discriminatory immigration laws ended in 1965, Asians have become one of our fastest-growing groups, expected to reach 10 million (4 percent of the U.S. population) by the year 2000. The largest of the many groups are Chinese, Japanese, Korean, Asian Indian, Filipino, and Vietnamese. Asian Americans have made major contributions to the economies of the American West and Hawaii.

MEXICAN AMERICANS

Hispanics made up 12 percent of the U.S. population in 1990. The fastest-growing Hispanic group is Mexican Americans (almost 13 million). Mexican Americans have deep roots in the American Southwest from past centuries when that region belonged to Mexico and Spain. More than half of Mexican Americans live in Texas and California.

PUERTO RICANS AND CUBAN AMERICANS

Around 1990, Puerto Ricans living on the U.S. mainland numbered 2.3 million, and those living in Puerto Rico 3.3 million. All are U.S. citizens. There are more than a million Cuban Americans, mainly in Florida.

Of course, many millions of individual "white" and minority Americans can claim a blended heritage of European, African, Asian, and Native American ancestors.

[*]Quality Education for Minorities Project, *Education That Works* (Cambridge: Massachusetts Institute of Technology, 1990).

[†]This and other figures below come from the U.S. Bureau of the Census.

Photo courtesy of Earlham College

work with each of the races—even those they felt they had the least in common with—to advance race relations."*

In addition to being morally and personally repugnant, you should know that *discrimination is illegal*. Most colleges and universities have established policies against all forms of racism, anti-Semitism, and ethnic and cultural intolerance. These policies prohibit racist actions or omissions including verbal harassment or abuse that might deny "anyone his/her rights to equity, dignity, culture or religion." Anyone found in violation of such policies faces "corrective action including appropriate disciplinary action."

EXERCISE 17.5 Checking Your Understanding

How clear is your understanding of discrimination and prejudice? Check your knowledge by circling T (true) or F (false) for each of the following:

T F 1. Positive stereotypes aren't harmful.

T F 2. Prejudice is personal preference usually based on inaccurate or insufficient information.

T F 3. The American Psychiatric Association lists homosexuality as a mental disorder.

T F 4. Racism combines prejudice with power.

T F 5. The problem of racism was solved years ago.

T F 6. Racism hurts everyone.

(See page 302 for the answers.)

*"Survey Finds Minorities Resent Whites and Each Other," *Jet*, 28 March 1994.

On Campus: No Racial Conflict—or Contact

Throughout my life most of my close friends have been black and Latino. I did not choose to change that when I came to college; yet I found myself in my senior year without one friend who was non-white. This occurred so swiftly and naturally that I did not know how to stop it.

When I first arrived at college, I moved into a dormitory with all white students. Although there were minority students in some of my courses, I rarely saw them outside of class. When I was looking for someone to eat with, study with, or play basketball with, it seemed that I had only white students to choose from. I look at the homogeneity of my social life now and realize that it does not reflect the person I am.

Never before did I have to consciously pursue diversity. I grew up in Brooklyn, N.Y., and attended public school there through junior high school, where I was one of only three white students. Because there were so few white students, integration was not an issue. I attended a Quaker high school that was not only numerically well integrated but also a successful, interacting community. Students seemed to choose their friends without thinking about race and certainly didn't feel separated from one another.

I assumed that I would continue to have a diverse group of friends.

At college there is no obvious tension between white and minority students, yet race still creates a barrier in personal relationships. While some students are able to cross the lines that separate white and minority students—for example, those who participate in highly integrated organizations like student government—most are not. Outside of classes the majority of students choose to associate with students who are just like them.

The natural pattern of campus life leads to racial separation. It takes more than an open mind to overcome racial boundaries, more than good intentions, more, even, than a genuine desire to surround yourself with a diverse group of friends.

Students cannot passively wait for chance meetings after class to take place because white and minority students do not socialize together. Nowhere is this more apparent than at the fraternity parties that are the dominant social outlet; white and minority students attend separate parties. The patterns of social separation are not challenged, and race relations are only discussed when controversy arises.

I wrote an article about campus race relations for the college newspaper. I knew that if a student who wanted to lead a diverse life could not succeed, then something must be standing in the way of improving race relations.

The discussions I had with twenty of my schoolmates confirmed what I knew to be true after three years of college: Successful race relations, those that are meaningful and lasting, do not seem to happen naturally. Unfortunately forging positive race relations requires an effort that many students are unwilling or afraid to make.

The article gave me a way to meet minority students. In fact I spoke to more minority students in two days of interviews than I had in my previous three years of college. I enjoyed those conversations, but they troubled me as well because I saw what I had been missing in not hearing perspectives much different from my own. It was disheartening that the atmosphere on campus made me feel that I needed an excuse to speak with members of another race.

I thought about students, both white and minority, who did not have experiences like mine before coming to college.

If college was their first sustained interaction with people of other races, they would be less likely to find separation unusual or problematic, and less motivated to work for change.

I fear that college was probably more similar to the real world than my life until then had been. It is clear that I would have to actively pursue a lifestyle that I once took for granted. If we don't get to know one another at college, how would we in the outside world?

SOURCE: By Adam Cahill, Trinity College. Adapted, with permission, from *The Courant* (Hartford, Conn.), November 14, 1993.

Combating Discrimination and Prejudice on Campus

What experiences have you had dealing with discrimination or prejudice on campus? Write briefly about the incident. Describe what happened and how you felt about it. Did you or anyone you know do anything about it? Did any administrator or faculty member do anything about it? Describe what was done. Do you think this was an effective way to deal with the incident? Explain.

If you have not experienced any problems like this, find out how your college would deal with acts of discrimination and prejudice. You may want to contact the college affirmative action/equal opportunity office for information. Find out what steps students would need to take if they wished to follow up on an incident.

Share your answers and information with other class members.

You don't have to wait for your school to take the lead in making your campus a more welcoming place. Everyone can work to create a community where diverse groups feel celebrated by "advocating for pluralism." For example, Cristina can stop laughing at her friends' racial jokes; Baidah can ask her English instructor to include some works by writers of color. Eric and Terrell can attend the gay, lesbian, and allies support group on campus with Gary.

Constructive Steps: Advocating for Pluralism

As a class come up with a list of steps that students could take at your school to "advocate for pluralism."

Is Hate Speech Permitted on Your Campus?

In a small group, evaluate your campus policy on "hate speech." Develop an argument for or against complete freedom of expression on Internet newsgroups accessible on campus computers. What values and what ideas about the nature of college or society does your argument reflect?

JOURNAL

You may know a great deal about the contributions of Native Americans to U.S. history but know little about the role Asian Americans have played. You may know a lot about African American artists but little about classical music. Consider some specific activities that would further your knowledge and understanding. For example, you could plan to attend a lecture that challenges your present thinking, interview a fellow student about his or her experiences on campus, switch the dial on your radio, or make a meal!

Reflect on your thoughts and feelings about your racial and ethnic background and diversity issues on campus. Is there something that came up in one of the class discussions that you would like to comment on? Is there some idea that remains problematic for you?

SUGGESTIONS FOR FURTHER READING

Bell, D. *Faces at the Bottom of the Well: The Permanence of Racism.* New York: Basic Books, 1992.

Bennett, C. *Comprehensive Multicultural Education,* 2nd ed. Boston: Allyn & Bacon, 1990.

Boswell, J. *Same Sex Unions in Pre-Modern Europe.* New York: Villard, 1994.

Carrion, A. M. *Puerto Rico: A Political and Cultural History.* New York: Norton, 1983.

De Lauretis, T. *The Practice of Love: Lesbian Sexuality and Perverse Desire.* Bloomington, Ind.: Indiana University Press, 1994.

DeVita, P. R., and J. D. Armstrong. *Distant Mirrors: American as a Foreign Culture.* Belmont, Calif.: Wadsworth, 1993.

Divoky, D. "The Model Minority Goes to School." *Phi Delta Kappan* (November 1988): 219–22.

Fisk, E. B. "The Undergraduate Hispanic Experience." *Change* (May/June 1988): 29–33.

Giovanni, N. "Campus Racism 101." *Essence* (August 1991): 71–72.

Halpern, J. M., and L. Nguyen-Hong-Nhiem, eds. *The Far East Comes Near: Autobiographical Accounts of Southeast Asian Students in America.* Amherst: University of Massachusetts Press, 1989.

Mathews, J. *Escalante: The Best Teacher in America.* New York: Holt, Rinehart & Winston, 1988.

Paley, V. G. *White Teacher.* Cambridge, Mass.: Harvard University Press, 1989.

Smith, S. G. *Gender Thinking.* Philadelphia: Temple University Press, 1992.

Stalvey, L. M. *The Education of a WASP.* Madison: University of Wisconsin Press, 1989.

Tatum, B. D. "Teaching About Race, Learning About Racism: The Application of Racial Identity Development in the Classroom." *Harvard Educational Review* 62, no. 1 (1992): 1–24.

Wiley, E. "Institutional Concern About Implications of Black Male Crisis Questioned by Scholar." *Black Issues in Higher Education 7,* no. 9 (1990): 1, 8–9.

Zinn, H. *A People's History of the United States.* New York: Harper & Row, 1980.

ANSWERS (to Exercise 17.5):
1. *False.* Stereotypes, even if positive, assume that all members of a group are the same.
2. *True.* Racism reflects attitudes and actions rooted in ignorance.
3. *False.* The American Psychiatric Association removed homosexuality from its list of disorders in 1973.
4. *True.* Racism occurs when individuals use their prejudice to deny others their civil rights.
5. *False.* Check current newspapers, periodicals, and television reports for the latest incidents of racism.
6. *True.* Everyone benefits when all individuals are allowed to reach their full potential. A victim of racism might just be the person who could find a cure for AIDS.

CHAPTER

Relationships and Campus Involvement

Tom Carskadon
Mississippi State University

Nancy McCarley
Mississippi State University

*N*o way am I going to give up
living for four or five years
just because college is work. I need
people. I need fun. I need to get
involved in something besides
books!

Chapter Goals

This chapter reminds you that relationships in college go beyond your social life and can have a bearing on your academic success. The relationships you develop in college may even set a pattern for handling relationships throughout your life. You will also learn that through involvement in campus activities, you can meet all sorts of people who may change your view of what the world is like and what the future holds.

The Beatles. The Beach Boys. The Stones. The Supremes. Thirty years ago, we loved to play those groups and many more on our college radio station's Top 40 show. As amateur disc jockeys, we were no competition for Wolfman Jack, but it didn't matter; the music was so good, it carried every show. A generation later, the groups have changed, but one thing hasn't: Almost all the songs are still about love. Good love, bad love, lost love, yearning for love—how many hit songs are there about college algebra?

Once in a while, we teach a class that is so good or so bad that students spontaneously write about it in their journals. Most of the time, though, they write about relationships: with dates, lovers, or lifelong partners; with friends and enemies; with parents and family; with roommates and classmates; and with new people and new groups.

In this chapter, we look at these relationships, for they are more than just aspects of your social life—they also bear on your survival and success in college. Distracted by bad relationships, you will find it difficult to concentrate on your studies, and college will be much less satisfying. Supported by good relationships, you will be better able to get through the rough times, succeed to your full potential, remain in college—and enjoy it. Thus, one of the most important things you can work on is making good relationships.

■ DATING AND MATING

Loving an Idealized Image

Carl Gustav Jung, the Swiss psychiatrist who first described the psychological types you read about in Chapter 5, "Learning Styles," also identified a key aspect of love: the idealized image we have of the perfect partner, which we project onto potential partners we meet. Instead of seeing the person who is really there, we may fall in love with the image we have put there—and become disappointed when the real person turns out to be quite different. Jung described archetypes as universal ideas or images, charged with emotion, that predispose us to see and react to the world in certain ways. He called a man's archetypal, idealized image of women the *anima,* and a woman's archetypal, idealized image of men the *animus.*

Some men, for instance, keep falling for women they see as motherly and nurturing; or as angelic and pure; or as romantic and exciting; or as knowing and wise. Women may complain about men who expect them to be an Earth Mother; or men who put them on a pedestal—which is flattering at first but impossible to live up to; or men who expect constant romance and excitement; or men who expect the woman to know everything. Women may keep falling for men they see as animally magnetic; or masterfully together and in control; or romantic and exciting; or knowing and wise. But no man can live up to the idealized image for long.

The first task of any romantic relationship, then, is to see that the person you are in love with really exists. You not only must avoid the trap of the anima and the animus, but also must be sure you are understanding your own reactions. Specifically, you need to see beyond sex to who is really there. If Joe thinks Susie has a divine set of curves, he will (if he is like college students in countless social psychology studies) see Susie not only as sexy, but also as intelligent, considerate, interesting, and likely to succeed—even if she is none of those things. Face it: Sex drives can be very powerful. Anything that can make your knees go weak and your mouth go dry at a single glance can affect your perceptions as well as your body. Are you in love, or are you in lust? People in lust often sincerely believe they are in love, and more than a few will say almost anything to get what they want. But would you still want that person if sex were out of the question? Would that person still want you? An answer of "No" bodes poorly for a relationship.

Folklore says, "Love is blind." Believe it. Check out your perceptions with trusted friends; if they see a lot of problems that you do not, listen to them. Another good reality check is to look at a person's friends. Exceptional people rarely surround themselves with jerks and losers; if the person of your dreams tends to collect friends from your nightmares, watch out!

You should think carefully and repeatedly about what kind of person you really want in a relationship. If a prospective partner does not have the qualities you desire, don't pursue the relationship. Also, pay attention to where you are looking. You won't catch mountain trout if you fish in a sewer.

EXERCISE 18.1 **Dating Games**

A Three-by-Five. Think about your own dating experiences and others that you have observed. Then:

1. List the five worst and five best "opening lines" that you have encountered.

2. List your five biggest dating gripes.

3. List five things you really like from a dating partner.

Be prepared to share your lists with the class.

B What Women Love and Hate. Dating games have been with us since forever; they may even be built into our biology. When we survey our students about their dating lives, certain themes emerge again and again.

Relationships and Campus Involvement　　**305**

Here are the most common gripes women have about men. Which ones are true and which are false? Which are you particularly sensitive to? Which don't bother you at all? Is there anything wrong with such complaints?

1. Why won't men express their feelings?
2. Why don't men talk about the relationship?
3. Why do men give you advice when what you want is sympathy?
4. Why do men always have sex on their minds?
5. Why do men say they want to be friends, but then make a move on you?
6. Why will men have sex with practically anyone?
7. Why do men say they'll call and then never do?
8. Why do men pull that macho crap?
9. Why do men try to dominate women?
10. Why are men obsessed with breasts?
11. Why are men obsessed with sports?
12. Why are men so immature—do they ever grow up?

Whether you're male or female, reflect on these questions in a brief essay, in which you either agree with or refute such statements.

C What Men Love and Hate. Here are common gripes from the men about women. Again, which ones are true and which are false? Which are you particularly sensitive to? Which don't bother you at all? Is there anything wrong with such complaints?

1. Why do women play games, tease you, and lead you on when they don't mean it?
2. Why won't women have sex with you, when they know you're dying for it? Why does it have to be such a big deal—can't we just do it?
3. Why are women so sensitive, moody, emotional, and unpredictable?
4. Why are women so illogical and irrational?
5. Why do women expect you to read their minds?
6. Why do women say they want nice guys but go for jerks who treat them like dirt?
7. Why don't women ask men out?
8. Why are women obsessed with their bodies and looks?
9. Why do women always go in pairs or groups—even to the bathroom?

Whether you're male or female, reflect on these questions in a brief essay, in which you either agree with or refute such statements.

Typically, women tend to want men to show consideration, affection, understanding, communication, romance, sensitivity, and maturity, with sex in the background. Men tend to prize women who are straightforward, enthusiastic, even tempered, logical, predictable, interested in sex, and comfortable with it (but not with anyone else but them).

Consider two things. First, now that you have read the typical gripes, turn to Chapter 5 and review the psychological types. Is it any coincidence that most women are feeling types, whereas most men tend to be thinking types? Many gender differences are really type differences in disguise, and they often show up in relationships. For thinking men who are dealing with feeling

© Joseph Nettis/Stock Boston

women, it often helps to be more feeling: Be emotionally affectionate—even if it feels a little silly at first—and do it often. Be more praising than critical—try to make her feel special. Feeling women dealing with thinking men should remember that disagreement or criticism generally is not meant maliciously and does not imply any loss of affection. Feeling women should try to present their desires coolly and succinctly, and realize that for thinking types, logical reasons or explanations help them understand better and show respect.

Second, men and women differ in their approach to sex. As a memorable cartoon suggested, for men "sex is the default mode." The average Joe awash in hormones can take one look at a woman and want to have sex, and he will interpret nearly any friendly response as sexual hope or encouragement. The average Susie doesn't do it that way. For her, sex is more likely to be in the background. There are exceptions, to be sure. Some Joes are genteel to a Victorian degree, and some Susies will pounce on anything that moves; but overall, a sensitivity to different approaches to sex could improve many a potential relationship.

Developing a Relationship

Usually, relationships develop in stages. Early in a relationship, you may be wildly "in love." You may find yourself preoccupied—if not obsessed—with the other person, with feelings of intense longing when you are apart. When you are together, you may feel thrilled, blissful, yet also insecure and demanding. You are likely to idealize the other person—the anima and the animus are probably running wild—yet you may overreact to faults or disappointments. If the relationship sours, your misery is likely to be intense, and the only apparent relief from your pain lies in the hands of the very person who rejected you. Social psychologist Elaine Walster calls this the stage of *passionate love.*

Most experts see the first stage as being unsustainable—and that may be a blessing! A successful relationship will move on to a calmer, more stable stage. At this next stage, your picture of your partner is much more realistic. You feel comfortable and secure with each other. Your mutual love and respect stem from predictably satisfying companionship. Walster calls this more comfortable, long-lasting stage *companionate love.*

Communication is always a key. If a relationship is to last, it is vital to talk about it as you go along. What are you enjoying, and why? What is disappointing you, and what would make it better? Is there anything you need to know? If you set aside a regular time and place to talk, communication will be more comfortable. Do this every week or two as the relationship first becomes serious. Never let more than a month or two go by without one of these talks—even if all you have to say is that things are going great!

Most relationships change significantly when they turn into long-distance relationships. Many students arrive at college carrying on a relationship with someone back home or at another school. If you are in your late teens or early twenties, such relationships have meager odds of lasting—as do all relationships at that age. College is an exciting scene with many social opportunities. If you restrict yourself to a single, absent partner, you may miss out on a lot; and cheating or resentment often ensues.

Our advice for long-distance relationships: Keep seeing each other as long you want to, but with the freedom to pursue other relationships, too. If the best person for you turns out to be the person you are separated from, then this will become evident, and you can reevaluate the situation in a couple of years. Meanwhile, keep your options open.

Occasionally, a potential relationship will present unusual possibilities—and perils. A prime example is relationships with teachers. Entering into a romantic relationship with one of your teachers can swiftly lead to major problems. Instructors and teaching assistants are hired to have a professional relationship with you that includes certain authority. It is tempting fate to enter into a personal, romantic relationship with someone who has power or authority over you—as you may learn when the relationship goes bad. For this reason, it is best to avoid such entanglements. (See Chapter 20, "Sexual Decisions," if an instructor isn't leaving *you* alone.)

Becoming Intimate

Sexual intimacy inevitably adds a new and powerful dimension to a relationship. That's why this book has an entire chapter about sexual decisions, which we urge you to read. At the risk of slight repetition, we think there are several key ideas with regard to sexual relationships:

- **Don't hurry into sexual intimacy.**
- **If sexual activity would violate your morals or values, don't do it—and don't expect others to violate theirs.** It is reasonable to explain your values so that your partner will understand your decision; but you do not owe anyone a justification, nor should you put up with attempts to argue you into submission.

- **If you have to ply your partner with alcohol or other drugs to get the ball rolling, you aren't engaging in sex—you are committing rape.** Read Chapter 21 for more information about alcohol and other drugs.
- **A pregnancy will curtail your youth and social life.** Pregnancy is a common consequence for students, even when they take some precautions. If you are sexually active for five years of college, and you use condoms for birth control all five years, data based on real-life use indicate that you have around a 50–50 chance of becoming pregnant while at college.

Here also are some warning signs that should concern you:

- **Having sex when you don't really want to or enjoy it.** If desire and pleasure are missing, you are doing the wrong thing.
- **Guilt or anxiety afterward.** This is a sign of a wrong decision—or at least a premature one.
- **Having sex because your partner expects or demands it.**
- **Having sex with people to attract or keep them.** This is generally short-sighted and unwise. It will almost surely lower your self-esteem. If sex is what is keeping someone with you, that someone is likely to go looking elsewhere soon.
- **Becoming physically intimate when what you really want is emotional intimacy.**

When you are between the sheets and having fun, with passions running high, physical intimacy can surely feel like emotional intimacy, but sex is an unsatisfying substitute for love or friendship. Genuine emotional intimacy is knowing, trusting, loving, and respecting each other at the deepest levels, day in and day out, independent of sex. Establishing emotional intimacy takes time—and, we think, more real courage. If you build the emotional intimacy first, not only the relationship but also the sex will be better.

An interesting question is whether sex actually adds to your overall happiness. Believe it or not, a thorough review of the literature on happiness finds no evidence that becoming sexually active increases your general happiness. If this seems impossible, consider this: Back when most of your teachers were students, most of them were not sexually active; yet their overall level of happiness was no different from yours now. If you are expecting sex to make you happy, or to make your partner happy, the fact is that it probably won't for long. Sex relieves horniness, but it doesn't make happiness. Loving relationships, on the other hand, are powerfully related to happiness.

One option from the past is being used more and more today. If you want sexual activity, but you don't want all the medical risks of sex, consider the practice of "outercourse": mutual and loving stimulation between partners that allows sexual release but involves no exchange of bodily fluids. This will definitely require direct and effective communication, but we think it is an option that may be helpful to students today.

Getting Serious

You may have a relationship you feel is really working. Should you make it exclusive? Don't do it just because it has become a habit. Ask yourself, Why should this relationship be exclusive? For security? To prevent jealousy? To

Think about it. An exclusive relationship means giving up a lot. Are you really prepared to do so?

© Frank Siteman/Stock Boston

build depth and trust? As a prelude to permanent commitment? To pursue a relationship exclusively, you are giving up a lot; before you do that, make sure it is necessary and advisable. You may find that you treat each other best and appreciate each other most when you have other opportunities; and checking out others can help you decide whether you truly want to stay with someone.

We emphatically do *not* recommend multiple, simultaneous sexual relationships. Besides the health risks involved, we have never seen a good, working relationship where the partners had sex with others as well. Sexual jealousy is very powerful, and it arouses insecurities, anger, and hurt.

Being exclusive can provide the chance to explore a relationship in depth and even get a taste of what marriage might be like. If you are seriously considering marriage, consider this: Studies show that the younger you are, the worse your odds of a successful marriage are. Also, you may be surprised to learn that "trial marriage" or "living together" does not decrease your risk of later divorce.

Above all, beware of what we call "The Fundamental Marriage Error": marrying before both you and your partner know who you are and what you want to do in life. Many 18- to 20-year-olds change their outlook and life goals drastically later on. The person who seems just right for you now may be terribly wrong for you within five or ten years. Although people may change at any age, that risk is particularly great in the teens and twenties. We suggest that you wait until you are past that stage. This doesn't mean you shouldn't have close relationships in the meantime; just hold off on permanent commitments.

Whatever you do, don't marry someone while you are in the first, or passionate, stage of love. In that stage, your brains are often out to lunch, and as we mentioned earlier, the person you are "in love" with probably doesn't exist. Here is some more good advice: If you want to marry, the person to marry is someone you could call your best friend—the one who knows you inside and out, the one you don't have to play games with (the one who'd know right away if you tried to), the one who prizes your company without physical rewards, the one who over a period of years has come to know, love, and respect who you are and what you want to be. This is what a good marriage becomes, so if you can start with this, you have it made.

Seeing Warning Signs in Relationships

Folklore says you can put a frog in a pan of water and heat it on a stove; do it gradually enough, and the frog won't hop out—he'll stay until he's dinner. We've never tried it, but we have seen good people destroyed as they remained in steadily worsening relationships so long that they forgot what normal, healthy, happy ones were like. Don't be that frog! The key is to be alert to warning signs and act on them. If you encounter the following in a relationship, get out.

- **Never tolerate violence or threats in a relationship.** Drunkenness or rage is not an excuse. We recommend against giving second chances after any significant episode of threat or violence, but if you forgive the first incident and abuse reoccurs, end the relationship immediately and permanently, *no matter what*. If you need counseling or legal help, get it, but get out of the relationship.

- **Anyone who drinks heavily or takes drugs on a regular basis is not someone with whom you should invest in a relationship.** If your partner is into addictive or dangerous drugs (such as heroin, cocaine, or LSD) or is an alcoholic, forget him or her. Addicts and users are often dangerous and seldom cured; don't let yourself believe that with your love and support, they will change. If your partner has big plans to change you, the same rules apply. Get out of the relationship!

- **Beware of pressure to split from your friends or family.** This takes you away from people who can recognize a bad situation and help you see and deal with the truth.

- **If your partner does not respect the sexual decisions you have made and pressures you to change them, find someone who will love you as you are.** Unwelcome sexual pressure is not part of a healthy relationship.

- **Cheating in a serious, exclusive relationship will surely destroy it.** Someone who will cheat on you now will do more of it later.

- **If being in a relationship is making you feel bad about yourself instead of good, this is not a relationship to continue.** Healthy relationships enhance your self-esteem; they do not diminish it.

- **If you are increasingly disappointed in your partner, and find yourself respecting that person less and less, the relationship is bad for both of you.**

- **Just passing time until someone better comes along is unfair to both you and your partner.** In fact, most of the best prospects won't approach someone already in another relationship.

- **If a relationship has become boring and seems to be inhibiting your personal growth, evaluate it carefully.** If it's just a temporary lull, then things will be better again soon; but if these feelings persist, it is time to move on.

Breaking Up

Change can be scary to think about and painful to create, but that doesn't make it less necessary. When you break up, you lose not only what you had, but also everything you *thought* you had (remember the anima and the animus), including a lot of hopes and dreams. No wonder it hurts. But remember that you are also opening up a world of new possibilities. You may not see them right away, but sooner or later you will.

If it is time to break up, break up cleanly and calmly. Don't do it impulsively or in anger. Explain your feelings and talk it out once. If you don't get a mature reaction, take the high road; don't join someone else in the mud. If a relationship does not work the first time, it probably will not work a second time, either. If you do decide to reunite after a trial separation, however, be sure enough time has passed for you to evaluate the situation effectively; and if things fail a second time, you really do need to forget it.

What about being "just friends"? You may want to remain friends with your partner, especially if you have shared and invested a lot. You can't really be friends, however, until you have both healed from the hurt and neither of you wants the old relationship back. That usually takes at least a year or two. Don't rush it.

Beware of intermittent reinforcement! Often, the hardest relationships to end are those that alternate unpredictably between bliss and misery. People will repeatedly let themselves be treated like dirt if every now and then they are treated like royalty. Unfortunately, some people are quite skillful at manipulating their partners with intermittent reinforcement. Good relationships are good most of the time and seldom, if ever, poor.

If you are having trouble getting out of a relationship or dealing with its end, get help. Expect some pain, anger, and depression, but if they are intense, get help. Your college counseling center has assisted many students through similar difficulties, and particular techniques can alleviate these problems. It is also a good time to get moral support from friends and family. There are good books on the subject, including our favorite, *How to Survive the Loss of a Love* (see "Suggestions for Further Reading").

Establishing Sexual Orientation

Just as people are very different, so are people's ideas about what relationships should be like. You will need to find someone whose ideas are truly compatible with your own. Of course, there is no single prescription. Other people have other needs, and you can understand them and tolerate them without having those needs yourself.

Differences in sexual orientation may be the most important instance of this. Chapter 17, "Diversity on Campus," contains more about this topic. If homosexuality is contrary to your religious beliefs, remember that homosexuals will not impose their beliefs on you; try to treat them likewise in return. If you find this difficult, ask yourself, "Why should I focus my attention on where other people prospect for love? Will time spent focusing on their behavior add to my happiness or improve my relationships?"

Learning Axioms of Relationships

After nearly a quarter century of helping students deal with relationships, we have come up with these basic principles:

1. **If it is the right relationship, it will work; if it doesn't work, it isn't the right relationship.** If it doesn't work, whatever the reason, get out of it.

2. **Every bad relationship has warning signs.** Learn to put aside your desires or dreams long enough to be sensitive to the warning signs; then believe them and act.

3. **No relationship is better than a bad relationship.** Not having a special someone can be a downer, but that pales in comparison to the grief a bad relationship will bring you.

4. **Don't settle for less than you deserve.** Sometimes the finest people have to wait the longest, because there are fewer people as good as they. Be patient.

5. **Get it right the first time.** Divorce is hell, and all those dating games will feel even sillier when you are 30 or 40 or 50. Don't marry too young. Don't marry in a hurry. Don't marry if you have doubts. If you do marry the wrong person, there's nothing noble about a lifetime of emotional suffering for you and your family. Try your best, but if it is hopeless, get out and rebuild your life.

6. **You'll have the best relationship when you don't need one.** First establish your own independence, confidence, achievement, and happiness. After that, potential relationships will abound—people are attracted to people who are happy and secure—and you can take your pick of the very best. It is much better to want someone than to need someone.

■ MARRIED LIFE IN COLLEGE

Both marriage and college are challenges. With so many demands, it is critically important that you and your partner share the burdens equally; you can't expect a harried partner to spoil or pamper you. Academic and financial pressures are likely to put extra strain on any relationship, so you are going to have to work extra hard at attending to each other's needs.

If you are in college but your spouse is not, it is important to bring your partner into your college life. Directly or indirectly, your partner is probably helping you get through college. Share what you are learning in your courses. See if your partner can take a course, too—maybe just to audit for the fun of it. Take your partner to cultural events—lectures, plays, concerts—on your campus. If your campus has social organizations for students' spouses, try them out.

Relationships with spouses and children can suffer when you are in college because you are tempted to take time you would normally spend with your loved ones and put it into your studies instead. You obviously will not profit if you gain your degree but lose your family. It's very important to schedule time for your partner and family just as you schedule your classes, and keep to the schedule just as carefully.

EXERCISE 18.2 Grounds for Marriage and College

A For personal writing and group discussion: If you are a married student, what are the greatest concerns you have about balancing your educational responsibilities with your responsibilities to your family? What can you do to improve the

If you are married or have children, take steps to involve your loved ones in your college life.

Dollarhide/Monkmeyer Press Photo

situation? Is there someone on campus you can seek for counseling? If you need counseling but aren't sure where to turn, ask your instructor to help you find that person.

B If you are married, write a letter to your spouse and another to your children, explaining why you must often devote time to your studies instead of to them. Don't deliver the letters; read them first and keep revising them until they sound realistic and convincing. Attempt to strike a sensible balance between your commitments to family and to your future academic and professional growth. If there are other married students in your class, share letters and get reactions. Then decide whether it's prudent to actually share these thoughts with spouses and children.

■YOU AND YOUR PARENTS

You may have heard of the "Empty Nest Syndrome": Children grow up and leave for college, and parents come unglued and launch into various midlife crises. Actually, it's a myth. Crises happen to parents sometimes, but no more often than at any other stage of adulthood. If you are on your own for the first time, now an independent adult, you are the one who will change. Thomas Wolfe said it in the title of his famous novel: *You Can't Go Home Again.* Home will never be as you left it, and you will not be who you were before. So how can you have good relationships with your parents during this period of major changes?

A first step in establishing a good relationship with your parents is to be aware of their perceptions. The most common perceptions are as follows:

1. **Younger students feel they are immortal.** You're not, of course, but you may act that way, taking risks that make older people shudder. You'll probably shudder, too, when you look back on some of your stunts. Sometimes your parents have reason to worry.

2. **Parents think their daughter is still a young innocent.** Some things parents wonder about, they don't really want to know. And yes, the old double standard (differing expectations for men than women, particularly regarding sex) is alive and well.

3. **Parents know you're 20 but picture you as 10.** Somehow, the parental clock always lags behind reality. Maybe it's because they loved you so much as children, they can't erase that image. Humor them a bit, and enlighten them gently.

4. **Parents mean well.** It's generally true. Most love their children, even if it doesn't come out right; very few are really indifferent or hateful, even if they seem that way at times.

5. **Not every family works.** If your family is like "The Brady Bunch," you are blessed. If it is even halfway normal, you will succeed. But a few families are truly dysfunctional. If love, respect, enthusiasm, and encouragement just are not in the cards, look around you: Other people will give you these things, and you can create the family you need. With your emotional needs satisfied, your reactions to your real family will be much less painful.

6. **The old have been young, but the young haven't been old.** Parental memories of youth may be hazy and distorted, but at least they have been there. A traditionally aged student has yet to experience the adult perspective.

To paraphrase Mark Twain, when you are beginning college, you may think your parents rather foolish; but when you graduate, you'll be surprised how much they've learned in four years! Your parents probably do have experience, wisdom, and love. Why not take advantage of it? Try setting aside regular times to update them on how college and your life in general are going. Actually ask for and consider their advice. You don't have to take it. If they know these conversations are coming, there may be less nagging in between.

Finally, realize that your parents are not here forever. Don't get hung up on inconsequential quarrels: "Don't let the sun set on your anger." Mend fences whenever you can. Don't let a kind word go unspoken, or love go unexpressed.

EXERCISE 18.3 Gripes

A Student Gripes. In our surveys, these are the most frequent student gripes about parents. Check off the ones that hit "closest to home" for you.

1. Why are parents so overbearing and controlling, telling you everything from what to major in to whom to date?

2. Why do parents treat you like a child? Why are they so overprotective?

3. Why do parents worry so much?

4. Why do parents complain so much about money?

5. Why are parents so hard to talk to?

6. Parents say they want to know what's going on in my life, but if I told them everything, they'd go ballistic and I'd never hear the end of it!

Reflect on the gripes you checked. Why do you think your parents are like that? How do your thoughts affect your relations with them?

B Parent Gripes. Looking at things from the other side, students report the following as the most common gripes their parents have about them. Check off those that ring true for your parents.

1. Why don't you call and visit more?

2. Why don't you tell us more about what is going on?

3. When you are home, why do you ignore us and spend all your time with your friends?

4. (If dating seriously) Why do you spend so much time with your boyfriend or girlfriend?

5. Why do you need so much money?

6. Why aren't your grades better, and why don't you appreciate the importance of school?

7. Why don't you listen to us about getting into the right major and courses? You'll never get a good job if you don't.

8. What have you done to yourself? Where did you get that (haircut, tattoo, style of clothes, and so on)?

9. Why don't you listen to us and do what we tell you? You need a better attitude!

How do such thoughts affect your parents? What do you think they are really trying to tell you?

EXERCISE 18.4 **Five over 30**

Select five adults over 30 whom you respect. Ask each the following questions.

- What were the best decisions you made when you were 18 to 22?
- What were the biggest mistakes you made in those years?
- What advice would you give someone who is 18?

Are there common themes in what they say? How good is their advice? Bring a summary of what you were told to class, and be prepared to share it.

■FRIENDS

You are what you run with—or soon will be. Studies of students across the country clearly show that the people who influence you the most are your friends. Choose them carefully, because social psychology suggests that your personality and behavior will be profoundly influenced by the people you choose to surround you.

If you want a friend, be a friend. Learn to be an attentive listener. Give your opinion when people ask for it. Keep your comments polite and positive. Never violate a confidence. Give an encouraging word and a helping hand whenever you can. You'll be amazed how many people will respect your opinions and seek your friendship.

Your friends are usually people whose attitudes, goals, and experiences are similar to your own. But in your personal life, just as in the classroom, you have the most to learn from people who are different from you. To truly enrich your college experience, try this. Make a conscious effort to make at least one good friend who is someone:

"They Didn't Know Me"

I was never that popular in high school—in fact, I hardly dated. Suddenly in college all these guys were asking me out. They didn't know me. About all they knew was that I looked Asian.

In fact, my father's Caucasian. He met my mother in Japan when he was in the merchant marine. He had one day of leave in Japan. They met for one afternoon, standing in line at a shrine in Kyoto when she was still in high school. They wrote to each other for four years before he went back and proposed. With that kind of courtship you might think they didn't know each other all that well, but I'm sure they did because I've seen the stacks of letters. They got married and came back to the States. My brother and I were born here.

I like to think that if I'm an unusual person it's not just because of things like my hair or the shape of my eyes. But you would be surprised how many guys in college would see me once and act like they already knew everything about me.

My freshman roommate had another kind of problem. She's African American, and in the first couple weeks she started dating someone who was also African American. Then he kind of left her alone and started going out with whites. She might not have minded so much if there had been as many African American men on campus as there were African American women. But there weren't. She got pretty fed up with it—I guess lonely is the word.

My brother visited me one weekend in January, and we got to talking about this. He said his experience in college had been more like hers than like mine. Some women seemed to reject him simply because he looked Asian. At the same time, the Asian and Asian American women were going out with whites. I was glad to hear him talk about this finally, but it also made me sad. My brother's a very sweet person, and I don't see why I should be accepted if he's not accepted also.

    of the opposite sex
    of another race
    of another nationality
    of a different sexual orientation
    with a physical handicap
    on an athletic scholarship
    of a much different age
    from a much different religion
    with much different politics

These friendships may take more time and effort, but you will have more than just nine new friends; you will have learned to know, appreciate, and get along with a much wider variety of people than you probably have before. This will serve you well in your later career as well as in your personal life.

ROOMMATES

Adjusting to a roommate on or off campus can be very difficult at the start of college. Roommates range from the ridiculous to the sublime. You may make a lifetime friend—or an exasperating acquaintance you wish you'd never known. If nothing else, it is good training for later adjustments, such as marriage.

Many students choose roommates they already know and like; but that is no guarantee that your personal habits will be compatible. A roommate doesn't have to be a best friend, just someone with whom you can share your living space comfortably. Your best friend may not make the best roommate at all, and in fact more than a few students have lost friends by rooming together.

EXERCISE 18.5 Common Roommate Gripes

Housing authorities report that the most common areas of conflict between roommates are those listed below. Check those that are true for you.

1. One roommate needs quiet to study; the other needs music or other stimulation.
2. One roommate is neat; the other is messy.
3. One roommate smokes; the other resents breathing or smelling smoke.
4. One roommate feels free to bring in lots of guests; the other finds them obnoxious.
5. One roommate brings in romantic bedmates and wants privacy—or goes at it right in front of the other; the other is uncomfortable with this and feels banished from the room that he or she paid for.
6. One roommate likes it warm; the other likes it cool.
7. One roommate considers the room a place to have fun; the other considers it a place to get studying done.
8. One roommate likes to borrow the other's things; the other isn't comfortable with that.
9. One roommate is a "morning person"; the other is a "night owl."
10. One roommate wants silence while sleeping; the other feels free to make noise.
11. One roommate wants to follow all the residence hall rules; the other wants to break them.

If you are rooming with someone, review your checks and write about what you and your roommate(s) can do to improve the situation. If you live alone, which of these gripes would be reason enough for you to not want to share your home with another? How might you overcome such situations if they arose?

For your next roommate situation, try to find someone you already know to be compatible on the issues listed in Exercise 18.5. If you are rooming with a stranger now, you can do things to get along better. Now or at the next outset, establish your mutual rights and responsibilities in writing. Many colleges provide "contract" forms that you and your roommate can use. If things go wrong later, you will have something to point to.

If you have problems, talk them out promptly. Too often, small, solvable problems become big, unsolvable ones. Dropping subtle hints is not dealing with problems. Talk about the problem directly—politely but plainly. If problems persist, or if you don't know how to talk them out, ask your residence hall counselor for help; he or she is trained to do this.

Normally, you can tolerate (and learn from) a less than ideal situation; but if things get seriously bad, insist on a change—your residence counselor will have ways of dealing with it.

If you find your roommate peculiar, probably your roommate is reacting the same way to you! Just because your roommate is different doesn't mean he or she is wrong. Part of college is learning how to get along with different people, so give it your best try.

EXERCISE 18.6   Roommate Roulette

Pick five persons of the same sex, whom you could imagine sharing a room with, and interview them using the list of common roommate conflicts in Exercise 18.5. See how many points of commonality and difference you would have. Try to determine whether there really exists an "ideal" roommate.

For each of the conflicts on the list, write down the best compromise solutions you can. Bring your solutions to class and be prepared to have your classmates—some of whom are probably facing these very problems—judge how well they might work.

■ CAMPUS INVOLVEMENT

Many organizations make it easy to form relationships.

Classes and Study Groups

Your classes are filled with people who have something in common. Many studies prove that studying in groups with them can help you succeed, earn higher grades, and meet people. Be sure that when you form a study group, you pick people whose goals and seriousness match your own. (See Chapter 5, "Learning Styles.")

Campus Organizations

Almost every college has a wide variety of organizations you may join. Usually, there are organized ways for you to check them out—activity fairs, printed guides, open houses, and so on. Organizations allow you to find friends with similar interests and try things you might never again have a chance to try. New students who become significantly involved with at least one organization are more likely to survive their first year and remain in college. Choosing to participate in campus organizations is one of the wisest moves you can make.

"To Greek or not to Greek?" may be a question on your campus. Fraternities and sororities can be a rich source of friends and support. Some students love them; others find them either philosophically distasteful or else too demanding of time and finances and too constricting of members' freedom. Fraternities and sororities are powerful social influences, so you'll probably want to take a good look at the upper-class students in them. If what you see is what you want to be, consider joining; but if it isn't, steer clear. Even if you aren't like the other members when you start, you are likely to become much more like them before you leave.

Getting Involved on Campus

Marie-Louise Ramsdale

Six Reasons to Join a Campus Organization

1. **You'll meet people with interests and ideas similar to yours.** You'll also meet people who are different.

2. **You'll gain experience.** College is the ideal place to try things you might never do otherwise. Audition for a play. Try hiking or mountain climbing. You don't have to be great to begin.

3. **You'll improve your communication skills.** Giving an impromptu speech at a club meeting will prepare you for speaking up in class. Editing the campus newspaper will teach you a lot about writing.

4. **You'll improve your resume.** Employers and graduate schools usually prefer well-rounded individuals to people with straight A's who hung around the library all the time.

5. **You'll meet advisors who generally are instructors or staff of the college and may be helpful to you in other areas of your college experience.**

6. **There's more to life than working.** If you spend all your time in college studying, what are you going to do later in life?

Five Things to Ask Before Choosing an Organization

1. **What am I already interested in?** Have you always loved to ski? Find out if there's a ski club.

2. **What do I still want to learn?** If you've always wanted to sing but never had the nerve, maybe it's time to join the chorus.

3. **How much time can I commit?** Find out when the group meets and how often, and determine whether you can work your schedule around it. If not, either make some adjustments or seek another group.

4. **What's the cost?** Most college activities are designed with a student's budget in mind.

Some groups may not charge fees. If dues are high, is there a payment plan?

5. **What is required for membership?** Must you attend a set number of meetings, maintain a certain grade point average, or take a special class in order to qualify for membership?

What If You Can't Find the Right Organization for You?

Start one. Ask your campus activities center for guidelines for starting a new group. Find out who's in charge of this activity, and get advice from him or her. Circulate the word to other students, on bulletin boards and in the campus events calendar. Ask the student media to run a story about your group.

Set goals for your group, even if it is small at first. Having goals lends structure to your group and gives members something to strive for. Set activities that are in line with the goals you have set. If your club was designed to promote environmental awareness, some activities could include sponsoring lunchtime forums with environmental activists as speakers or holding monthly recycling days during which students could bring recyclables to a central location staffed by club members.

Plan how your group is to be funded. Look into your school's procedure for funding student organizations. At many colleges, organizations must be established for a certain period of time before they can receive funding from student activity fees. Also consider fund-raisers. Your campus activities center should be able to provide ideas for fund-raising.

Serving as You Learn

Service learning is a recent trend in colleges and universities that helps students gain life skills and knowledge while making a difference in their communities. First, identify a community service project, perhaps in your area of career interest. If you are majoring in health, you might volunteer at the local soup kitchen or food bank. As you prepare meals for people, you'll also receive a good education in nutrition. Future teachers may want to tutor at a local

(continued)

school; future structural engineers can help build or renovate low-income housing. It's a win–win situation: You help other people as you learn. The community service center at your school should be able to link you with worthwhile organizations. Your local United Way is often another good source for such referrals. Many campus organizations are already involved in community activities.

© 1992 Chuck Savage/photo courtesy of Beloit College

Many students go through Greek rush even with no intention of joining, simply because it is a good way to meet a lot of people quickly. Try to approach Greek organizations with an open mind. They are among the most stereotyped groups on campus, and the things you hear may not be true. Greek organizations are not all alike, nor are their members. You are certainly not inferior if you do not join a fraternity or sorority. Nor are you hot stuff if you do.

Residence Halls

They may be noisy, chaotic, and spartan, with neither privacy nor peace, but you're all in that social adventure together, and a residence hall is probably the easiest of all places to make new friends. Don't hesitate to visit new people. Take advantage of residence hall programs, too.

Jobs and Co-op Placements

Another good place to make friends is on the job. Working together on a common task, you get to know people quickly and well. Avoid starting romantic relationships on the job, though. Dating someone who works over you or under you creates problems in a hurry, and even if both of you are on the same level, you may feel awkward or miserable if the relationship ends but the two of you must still work together.

Always give a job your best because future employers may ask your past employers about you. Also, you probably will want to use them as a reference. A special kind of job available at many schools is the co-op placement. Find out whether your school has a cooperative education program at the career center. If so, be sure to check it out. These programs place you in temporary but paid positions with organizations that hire graduates in your major. Not only will you get excellent firsthand experience working in your field, but also you will form relationships and make contacts that may help a lot when you are looking for a permanent position after graduation.

EXERCISE 18.7   Connecting with Campus Organizations

Get a list of your campus organizations from your campus student center. Choose six that you might enjoy participating in. Find out more about each: Attend a meeting, talk to an officer, and/or obtain and read detailed information. Choose two you would like to get involved with this term. Bring your list to class, and be prepared to discuss what you found and your reasons for the selections you made.

■A PARTING THOUGHT

You are here for your college education; but relationships are an integral part of it and can consume up to two-thirds of your waking hours. Whether you're a traditional-age new student or a returning student with family responsibilities, be sure to approach your relationships with the same effort and planning as you would approach your course work. "Take life as it happens, but try to make it happen the way you want to take it." Long after you have forgotten whole courses you took, you will remember relationships that began or continued in college.

JOURNAL

It is often easy to gripe about parents, and you probably do it now and then; but what about a celebration of your parents, what they have done for you and what they have meant to you? For this journal entry, imagine yourself away from your parents for a year or two, perhaps in the service, at school, or on a job abroad. After careful reflection, write your parents a letter of appreciation to let them know what they have done for you and what they mean to you. Add anything else you may have left unsaid or unforgiven for too long. Now that you have written it, consider sending it to them. Sending that letter might be one of the most profoundly rewarding acts in your relationship with your parents—but that's up to you.

SUGGESTIONS FOR FURTHER READING

Cosgrove, Melba, Harold Bloomfield, and Peter McWilliams. *How to Survive the Loss of a Love*. New York: Bantam Books, 1976.

Kummerow, Jean, and Sandra Hirsh. *LifeTypes*. New York: Warner Books, 1989.

Myers, David G. *The Pursuit of Happiness: Who Is Happy and Why*. New York: William Morrow & Co., 1992.

Managing Stress

Kevin W. King
Counseling Psychologist

*H*ey you! Yeah I said you! Watch where you're going. I mean, move and let me get by. I've gotta get to class, and I don't have time to hassle with you. What's the big rush? . . . What? Who are you tellin' to slow down, mister? I am not stressed out. Hey, I was up till four gettin' ready for class . . . so maybe I'm a little edgy today. So butt out, will ya?

Chapter Goals

This chapter focuses on stress as practically unavoidable yet something you can control. It even suggests that stress, in small doses, can be beneficial, although excessive stress can interfere with your success in college. You will learn how to identify the warning signs of stress and subsequently to manage it in positive ways, either by yourself or with assistance available on campus.

Stress is natural. So, to the extent that stress is a sign of vitality, stress is good. Yet most of us never really learn how to cope effectively with stress-producing situations, and the result is that stress can overwhelm us, undermining our ability to perform. The primary way to manage stress is to modify it with something that enhances our feeling of control in the situation. For me relaxation is also very important in counteracting stress. It's impossible to be tense and relaxed at the same time, and relaxation is a skill that we can learn just like any other skill.

Did you realize you have actually *learned* to be tense in most stress-producing situations? Now you can learn how to identify the warning signs or symptoms of stress. And once you are aware of the warning signs, you can *choose* how you will react. That's what this chapter is all about.

■ A HEALTHY LIFESTYLE

The best starting point for handling stress is to be in good shape physically and mentally, by eating, sleeping, and exercising to reasonable degrees. If you are uncertain about what constitutes a healthy diet or whether yours is healthy, ask your campus health or counseling office for information, consult the library, or take a brief wellness course. Also, use the box on page 325 to determine how much caffeine you may be consuming on a regular basis. In moderate amounts (50–200 milligrams per day), caffeine increases alertness and reduces feelings of fatigue, but even at this low dosage it tends to make you perkier during one part of the day and more tired later and may give you headaches when you try to cut down. Consumed in larger quantities, it may cause nervousness, headaches, irritability, stomach irritation, and insomnia. Don't overdo caffeine.

If starting college means a major change in your sleep habits, consider whether these are entirely necessary or due to a lifestyle choice that you may

Start Healthy

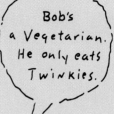

Bob's a Vegetarian. He only eats Twinkies.

GOOD EXERCISE

1. **Mode.** Pick something you enjoy and will stick with. You can cross-train doing different exercises as long as they cumulatively meet the next three criteria. Find exercise partners to help you keep going.

2. **Frequency.** Exercise at least three times weekly. You will see even greater improvements if you build gradually to four to six times weekly. Give yourself at least one day a week free of exercise so your body can recover.

3. **Duration.** Exercise for at least 20–30 minutes at a time. Even when you begin, maintain exercise for at least 20 minutes.

4. **Intensity.** Monitor the intensity of your workout. In order to get aerobic benefits, your heart must be beating at a target rate. To determine this rate, subtract your age from 220 and multiply by .60. Then subtract your age again from 220 and multiply this time by .75. These two answers are the high and low limits of what your heart rate (pulse) should be during exercise.

CAFFEINE CONTENT

ITEM	CAFFEINE (MILLIGRAMS)
1 cup brewed coffee	85
1 cup instant coffee	60
1 cup tea	30–50
12-ounce cola drinks	35–65
Many aspirin compounds	30–60
Various cold preparations	30
1 cup cocoa	2–10
1 cup decaffeinated coffee	3

need to modify. You probably already know how much sleep you need to maintain a good daily routine. Being rested makes you more efficient when you are awake. It also helps to make a lot of other activities more enjoyable and cuts down the likelihood that you'll succumb to annoying diseases that enjoy preying on fatigued students, such as infectious mononucleosis.

Exercise regularly. The box "Start Healthy" suggests how. You may feel that you have no time for regular exercise, but even a daily regimen of stretches each morning can help lower stress, keep you looking and feeling trim, and make you feel better. Most often, regular exercise enhances your energy.

Although competitive sports are fun and a great way to meet friends, and although weight training may be appealing, it's more beneficial to find an *aerobic* activity—swimming, jogging, brisk walking, cycling, or vigorous racquet sports—that strengthens your cardiovascular system and gives other physiological benefits. People who undertake aerobic exercise report more energy, less stress, better sleep, weight loss, and an improved self-image.

■ WHAT HAPPENS WHEN YOU ARE TENSE

The signs of stress are easy to recognize and differ little from person to person. Basically your rate of breathing becomes more rapid and shallower; your heart rate begins to speed up; and the muscles in your shoulders and forehead, the back of your neck, and perhaps even across your chest begin to tighten. Probably your hands and perhaps your feet become cold and sweaty. There are likely to be disturbances in your gastrointestinal system, such as a "butterfly" stomach or diarrhea, vomiting, and frequent urination. Your mouth may become parched, your lips may dry out, and your hands and knees may begin to shake or tremble. Your voice may quiver or even go up an octave.

A number of psychological changes also occur when you are under stress. These changes are the result of your body and mind trying to "defend" you from some real or imagined threat. The threat could be from an actual situation, such as someone approaching you with a gun in hand. Or it could come from something that hasn't actually happened but that you are worried about, because the part of the brain that controls your defensive reactions doesn't do any thinking—it simply reacts. The stress you typically feel is just part of that defensive reaction. As a result, you're more easily confused, your memory becomes blocked, and your thinking becomes less flexible and more critical. Along with these reactions, your body's adrenal glands produce adrenalin and a group of hormones called corticoids. If the situation persists over a long time, you may also find it difficult to concentrate, and you may experience a general sense of fear or anxiety, insomnia, early waking, changes in eating habits, excessive worrying, fatigue, and an urge to run away.

EXERCISE 19.1 ### Your Signs of Stress

Recall your last troublesome experience. What signals from your mind or body (for example, worry, frightening thoughts, tense muscles, headache, stomach distress) let you know this was a distressing situation? How did you respond to those signals? What might you do next time to handle the situation more effectively?

The urges to stand and fight or to run away are two of the human body's basic responses to stress. But many times both urges must be suppressed because they would be inappropriate. For instance, a person taking an exam may want to bolt from the exam room, but it probably would not help the grade to do so, and it's pointless to fight with a piece of paper. So we often find we must cope with a situation in a way that allows us to stay and face it, and to do so using our potential and skills to the maximum. This is where learning to manage stress effectively can make a difference!

■ IDENTIFYING YOUR STRESS

Stress has many sources, but there are two prevailing theories as to its origin. The first is the life events theory, which attributes health risks and life span reduction to an accumulation of effects from events that have occurred in the previous twelve months of a person's life.

EXERCISE 19.2 The College Readjustment Rating Scale

The College Readjustment Rating Scale is an adaptation of Holmes and Rahe's Life Events Scale. It has been modified for college-age adults and should be considered as a rough indication of stress levels and possible health consequences.

In the College Readjustment Rating Scale, each event, such as one's first term in college, is assigned a value that represents the amount of readjustment a person has to make in life as a result of change. In some studies, people with serious illnesses have been found to have high scores on similar scales. Persons with scores of 300 and higher have a high health risk. Persons scoring between 150 and 300 points have about a 50–50 chance of serious health change within two years. Subjects scoring 150 and below have a 1 in 3 chance of a serious health change.

To determine your stress score, circle the number of points corresponding to the events you have experienced in the past six months or are likely to experience in the next six months. Then add up the circled numbers.

Event	Points	Event	Points
Death of spouse	100	Sexual difficulties	45
Female unwed pregnancy	92	Serious argument with significant other	40
Death of parent	80	Academic probation	39
Male partner in unwed pregnancy	77	Change in major	37
Divorce	73	New love interest	36
Death of a close family member	70	Increased work load in college	31
Death of a close friend	65	Outstanding personal achievement	29
Divorce between parents	63	First term in college	28
Jail term	61	Serious conflict with instructor	27
Major personal injury or illness	60	Lower grades than expected	25
Flunk out of college	58	Change in colleges (transfer)	24
Marriage	55	Change in social activities	22
Fired from job	50	Change in sleeping habits	21
Loss of financial support for college (scholarship)	48	Change in eating habits	19
Failing grade in important or required course	47	Minor violations of the law (for example, traffic ticket)	15

If your score indicates potential health problems, it would be to your benefit to seriously review the "stress relief smorgasbord" that appears later in this chapter and select and implement some strategies to reduce your stress.

NOTE: Adapted with permission from T. H. Holmes and R. H. Rahe, "The Social Readjustment Scale," in Carol L. Otis and Roger Goldingay, *Campus Health Guide* (New York: CEEB, 1989).

If you find that your score on the preceding exercise is 150 or higher, it would be good preventive health care to think about why you experienced each of the scored events. In addition, you might consider what skills you need to learn either to repair the damage that these events caused or to prevent their recurrence. It would also be interesting to find out how the rest of the class scored on the scale. If there seems to be a need, the class might draw upon a resource person to help everyone develop better coping or learning skills. You might also find out that you already have experts within the class who might share with you how they have handled these or similar events.

The other major theory about the sources of stress attributes our general level of stress to an overload of personal hassles and a deficit of uplifts or reliefs. This theory encourages us to evaluate our immediate problems but, while doing so, to focus on what's good about our lives and to strive to notice positive events instead of taking them for granted. We are all going to experience reversals, whether it's because we don't get along with our roommate, can't register for the course or time slot we want, can't find a parking space, can't find the classroom, can't seem to handle the freedom of college, can't find the time to do all that we might, can't get into the "right" Greek or social organization, can't get our parents to "understand," can't find the money to do it all, and so on. What we can control is our *reaction* to these hassles. If we can adopt the attitude that we will do what we can do, seek help when appropriate, and not sweat the small stuff, we won't be as negatively affected by disappointments and hassles. It also helps to keep a mental tally of the positive things in our lives. The following exercise will help you to take positive stock of your life and to become more aware of the barriers to letting go of useless worries.

EXERCISE 19.3 Protection from Stress

A Feeling good about yourself can be an effective buffer against stress. Begin here by identifying some of your personal strengths.

_____

_____

_____

Expand this into a longer list of what you like about yourself, and keep the list in a private place. Every day, whether you feel the need or not, review your list and try to add a new positive thought about yourself to it.

B Likewise, it's important to eliminate unnecessary worries. Most of our worries are either passed on to us by other people or conjured up in our imaginations. What are some of your current worries?

_____

_____

_____

What can you do to eliminate one or more of them?

_____

_____

_____

Physical activity, especially when it's fun, can serve as a remedy for stress.

Lynn Howlett Photography/photo courtesy of Willamette University

■A STRESS RELIEF SMORGASBORD

Everyone finds different activities relaxing. To provide yourself with a sense of relief, you need to do those things that help you to let go of stress or invigorate your mind and body. However, many of the traditional things that people do with the intention of relieving stress—such as drinking alcohol, taking drugs, sleeping, or eating—don't relieve stress and may actually increase it! There are many other ways of handling stress that actually work. I offer the following as more effective methods.

Get Physical

1. **Relax your neck and shoulders.** Slowly drop your head forward, roll it gently to the center of your right shoulder, and pause; gently roll it backward to the center of your shoulders and pause; gently roll it to the center of your left shoulder and pause; gently roll it forward to the center of your chest and pause. Then reverse direction and go back around your shoulders from left to right. Remember that your goal is to slowly stretch muscles into relaxation.

2. **Take a stretch.** In any situation, if you pause to stretch your body you will feel it loosen up and become more relaxed, so stand up and reach for the sky!

3. **Get a massage.** Physical touch can feel wonderful when you are tense, and having someone else help you to relax can feel very supportive.

4. **Exercise.** Physical exercise strengthens both mind and body. Aerobic exercise is the most effective type for stress relief.

Get Mental

1. **Count to ten.** Many people discount this method because it sounds too simple. Your purpose is to master self-control and gain a more realistic

Road Warrior

A student who commuted twenty-three miles to school was tailgated just before arriving on campus one day. The accident was minor, but unfortunately she had been sipping coffee at the time of the collision, and it splashed all over her dress. She was so embarrassed that she didn't go to class. Unfortunately, that was a particularly important class, and her absence eventually cost her a full letter grade.

If you commute a long distance, carry a store of supplies. Leave your "survival" kit in your car if you drive, or in a locker at school if possible. Here are some things you should have in your kit. Talk with other students about other items that might be useful and add them to the list.

1. Emergency medical supplies
2. Flashlight
3. One dollar in change
4. Some pencils and paper
5. Jumper cables
6. Local bus schedule
7. Rag or towel
8. Spare set of clothes
9. _____
10. _____
11. _____
12. _____

perspective or outlook. To give yourself time to gain that new outlook or to come up with a "better" way to handle the situation, count slowly while asking yourself, "How can I best handle this situation?"

2. **Control your thoughts.** The imagination can be *very* creative—it can veer off in frightening directions if allowed to do so. To gain control of negative thoughts or worries, imagine yelling "STOP!" as loudly as you can in your mind. You may have to repeat this process quite a few times until you master it, but gradually it will help you to shut out angry or frightening thoughts.

3. **Fantasize.** Give yourself a few moments to take a "minivacation." Remember the pleasure of an experience you enjoy, or listen to a child laugh, or just let your mind be creative. Make a list of some places or activities that make you feel relaxed and good about yourself. Next time you need to "get away," refer to the list, close your eyes, and take a minibreak.

4. **Congratulate yourself.** Give yourself pats on the back. No one knows how difficult a situation may have been for you to handle, or even how well you may have handled it, so tell yourself, "Good going."

5. **Ignore the problem.** This may sound strange at first, but many problems just don't need to be dealt with or can't be solved right now. Forget about the problem at hand and do something more important or something nice for yourself.

6. **Perform self-maintenance.** Stress is a daily issue, so the more you plan for its reduction, the more likely it will be reduced.

Photo by Jason Jones/courtesy of Lyon College

Get Spiritual

1. **Meditate.** All that meditation requires is slow breathing and concentration! Look at something in front of you or make a mental picture while you gradually breathe slower and slower, and feel the relief spread through your body and mind.

2. **Pray.** You don't need to go through life feeling alone. Prayer can be a great source of comfort and strength.

3. **Remember your purpose.** Sometimes it is very valuable to remind ourselves why we are in a particular situation. Even though it may be a difficult situation, you may need to remind yourself that you have to be there and to realize that the situation's importance outweighs its difficulty.

Use Mind and Body Together

1. **Take a break.** If possible, get up from what you are doing and walk away for a while. Don't let yourself think about the source of the problem until after a short walk.

2. **Get hug therapy.** We need at least four hugs a day to survive, eight hugs to feel okay, and twelve hugs to tackle the world. "Hugs" can come from many different sources and they can take many different forms. They can be bear hugs, smiles, compliments, or kind words or thoughts. If you have forgotten how to hug, ask a small child you know to teach you. Young children know that every time you give a hug, you get one back as a fringe benefit!

3. **Try progressive relaxation.** Perform a mental massage of each muscle in your body from your feet up to your head. Take the time to allow each muscle to relax and unwind. Imagine that the muscles that were all knotted and tense are now long, smooth, and relaxed.

4. **Laugh.** Nothing is so important that we must suffer self-damage. The ability to laugh at your own mistakes lightens your load and gives you the energy to return to a difficult task.

5. Find a pet. Countless studies have demonstrated that caring for, talking to, holding, and stroking pets can help to reduce stress.

Develop New Skills

1. Learn something. Sometimes your problem is that you lack information or skills in a certain area. The sooner you remedy your deficiency, the sooner your distress will end.

2. Practice a hobby. If you have one, use it; if you don't currently have one, then it's time that you did. The purpose of a hobby is to immerse yourself in an activity of your choice that provides you with a sense of accomplishment and pleasure.

EXERCISE 19.4 Adding to and Using the Stress Reduction List

A Over your lifetime you've discovered some additional things that work to relieve stress for you. List them here:

_____

_____

_____

Expand your list by comparing notes with other students in the class.

B Try at least one stress relief technique suggested in this section for two weeks. Give it a good try. To assist yourself in changing from a stress habit to a control habit, resolve in your mind that you deserve to be a more relaxed, confident person. Share your experience with someone.

The stress management habits that you are currently acquiring and practicing are likely to be the same ones that you will use for the rest of your life! Learning to handle stress in a healthy fashion is important not only to survive your first year and do well but to cope with the demands and opportunities of adulthood. A healthy adult is one who treats his or her body and mind in a respectful manner. When you do that, you communicate to all other adults that you are handling yourself well and don't need them to "baby" you or to tell you how to live your life.

Sometimes our lives or problems are either too overwhelming or too complex to resolve by ourselves. If you find that to be the case, you might benefit from checking out the services provided by your college counseling center. Counseling centers often offer individual or group sessions on handling difficult times or situations in our lives, and the support and skills of a trained professional can help make the most difficult issues a lot more manageable.

EXERCISE 19.5 Your Social Support Network

Your social support network can be extremely helpful to you in difficult times, but many people aren't sure whom to count on for support or how to ask for it.

You first learned about getting support from your family. Think back to a time when you felt you really needed support. Was it when you were trying to accomplish something or when you felt discouraged or defeated? Whom did you ask for support? How did you ask? Did they respond in the way that you needed them to? Did you get the caring or comfort that you wanted?

Life's early lessons usually get reinforced over the years. Probably by now either you feel good about the level of support in your life or you don't.

Imagine you have a problem with a roommate that you want to discuss with someone else. Whom would you choose? Would you expect that discussion to leave you feeling the way you want to feel, or are you just used to feeling that you never get the support you need to feel good about yourself?

In different situations, you may need different people for support. Are you still relying primarily on your family, or have you expanded your resources to get support from friends, professors, co-workers, and so on? Who is in your support network? Make a list of people you would support. Make a list of situations in which you sometimes need support. List the people who support you in them. Do you need to add someone to your network? Write yourself a note about how to get that person's support.

You may also want to consider the values that your current physical, emotional, and spiritual circumstances reflect. Are those values similar to or different from those of your family and friends? Are you acting in accordance with your values? Is this a source of stress? Remember, whatever you do to cope with stress, you will be coping either productively or counterproductively—it's your choice. Go forth and manage stress!

EXERCISE 19.6 A One-Week Checkup

To control stress, we need to heed its warning signs. Photocopy the chart on the next page and use it for one week to keep track of troublesome experiences and your *reactions* and *responses* to them. If at first you don't notice any reactions, pay attention to your general state during the day. Times when you feel suddenly fatigued, tense, angry, upset, frightened, and so on are stress points in your day.

After the week is over, analyze the chart. Look for both positive and negative patterns. Based on this information, write down a plan for stress management:

I will _____

_____

I will _____

_____

I will not _____

_____

I will not _____

_____

| | Signals | | Your | What (If Anything) Would You |
Event	Physical	Emotional	Response	Do Differently Next Time?

A Relaxation Process

Settle back and get comfortable. Take a few moments to allow yourself to listen to your thoughts and to your body. If your thoughts get in the way of relaxing, imagine a blackboard in your mind and visualize yourself writing down all of your thoughts on the blackboard. By doing this, you can put those thoughts aside for a while and know that you will be able to retrieve them later.

Now that you are more ready to relax, begin by closing your eyes. Allow your breathing to become a little slower and a little deeper. As you continue breathing slowly and deeply, let your mind drift back into a tranquil, safe place that you have been in before. Try to recall everything that you could see, hear, and feel back there. Let those pleasant memories wash away any tension or discomfort.

To help yourself relax even further, take a brief journey through your body, allowing all of your muscles to become as comfortable and as relaxed as possible.

Let's begin that journey down at your feet. Begin by focusing on your feet up to your ankles, wiggling your feet or toes to help them to relax, then allowing that growing wave of relaxation to continue up into the muscles of the calves. As muscles relax, they stretch out and allow more blood to flow into them; therefore they gradually feel warmer and heavier. Continue the process on up into the muscles of the thighs; gradually your legs should feel more and more comfortable, more and more relaxed.

Then concentrate on all of the muscles up and down your spine, and feel the relaxation moving into your abdomen; as you do so you might also feel a pleasant sense of warmth moving out to every part of your body. Next focus on the muscles of the chest. Each time that you exhale, your chest muscles will relax just a little more. Let the feeling flow up into the muscles of the shoulders, washing away any tightness or tension, allowing the shoulder muscles to become loose and limp. And now the relaxation can seep out into the muscles of the arms and hands; gradually your arms and hands become heavy, limp, and warm.

Now move on to the muscles of the neck—front, sides, and back—imagining perhaps that your neck muscles are as floppy as a handful of rubber bands. And now relax the muscles of the face, letting the jaw, cheeks, and sides of the face hang loose and limp. Now relax the eyes and the nose, and now the forehead and the scalp. Let any wrinkles just melt away. And now, by taking a long, slow, deep breath, cleanse yourself of any remaining tension.

JOURNAL

Which stress theory described in this section makes the most sense to you? Explore your reaction by recording some personal examples or experiences. Comment on some of your stress relief strategies. How effective are they for you?

SUGGESTIONS FOR FURTHER READING

Benson, H., and M. Z. Klipper. *The Relaxation Response.* New York: Morrow, 1976.

Brown, B. *Supermind.* New York: Harper & Row, 1980.

Butler, P. *Talking to Yourself.* New York: Stein & Day, 1981.

Clum, George A. *Coping with Panic: A Drug Free Approach to Dealing with Anxiety Attacks.* Pacific Grove, Calif.: Brooks/Cole, 1990.

Emmons, M. *The Inner Source.* San Luis Obispo, Calif.: Impact, 1978.

Glasser, W. *Positive Addiction.* New York: Harper & Row, 1979.

Green, E., and A. Green. *Beyond Biofeedback.* New York: Delta, 1977.

Hyatt, C., and L. Gottlieb. *When Smart People Fail.* New York: Simon & Schuster, 1987.

Kinser, N. S. *Stress and the American Woman.* New York: Ballantine Books, 1980.

Martin, R. A., and E. Y. Pollard. *Learning to Change.* New York: McGraw-Hill, 1980.

Otis, C. L., and R. Goldingay. *Campus Health Guide.* New York: College Entrance Examination Board, 1989.

Pennebaker, James W. *Opening Up: The Healing Power of Confiding in Others.* New York: Morrow, 1990.

Powell, Trevor J. *Anxiety and Stress Management.* New York: Routledge, 1990.

Smith, Jonathan C. *Stress Scripting: A Guide to Stress Management.* New York: Praeger, 1991.

Sutherland, Valerie J., and Cary L. Cooper. *Understanding Stress.* New York: Chapman & Hall, 1990.

Vorst, J. *Necessary Losses.* New York: Fawcett, 1986.

CHAPTER 20

Sexual Decisions

Lisa Ann Mohn
University of South Carolina

A few of my friends are always bragging about who they were with last night. I'm not into that. Some women around here turn me on, but I just don't want a sexual relationship right now. I have enough to deal with. Down the road a little, if I find the right person, who knows?

Chapter Goals

Your first thought may be, "I've heard all this before." Nonetheless, we hope you'll read this chapter carefully so that you'll be better prepared to make adult choices about sexuality. This includes deciding whether to have sex or not, what precautions to take if you choose to have sex, and the consequences of engaging in unprotected sex.

Because the goal of this book is to help you survive your first year in college, a chapter on sexual decision making seems almost a given. The main reason is that we know from numerous studies that about 75 percent of traditional-age college students have engaged in sexual intercourse at least once. Another reason is that, depending on where you are from, what your family background is, what your school district's policies on sex education were, and so on, you may or may not have some critical information.

You may be wondering what our point of view will be. Are we urging you to fight "that urge"? Providing you some answers in case you find yourself in a compromising situation? Telling you that sex in college is inevitable, so learn all you can now? No. We will neither condone nor condemn your sexual decisions. But we will encourage you to know your options, to recognize that you have the right to choose what's comfortable for you, and to accept that, should you choose to have sex, you should also choose to protect yourself against unwanted pregnancy and sexually transmitted diseases.

■ SEXUAL DECISION MAKING

The first thing we need to say is that not all first-year students are sexually active, so if you're in this category you need not feel alone. However, college seems to be a time when recent high school graduates begin at least to think more seriously about sex. Perhaps this has to do with peer pressure or a sense of one's newfound independence, or maybe it's just hormones. Regardless of the reasons, it can be quite helpful to explore your sexual values and to consider whether sex is right for you at this time.

Although the "sexual revolution" of the 1960s and 1970s may have made premarital sex more socially acceptable, people have not necessarily become better equipped to deal with this sexual freedom. One sign of this is the alarming increase in the rate of sexually transmitted diseases (STDs) among college students. Another is the fact that unwanted pregnancies are not uncommon. More difficult to quantify is the degree to which young people may later regret impulsive decisions to have sex.

Why is it that otherwise intelligent people choose to take sexual risks? Well, sex isn't the only thing that college students take risks with. If you are 18 or so, you may feel you are invincible or immune from danger. Although you know certain risks exist, you may never have been sufficiently exposed to them personally to believe your own life could be touched. Or perhaps it's simply that sex and relationships are a confusing business. While there are many pressures to become sexually active, certainly many factors may discourage sexual activity as well. The following list compares these factors:

Encouragers	Discouragers
Hormones	Family values/expectations
Peer pressure	Religious values
Alcohol/other drugs	Sexually transmitted diseases
Curiosity	Fear of pregnancy
The media	Concern for reputation
An intimate relationship	Feeling of unreadiness
Sexual pleasure	Fear of being hurt or "used"

As you can see, there are powerful pressures on each side. Consequently, some people get confused and frustrated and fail to make any decision. Or they may allow the encouragers to persuade them but not feel comfortable enough with that decision to take responsibility for their actions—the "If I don't think or talk about it, then I can pretend I'm not really doing it" syndrome. This irresponsibility or indecisiveness carries a risk: that sex will occur without the means to prevent pregnancy or STDs.

For your protection, try to clarify your own values and then act in accordance with them. Those who do this usually wind up happier with their decisions. Take a moment now to reflect on whether you plan to be sexually active. Whatever you decide, think about how you will reinforce your resolve to abstain from sex or only practice safer sex and how you plan on communicating that decision to your partner.

EXERCISE 20.1 Personal Reflection on Sexuality

A Ask yourself the following questions to prepare for part B: Have you taken time to sort out your own values about sexual activity? If you aren't willing to commit to a particular plan of action at this time, what keeps you from doing so? If you are sexually active, do your values take into account your own and your partner's health? If that's not a priority for you, what would it take to get you to a point where safer sex took priority over unsafe sex?

B Write down some of your thoughts and intentions about sexuality. This should be for you alone to read. The act of writing may help you organize your thoughts. Committing your values to paper may also help you live by them when faced with tough decisions.

Birth Control

One sexuality issue that heterosexual students need to be concerned about is preventing an unwanted pregnancy.

What is the best method of contraception? It is any method that you use correctly and consistently, each time you have intercourse. Although one

Table 20.1 Methods of Contraception

ABSTINENCE (100%)*
What It Is
Choosing not to have intercourse.
Advantages
Only method that provides total protection against pregnancy and STDs.
Disadvantages
Does not allow for the benefits people look for from sexual intercourse.
Comments
Not an acceptable practice for many people.

NORPLANT (99.9%)
What It Is
Six matchstick-sized silicone rubber capsules, inserted into a woman's arm, that continually release a very low dose of progesterone.
Advantages
Highly effective. Works for up to five years. Allows for sexual spontaneity. Low dose of hormones make this medically safer than other hormonal methods.
Disadvantages
Removal may be difficult. Very expensive to obtain initially.
Comments
Users may have typical side effects of hormonal methods, causing them to discontinue during the first year. This makes it somewhat risky due to the high initial cost.

DEPO-PROVERA (99.7%)
What It Is
A progestin-only method, administered to women by injection, every three months.
Advantages
Highly effective. Allows for sexual spontaneity. Relatively low yearly cost.
Disadvantages
A variety of side effects typical of progestin-type contraceptives may be present and persist up to six to eight months after termination.
Comments
Method is easy and spontaneous, but users must remember to get their shots.

STERILIZATION (99.5%)
What It Is
Tubal ligation in women; vasectomy in men.
Advantages
Provides nearly permanent protection from future pregnancies.
Disadvantages
Not considered reversible and therefore not a good option for anyone wanting children at a later date.
Comments
Although this is a common method for people over age 30, most college students would not choose it.

ORAL CONTRACEPTIVES (97–99%)
What They Are
Birth control pills.
Advantages
Highly effective. Allows for sexual spontaneity. Most women have lighter and shorter periods.

Disadvantages
Many minor side effects (nausea, weight gain), which cause a significant percentage of users to discontinue. Provides no protection against STDs.
Comments
Available by prescription only, after a gynecological exam.

INTRAUTERINE DEVICE (IUD) (98–99%)
What It Is
Device inserted into the uterus by a physician.
Advantages
Once inserted, may be left in for one to eight years, depending upon the type. Less expensive than other long-term methods.
Disadvantages
Increased risk of certain complications such as pelvic inflammatory disease and menstrual problems. Possible increased risk of contracting HIV, if exposed.
Comments
Women who have not had a child may have a difficult time finding a doctor willing to prescribe it.

CONDOM (88–98%)
What It Is
Rubber sheath that fits over the penis.
Advantages
Only birth control method that also provides good protection against STDs, including HIV. Actively involves male partner.
Disadvantages
Less spontaneous than some other methods because it must be put on right before intercourse. Belief of some men that it cuts down on pleasurable sensations.
Comments
Experts believe that most condom failure is due to misuse of condoms rather than breakage. Using condoms in conjunction with additional spermicide can increase effectiveness to nearly 100 percent.

DIAPHRAGM (80–95%)
What It Is
Dome-shaped rubber cap that is inserted into the vagina and covers the cervix.
Advantages
Safe method of birth control with virtually no side effects. May be inserted up to 2 hours prior to intercourse, making it somewhat spontaneous. May provide some protection against STDs.
Disadvantages
Wide variance of effectiveness based on consistent use, the fit of the diaphragm, and frequency of intercourse. Multiple acts of intercourse require use of additional spermicide.
Comments
Must be prescribed by a physician. Must always be used with a spermicidal jelly and left in for 6–8 hours after intercourse.

FEMALE CONDOM (80–95%)
What It Is
A polyurethane sheath that completely lines the vagina acting as a complete barrier. Two rings hold it in place, one inside and one outside the vagina.

(continued)

Advantages

Highly safe medically. Does not require any spermicide. Theoretically provides excellent protection against STDs—almost perfectly leakproof and better than the male condom in this regard.

Disadvantages

Lower effectiveness rate than many other methods. Visible outer ring can be aesthetically displeasing.

Comments

While the research is not yet conclusive, this method seems to offer good STD protection that is controllable by the woman.

CONTRACEPTIVE SPONGE (80–90%)
What It Is

Small polyurethane sponge containing the spermicide Nonoxynol-9.

Advantages

Easy to obtain (over the counter) and use. Once inserted, effective for 24 hours with no additional spermicide needed.

Disadvantages

Frequent difficulty with removal. For women who have had a child, effectiveness is less than indicated here.

Comments

Must be left in for 6–8 hours after intercourse.

CERVICAL CAP (80–90%)
What It Is

Cup-shaped device that fits over the cervix.

Advantages

Similar to diaphragm, but may be worn longer—up to 48 hours.

Disadvantages

Not widely available due to lack of practitioners trained in fitting them.

Comments

Longer wearing time increases risk of vaginal infections.

SPERMICIDAL FOAMS, CREAMS, AND JELLIES (80–90%)

What They Are

Sperm-killing chemicals inserted into the vagina.

Advantages

Easy to purchase and use. Provide some protection against STDs, including HIV.

Disadvantages

Lower effectiveness than many methods. Can be messy. May increase likelihood of birth defects should pregnancy occur.

Comments

As with condoms, it is suspected that failure is due to misuse. However, spermicides seem to work better in combination with other methods (such as condoms).

NATURAL FAMILY PLANNING (80%)
What It Is

Periodic abstinence based on when ovulation is predicted.

Advantages

Requires no devices or chemicals.

Disadvantages

Requires a period of abstinence each month, when ovulation is expected. Also, requires diligent record-keeping.

Comments

For maximum effectiveness, consult a trained practitioner for guidance in using this method.

COITUS INTERRUPTUS (80%)
What It Is

Withdrawal.

Advantages

Requires no devices or chemicals. Can be used at any time, at no cost.

Disadvantages

Relies heavily on the man having enough control and knowing when ejaculation will occur to remove his penis from the vagina in time. Also may diminish pleasure for the couple.

Comments

Ejaculation must be far enough away from partner's genitals so that no semen can enter the vagina. Provides no protection against STDs.

*Percentages in parentheses refer to approximate effectiveness rates based on one year of using the method. Where two numbers are given, the lower percentage refers to the *typical* effectiveness, while the higher number refers to the *possible* effectiveness if used correctly and consistently.

method may be more effective than another, if a couple does not prefer it, they will be less likely to use it consistently and correctly, and therefore it's not better for them. When choosing a method of birth control, consider all aspects of the method before you decide. Table 20.1 compares the major features of some common methods. Note the table's emphasis on whether each method protects against STDs. For most college students, this is important in choosing one or more methods of birth control. Because of their importance in preventing disease, more information about condoms is included later in this chapter.

As the table indicates, all methods have advantages and disadvantages. Make sure that whatever method you choose, you feel comfortable using it.

Consult your physician for the methods requiring a prescription, and make sure to read all package inserts thoroughly, particularly for any products you buy over the counter.

Always discuss birth control with your partner so that you both feel comfortable with the option you have selected. For more information about a particular method, consult a pharmacist, a medical practitioner at your student health center, a local family planning clinic or Planned Parenthood affiliate, the local health department, or your private physician. The main thing is to get information somewhere and to resolve to protect yourself and your partner each and every time you choose to have sexual intercourse.

If you've already chosen a method, or have one in mind, the next exercise can help you decide whether it's truly the best method for you.

EXERCISE 20.2 Which Birth Control Method Is Best?

If you're choosing to be sexually active and don't desire to have children at this time, it's time to choose a method of birth control. Both partners should be involved in this decision. Consider various factors to decide what's right for you, your partner, and your relationship. You can answer these questions on your own and then have your partner complete the exercise, with both of you keeping in mind a particular method you're considering. Or you can complete it together, discussing the issue as you go.

	Me	My Partner
1. Has a pregnancy ever occurred despite using this preferred method of birth control?	_____	_____
2. Will I have difficulty using this method?	_____	_____
3. If this method interrupts lovemaking, will I be less likely to use it?	_____	_____
4. Is there anything about my behavior or habits that could lead me to use this method incorrectly?	_____	_____
5. Am I at risk of being exposed to HIV or other STDs if I use this method?	_____	_____
6. Am I concerned about potential side effects associated with this method?	_____	_____
7. Does this method cost more than I can afford?	_____	_____
8. Would I really rather not use this method?	_____	_____

Sexually Transmitted Diseases (STDs)

The problem of STDs on college campuses has been receiving growing attention in recent years, as an epidemic number of students have become infected. The consequences of the most common STDs reach far beyond the embarrassment most students feel when diagnosed with a sexually related illness. The idea that "nice" young men and women don't catch these sorts of diseases is more dangerous and inaccurate than ever before. If you choose to be sexually active, particularly with more than one partner, exposure to an STD is a very real possibility.

The most important thing you can do for yourself with regard to sexuality is simply to live consistently in keeping with your own values. Intimacy, belongingness, mutual acceptance, and support are all possible regardless of a person's sexual choices.

Photo courtesy of Earlham College

This section will discuss the STDs students need to be most aware of. Chlamydia, herpes, and human papillomavirus are important because of their high rates and potential consequences. Gonorrhea is discussed briefly because it is so similar to and often accompanies chlamydia, although its rates are much higher in the general population than among college students. Hepatitis B can lead to serious illness and is on the rise, but a preventive vaccine is available. Naturally, HIV/AIDS is a concern, not only because of its deadly consequences but also because of its increasing incidence among the college-age population.

In general, STDs continue to increase faster than other illnesses on campuses today. Approximately 5–10 percent of visits to college health services nationally are for the diagnosis and treatment of STDs. For more information about any of these diseases, or others, contact your student health center, your local health department, or the National STD Hotline (1-800-227-8922).

CHLAMYDIA

The most common STD in the United States is chlamydia. Over 4 million new cases are diagnosed each year. Chlamydia is particularly threatening to women because a large proportion of women who are infected do not show symptoms, allowing the disease to progress to pelvic inflammatory disease (PID), now thought to be the leading cause of infertility in women. When chlamydia does produce symptoms in women, the symptoms may include mild abdominal pain, change in vaginal discharge, and pain and burning with urination.

In men, symptoms are typically pain and burning with urination, and sometimes a discharge from the penis. Occasionally, the symptoms will be too mild to notice. Men who go without treatment may also become infertile, although this happens much more rarely than it does in women. In both sexes, symptoms usually appear one to three weeks after exposure. Even if symptoms are not apparent, an individual infected with chlamydia is still contagious and may transmit the disease to subsequent sexual partners. If detected, chlamydia is completely treatable with antibiotics.

GONORRHEA

Gonorrhea is a bacterial infection that produces symptoms similar to chlamydia. Although not quite as common as chlamydia, with approximately 2 million new cases nationwide per year, it still has a significant impact on the health of Americans. As with chlamydia, men will usually show symptoms, but women often do not. Gonorrhea is treatable with antibiotics, but in recent years new, more resistant strains of gonorrhea have made this process more difficult. Untreated gonorrhea, like chlamydia, can lead to more severe infections in men and women.

HERPES

Before AIDS came along, herpes was considered the worst STD one could get, because there is no cure. There are approximately 200,000 new cases nationwide per year, but it's estimated that 30 million people are infected with genital herpes, many of them asymptomatic (showing no symptoms). The characteristic blisters one gets on the genitals are very similar to the cold sores and fever blisters people get on their mouths, and in fact they are both caused by varieties of the herpes virus. (The strains of the virus are even interchangeable above and below the waist if transmitted through oral sex.)

Symptoms appear on the genitals two days to two weeks after exposure in the form of small blisters or lesions that erupt into painful sores. The first outbreak is usually the most severe, and about 50 percent of those infected will never have another outbreak. The other 50 percent are likely to have outbreaks several times a year, particularly when they are under stress or their immune system is being taxed.

Although there is no cure, the prescription drug Zovirax seems to reduce the length and severity of herpes outbreaks. People are most contagious to a partner after or right before lesions erupt, so it is important to abstain from any sexual contact at this time. It is difficult to determine exactly how contagious a person is at other times, but asymptomatic people can transmit the disease because the virus continues to live in the body. Some experts believe that most cases of herpes are transmitted this way.

HUMAN PAPILLOMAVIRUS (HPV)

Although chlamydia may still be the most prevalent STD nationwide, HPV has become the leading STD affecting the health of college students. There has been a 600 percent increase of HPV in this population in the past twenty years, and some recent studies show that as many as 40–50 percent of sexually active college students may be infected.

HPV is the cause of venereal warts, which affect both men and women on their outer genitals and in the rectum of those who practice anal receptive intercourse, and it may even grow inside a man's urethra or a woman's vagina. A typical incubation period for venereal warts is one to three months, though symptoms may not appear for several months or years after exposure. Genital warts may be small, flat, pink growths, or they may be larger, with a cauliflowerlike appearance. In either case they are usually not painful.

Because HPV is a virus, there is no cure, but treatment is available in the form of burning, freezing, chemical destruction, and, in severe cases, laser surgery. Wart removal often takes multiple treatments, which can be painful but are less disruptive to a busy student's schedule. As with herpes, the virus remains in the body and may cause recurrences and be transmitted to a partner over an indefinite period of time.

The major long-term health concern associated with HPV affects women. Certain strains of HPV don't cause the visible warts but invade the cervix and incorporate themselves into the DNA of the cells there. The subsequent cervical cell changes produce dysplasia, a precancerous condition that can lead to cervical cancer. In the past few years, the correlation between cervical cancer and HPV has become very strong, and most experts believe HPV is responsible for the large majority of cases of cervical cancer in our country today. The incubation period for these changes can take many years. Fortunately, if women are screened regularly with Pap smears, precancerous changes can be detected and treated before they lead to cervical cancer.

HEPATITIS B

There are about 300,000 new cases of hepatitis B nationwide each year, most of them in adolescents and young adults. Hepatitis B is transmitted through unprotected sex and through contact with infected blood, and it is 100 times more infectious than HIV. This means you have a much greater risk of contracting it if you are exposed.

People who are infected with hepatitis B can have varying symptoms. In fact, it's common to show no symptoms. When present, symptoms may include those similar to a stomach virus, in addition to yellowing of the skin and eyes. Occasionally, people become very ill and are disabled for weeks or months. Most people will recover completely, but some remain carriers for life, able to transmit the virus to others. A small percentage of infected people go on to get chronic liver disease, which puts them at risk for cirrhosis and liver cancer.

There is no cure for hepatitis B, and no treatment other than rest and a healthy diet. What makes this STD unusual is that there is a vaccine available to prevent it. The series of three shots is recommended by the Centers for Disease Control and the American Academy of Pediatrics for all young adults. The major drawback to the vaccine is that it's very costly—up to $150 for the three shots—making it unlikely that many college students will invest in it.

HIV/AIDS

HIV/AIDS is very difficult to discuss briefly. We must assume that you have already been exposed to a good deal of information on this STD. The main thing we want to stress is that AIDS and the virus that causes it—HIV—continue to increase. During 1994, in the thirteenth year of the epidemic, the number of cases of AIDS had grown to almost 400,000, more than twice the number there were in 1990! The Centers for Disease Control estimate that there are at least 1–1½ million people infected with HIV. The routes of transmission for HIV are through blood, semen, vaginal fluids, and breast milk, or by being born to an HIV-infected mother.

While men who have sex with men and intravenous drug users still make up the majority of AIDS cases to date, other groups have rapidly increasing rates of infection, including women, teens, heterosexuals, Hispanics, and African Americans (who continue to be disproportionately represented among those with AIDS). Although we're discussing "risk groups" here, it's important to keep in mind that it's not who you are but what you do that puts you at risk for contracting HIV.

AIDS had not been a major problem on most college campuses as of the early 1990s. However, as more and more people become infected with HIV,

Living with AIDS

Most people only die once. I've already died twice. The first time was in the fall of 1981 when I surrendered to the fact that I was an alcoholic and pillhead. The second time was on a warm, sunny day in late April 1987, when my doctor said, "With these symptoms, I have to conclude that it's the AIDS virus."

Being dead can have its advantages. Sometimes I say to myself, "You're dead, you can do whatever you want. What are they going to do, shoot you?" You get to eat what you like. In fact, like the scene from Sleeper, *the doctors encourage you to eat steaks and ice cream. People don't castigate you when you sleep in. Planning for the future means drawing up a will. You don't save for retirement; you should live that long. I have a friend who went $27,000 into debt and then kicked the bucket. Now, he got the joke.*

Generally, though, being dead isn't much fun. Old friends often treat you like the proverbial hot potato, or like a time bomb. They pass you around, hoping you don't go off around them. Not that I blame them: We've all gone to too many funerals.

So you find yourself gravitating to the other HIVs. Then the game becomes more like musical chairs. Who's the next one out? When your friends start the

fast slide, they are instantly old men, the shadow-dead. Hair turns into fragile wisps, bodies become gaunt, eyes disappear into the recesses of emaciated faces. Then everyone knows, not much longer for this one.

Some are deserted by their families. More often, families kill with a kind of kindness. Well-intentioned, misguided, they nurse you through the last months, but they really want you to go out on their terms. I have a friend who was an invalid for his last six months while his . . . family screened out all gay callers and "converted" him to Christ and prayer and away from the gay life.

Another unpleasant thing about being dead is that people objectify you, treat you like a thing rather than a person. This is, of course, what we do to dead things. Bad enough that the doctors and hospital medical staff treat you like a faulty piece of equipment to keep running and keep clean (although I've had indigent friends who were denied even that slim dignity in the final countdown). You begin to wonder how to justify all this expense and bother. Soon you hear subtle messages like, "Do you realize how much your decision to stay alive is costing us?"

Then there is all the shame that goes with being too sick to meet obligations, with losing your looks,

college students are more likely to be exposed and to contract the virus. Because of the long incubation period suspected for AIDS, students may become infected with the virus while they are in college but not become sick until several years afterward.

Because other STDs are occurring at such a high rate, many students obviously are engaging in the behaviors that put them at risk for STDs, including HIV. In addition, having other STDs may actually predispose people to contract HIV more readily if they are exposed to the virus. Each person must try to evaluate his or her own risk of becoming infected and take precautions.

As with other STDs, abstinence, monogamy, and condoms (in that order) are the best ways to prevent the sexual spread of AIDS. Get as much information as you can through your student health service, your local health department, or the National AIDS Hotline (1-800-342-AIDS).

Preventing STDs

Although the sexually transmitted diseases discussed here can be very serious and very scary, it's not all bad news. Good methods of protection are *with becoming helpless. Shame is an awesome thing. My mother, who has otherwise been remarkable, cannot tell her friends that her son has this virus and is probably dying. She simply cannot do it.*

Then there are all the lies. I lost a job because they found out why I was sick. I lost a job because I couldn't risk telling them I was sick. Better to leave with a question mark than with that trailing after you. Outside of the gay community I tell only a select few. I'll be [damned] if I'll surrender my personal power. . . .

Gradually the gritty process of closing out a life begins. Can't make it into the office at nine? Go on disability. Can't keep your apartment up? Move in with Mom and Dad. Learn to like daytime television. Let's not even talk about a sex life. You end up disempowered, nudged to the edge of things by the busy, ignored, untouched, living in limbo. . . .

Memorize this equation: silence = death. The mountains of medicine labor to bring forth a mouse. When you get an undeserved death sentence, you have the right to be angry. It is only the most belligerent and unpleasant among the sick who can hope to hope.

SOURCE: Adapted and reproduced, with permission, from *the Student Union* (a publication by students at Carnegie-Mellon University), 6, no. 3 (1990).

Cassandra Ecker/photo courtesy of Illinois Media Company

The Names Project has toured many American campuses. It is both an urgent appeal for everyone to face the reality of AIDS and a moving celebration of the lives of thousands of people—male, female, gay, straight—cut short by HIV.

available, and you can choose what's right for you. The worst thing you can do is nothing. If you let concerns about sexual risks overwhelm you, they will. People who do not make conscious choices in advance are often caught making a decision that doesn't suit their values and may compromise their health.

ABSTINENCE

The first choice you always have is to abstain from sex. Even if three-quarters of college students are having sex, that still leaves a solid one-quarter who are not. If you currently fall in this group, congratulations! It can be difficult to choose a behavior when you're in the minority, but you are surely reaping benefits.

One thing that can make the decision to remain abstinent easier is realizing that abstinence doesn't have to mean a lack of intimacy, or even of sexual pleasure, for that matter. Abstinence (with a partner) encompasses a wide variety of behaviors from holding hands to more sexually intimate behaviors short of intercourse. These carry a lower risk of spreading disease, having an unwanted pregnancy, or possibly regretting sex than do vaginal or anal intercourse. Even if you've had intercourse in the past, you can return to a "secondary virginity" if you choose.

Condoms

When selecting a condom, always consider the following:

1. **Use condoms made of latex rubber.** Latex serves as a barrier to the virus. "Lambskin" or "natural membrane" condoms are not good because of the pores in the material. Look for "latex" on the package.

2. **Use condoms with a spermicide to get more protection.** Spermicides have been shown in laboratory tests to kill viruses. Use the spermicide in the tip and outside the condom.

3. **Use a lubricant with a condom.** Check the list of ingredients on the back of the lubricant package to make sure the lubricant is water-based. Do not use petroleum-based jelly, cold cream, baby oil, or cooking shortening. These can weaken the condom and cause it to break.

SOURCE: Adapted from *Understanding AIDS: A Message from the Surgeon General.* HHA Publication No. (CDC) HHS-88-8404 (Washington, D.C.: Government Printing Office).

MONOGAMY

Another very safe behavior, in terms of disease prevention, is having sex exclusively with one partner who is uninfected. However, students find it difficult to practice this type of monogamy successfully for two reasons. The first is that having a long-term monogamous relationship is not always practical because college is a time when many people want to date and either aren't interested in becoming "serious" or just don't find the right person. And the "love of your life" this fall may not be the same next spring. The second reason is that it is hard to know for sure that your partner was not infected to begin with. Unless you're both virgins, you can't be certain, but your chances of remaining healthy are better the more limited the number of your prior sexual partners and the longer you progress in the relationship disease-free.

CONDOMS

Lastly, there's the condom. In the 1990s, the condom needs to be a "given" for those who are sexually active. Other than providing very good pregnancy protection, it can help to prevent the spread of STDs, including HIV/AIDS. The condom's effectiveness against disease holds true for anal, vaginal, and oral intercourse. The most current research indicates that the rate of protection provided by condoms against STDs is similar to its rate of protection against pregnancy (90–99 percent). This was supported in 1993 when the National Centers for Disease Control endorsed condom use as a safe and effective method when used correctly and consistently.

Other methods of birth control, particularly those with spermicides containing Nonoxynol-9, may provide some extra protection against STDs, but no other method rivals the protection offered by condoms. Because STDs are epidemic on most college campuses, and because AIDS is a deadly disease, it becomes more and more important to use condoms.

Almost no one finds it easy to talk about sex with a potential partner. That's no excuse. Express your needs and concerns. Be sure you understand the other person's feelings and concerns as well.

Photo by Hilary Smith

To some degree, however, this is easier said than done. The condom has long had a reputation of being a less spontaneous method and of diminishing pleasurable sensations. It may take some discussion to convince your partner that using condoms is the right thing to do. Perhaps he or she will respond negatively to the suggestion. If this happens, here are some comments that may help you in your discussion:

Your partner: Condoms aren't spontaneous. They ruin the moment.

You: If you think they're not spontaneous, maybe we're not being creative enough. If you let me put it on you, I bet you won't notice that it's not spontaneous!

Your partner: Condoms aren't natural.

You: What's not natural is to be uptight during sex. If we know we're protected against unwanted pregnancy and disease, we'll both be more relaxed.

Your partner: It just doesn't feel as good with a condom. It's like taking a shower with a raincoat on.

You: I know it may not feel exactly the same, but I'm sure we can both work toward making it feel really *good*. Besides we can't have sex without one. Using a condom is going to feel a lot better than not having sex at all.

Your partner: I can't believe you carry condoms with you. Does this mean you'll "do it" with anyone?

You: Of course not! In fact I carry condoms because I think sex is special. I want to be responsible about it. Also I care about you, and if we decide to have sex, I want to make sure we're both protected.

Your partner: I won't have sex with a condom on.

You: Well, we can't have sex without one. There are other things we can do without having intercourse. Why don't we stick to "outer-course" until we can resolve our differences?

EXERCISE 20.3 What's Your Decision?

Although you might know about the strategies to keep yourself from contracting a sexually transmitted disease, knowledge doesn't always translate into behavior. Use the following chart to brainstorm all the reasons you can think of that people *wouldn't* practice each of the prevention strategies: abstinence, monogamy, or condom use. In other words, think about the *barriers* to safer sex. Then go back over your list, and consider whether the barrier would apply to you (Yes, No, or Maybe). In this way you can better evaluate where you stand on the issue of safer sex and determine what areas you may need to work on to ensure that you protect yourself—always!

Barriers   **Does This Apply?**

_____   _____

_____   _____

_____   _____

_____   _____

_____   _____

_____   _____

_____   _____

_____   _____

_____   _____

■SEXUAL ASSAULT

To this point our assumption has been that both partners were interested in having sex. An issue gaining much attention on college campuses lately, though, is nonconsensual sex. Sexual assault, which includes but is not limited to rape (forced intercourse), seems to be increasing on campus. At the least, victims are beginning to come forward in greater numbers, demanding that administrators take the issue more seriously. As a result more and more schools are developing sexual assault policies and procedures, designating specific personnel to deal with the issue, and providing more education for both men and women about how they can reduce their risk of becoming involved in a sexual assault.

Knowing a bit more about the profile of rape on campus may help reduce your risk. Anyone is at risk for being raped, but the majority of victims are women. By the time they graduate, an estimated 1 out of 4 college women will be the victim of attempted rape, and 1 out of 6 will be raped. Most women will be raped by someone they know, a date or acquaintance, and most do not report the crime. Alcohol is a factor in nearly three-quarters of the incidents. Whether raped by a date or a stranger, the victim can suffer long-term traumatic effects.

Rape Does Happen

I can remember a friend of mine talking about a party that she went to this summer. She was telling me about how she liked this guy and was flirting with him a little bit. She ended up having too much to drink and passed out in a friend's room. In the morning she woke up next to the guy she had been flirting with the night before. She thought that she was OK because she had all her clothes on, but when she was walking home she noticed that her underwear was in her pocket.

Every day I walk to school and in the past couple of weeks I have noticed stencils on the sidewalk—one saying "stop raping" and the other saying "sex – yes = rape." The sight of these are kind of eerie to me. Where are the rape victims on our campus? Do they have no one to turn to and therefore resort to making their concerns and hurts on the sidewalk?

This graffiti makes me think of the statistics that I hear floating around about 1 out of every 3 women getting sexually assaulted by the time they graduate from college. Sometimes I feel lucky because I got my one time over with already and the person did not get very far except for scaring me. But then I tell myself I am not that lucky—this could happen again at any time.

I was standing against a fraternity wall and someone that I knew pretty well came up to me and pushed his body against mine and started putting his hand up my shirt while trying to kiss me. I kept turning my head against the wall so he couldn't kiss me on the lips and I was trying to push him away by pushing on his shoulders. It was scary because he was bigger and stronger than I was. Even though I was pushing as hard as I could, he was stronger. After about a minute, which felt like an eternity, he got really embarrassed and backed off and said, "I'm sorry, I'm sorry, I know I shouldn't do that to you," and then he ran away.

That incident made me feel very uncomfortable and very scared. Uncomfortable because I felt a little guilty—like maybe it was my fault. I asked myself, "Why didn't I scream? What if someone else saw?" I was scared because something like that could happen to me and I was not strong enough to stop it. Also it scared me that this was someone that I knew. I had spent time alone with him in his room in the past and he had never touched me. I was confused about why all of a sudden, in the middle of this party, he would attack me. I became distrusting of him, but also of other men that I am not very close to.

It's very frightening to think about, but too often there comes a time when a woman's resistance to sexual advances is simply chalked up to her need for further seduction, for further convincing. Suddenly the female in question is no longer a feeling individual, she's just a woman, one of the ones who would eventually say "yes" anyway. At this point an act of what might have been sexual desire turns into a desire to control the situation and the woman. It is in these cases, when the someone is denied the right to say NO, that sexual assault occurs.

To understand even faintly what the experience of sexual assault is like, you must consider what it would be like to be robbed of something very personal. There are very few things that we can personally exert control over in this life, and when someone takes the control of your own body away from you, it is devastating. When something that you own is stolen, you will be justifiably upset and insecure. When your body is violated and control over your own person is taken from you, you can never regain the security of knowing that your self (physical, emotional, mental) is your own.

SOURCE: Reproduced, with permission, from Ingrid Bromberg, "Rape Does Happen at CMU," the Student Union (a publication by students at Carnegie-Mellon University), 6, no. 3 (1990).

First-year students are at particular risk for being raped because they are in a new and unfamiliar environment, may not realize the risks, want to fit in, and may even appear to be easy targets. Knowledge is important, but there are also concrete actions you can take to avoid being raped or being accused of raping someone. These are presented here with the assumption that it is women who are being raped, and men who are doing the raping.

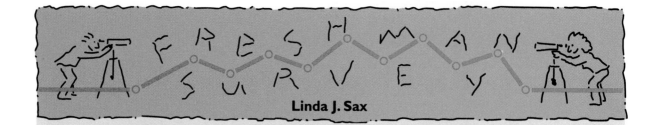

Linda J. Sax

"Date Rape" Unacceptable

As this graph shows, most students do *not* believe that a man is entitled to have sex with a woman just because he feels she has "led him on." Although women are more likely than men to oppose such nonconsensual sex, first-year males have become significantly more likely to oppose it in the eight years since the question was first introduced on the CIRP Freshman Survey.

Attitudes on Date Rape, 1988–1995 (percent agreeing "somewhat" or "strongly" that "just because a man feels a woman has 'led him on' does not entitle him to have sex with her")

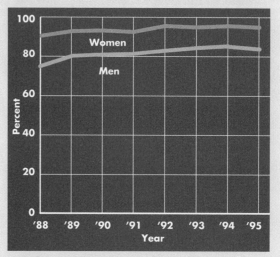

SOURCE: Higher Education Research Institute, UCLA

Potential Victim of Sexual Assault

1. Know what you want and do not want sexually, and when the issue comes up, communicate it loudly and clearly to a partner.
2. Go to parties or social gatherings with friends, and leave with them. Sexual assaults happen when people get isolated.
3. Avoid being alone with people you don't know very well, such as accepting a ride home with someone you just met or studying alone in your room with a classmate.
4. Trust your gut. If a situation feels uncomfortable in some way, don't take chances. Get out of it even if it means a few minutes of embarrassment.

5. Be alert to unconscious messages you may be sending. Although it in no way justifies someone taking advantage of you, be aware that if you dress in a sexy manner, spend the evening drinking together, and then go back to your friend's room, that person may think you want something you are not necessarily interested in.

6. Be conscious of how much alcohol you drink, if any. It is easier to make decisions and communicate them when you are sober, and also easier to sense a dangerous situation.

Person Potentially Accused of Sexual Assault

1. Realize that it is never okay to force yourself sexually on someone.

2. Don't assume you know what your date wants. He or she may want a different degree of intimacy than you do in the same situation. If you're not sure, ask.

3. If you're getting mixed messages, also ask. You have nothing to lose by stopping. If someone really wants you, he or she will let you know. And if he or she doesn't, then it's the right decision to stop.

4. Be aware of the effects of alcohol. It makes it more difficult to understand the communication you're receiving, and it is more likely to instigate violent behavior.

5. Remember that rape is legally, morally, and ethically wrong. If you have the slightest doubt about whether what you're doing is right, it's probably not.

Regardless of whether a victim chooses to report the rape to the police or get a medical exam, it is very helpful to seek some type of counseling to begin working through this traumatic event.

The following is a list of people or offices that may be available on or near your campus to deal with a sexual assault:

- Campus sexual assault coordinator
- Local rape crisis center
- Campus police department
- Counseling center
- Student health services
- Student affairs professionals
- Women's student services office
- Residence life staff
- Local hospital emergency rooms
- Campus chaplains

Perhaps the most important thing to remember about sex is that when it happens in ignorance, in haste, or without regard for the other party involved, it may leave emotional scars that are difficult to erase. On the other hand, when individuals who have genuine feelings for each other can agree on the degree of intimacy and involvement, be knowledgeable and candid about all possible outcomes, take precautions to benefit both partners, and show respect for each other's needs and feelings, sex can be wonderful indeed.

JOURNAL

Reread the comments at the beginning of the chapter about our reasons for discussing sexuality and our promise to be open-minded. Rate us on how well we did. What specific information benefited you the most? How did your class react to the presentation of the material? What do you believe could have been omitted or told in a different way?

SUGGESTIONS FOR FURTHER READING

Boston Women's Health Collective. *The New Our Bodies, Our Selves.* New York: Simon & Schuster, 1984.

Hatcher, Robert, et al. *Sexual Etiquette 101.* Decatur, Ga.: Bridging the Gap Communications, 1993.

Lindquist, Scott. *Before He Takes You Out.* Marietta, Ga.: Vigal Publishers, 1989.

Parrot, Andrea. *Coping with Date Rape and Acquaintance Rape.* New York: Rosen, 1988.

Rathus, Spencer A., and S. Boughn. *AIDS—What Every Student Needs to Know.* Ft. Worth, Tex.: Harcourt Brace Jovanovich, 1993.

CHAPTER 21

Alcohol, Other Drugs, and You

N. Peter Johnson
University of South Carolina

Preston E. Johnson

I'm sick of hearing how bad it is to drink. You have to loosen up sometimes. So I have a couple of beers before I go to sleep. The way I see it, I'm old enough to make decisions on my own. So what if I drink a few beers every night? What's the big deal?

Chapter Goals

This chapter pulls no punches. Although you may not agree with some of its statements, we hope you will be open to hearing about the effects of alcohol and drugs as they relate to college success and to your general health and well-being throughout life. It is true enough that college is a time to seek new experiences, but the ultimate decision as to whether an experience is the right one is up to you.

Writing a piece on alcohol and other drugs for students entering college is hardly an easy task. It's very tempting to come down hard on anyone who uses any form of drugs. For example, I could share with you my beliefs that alcohol is the most dangerous drug, that there is no such thing as "recreational use of drugs," and that even the caffeine in coffee can produce effects that will inhibit your chances for success in college and beyond.

If that's all I wrote, however, no matter how strongly I might believe it, you probably would think, "There's another guy preaching to me like he's my parent." I could hardly blame you. I gave considerable thought to this issue when my own son, Preston, began his college career at Emory University. I decided to write to Preston about my feelings on this subject. As an alcohol and drug educator, I felt professionally obligated to let him know all I knew about alcohol and other drugs, yet the parent in me warned me not to overdo it.

After much thought, and reams of drafts that ended up in the trash, I finally began to make sense to myself as well as to my son. I began by telling him that, in spite of what we read in the newspapers, college students use drugs far less frequently than young people who do not attend college. Over the past ten years, the number of college students using drugs other than alcohol has actually fallen. The only people you hear saying things like "Duh, like wow man, this is really heavy" either are truly dumb or are smoking marijuana, a topic we shall get to in due time.

However, heavy drinking has been increasing on campus even as it declines among young people not in college. So college students use fewer drugs, but drink more alcohol. Male college students use more drugs and alcohol than female college students, with one exception: More college women than men are smokers.

EXERCISE 21.1 Alcohol and Drug Use on Your Campus

In a small group, review the following list of questions, and add three or four of your own.

1. What percentage of students on this campus do you think are problem drinkers?

2. What percentage of students do you think use illegal drugs?

3. What drugs, excluding alcohol, are most popular on your campus?

4. What are the rules pertaining to alcohol and other drugs on your campus?

5. How many students have discipline problems due to alcohol and drug use?

6. What are the consequences of these discipline problems?

7. Why do students use alcohol and other drugs?

8. _____

9. _____

10. _____

11. _____

Now, using these questions, interview people from at least three of the following seven categories and note their answers. Each group member should report at least one interview.

First-year student   Dean of students or person in that office
Upper-class student   Health center staff person
Alcohol/drug educator   Discipline officer
Counseling center staff person

Discuss your findings. How are their answers similar? What would account for any differences in their answers? What did you learn that surprised you about alcohol and drug use on your campus?

I went on to tell Preston about several basic principles that have been important in my life. First, I believe in a "no use" drug policy because of the effects of drugs on the thought process, on academic performance, and on life in general. Second, I recommend a "no use" alcohol policy because not only does alcohol affect mental and physical performance for several days, it blocks long-term memory. I believe in this principle even though I know that approximately 80 percent of college students drink alcoholic beverages at some time.

I refuse to minimize the consequences of using drugs and alcohol, and I detest the term *responsible drinking*. I don't support the term *recreational drug use* either, because there is no such thing. The word *recreation* derives from the Latin *recreatio,* meaning "to restore to health." Its use here implies that health is somehow related to drug use, when the exact opposite is true.

So, now that I've stated my opinions, let me pass on some further information about specific drugs to help you decide where you stand.

■ALCOHOL

Alcohol consumption is the number-one cause of problems for college students. In fact, drinking alcohol has become such an expected part of life on many campuses that some consider it to be "normal." Most of us forget or ignore its consequences until forcefully reminded by friends who suffer discipline problems, broken bones, head injuries, automobile accidents, sexual assaults

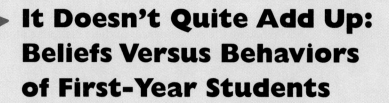

It Doesn't Quite Add Up: Beliefs Versus Behaviors of First-Year Students

In a recent survey of 500 first-year university students, only 1 percent felt they had a problem with alcohol, and only 0.2 percent felt they had a problem with other drugs.

But their answers to other questions suggested a striking lack of awareness of what constitutes a problem with alcohol and other drugs.

The survey asked about alcohol and other drug use, along with related problems that had occurred in the *previous six-month period*. The graphs show the results.

Thirteen percent of the students admitted to seven or more of the risk factor behaviors. Another 27 percent indicated four to six risk factors. Only 23 percent had no risk factors.

How would you explain the discrepancy between the students' beliefs and their behaviors?

Beliefs

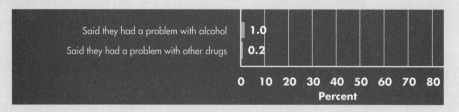

Behaviors

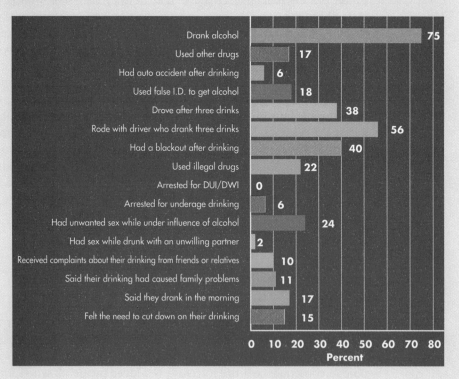

including acquaintance rape, academic failure, near deaths, and death itself. Then in six months we ignore or forget again until still another tragedy strikes.

Many people can paraphrase the 1985 report (widely publicized by the alcohol industry) indicating that moderate drinking had positive health consequences. Fewer people know about other research since then showing that even moderate drinking can negatively affect the heart (enlarging and weakening the ventricles) and skeletal muscles.

Let's talk about alcoholism. Alcoholism is a disease in which a person consistently and continually causes harm to him- or herself or others as a result of drinking. Alcoholics are people who cannot resist drinking frequently or who cannot limit themselves when they do drink. In general terms, the alcoholic drinks four or more days per week or has five or more drinks in a row. Six percent of adults in the United States are alcoholics—10 percent of all drinkers in this country.

You or a friend might say, "That definition doesn't apply to me. Everybody I know drinks that way." My answer is, "Birds of a feather flock together." Drinkers tend to hang out with drinkers, while nondrinkers tend to prefer the company of others like themselves.

But what if you drink? Even then, a little knowledge may lessen the damage you can inflict. For example, you should know that the alcohol in beer, wine coolers, wine, and distilled liquors is all the same alcohol. You can become intoxicated, or alcoholic, just as easily from drinking *any* alcoholic beverage.

You should also know that there are ways to reduce the quantity of alcohol you consume per hour. If you tend to gulp drinks, try alternating noncarbonated, nonalcoholic drinks with mixed drinks to keep the alcohol quantity down. Stay away from college drinking games, such as "quarters," "thumper," and "Indian," in which participants must consume large quantities of alcohol in short periods of time. Heavy drinkers frequently begin these games so that their drinking will appear normal. The games require that others become involved; try to be the student who is not enticed. And never drink on an empty stomach; the stomach rapidly absorbs alcohol, especially from carbonated beverages, when empty.

EXERCISE 21.2 Responses to Peer Pressure

Sometimes it's difficult to be the only one in the group not drinking. You may not receive *direct* pressure from others, but more often there is a subtle message that you should drink to "be like everyone else." Write potential responses to these remarks, made in situations in which you choose not to drink.

1. C'mon, you're not gonna be any fun if you don't loosen up and down a

   couple! _____

   _____

2. Are you going to drink that? It's getting (cold/warm). _____

   _____

3. Hey—alcohol is *healthy* for you! _____

   _____

4. Man, you don't want to be sober all by yourself, do you? _____

   _____

Beer, Wine, or Liquor—Alcohol Is Alcohol

If you drink, know how much alcohol you are consuming. The absolute alcohol content varies according to the type of alcoholic beverage.

• Can of beer (2.3 percent alcohol)	12 oz	× .023	=	.28 oz absolute alcohol
• Can of beer (5 percent alcohol)*	12 oz	× .05	=	.60 oz absolute alcohol
• Wine cooler (5 percent alcohol)	6 oz	× .05	=	.30 oz absolute alcohol
• Glass of wine (12 percent alcohol)	5 oz	× .12	=	.60 oz absolute alcohol
• Glass of wine (15 percent alcohol)	5 oz	× .15	=	.75 oz absolute alcohol
• MD 20/20 (20 percent alcohol)	6 oz	× .20	=	1.20 oz absolute alcohol
• Liquor (80 proof/40 percent alcohol)	1 oz	× .40	=	.40 oz absolute alcohol
• Liquor (100 proof/50 percent alcohol)	1 oz	× .50	=	.50 oz absolute alcohol
• 151 rum (75.5 percent alcohol)	1 oz	× .75	=	.75 oz absolute alcohol

*Alcohol content in some "light" beers is greater than in nonlight beers.

5. No, don't give _____ any—(he's/she's) not
    (your name)

  drinking tonight! _____

_____

You should also know that the passage of time is the only thing that will sober you up after drinking. The enzymes in your liver process alcohol at a rate of about half a regular drink per hour. Cold showers, coffee, and exercise will not help at all. The joke is that coffee only makes for a more wide-awake drunk, but it really isn't funny.

Just as important is that rate of intoxication depends on age, body weight, gender, and tolerance levels. For example, women and older persons produce higher blood alcohol levels for the same amount of alcohol consumption, even if body weights are the same as those of younger men. Also, because of differences in body fat distribution, a stomach enzyme, and hormones, a woman weighing the same as a man may need only drink 45 percent of what the man drinks to reach the same level of intoxication.

If you play sports, be aware that moderate drinking results in loss of muscle coordination for at least 12–18 hours after consumption. The decreased muscle tone and other effects last for days, long after the alcohol is undetectable in the bloodstream. And since processing alcohol disrupts the liver from its normal process of making fuel for the body, muscles tend to tire faster. For 48 hours or longer, you can also expect impaired reaction time, balance, and hand–eye coordination; distorted perception; reduced ability to make smooth, easy movements; decreased strength; increased fatigue; and a host of other problems. Alcohol impairs memory, too; isn't college tough enough as it is?

Drinking and driving is a special problem for college students. Were you aware that the highest automobile accident rates are for persons ages 18–24? This age group also ranks highest in binge drinking and per capita alcohol consumption. Almost 250,000 college students are arrested for driving under the influence (DUI) each year, and 75 percent of first-time DUI offenders will later be diagnosed as alcoholic. The likelihood of alcoholism for second-time DUI offenders is 90 percent. Driving a motor vehicle under the influence of alcohol also costs in many ways: jail time, legal fees (at least $500), and increased insurance costs (up to $1,000). The estimated lifetime cost in 1991 for DUI offenses was $10,000, even if no repeat occurrences take place.

Alcoholism should be a special concern for you if alcohol problems have occurred in your immediate family. If a parent, sibling, aunt, uncle, or grandparent has a problem, your likelihood increases. At the end of the chapter is a test that may help you determine whether you have a family problem with alcoholism. People who score above 3 on the test should be particularly careful about drinking or avoid it entirely.

■MARIJUANA

I read recently that a custodian at a college campus was busted for possession of marijuana. Seems marijuana is everywhere and everyone is using it, doesn't it? Actually that's not so. Less than 20 percent of college students use marijuana, but about 5 percent of all college students develop pretty serious habits. That's disturbing, because marijuana is a strange drug. When I was in college, the authorities warned us about "killer weed," and since most of us knew it wasn't deadly—at least in the short term—we disregarded everything anyone told us. Actually, marijuana has some pretty negative attributes. The ingredient most responsible for the "high" is delta-9-tetrahydrocannabinol, or THC, which is absorbed through the lungs and into the bloodstream immediately. If you detest tobacco smoking for what it does to the body, you should know that smoking marijuana has the same effect on the lungs. In fact, it is even more cancer-causing than tobacco, though people generally smoke less of it. In addition, strains of marijuana available today contain higher levels of THC than ever before. For example, sinsemilla reportedly is as much as 15 times stronger than the marijuana of the 1960s and 1970s.

Once in the bloodstream, THC is absorbed by, stored in, and gradually released by fat cells. A single puff of marijuana has a half-life in the body of between three and seven days, depending on the potency and the smoker. After a period of chronic, heavy use, it can take as long as a month for THC to clear your system. One acquaintance of mine lost a job because marijuana showed up on a drug test even though he was not a user. Rather, for the previous year he had been regularly exposed to the secondhand smoke of a roommate and

It Isn't Over Till It's Over

How long do the behavioral effects of marijuana last?

A group of scientists wanted to determine how long after smoking marijuana a person's judgment and performance might still be impaired. To do this, they trained ten experienced, licensed private pilots for 8 hours to perform a simple takeoff and landing procedure on a flight simulator. After this training, each pilot smoked a cigarette containing THC, the principal active ingredient in marijuana. Each cigarette contained 19 milligrams of the drug, roughly the same amount a person is likely to smoke in a social setting. After smoking this drug, the pilots tried the landing task again.

The pilots' mean performance on the landing task showed impairment on all variables, including significant impairment in vertical and lateral deviation on approach to landing and distance off center from the runway.*

The pilots reported no awareness of impaired performance.

How long after they had smoked the drug would you guess that the pilots were tested?

a. 3 hours   c. 12 hours
b. 6 hours   d. 24 hours

(The answer may be found in the footnote on page 363.)

*Jerome A. Yasavage et al., "Carry-Over Effects of Marijuana Intoxification on Aircraft Pilot Performance: A Preliminary Report," *American Journal of Psychiatry* 142, no. 11: 1325–29.

family members. He had stored up so much THC in his fat cells that it was as if he were smoking marijuana himself.

Recently, a student with a very high grade point average asked me to help him stop smoking marijuana. He was about to graduate and was afraid he might be tested for drugs during his preemployment physical. He wanted to stop at least long enough to clear his system. He said he wasn't sure he could stop smoking that long, since it had been several years since he had gone without marijuana. We worked together, and after a month of abstinence, he commented that he could now think and remember much more clearly. The decrease in his thinking abilities had occurred so gradually that he was unaware of it. This can be a major problem for students who need to memorize quantities of information. Recent research shows that the measurable pharmacologic effects of marijuana can last for one full day, and the behavioral effects may last much longer.

COCAINE

Cocaine is a powerful chemical extracted from the leaves of the coca plant. People in the Andes Mountains use coca mixed with a little lime to avoid hunger pangs and to make work at high altitudes go easier. In concentrated

Effects of Marijuana

If you think marijuana isn't really that bad for you, perhaps you should consider the following list of potential adverse effects from chronic use.

- Chronically slowed reaction times
- Decreased tracking capability by the eyes
- Impaired hand–eye coordination
- Altered perception of time (for example, "slow motion" sensations)
- Impairment of depth perception
- Impairment of recent memory
- Increased suggestibility, suspiciousness, and fearfulness

- Apathy, loss of drive, unwillingness or inability to complete tasks, low frustration tolerance, unrealistic thinking, increased shyness, total involvement in the present at the expense of future goals
- Increased number of lung infections
- Increased likelihood of cancer (marijuana contains *ten times* more cancer-causing agents than found in cigarettes)
- Breast enlargement in males

form, cocaine is a powerful stimulant; it overstimulates the pleasure centers of the brain. The user literally loses touch with even basic biological needs during a cocaine "high." Laboratory animals have been observed to self-administer cocaine until they die of thirst or starvation, ignoring their needs for food, water, and sex. Cocaine is one of the most addictive drugs known.

The street drug cocaine hydrochloride (what most people call cocaine) is sniffed into the nose. "Crack" is smokable cocaine from which the hydrochloride has been removed. Once the drug is in the bloodstream, both forms produce the same symptoms although the way the drug is delivered (smoked or snorted) causes differences in the immediate severity. Snorting cocaine causes runny noses, and in the long term it can "burn" a hole through the septum of the nose. Smoking crack causes respiratory problems and has destructive effects on the lungs and breathing tubes. Incidentally, these same problems occur with methamphetamine, or "ice," its smokable form.

Cocaine produces an intense experience by enhancing certain chemical processes in the brain. For the cocaine user, thoughts seem to come more quickly, each of the five senses seems heightened, physical energy seems unlimited, attitude becomes one of unwavering self-assurance, and fatigue and hunger disappear. It is easy to see why some students are attracted to this potent drug.

However, what goes up must come down—and in this case, rather quickly. A cocaine high starts in a few minutes, peaks in 15–20 minutes, and goes away in less than an hour. A crack high peaks within seconds and lasts about

ANSWER (to question in box on page 362): d. The pilots were tested one full day after smoking. At this time they were still clearly impaired in their ability to perform the flight simulation. Yet they were unaware of their impairment or of any continuing effect of the THC on performance, mood, or alertness.

Effects of Cocaine

Cocaine use can lead to a staggering number of physical, mental, and emotional problems, both short- and long-term. Consider the following:

ADVERSE EFFECTS FROM THE COCAINE "HIGH"

- Accelerated but unfocused thinking, disrupted concentration
- Misjudgment of timing and accuracy
- Misjudgment of physical and mental power
- Jumpiness
- Covered-up pain, increasing the possibility of injury
- Increased aggressiveness and sense of hostility toward others
- Extreme rises in body temperature (heat prostration)
- Heavy sweating, dehydration, and muscle cramping
- Rapid heart rate
- Heart irregularities and heart attack
- Stroke and seizures due to increased blood pressure
- Increased rate and depth of breathing (hyperventilation)
- Visual hallucinations ("coke lights")
- Restlessness and insomnia
- Shakes
- Convulsions
- Mental problems similar to schizophrenia (including hallucinations)
- Loss of appetite
- Cross-problems with alcohol including heavy drinking

ADVERSE EFFECTS FROM THE POSTCOCAINE "CRASH"

- Auto and other accidents from too much alcohol consumption while using cocaine
- Extreme hunger
- Decrease in energy
- Loss of motivation
- Inability to concentrate on specific tasks
- Depression ("coke blues")
- Suicidal thoughts and attempts

ADVERSE EFFECTS FROM CHRONIC COCAINE USE

- Restlessness and inability to consistently study
- Continued insomnia and loss of sleep, leading to an increased use of cocaine and/or alcohol for sleep and other reasons
- Isolation from other people
- Irritability and fear
- Profound depression
- Seizures and convulsions
- Suicidal thoughts and actions
- Feeling that something is crawling under the skin ("coke bugs")
- Extreme hunger and self-induced vomiting in response to overeating

CAUSES OF DEATH RELATED TO STIMULANTS INCLUDING COCAINE

- Convulsions (seizures)
- Coma (loss of consciousness)
- Heart attack
- Stroke

a minute. It is this speed of delivery that causes rapid addiction for many people. During the crash, the user may feel tired and unmotivated. Mood may swing rapidly to depression and agitation, and the user may feel paranoid and restless and be unable to sleep.

■TOBACCO

Although tobacco is the number-one killer drug, very few college students smoke. Because more women than men now smoke, the rate of cancer in women has surpassed that in men. The easiest time to break an addiction is before it starts. After that it takes courage and willpower, but in the long run, it's worth it.

■BE INFORMED

The best defense against alcohol and drug abuse is information, and there's plenty of it available. You can start by contacting the alcohol and drug program on your campus. Hospitals are another excellent source of information. You can also call the National Clearinghouse on Alcohol and Drug Information at 1-800-729-6686. For cocaine information call 1-800-COCAINE.

College is a valuable time in the lives of each of us fortunate enough to reap its rewards. The more you remember the value of education, the less likely you are to take risks that could devalue that experience. This is why I hope you will think long and hard about what I have said in these few pages. I've tried not to preach to you, and I hope I have succeeded in presenting the facts as objectively as possible. As an alcohol and drug educator, I obviously have strong feelings about alcohol and drug use. As a human being, so may you. All I ask is that you consider what I have written, discuss it with people you admire, and make a decision for yourself based on *your own* values, not on the prevailing attitudes of others.

EXERCISE 21.3

Campus Resources

Visit the places on your campus where resources and assistance related to alcohol and other drugs are available. You may find help in these places:

Health center	Counseling center
Student activities office	Drug/alcohol education office
Residence life office	Discipline office
Minister or chaplain's office	

Note below the offices you visited, their phone numbers and hours, and the types of resources they offer to students.

Office: _____

Phone: _____ Hours: _____

Resources: _____

Office: _____

Phone: _____ Hours: _____

Resources: _____

Office: _____

Phone: _____ Hours: _____

Resources: _____

EXERCISE 21.4   Michigan Alcoholism Screening Test (MAST)

For each of the following items, answer Y for yes or N for no.

_____ 1. Do you feel you are a normal drinker? ("Normal" means you drink less than or as much as most other people and you have not developed recurring trouble while drinking.)

_____ 2. Have you ever awakened the morning after some drinking the night before and found that you could not remember part of the evening?

_____ 3. Do either you, your parents, any other close relatives, your spouse, or any girlfriend or boyfriend ever worry or complain about your drinking?

_____ 4. Can you stop drinking without a struggle after one or two drinks?

_____ 5. Do you feel guilty about your drinking?

_____ 6. Do friends or relatives think you are a normal drinker?

_____ 7. Are you able to stop drinking when you want to?

_____ 8. Have you ever attended a meeting of Alcoholics Anonymous (AA)?

_____ 9. Have you been in physical fights when you have been drinking?

_____ 10. Has your drinking ever created problems between you and either your parents, another relative, your spouse, or any girlfriend or boyfriend?

_____ 11. Has any family member of yours ever gone to anyone for help about your drinking?

_____ 12. Have you ever lost friends because of your drinking?

_____ 13. Have you ever been in trouble at work or at school because of drinking?

_____ 14. Have you ever lost a job because of drinking?

_____ 15. Have you ever neglected your obligations, your schoolwork, your family, or your job for two or more days in a row because you were drinking?

_____ 16. Do you drink before noon fairly often?

_____ 17. Have you ever been told you have liver trouble or cirrhosis?

_____ 18. After heavy drinking, have you ever had severe shaking or heard voices or seen things that really weren't there?

_____ 19. Have you ever gone to anyone for help about your drinking?

_____ 20. Have you ever been in a hospital because of drinking?

_____ 21. Have you ever been a patient in a psychiatric hospital or in a psychiatric ward of a general hospital where drinking was part of the problem that resulted in hospitalization?

_____ 22. Have you ever gone to a psychiatric or mental health clinic or to any doctor, social worker, or clergy for help with any emotional problem where drinking was a part of the problem?

_____ 23. Have you ever been arrested for drunk driving, driving while intoxicated, or driving under the influence of alcoholic beverages or any other drug? (If yes, how many times? _____)

_____ 24. Have you ever been arrested or taken into custody, even for a few hours, because of other drunk behavior, whether due to alcohol or another drug? (If yes, how many times? _____)

Now compute your total score based on the point values listed here for each Y or N answer.

1. N2	5. Y1	9. Y1	13. Y2	17. Y2	21. Y2
2. Y2	6. N2	10. Y2	14. Y2	18. Y2	22. Y2
3. Y1	7. N2	11. Y2	15. Y2	19. Y5	23. Y2*
4. N2	8. Y5	12. Y2	16. Y1	20. Y5	24. Y2*

*Score 2 points for each time.

Compare your total score with the numbers listed below.

0–3 points = probable normal drinker

4 points = borderline score

5–9 points = 80 percent associated with alcoholism

10 or more = 100 percent associated with alcoholism

Regardless of your score, if you have some concerns about your drinking, assistance is available. Make an appointment to talk with someone on your campus who can help. This may be a counselor, alcohol/drug educator, campus physician, minister, or someone else with whom you feel comfortable. Take advantage of the assistance they can provide.

EXERCISE 21.5 Children of Alcoholics Screening Test

Place a Y for yes next to each question that you answer affirmatively.

_____ 1. Have you ever thought that one of your parents had a drinking problem?

_____ 2. Have you ever lost sleep because of a parent's drinking?

_____ 3. Did you ever encourage one of your parents to quit drinking?

_____ 4. Did you ever feel alone, scared, nervous, angry, or frustrated because a parent was not able to stop drinking?

_____ 5. Did you ever argue or fight with a parent when he or she was drinking?

_____ 6. Did you ever threaten to or actually run away from home because of a parent's drinking?

_____ 7. Has a parent ever yelled at or hit you or other family members when drinking?

_____ 8. Have you ever heard your parents fight when one of them was drunk?

_____ 9. Did you ever protect another family member from a parent who was drinking?

_____ 10. Did you ever feel like hiding or emptying a parent's bottle of liquor?

_____ 11. Do any of your thoughts revolve around a problem-drinking parent or do difficulties arise because of his or her drinking?

_____ 12. Did you ever wish that a parent would stop drinking?

_____ 13. Did you ever feel responsible for and guilty about a parent's drinking?

_____ 14. Did you ever fear that your parents would get divorced due to alcohol abuse?

_____ 15. Have you ever withdrawn from and avoided outside activities and friends because of embarrassment and shame over a parent's drinking problem?

_____ 16. Did you ever feel caught in the middle of an argument or fight between a problem-drinking parent and your other parent?

_____ 17. Did you ever feel that you made a parent drink alcohol?

_____ 18. Have you ever felt that a problem-drinking parent did not really love you?

_____ 19. Did you ever resent a parent's drinking?

_____ 20. Have you ever worried about a parent's health because of his or her alcohol use?

_____ 21. Have you ever been blamed for a parent's drinking?

_____ 22. Did you ever think your father was an alcoholic?

_____ 23. Did you ever think your mother was an alcoholic?

_____ 24. Did you ever wish your home could be more like the homes of your friends who did not have a parent with a drinking problem?

_____ 25. Did a parent ever make promises to you that he or she did not keep because of drinking?

_____ 26. Did you ever wish that you could talk to someone who could understand and help with the alcohol-related problems in your family?

_____ 27. Did you ever fight with your brothers and sisters about a parent's drinking?

_____ 28. Did you ever stay away from home to avoid the drinking parent or your other parent's reaction to the drinking?

_____ 29. Have you ever felt sick, cried, or had a "knot" in your stomach after worrying about a parent's drinking?

_____ 30. Did you ever take over any chores or duties at home that were usually done by a parent before he or she developed a drinking problem?

Now compute your score by as signing 1 point for each Y answer, and compare the total with the numbers listed below. (*Note:* This test is *not* nationally standardized.)

0–3 points = probably normal family

4–9 points = indication that a family member *does* have a drinking problem

10 or more points = severe dysfunction

Again, if you are concerned about family alcohol use and/or the effect it has had on you, visit with someone on your campus who is qualified to help.

JOURNAL

You probably found the author of this chapter very straightforward in saying what he believes. Be equally direct in discussing your views on alcohol and other drugs. In what respects do you agree? In what ways do you disagree? Try writing in response to specific new information you may have gathered from the reading. For instance, what do you make of the study of marijuana use by airplane pilots?

SUGGESTIONS FOR FURTHER READING

Cohen, S. "The Effects of Combined Alcohol/Drug Abuse on Human Behavior." Chapter 1 in *Treatment Research Monograph Series: Drug and Alcohol Abuse—Implications for Treatment.* Washington, D.C.: Department of Health and Human Services, Alcohol, Drug Abuse, and Mental Health Administration, 1981.

Gilbert, R. M. "Caffeine as a Drug of Abuse." In R. J. Gibbins et al., *Research Advances in Alcohol and Drug Problems,* Vol. 3. New York: Wiley, 1976.

Gold, M. S. *800-COCAINE.* New York: Bantam Books, 1984.

———. *Facts About Drugs and Alcohol.* New York: Bantam Books, 1986.

Griffin, T. M. *Paying the Price.* Center City, Minn.: Hazelden Foundation Press, 1985.

Johnson, Peter, ed. *Dictionary of Street Alcohol and Drug Terms,* 4th ed. Upland, Pa.: Diane, 1993.

Johnston, L. D., P. M. O'Malley, and J. G. Bachman. *National Trends in Drug Use and Related Factors Among American High School Students and Young Adults, 1975–86.* Publication No. 87-1535. Washington, D.C.: Department of Health and Human Services, 1987.

Kaufman, D. W., L. Rosenberg, S. P. Helmrich, and S. Shapiro. "Alcoholic Beverages and Myocardial Infarction in Young Men." *American Journal of Epidemiology* 121 (1985): 548–54.

Kinney, J., and G. Leaton, eds. *Understanding Alcohol: A Handbook of Alcohol Information,* 3rd ed. St. Louis: Mosby, 1987.

Schwartz, R. H. "Marijuana: An Overview." *Pediatric Clinics of North America,* 34, no. 2: 305–17.

Strauss, R. H., ed. *Drugs and Performance in Sports.* Philadelphia: Saunders, 1987.

Whitfield, C. L., J. E. Davis, and L. R. Barker. "Alcoholism." Chapter 21 in *Principles of Ambulatory Medicine,* 2nd ed. L. R. Barker, J. R. Burton, and P. D. Zieve, eds. Baltimore: Williams and Wilkins, 1987.

Managing Money

Ray Edwards
Gunnison Country Partners, Inc.

Money's no problem for me. Either I have it or I don't. If I have it, I spend it. Once it's gone, I stop. By the way, can you lend me fifty bucks until I get paid next week?

Chapter Goals

Being in control of your finances will make other aspects of your life in college easier to cope with. This chapter guides you in conducting an analysis of your financial resources versus expenses and setting financial priorities. You will also learn about different types of financial aid or scholarships available on your campus and how to apply for them.

If you are putting yourself through school, you probably have more expenses and less income than you had in the past. If your parents are helping you pay for college, you are probably responsible for making and spending more money now than you ever were before.

This chapter will help you take control of your money so that you can worry less about it and focus more on your education. The first part is about managing what you have. The second part is about making up the difference if your budget doesn't balance.

■ SOME BASIC MISCONCEPTIONS

There are several common misconceptions about the management of money.

- **Misconception 1:** Financial management is a magical process known only by a few wizards. (The truth is, there's nothing mysterious about it. Financial management is a skill that you can learn.)

- **Misconception 2:** In order to *manage* money, you need a lot more of it. Otherwise what is there to manage? (Actually it is probably more important to manage your money well when you don't have much than it is when you have money to burn.)

- **Misconception 3:** If you have enough money, you don't need to worry about how you spend it. (If you are handling most of your own finances for the first time now—paying for your room and board, buying expensive books, and so on—you may feel that you have more money than you need. Nevertheless, you need to keep track of where that money is going.)

- **Misconception 4:** You can keep track of your personal finances just by balancing your checkbook. (Balancing your checkbook is certainly important, but it has little value in relation to planning for your financial needs.)

Fortunately, money management represents nothing more than the application of common sense, planning, and self-discipline—applying some simple techniques in an organized, logical way.

THE MONEY-MANAGING PROCESS

Money management boils down to three primary activities: analysis, planning, and budgeting.

Analysis

Analyze your finances by identifying and comparing your expenses with your resources. Unless you know what your costs are and how much you have available, you are not going to be in control of anything. Think in terms of your academic year (August or September through May or June).

EXPENSES

Start by making a list of all the expenses you can think of, under two main categories of costs: educational and noneducational. *Educational expenses* are those you incur because you are a student, including tuition, fees, books, supplies, lab equipment, and so on. *Noneducational expenses* include all your other costs: housing, food, transportation, and miscellaneous and personal needs.

Be especially careful as you identify noneducational expenses because these costs are often hard to estimate. For example, it is easy to determine how much your tuition and fees are going to be (you need only consult your institution's published schedule of costs), but it is not so easy to estimate utility bills or food and transportation costs. Be as methodical as you can. If you are careless, you may end up being "nickeled and dimed to debt."

Table 22.1 shows most of the types of costs you will face. If you have other expenses, add them to the list.

EXERCISE 22.1 Listing Your Expenses

Note: If you're doing the exercises in this chapter on paper, be sure to use a pencil so that you can revise your numbers as you go. Better yet, use a computer word processing or spreadsheet program. Creating your own budget is a great way to learn how to use a simple computer spreadsheet.

1. Spend a few minutes writing down all the types of expenses you can think of that will apply to you during this term or academic year. Then compare your list with the list in Table 22.1.
2. Using Table 22.1 as a rough model, list your expenses. Find the total.

If you have trouble deciding how much to put down for a category such as clothing or personal items, try listing specific items you will need and estimate a cost for each. Use the estimates to help decide on a dollar total for the category.

RESOURCES

Next, identify your resources. Again, list your sources of financial support by category (savings, employment, financial aid, parents, spouse, and so on). Be realistic—neither overly optimistic nor too pessimistic—about your resources. Table 22.2 lists some common types of monetary support. List any additional sources.

Table 22.1 Typical Expenses (academic year)

Educational Expenses

Tuition	$ 800
Fees	1,200
Books	325
Supplies	75
Subtotal educational expenses	$2,400

Noneducational Expenses

Housing	$1,250
Food	1,500
Personal	100
Phone	120
Transportation	750
Clothing	450
Social/entertainment	360
Savings	250
Subtotal noneducational expenses	$4,780
Total educational and noneducational expenses	$7,180

Table 22.2 Typical Resources (academic year)

A. Parents/Spouse	
Cash	$1,000
Credit union loan	1,500
B. Work	
Summer (savings after expenses)	1,000
Part-time during year	1,500
C. Savings	
Parents	0
Your own	150
D. Financial Aid	
Grants	400
Loans	700
Scholarships	0
E. Benefits	
Veterans	0
Other	0
F. Other	
ROTC	900
Relatives	0
Trusts	0
Total	$7,150

EXERCISE 22.2 Listing Your Resources

1. Spend a few minutes writing down all the types of resources you have that will apply to you during this academic year. Then compare your list with the list in Table 22.2.

2. Using Table 22.2 as a model, list your resources. Find the total.

COMPARING EXPENSES TO RESOURCES

Once you have identified your expenses and resources, compare the totals. Remember that this is a tentative tally, not a final evaluation. This is especially important to note if your costs exceed your resources.

EXERCISE 22.3 Comparing Resources with Expenses

1. Subtract your total expenses from your total resources (or resources from expenses). Do you have more money than you need (a positive balance)? Or do you have less (a negative balance)? Is the difference large enough to worry about?

2. If you have more money than you need, check your expenses to be sure that you are not seriously underestimating anything. Change any numbers that should be changed and compare totals again. If you still have more money than you need, increase the amount you plan to save so that your expense total equals your resources.

To bring your finances in focus, you must now complete the third step of your analysis: setting priorities and revising. To do this, classify your expenses as fixed or flexible. *Fixed expenses* are those over which you have no control; *flexible expenses* are those you can modify (flexible does not usually mean completely avoidable). Tuition, fees, and residence hall costs are generally fixed, since the institution requires you to pay specific amounts. Food may be fixed or flexible, depending on whether you are paying for a residential board plan or cooking on your own.

Table 22.3 shows some typical new-student costs divided into fixed and flexible expenses. The flexible expenses are listed in order of importance.

If the total of your expenses exceeds the total of your costs, you can start revising your flexible costs, such as telephone, clothing, and entertainment. Although cutting wardrobe and entertainment costs may be less than enjoyable, good money management means maintaining control and being realistic.

EXERCISE 22.4 Setting Priorities

Note: Do this exercise if Exercise 22.3 showed that your expenses are significantly higher than your resources.

1. Using Table 22.3 as a model, create a list that separates your costs into fixed versus flexible expenses. Then focus on the flexible costs and see which of them can be reduced. Change your figures to improve the balance of costs and resources. However, be realistic. Don't lower expenses that cannot realistically be lowered.

2. If your expenses are still greater than your resources, continue reading the chapter to see how you might add more to the resource side. Then come back and rework your figures to achieve a balance.

Planning

Having analyzed your costs and resources, you now have a good overall perspective on your financial situation. Next you need to plan how you will manage your money. Focus on timing, identifying *when* you will have to pay for various things and also when your resources will provide income.

For planning, you will need an academic schedule for your school (which probably appears in your college catalog or bulletin) and a calendar, preferably organized on an academic schedule such as August through July. First, review your institution's academic schedule for its overall time frame and specific dates. Determine your school's registration and payment schedules. When is the latest you can pay your housing deposit for living on campus? What is the deadline for tuition and fees? What is the school's refund policy and schedule? Enter these critical dates on your own planning calendar for the entire academic year. Find out if your school accepts credit cards for tuition payments.

Then turn your attention to other important dates that are not institutionally related. For example, if you pay auto insurance semi-annually, when is your next big premium due?

After you have recorded the important dates of your major expenditures, do the same thing for your revenue. This knowledge is essential for planning, since you can't very well plan *how* you're going to pay for things if you don't know *when* you'll have the money. For example, financial aid is typically disbursed in one lump sum at the beginning of each academic term, whereas paychecks come in smaller, more frequent installments.

Do you have any timing problems? Are there going to be points at which your costs exceed your cash? If there are, you must adjust either when you must pay or when your income will arrive. If you will be a bit strapped paying all of your tuition and fees at the start of the term, see if your school has an installment plan that will let you stretch out the payments or if you can reschedule semi-annual payments (such as car insurance premiums) as monthly payments. Many schools also allow payment by credit card, but be careful about "overloading" your cards. This is a major reason students drop out of college.

EXERCISE 22.5 — Timing Income and Expenses

Get the academic schedule for your school and any monthly calendar that is convenient.

1. On the academic schedule, find the dates when your school's registration fees, charges for room and board, and other charges are due. Record these amounts on the calendar.

   Look over your expenses to see whether there are any other dates when large payments may be due for things such as automobile insurance, license fees, and required course materials. Record these amounts also on the calendar.

2. Now look at your list of resources and record the dates and amounts on your calendar when portions of your resources will be available.

3. Are there any points in the term when your resources won't cover your expenses? After reading the rest of this chapter, use the goal-setting process in Chapter 1 to solve the problem.

Once you have determined the critical dates of income and expenses, planning becomes very simple. But keep in mind that most significant of all planning destroyers, the dreaded Murphy's law: If something can go wrong, it will—and at the worst moment. For example, you might leave the cap off your car's radiator and accidentally crack the engine block. Or a roommate might suddenly split for Bali, leaving you to pay extra rent.

How can you prepare for and minimize the damage caused by unscheduled calamities? Frankly, you can't do everything, but you can prepare to some extent by being emotionally ready to deal with such things when they happen, by building up an emergency fund (even a small one), and by not departing from your money management plan. These principles not only are important for you now, but also are good habits to follow throughout your life.

Having completed the process of planning your expenditures, you should feel much more in control of your finances. Being totally aware of where you are will alleviate much potential stress.

Budgeting

The last step in developing a sound money management plan is budgeting. Budgeting takes self-discipline. Develop both a monthly budget and an academic year budget.

Table 22.3 Typical Expense Priorities (academic year)

Fixed Expenses

Tuition	$ 800
Fees	1,200
Books	325
Supplies	75
Housing	1,250
Subtotal fixed expenses	$3,650

Flexible Expenses

Food	$1,500
Transportation	700
Clothing	450
Personal	100
Phone	120
Social/entertainment	360
Savings	250
Subtotal flexible expenses	3,530
Total fixed and flexible expenses	$7,180

Table 22.4 Sample Monthly Budget (September)

Resources

Summer savings	$1,000
Parents/spouse	750
Financial aid	500
ROTC	100
Part-time job	166
Total	$2,516

Fixed Expenses

Tuition and fees	$1,000
Books	175
Dorm room	625
Total	$1,800

Flexible Expenses

Food (meal cash card)	$150
Supplies	35
Personal	35
Phone	15
Transportation	10
Social	40
Total	$285

Summary

Total resources	$2,516
Less total expenses	2,085
Less savings	50
Balance	$ 381*

*Carried forward to October.

The budgeting process overlaps with the financial planning you did when you identified the timing of your "big ticket" items and income. The academic year budget transforms what you have on your academic calendar into a scheme that also includes your smaller, less dramatic, ongoing expenses.

The monthly budget is a specific plan for each month's income and outgo—the final details necessary to make your management system work. It eliminates any confusion about what you must do in the near future, within a manageable block of time. It is also your method for maintaining continual control over your finances. Since it coincides with the cycle of your checking account, it also facilitates monthly balancing and scheduling.

To develop your monthly budget, put your expenses and income together on one sheet, as shown above in Table 22.4. After listing your fixed expenses, your flexible expenses, and your resources, subtract expenses from resources to create a summary for the month. Settle your fixed outlays, and revise the flexible ones as necessary to achieve a reasonable balance. The September budget shown in the chart happens to include the major "start-up" costs for tuition, fees, and so on. Make sure your budget is comprehensive and keeps track of how you spend what you spend.

EXERCISE 22.6 A Monthly Budget

Create a sample monthly budget to plan your income and expenses on a monthly basis.

Note that Table 22.4 includes tuition, books, fees, and other expenses that may be paid in one lump sum at the beginning of the term. This means that your budget for the first month may be very different than for later months. For this reason, you may want to use the second or third month of the term for your sample monthly budget.

Once you have done this for a month or two, you will probably have a good idea of how things are going and will not need to go through such a formal process again, except in months when you foresee unusual expenses.

Financial worries can be stress-inducing, but you can minimize this stress by analyzing, planning, and budgeting well. Good money management supports your total health and well-being.

The way you handle your money in college says a lot about how you approach life in general. When you manage your personal finances well, you are facing up to realities that will confront you for the rest of your life. Developing the required seriousness and skill will continue to pay off long after you have finished college.

▉INCREASING RESOURCES

Once you're doing everything to manage your current finances well, you may still need more money. How you acquire more aid has both immediate and long-term implications. Even if you're fortunate enough to have parents helping you through college, don't leave the problem up to them. Paying for college is a major undertaking that should be shared. Not all students should work while they are in college, but most students find ways to pay at least part of their college expenses, and most work at least part-time.

Over the past twenty years, inflation has eroded the savings of many families. In fact, the United States currently has one of the lowest percentages of per capita savings among industrialized countries. Most American families today are not paying for their children's college education out of savings. Because of this, and because the price of a college education has risen sharply over the same period, most students must now rely mainly on their family's current income and loans to finance college.

Such overreliance on current income and loans has been harmful to parents and their student/dependents in two ways. First, families are forced to make difficult sacrifices. Second, the repayment "legacy" of educational loans usually extends long after the student has finished college.

For their part, colleges and universities have been caught by the same economic forces as families, and college expenses over the past twenty years have risen faster than the overall inflation rate. It simply costs more each year for schools to provide the same level of service. Both public and private

Most college students work at least part-time. Evidence suggests that students who hold part-time jobs generally do better academically than students with more free time.

Photo courtesy of University of Nevada, Las Vegas

colleges have had little choice but to increase fees, and you will likely have to pay more each year you are in college.

The average annual cost of an education (including room and board) at a public four-year university or college in 1996 was around $9,300, with some schools costing close to $17,000. Average annual costs at private colleges were around $20,000, with some schools costing over $27,000.

If you are commuting to a local public institution, the cost (not including any living expenses) may still be as low as a few thousand dollars a year. Of course, even that may be a large sum for you and your family to afford.

If you are going to be able to deal with your college expenses, it is essential that you see them realistically. Only by knowing how much your education is going to cost can you go about planning how to pay for it. If it is clear that you and/or your family cannot handle all of the costs, you should certainly apply for financial aid.

EXERCISE 22.7 **Applying Critical Thinking to the Money Management Process**

Write a critical analysis of your current approach to managing money. You will need to consider your expenses, resources, budgeting, priority-setting, planning, and timing of income and expenses. Try to be as objective as you can. How do you assess the logic and appropriateness of your most important financial decisions? Can you identify any alternative strategies you might consider? Discuss these.

EXERCISE 22.8 **Monitoring the Media**

For a week or so, keep track of advertisements you see on television, hear on radio, or read in newspapers or magazines that not only hype credit cards, but also suggest you need to own certain material things in order to be successful and happy. Subject these to a critical analysis. How do the positive outcomes

The Perils of Plastic

Believe it or not, credit card debt by first-year students has contributed significantly to the dropout rate for this group. You may have already received letters from banks and other businesses offering credit cards or other types of charge cards. Their goal is to lend you money so that you will pay high interest rates in return. They may also charge you annual or monthly fees. In 1994, the interest rates for such student accounts were generally over 15 percent. Rates often go as high as 20 percent, which is much higher than the interest you would pay for many student loans.

At the same time, credit cards and other charge cards are sometimes very convenient. Before you decide to use a credit card or which card to choose, consider this advice:

1. Don't accept or keep cards that you don't really need.

2. Choose the right card. Before you accept a card, be able to answer these questions:

    a. Is there an annual or monthly fee or any other charge apart from interest you may have to pay? What are these fees?

    b. What is the interest rate?

    c. Is there a grace period (the time between making a purchase and paying off the charge, before you will be charged interest)? How long is it?

    d. Does the card allow cash advances? What fees and interest rates apply? (Cash advances are generally the most expensive way to borrow money.)

    e. Are there any fringe benefits to the card that would clearly be valuable to you or your family? Some cards offer a lower rate on phone calls, small cash rebates, or credit miles on "frequent flyer" programs. Usually the benefits are not significant unless you are charging large amounts.

3. If you accept a card, sign it right away. Keep a separate record of the card's number and expiration date and the number to call if it is lost or stolen.

4. Destroy carbons or incorrect slips that have not been processed.

5. Save your charge slips so that you can be certain you have been correctly charged.

6. Never lend your card or tell its number to anyone except when necessary for a transaction. (If someone uses your number to make telephone purchases or to make a fraudulent card, you are not responsible for these charges, but you may go through a lot of trouble trying to show the bank which charges were yours and which were fraudulent.)

7. If the card is lost or stolen, you will probably have to pay no more than $50 of any charges made with the stolen card. Report any loss of the card or other problems immediately by phone.

depicted square with the impact of credit cards on your life? What essential facts, truths, and realities do these ads fail to portray? How would your life be different if credit cards or some other forms of borrowing money did not exist?

Financial Aid

This chapter will not go into detail about applying for financial aid because it is a complex process that varies from school to school and may change from year to year. What we will do is help you get started thinking about how financial aid works and about what questions you might ask at your school's financial aid office.

Financial aid refers to any type of funding you receive to assist yourself in paying for college. Most financial aid money is given on the basis of need, often according to "demonstrated financial need." *Demonstrated financial need* is eligibility determined by some specific financial scale, most commonly the federal needs analysis system called the "congressional methodology." Other types of financial aid awards may not depend on this type of eligibility.

Financial aid is categorized as either gift or self-help assistance. *Gift assistance* is that which does not have to be repaid. *Self-help assistance* requires you to do something in return, such as work or repay the money. An academic scholarship is gift assistance; a student loan is self-help assistance.

The basis upon which financial aid is awarded varies, but typical criteria are academic merit, financial need, or some combination of the two. The large federal aid programs and most state programs are based on financial need and acceptable progress toward a degree.

Financial aid can be further categorized into two types of gift assistance—grants and scholarships—and two types of self-help assistance—loans and work opportunities.

GRANTS

Grants are gift assistance and so do not have to be repaid. Most institutions offer numerous grants programs, the largest funded by the federal and state governments. Generally, grants are aimed at students with the greatest demonstrated financial need. Students can often receive more than one type of grant simultaneously, but institutions do place limits on the total amount of grant assistance they will award to any one individual, since such funds are limited. Most schools want to spread grants out among as many students as possible.

SCHOLARSHIPS

Scholarships are awarded on the basis of superior academic achievement or merit, although financial need may also be a criterion. Most colleges and universities have scholarships for new students as well as for students in the upper years. Thousands of scholarships are also available from hundreds of national foundations, organizations, state and federal agencies, businesses, corporations, churches, and civic clubs.

The best way to find scholarship opportunities is to start with your institution and work your way out. Check the availability of scholarships from groups and organizations in your home region. Review information from the primary education-related agency or organization in your state. Go to the library or financial aid office at your school to ask for assistance and to review publications listing scholarships. Our best advice is, *ask, ask, ask.*

LOANS

Over the past fifteen years, long-term, low-interest educational *loans* have become the major means for financing college. There are a number of public and private student loan programs, most of which allow extended repayment periods (up to ten years, depending on the amount borrowed) and very reasonable rates (5–10 percent). Though the practice is not recommended unless absolutely necessary, it is possible to receive assistance from more than one loan program at a time.

A Caution About Loans

Student loans are an extremely valuable component of the total financial aid picture, but it is important to remember that they are exactly what they are called: loans. They must be repaid. Failure to repay a student loan can have very negative consequences, including damaged credit, garnishment of wages, confiscation of income tax refunds, and litigation. Be very careful in assuming loan indebtedness during college, since a sizable monthly loan repayment can become a heavy burden. Take out student loans only to the extent that they are absolutely necessary for you to stay in school. Keep track of exactly how much you have borrowed as you go. Otherwise, the student loan that seems like such a boon now may be a tremendous bane later.

The large federal student loan programs are based primarily on need. In addition to student loans there is also a federally sponsored loan program for parents that does not require demonstrated need. The interest rate for this program can be as high as 12 percent, and repayment generally begins shortly after the loan is made. This program has become popular among parents whose dependents do not qualify for need-based aid.

WORK OPPORTUNITIES

Part-time work is a valuable type of self-help aid. The College Work–Study Program is a federal student aid program based on need that lets you earn some of the aid for which you may be eligible through employment, generally on campus. In addition, many schools have their own programs through which students earn money or in-kind support such as board. This type of assistance has two advantages. First, you are not indebted after graduation. Second, you may be able to work in areas related to your major, thereby gaining an edge in later job hunting.

Contrary to some opinion, a reasonable amount of part-time work does not interfere with the academic performance of most working students. Indeed some national studies have indicated just the opposite effect, because students who work must be more self-disciplined and must manage their time and energies more wisely.

Cooperative education (co-op) programs are another great opportunity for students at many institutions. These programs provide employment off campus in public and private agencies, business, and industry. Work may parallel education (part-time course load, part-time work) or alternate with it (full-time study one term, full-time work the next). This type of experience can also be invaluable when you look for that first job after graduation. Many graduates are offered permanent, full-time positions as a result of co-op experience.

The Financial Aid Process

Unfortunately, where there is money, there is bureaucracy. Consequently, you are going to have to deal with red tape. This may be frustrating, but remember that the potential payoff can be well worth the aggravation. Be prepared to fill out forms and to stand in lines.

The largest financial aid programs are those based upon need and regulated by state and/or federal agencies. For these most institutions require at least two basic documents: a needs analysis document and an institutional application/information form. Another routine financial aid form is the scholarship application. Such forms vary widely depending on the scholarship sought and the organization awarding it, but they usually gather information about past performance, honors, leadership, and so on.

THE NEEDS ANALYSIS DOCUMENT

The term *needs analysis* is sometimes used to refer to the general process of analyzing a student's financial resources in order to determine whether the student needs any further assistance to attend college. Frequently, however, it refers specifically to the federal system that provides a consistent national standard for deciding who will get federal financial aid. Because it is an extremely complex and sophisticated method for allocating limited financial aid resources, it really doesn't determine an individual's "need" in the pure sense, but merely one's eligibility. Of course need is relative. How much help a student or family may feel they need in order to send someone to college depends on many subjective opinions and feelings. At best, needs analysis is simply a relative measure comparing a given family's ability to pay for a college education with that of other families.

In order to operate this system, the federal government requires certain basic information for determining your eligibility, which you must provide on a needs analysis document. The two federal forms you are most likely to use are referred to by their acronyms—the "FAF" and the "FAFSA." Before you fill one out, however, check with the financial aid office at your school to determine which form or forms it uses.

THE INSTITUTIONAL APPLICATION/INFORMATION FORM

Many institutions have their own financial aid forms in addition to the needs analysis document. These forms typically ask for different information than is requested in the needs analysis.

APPLYING FOR FINANCIAL AID

When you apply for financial aid, remember to do the following:

1. **Plan ahead.** Planning is critical. Find out what is available at your institution, how to go about applying, and when you must apply. You also need to determine what information will be required and allow enough time to gather that information.

2. **Allow sufficient time for the process to work.** The financial aid application process is often slow, taking several weeks to several months, depending on the type of aid you are applying for, your school's application volume, processing mechanisms, and the time of year. (Summer is the peak season, so allow extra time in the summer.) After you have submitted your initial application, you may be asked to provide additional information to support or clarify it. Be prepared to do this promptly and to experience further delay.

3. **Keep copies of everything.** Maintain a file with copies of everything you complete or send regarding your application for aid, including the date it was completed or sent. This will help you avoid confusion and/or costly delays due to miscommunication or things getting lost in the mail.

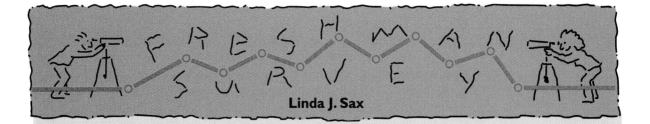

Linda J. Sax

Concerns About Money

Since 1978, the percentage of freshmen taking out loans to pay for college has increased dramatically from 25.7 percent to 54.8 percent. Given students' increasing financial responsibilities, it is not surprising that they are more concerned than ever about their ability to pay for college. The percentage of freshmen who have a "major" concern about having enough funds to complete college increased from 8.6 in 1966 to a new high of 19.1 in 1995. The percentage of students who believe they will have to get a job to pay for college expenses has reached a fifteen-year high of 39.5 percent.

What forces make students more concerned about money worries today than in the past? Why are more students relying on loans to pay for college? What, if anything, could happen that would make financial issues less of a concern for you and future college students?

Financial Concerns, 1966–1995

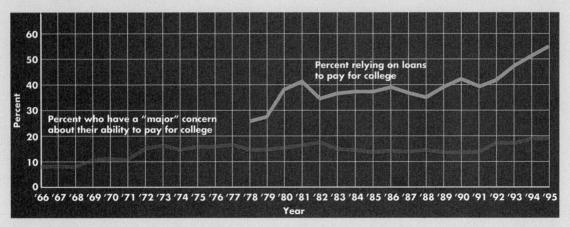

SOURCE: *Higher Education Research Institute, UCLA*

You are responsible for helping to finance your college education. Aside from working, whether from necessity or desire, to help earn some of what you need, you can contribute in two other ways.

First, you can stretch your dollars. Be as frugal as possible in areas where you can be flexible, such as personal expenses. Think twice before you spend your money. Is what you're spending it on necessary, or can you live without it? Budget and manage your money wisely.

Second, you can be serious about your college education. By applying yourself to the best of your abilities, managing your time wisely, keeping up in your classes, and, above all else, not having to repeat courses because of poor grades, you will get the most value possible for your investment. By going about your college education with dedication and focus, you will save both time and money.

If you need more resources to pay for college, first consult with your parents or anyone else who is helping you pay for college. Then visit your school financial aid office and talk with a financial aid counselor. If possible make an appointment so that the counselor can give you his or her full attention. Then use the goal-setting process in Chapter 1 to line up additional resources.

JOURNAL

How well are you controlling your finances at this point? What can you do now to improve your current money management and financial situations in the near future?

SUGGESTIONS FOR FURTHER READING

Adams, Janelle P., ed. *The A's and B's of Academic Scholarships.* Alexandria, Va.: Octameron Associates. Published yearly.

Chany, Kalman A., and Geoff Martz. *The Student Access Guide to Paying for College.* New York: Villard Books. Published yearly.

College Check Mate: Innovative Tuitions Plans That Make You a Winner. Alexandria, Va.: Octameron Associates. Published yearly.

The College Costs and Financial Aid Book. Princeton, N.J.: College Board Publications. Published yearly.

Dacyczyn, Amy. *The Tightwad Gazette: Promoting Thrift as a Viable Alternative Lifestyle.* New York: Villard Books, 1993.

Directory of Special Programs for Minority Group Members, 4th ed. Garrett Park, Md.: Garrett Park Press, 1986.

Earn and Learn: Cooperative Education Opportunities with the Federal Government. Alexandria, Va.: Octameron Associates. Published yearly.

Financial Aid Fin-Ancer: Expert Answers to College Financing Questions. Alexandria, Va.: Octameron Associates. Published yearly.

Keesler, Oreon. *Financial Aids for Higher Education,* 4th ed. Dubuque, Iowa: Brown, 1991.

Kennedy, Joyce, and Herm Davis. *The College Financial Aid Emergency Kit.* Cardiff, Calif.: Sun Features. Published yearly.

Paying Less for College. Princeton, N.J.: Peterson's. Published yearly.

Schlacter, Gail A. *Directory of Financial Aids for Women.* Santa Barbara, Calif.: Reference Service Press, 1991.

Schlacter, Gail A., and David R. Weber. *Directory of Financial Aids for Minorities.* Santa Barbara, Calif.: Reference Service Press, 1993.

Student Consumer Guide. Washington, D.C.: Government Printing Office. Published yearly.

Glossary/Index

In addition to other terms discussed in the text, this glossary defines terms that you may need to know.

demonstrate proficiency in various college subjects. Passing the test earns credit for certain college courses. CLEP subject exams cover individual courses, such as Introductory Psychology; CLEP general exams incorporate several courses, such as the one for social studies. Some colleges will accept CLEP subject exams but not general exams. CLEP tests are usually administered through the college testing office. Information may be available from the admissions office and/or an advisor.

Clubs. *See* **Co-curricular activities; Organizations, college**

Cocaine, 363–65

Cocaine hotline, 365

Co-curricular activities campus student activities provided by organizations, clubs, and so on, independent of a school's formal academic program. 9, 256, 319–21

Coeducation including both men and women in an educational program. 6

Cognate courses apart from but related to a student's major and approved by his or her advisor. Such courses are required for graduation at many colleges. Cognates are junior- and senior-level courses. Colleges that don't require a cognate may require a minor. *See also* **Minor**

Coitus interruptus, 341

Collaborative learning style, 73

College
attendance rates, 4
benefits of, 12–13
catalogs, 242–46
as challenge to personal values, 279–82
cost of, 245, 378–79
high school versus, 26–27, 39, 48, 193
keys to success in, 7–9
reasons for attending, 2–4, 13, 277–78
reasons for choosing, 277
support services, 7, 8, 9, 10, 15, 16
survival tests for, 38–45
value of, 11–13

College Readjustment Rating Scale, 327

College Work–Study Program, 382

Commencement graduation. A ceremony in which colleges award degrees to graduating students. Some schools hold two or three commencements annually, but the largest ones are held in May or early June.

Communication
and academic freedom, 30
in relationships, 308
with teachers, 8, 28, 29–30, 99, 100
of thought, 18, 19

Community college a two-year college; may also be known as a junior college or technical school. These colleges most often award associate degrees; technical colleges may offer other types of degrees or certificates as well. 249

Community service, 321

Commuter students students who live off campus and have to commute, or travel, to campus each day. Includes about 80 percent of all U.S. college students today.
campus involvement of, 5
handling of distractions by, 61–62
numbers of, 22
problems of, 5
services for, 15
survival kits for, 330
telephone directories for, 66–67
time management for, 61, 62–66

Commuting, costs of, 379

Companionate love, 308

Comparison and contrast, 165

Competitive learning style, 73

Comprehensive examination some schools use this term to describe final exams, which are given during the last days of the term. The word *comprehensive* means that all material covered during the term may be included on the exam. Graduate students may also take comprehensive exams covering information learned in all courses to earn the master's or doctoral degree.

Computation skills quantitative, or mathematical, skills.

Computers, 242
accessing, 209–10
accessing library resources with, 140
approaches to, 204–6
e-mail, 9, 10, 34–35, 129, 140, 242
ethical and legal issues, 224
etiquette for use of, 221–23
help with, 208, 210–12
home, 233
keyboarding, 209

in liberal arts education, 231
literacy assessment, 14
math and, 193, 194
note-taking and, 93
on-line exam schedules, 117
on-line services, 217–21
preventing disasters, 212–13
rates of using, 205
scheduling and, 53
skill in use of, 9, 10, 208–9
software for, 214–15
strategies for use of, 206–9
word processing, 9, 10, 215–16, 231

Computer science careers, 265

Condoms, 340, 346, 348–50

Conflicts
racial, 297, 299–301
values and, 279–82

Continuing education programs that enable the nontraditional college student to take classes without having to be admitted as a degree candidate. While continuing education students may take college courses for credit, some colleges have established noncredit learning programs under this name.

Contraception, 339–42

Contraceptive sponge, 341

Conventional personality type, 260, 263

Cooperative (co-op) education programs that provide an opportunity to work in academic major-related settings off campus in public and private agencies, as well as in business and industry, either by parallel scheduling (going to school part-time and working part-time) or by alternate scheduling (staying out of school for an academic term and working full-time). 8, 321, 382

Core courses/distribution requirements/basic requirements/general education a broad range of courses that a college may require mainly in the freshman and sophomore years, which introduce the student to a wide variety of subjects. *See also* **Prerequisite**

Counseling a wide variety of services to which students are entitled based on their payment of tuition. Most campuses provide confidential professional counseling and referral services in numerous different offices, including admissions, financial aid, residence halls, career planning, placement, veterans' affairs, study skills, academic advising, and counseling. 9, 246–54. *See also* **Academic advising**

jurisprudence) also require extensive study.

Dormitories. *See* **Residence hall**

Double-up schedule, 66

Downloading, 221

Drafting, 113, 166, 167, 168–69. *See also* **Writing**

Drinking. *See* Alcohol

Driving under the influence (DUI), 361

Drop most colleges allow students to drop (or quit) a course without penalty during specified periods of time. When dropping a course, you must follow the proper procedures, which include completing certain forms and obtaining official signatures. If you're receiving financial aid, your status may change if you drop a course. 136

Drugs
  alcohol, 9, 281, 350, 353, 356–61
  caffeine, 324, 325
  cocaine, 363–65
  effect on relationships, 311
  marijuana, 361–63
  risk factor behaviors, 358
  sex and, 309
  tobacco, 361, 365
  values and, 281

Drunk driving, 361

DUI/DWI police acronyms for driving under the influence of alcohol and driving while intoxicated. 361

Economy, student concerns about, 13

Editing, 169, 171

Education, college
  costs of, 245, 378–79
  liberal arts, 228–38
  necessity of, 4
  value of, 11–13

Einstein, Albert, 33

Electives an elective is a course you may select from an academic area of interest to you. Thecourse will not apply toward your core, major, or minor/cognate requirements. Each college determines the number of electives you may take, and you may take them at any time.

E-mail electronic mail. Various systems by which computers are linked so that personal computers can be used to send and receive messages and information. 214
  basics of, 219–21
  faculty addresses, 34–35, 129, 242

flaming, 222

forwarding, 222–23

learning to use, 9, 10, 140, 223–24

library research and, 152

replying to, 221–22

Emergencies, 129

Emotional intimacy, 309

Empathy, 43–44

Employment. *See also* **Careers**
  college education and, 11–13, 256
  forming relationships through, 321
  full-time course load and, 7
  liberal arts education and, 232–33

Empty Nest Syndrome, 314

Encyclopedias
  general, 146, 153–54
  subject, 146–47, 154

Engagement, in writing, 163–64

Engel, Elliot, 33

Engerman, Stanley L., 236

Engineering careers, 186, 196–97, 265

Enrollment, 4

Entering students. *See* **First-year students**

Enterprising personality type, 259–60, 263

Essay tests
  key task words and, 122–27
  principles for taking, 122–23
  studying for, 116–17, 119–22
  super recall columns and mind maps for, 120–22
  time management on, 122, 127

Ethnic groups, 289–90

Evaluation of courses. *See* **Validation of credits**

Examinations. *See* **Tests**

Examples, in oral presentations, 178, 182

Exchange program an arrangement for attending another college or university for a specific time period at the same cost and for the same credits as at your own institution. 9

Exercise, 325, 329

Expenses, 373–75

Experience, learning from, 44–45

Explanation an argument that relies mainly on a careful process of reasoning and statements of facts, as opposed to emotional appeal. 165

Extracurricular activities. *See* **Co-curricular activities**

Extroverted learning style, 73, 76, 77

Fabrication a form of academic misconduct that involves in-

tentionally inventing information or results in the course of academic work. 133

Factual learning style, 71, 72, 81

Faculty the teachers at a college.

FAF/FAFSA forms, 383

Failure, fear of, 236

Fallacy any one of several erroneous patterns of thinking or arguing; for example, the fallacy called "hasty generalization" occurs when a person assumes that if one member of a group behaves badly, then all members of the group will also behave in that way.

Family
  contact with, 9
  effect of college education on, 11, 12
  parents, 314–16
  as support network, 10
  values of, 278

Family planning, 341

Fantasizing, 330

FAQ in computing, a frequently asked question. 211

Feeling, thinking and, 237

Feeling learning style, 74, 76–77, 80, 85

Fees charges that a student may have to pay in addition to tuition. Fees may have to be charged for housing, health care, labs, parking, and so on. Most college catalogs list fees and say when they are due. 373. *See also* **Tuition**

Female condom, 340–41

Files
  for catalogs and academic documents, 242
  computer, 212
  of tests, 135

File Transfer Protocol (FTP), 152

Final exam a test administered at the end of most courses, usually written and often covering the entire content of the course.

Financial aid student scholarships, grants, and loans. Some forms of financial aid are gifts, but others are loans that must be repaid with interest. Some aid is offered only to new freshmen, while other sources of financial aid are available to all students. To determine your eligibility for any aid, see your financial aid counselor. The application process for financial aid for a fall semester usually begins during the preceding January. 15, 245, 373, 379, 380–84

Financial resources, 373–75, 378–79. *See also* **Money**

Fine arts   the range of academic fields or disciplines including mainly the study of art, music, dance, and theater. 147, 230, 238

First-year students
alcohol, drugs, and, 358
financial concerns of, 384
journals of, 20
problems of, 5
rape and, 351, 352
reading attention span of, 103
reasons for attending college, 2–4
self-esteem of, 43
sex and, 338–39
values of, 277, 280
word processing and, 215–16

Flaming   highly emotional, highly critical messages via e-mail. 222

Flashcards, 131

Flexibility, reading and, 111

Fogel, Robert W., 236

Footnotes, 170

Forgetting, 94
note-taking and, 89, 90
recitation and, 94–95

Forgetting curves, 89, 90

Fraternity. *See* **Greeks**

Freedom
academic, 30
newfound, dealing with, 4, 5, 40

Friends. *See also* **Peers**
choosing, 9, 316–17
values and, 279–82

Full-time student   students enrolled for a specified number of hours, such as 12 semester hours or more. At most schools, part-time students receive the same benefits as full-time students. At others, part-time students may receive limited benefits.

Gaffin, Adam, 140

Gay students. *See* Homosexual students

Gender-balanced curriculum   a curriculum that includes information about women equivalent to the quality and quantity of information about men.

Gender referencing   attributing occupational, personality, or other characteristics to individuals of a specific gender. For example, taken by itself, the

statement that "a nurse receives her training" seems to imply that nurses must be female.

General encyclopedias, 146, 153–54

Genital warts, 344–45

Gift assistance   any type of financial aid that does not have to be repaid. 381

Glenwick, David, 64

Goals
approach to setting, 42
for campus organizations, 320
life, 258–59, 277
in math/science courses, 195
realistic, 11, 136–37
short- and long-term, 14, 16–17, 20

Gonorrhea, 343, 344

Gopher, 152, 158

Grade point average (GPA)   sometimes called the cumulative average, grade point ratio (GPR),or quality point average (QPA). Most colleges base grades on a four-point scale, with points assigned to each grade (A = 4, B = 3, C = 2, D = 1, F = 0). To compute your GPA for one term, you need only complete three simple mathematical steps: multiply, add, divide. *Multiply* the number of points representing the grade you receive for each course by the number of credit hours for the course. *Add* the points for all courses to determine the total number of points you've earned for the term. *Divide* the total points by the number of credit hours you attempted that term. The result will be your GPA. Some colleges complicate this with a three-point system or by using grades in addition to A through F. College catalogs explain the system at individual schools.

Grades or **grading system**   most schools use the A–F system. A is the highest grade, and F means failure. A–D are passing grades for which you will earn points and credits. If you transfer colleges, however, the D grades may not transfer. Most colleges require a minimum 2.0 GPA, or C average, for graduation; in addition, you might lose financial aid, housing, and other benefits when your GPA falls below a certain level. Bad grades and low GPAs also may lead to

dismissal or suspension. Some schools have pass/fail grades (P/F or S/U) and an incomplete grade (I), the latter representing work not completed during the term it was taken.
academic advising and, 248
grading systems, 245
minority students and, 8
overestimating importance of, 136
realistic goals for, 10, 11
writing for, 169

Graduate student   a person who has earned at least a bachelor's degree (B.A. or B.S.) and is enrolled in a program granting a master's degree (M.A. or M.S.), a Ph.D., or other graduate degree, for example, in law or medicine.

Graduation check, 243

Granger's Index to Poetry, 149

Grants   a type of financial assistance that does not have to be repaid. 381

Graphics software, 215

Grasha, Tony, 73

Grasha-Riechmann instrument, 73

Greeks   fraternities or sororities whose names are based on Greek letters. 319, 321

Gripes, of students and parents, 315–16

Groups. *See* **Organizations, college; study groups**

Guess-and-check technique, 190

Guidance counselors, 84

GUIDE checklist, 175, 176–79

Hate speech, 301

Headings, subject, 149

Health. *See also* **Drugs; sex; stress**
college education and, 13
importance of, 9

Health enrichment services, 15

Health-related majors/careers, 264

Hepatitis B, 343, 345

Herpes, 343, 344

Higher education   any college courses you take or any degree you earn after completing high school (secondary education). Also called postsecondary education.

High school, college versus, 26–27, 39, 48, 193

Hispanic American students, 118, 298

HIV/AIDS, 343, 344, 345–47, 348

Hobbies, 332

Hogan, R. Craig, 78

occurs in the middle of the term prior to the one you're registering for. Preregistration gives students a greater chance of getting into the courses and sections they ask for.

Prerequisite   a course or courses that must be completed as a condition for taking another course. Catalogs state prerequisites. A GPA or class standing may constitute a prerequisite for certain courses.

Probation   a warning that you are not making satisfactory academic progress toward your degree or have violated certain standards of acceptable personal behavior. Probation is followed by suspension/dismissal unless the situation is corrected.

Professional degree   a degree awarded for study in fields such as business, journalism, pharmacology, nursing, or one of the sciences where what you learn is directly linked to actual work in the career field. 232

Professor   college teachers are ranked as teaching assistant, lecturer, instructor, or professor. Professor is the highest rank and includes three levels: assistant professor, associate professor, and (full) professor. When in doubt how to address a college teacher, say "professor." While many professors have earned a doctoral degree, this is not a rigid requirement for holding professorial rank. *See also* **Teacher**

Proficiency exam   a test that measures whether a student has reached a certain level of knowledge. Such exams may allow you to exempt, with or without credit, certain lower level courses. Math and foreign language departments often use proficiency exams.

Quantitative studies   the academic subjects that create systems for describing the physical world or human behavior in abstract or mathematical terms. They include mathematics, statistics, and computer science. 231

Quarter hour   a unit of credit given at colleges whose terms are called quarters, which last approximately ten weeks. *See also* **Semester hour**

Quarter system   a college scheduling system of four terms, or quarters: fall, winter, spring, and summer. If you attend full-time and plan to finish in four years without attending summer school, you'll take courses for twelve quarters. *See also* **Semester system**

Racism   discriminatory or differential treatment of individuals based on race. 289, 299

Registrar   the college administrator who maintains student transcripts and directs the registration process. When faculty submit final grades, the registrar posts them to your transcript and mails you a copy.

Registration   the act of scheduling classes for each term. *See also* **Preregistration**

Reinstatement or **Readmission**   a return to college following suspension or a leave of absence; you must apply for reinstatement or readmission. In some cases, you'll be readmitted with no restrictions. If your GPA is low, you may be readmitted on probation.

Residence hall   on-campus student housing provided by the school. Formerly called a dormitory. 321

career planning and, 258, 270
new, and stress relief, 332
time management and, 48–49
Slade, John, 135
Sleep, 324–25
Smileys, 222
Social personality type, 259, 263
Social sciences the range of academic disciplines, including mainly the scientific study of people and society, including such fields as sociology, psychology, and economics. 231
Software, 214–15
Sophomore. *See* **Class standing**
Sorority. *See* **Greeks**
Sources, in library research, 151
Speaking. *See* **Public speaking**
Special student in most colleges, this is a student who has not matriculated (has not been accepted into a degree program). A special student may have one degree but may wish to continue his or her education by selecting courses without regard to a degree program. Military personnel are often admitted as special students. Special students may be exempted from certain prerequisites, but they don't receive financial aid or other benefits enjoyed by full-time students.
Speech Index, 149
Spelling checker, 215, 216
Spermicidal foams, creams, and jellies, 341, 348
Split schedule, 66
Spreadsheet a computer application program used mainly for budgeting, financial planning, and other tasks requiring calculations based on lists of numerical information. 214
Squirrel exercise, 192
Standardized tests, 8
Statistics, in oral presentations, 178
STD sexually transmitted disease (AIDS, syphilis, gonorrhea, etc.). 338, 339, 342
chlamydia, 343–44
gonorrhea, 343, 344
hepatitis B, 345
herpes, 343, 344
HIV/AIDS, 343, 344, 345–47, 348
human papilloma virus (HPV), 343, 344–45
protection against, 340–41, 346–50
risk factors for, 339
Stereotypes
racial, 297

sexual orientation, 294
Stereotyping, in math and science, 193
Sterilization, 340
Stress
academic advising and, 247
finances and, 378
lifestyle and, 324–25
management of, 10, 13
mental relief of, 329–30
mind/body relief of, 331–32
physical relief of, 329
protection from, 328
relaxation and, 331, 335
signs and symptoms of, 326
social support network and, 332–33
sources of, 326–28
spiritual relief of, 331
Stretching, 329
Structure
in public speaking, 178–79
in writing, 167
Students
concerns of, 11
enrollment rates, 4
expectations of, by teachers, 25–27, 235
fears and problems of, 5, 38
learning styles of, 7, 70–71
persistence factors of, 7–9, 11
romantic relationship with teachers, 308
support networks for, 7, 10
support services for, 7, 8, 9, 10, 15, 16
Student union a campus building devoted to student co-curricular organizations, activities, stores, dining facilities, and various support services. Sometimes called the student center.
Study abroad a program that lets you attend a college or university in another country for a specific time, earning credit that will apply toward graduation requirements at your institution.
Study groups
forming, 118–19
importance of, 7, 201–2, 319
learning styles and, 79–8
Studying
assessing skills, 7, 14, 118–19
courses in, 10
throughout courses, 117–18
for essay exams, 116–17, 119–22
for lectures, 90–91
for multiple-choice tests, 128
procrastination and, 63
reducing distractions, 62

Styles. *See* **Learning styles; teaching styles**
Subject encyclopedias, 146–47, 154
Subject periodical indexes, 150, 156
Success
keys to college, 7–9, 11
in math and science courses, 192–93, 195–96
student responsibility for, 40
Super recall columns, 120, 122
Support networks, 332–33
Support services, 15, 16. *See also* **Academic advising**
for computer use, 210–12
counseling, 7, 9
for minority students, 8
for returning students, 10
Survival kits, for commuters, 330
Survival tests, for college success, 38–45
Suspension. *See* **Dismissal**
Syllabus one or more pages of class requirements that an instructor gives out on the first day of a course. The syllabus acts as a course outline, telling when you must complete assignments, readings, and so on. 53
Systematic thinking, 18, 99, 100

Tables, making, 190
Taking America's Pulse survey, 297
Task words, 122–27
Teachers
academic freedom and, 30
bad, 32
choosing, 8, 30–32
communication with, 8, 28, 29–30
duties and tasks of, 27–28
effective, characteristics, 29, 30–31
e-mail communication with, 223
expectations of students by, 25–27, 235
high school versus college, 26–27
interviewing, 33
lecture system of, 97
maximizing relationships with, 28
romantic relationships with students, 308
Teaching careers, 268
Teaching styles
assessing, 83–84
clues to, 81–82
exam preparation and, 82–84
Technical (tech) schools technical education systems established by many states offer specialized two-year degrees and certificates. While these schools may be accredited, course work may be so technically oriented that it won't

Work/study a federal student aid program based on need, which provides the opportunity for students to earn some of the aid for which they are eligible through employment, generally on campus. 382

WE'D LIKE TO HEAR FROM YOU

Thank you for using *Your College Experience*, 3rd Edition. We care a lot about how well you liked this book. Please let us know how we can improve the next edition! Return this page with your comments, using the postage-free label on the other side. Or send a letter. Either way, we'd like to hear your thoughts.

Overall, how valuable was the book as part of your course? _____

_____

_____

Circle each chapter that you used as part of your course assignments.

1 Keys to Success	7 Textbooks	13 Liberal Arts	19 Stress
2 Student/Teacher	8 Grades	14 Catalog/Advisor	20 Sexual Decisions
3 Surviving College	9 Library	15 Major/Career	21 Alcohol/Drugs
4 Time Management	10 Writing/Speaking	16 Values	22 Money
5 Learning Styles	11 Math/Sciences	17 Diversity	
6 Listening/Learning	12 Computing	18 Relationships	

Mark an X by any chapter that you read in addition to the course assignments. Mark an O by any other chapter that your class didn't cover but you wish it *had*.

Did you find some parts or exercises particularly helpful? Which? _____

_____

_____

Are there any parts or exercises that you think should be changed? _____

_____

_____

Are there any topics not covered in this book that you think should be added? _____

_____

_____

How else can we improve *Your College Experience?* _____

_____

_____

This book contains a number of firsthand experiences from first-year students. Have you had some experience this year that you would like to write about and possibly see published in a future edition?

Please let us know! _____

_____

_____

Thanks and good luck!

John Gardner

Jerry Jewler

Your name _____ School _____

Your address _____

City/State _____ Zip _____

Your instructor's name _____

FOLD HERE

FOLD HERE

NO POSTAGE
NECESSARY
IF MAILED
IN THE
UNITED STATES

BUSINESS REPLY MAIL
FIRST CLASS   PERMIT NO. 34   BELMONT, CA

POSTAGE WILL BE PAID BY ADDRESSEE

John N. Gardner / A. Jerome Jewler
Your College Experience, 3rd Edition
℅ College Success Editor
Wadsworth Publishing Company
10 Davis Drive
Belmont, CA 94002-9801